The Modern Terminal

Brian Edwards

The Modern Terminal

New approaches to airport architecture

E & FN SPON
An Imprint of Routledge

London and New York

Published by E & FN Spon, an imprint of Routledge
11 New Fetter Lane, London EC4P 4EE

Simultaneously published in the USA and Canada by Routledge
29 West 35th Street, New York, NY 10001

© 1998 Brian Edwards

Typeset in 9.5/12pt Helvetica 45 by Fox Design, Godalming, Surrey
Printed in Great Britain by Alden Press, Oxford

British Library Cataloguing in Publication Data
A catalogue record for this book is available from the British Library

ISBN 0 419 21750 9

Contents

Contents

Acknowledgements

My chief debt is to the many architects in the UK and abroad who have furnished me with details of airport terminals either built or at the design stage. They are too many to list in full, but I wish to single out Foster and Partners, Nicholas Grimshaw & Partners, Richard Rogers Partnership, Renzo Piano Building Workshop, Terry Farrell and Partners, Ove Arup and Partners, Scott Brownrigg and Turner, Murphy/Jahn, RMJM, Parr Partnership, Calatrava Valls, and Manser Associates.

In addition I am greatly indebted to BAA for the assistance provided by the staff at Gatwick, Heathrow, Stansted, Glasgow and Edinburgh.

Airport authorities worldwide have assisted in various ways, and I wish to single out in particular the City of Chicago Department of Aviation, Dallas/Fort Worth International Airport Authority, Airport CCI Marseilles, and Kansai International Airport.

Three people went out of their way to guide me towards the future direction of airport design: Emma Boulby at BAA International, Graham Jordan at BAA, and Christopher Blow at Scott Brownrigg and Turner.

Finally, I am greatly indebted to my secretary Karen Beaumont, who typed the manuscript, made copious corrections without complaint, and dealt with the flood of responses from airport authorities and designers.

Introduction

Air travel has been described as the defining mode of transportation of the twentieth century.[1] No other form of travel compares with the speed, scale and glamour of contemporary air travel. Flight has opened up continents and allowed mass accessibility much as the railways did on a smaller scale, a century earlier. In the process, air travel has altered our experience of place and time: it has broadened our sense of geography and human experience.

The airport terminal is the central building of the air transport system. Its architecture reflects the glamour, scale and technological prowess of this fast-growing industry. As air travel becomes more popular and accessible, the airport has assumed greater importance as a fundamentally new and challenging building type. Rather like the railway station and theatre combined, the modern airport terminal is a highly charged and symbolic building. It is a miniature city reflecting the values and aspirations of society at large. National image is reflected more directly in the design of airports than in any other building type, with the passenger terminal the key element in public perception.

On the stage of world architecture the airport holds an important place. Airport authorities have been, for half a century, one of the most adventurous patrons of modern architecture. From Eero Saarinen's TWA Terminal of 1959 at Kennedy Airport to Renzo Piano's Kansai Airport of 1995, airport developers have been consistent in their support of innovative design, whether expressed in formal or in technological terms. The airport of the future will continue to push forward the frontiers of architectural design, creating

0.1 Stansted Airport, UK, by Foster and Partners marked the emergence of a new generation of airport terminals.

images and structural solutions that become adopted in other building types. Such is the link between the thrill of air travel and the design of the airport, and between the technology of the aeroplane and that of the terminal, that the next generation of airports will continue to stretch architecture and engineering to its limits.

Reference

1. *Interbuild Preview*, November 1995, p. 4.

Part one

Airport design

CHAPTER 1   The airport industry

Aviation is a major international industry, which in 1995 carried over a billion passengers. Of all forms of transport, flying is the most glamorous, the fastest and increasingly the safest form of long-distance travel. For most international journeys travel by air is the only option, and to make it comfortable and reliable, international standards and regulations apply. These influence the layout, engineering and infrastructure of airports, the design of terminal buildings, and the design of the aircraft themselves. Civil aviation is therefore a highly regulated and efficient industry, which recognizes few national boundaries or customs. The standardization of operational practices leads to greater safety on and off the ground, and provides an element of uniformity in the criteria that shape airports themselves. Hence runways, taxiing areas, safety zones, passenger piers and terminal buildings all confirm to relatively standardized operational parameters.

The infrastructure of airports consists of five basic zones: the runway, the aircraft fuelling and maintenance areas, the aircraft stands, the passenger piers and the terminal buildings. These are the primary functional divisions that establish the layout and operation of the airport. Secondary areas or buildings may include the

1.1   Marseille Airport, France, extended in 1994 by the Richard Rogers Partnership.

2

flight control tower, connecting forms of transport (such as railway stations or light rail systems), the road system, car parks and hotels.

To regulate the aircraft industry, governments have tended to delegate control to industrial organizations in the air transport business. There are three prime international bodies:

- the *International Air Transport Association* (IATA), which represents the interests of aircraft carrier members, such as British Airways and Pan Am
- the *Airports Association Council International* (AACI), which represents civil airport authorities such as the BAA (previously British Airports Authority).
- the *Institute of Air Transport* (ITA), which represents those other than carriers and airport owners, such as managers, manufacturers and designers.

These three bodies effectively self-regulate and provide a policy framework for the aircraft industry. Because many national governments are little bigger (in GNP terms) than the larger carriers, or generate less wealth than a major international airport such as Heathrow, most governments accept the beneficial influence of these powerful industrial organizations.

Ownership of airports

The trend these days is away from ownership of airports by the state (either central or regional government) towards either private ownership or partnership between government and private investors. London Stansted is owned by BAA (which is wholly private and quoted on the Stock Exchange), and other major airports, such as Stuttgart in Germany and Milan in Italy, have been denationalized and are now no longer state owned. The reasons are clear: airports require massive injections of funds to adapt to changing regulation, market conditions and commercial opportunity. Only with private capital can the outmoded infrastructure of airports be kept up to date – or so most Western governments believe. In the developing world it is still commonplace for the state or local authority to own and manage airports, but

1.2 Kansai Airport, Osaka, Japan: a major public investment in transport infrastructure with private stakeholders. Architects: Renzo Piano Building Workshop.

as soon as they become profitable they are quickly sold, often to international organizations. Although many governments cling to the idea that their major airports are part of the state infrastructure of public utilities, in reality the past 10 years have seen a shift worldwide away from government ownership towards some sort of consortium ownership or total private ownership. The prime question, however, is not about who owns the airport, but rather: does the air transport industry exist to provide a public service, or profit for the shareholders? The pattern of ownership throughout the world tends to follow the varying ideologies of the respective governments rather than any obvious regional or subcontinental pattern.

If ownership of airports by governments is declining, there remains a strong group of airports (such as Kansai in Japan) run by a consortium of state and local government, with private companies having a financial stake. Sometimes the airport may be owned by an arm of government, but the principal buildings (such as the passenger termini) are owned, leased or managed by a private organization such as an airline company. The mix of ownership has implications for the operation of the airport and – to some extent – for the design of the parts. Where ownership is vested in government there tends to be a controlling hand over the appearance of the whole airport estate, from hotels to car parks, terminal buildings to control towers. Where ownership is fragmented, or resides in a consortium, there is

1.3 Retail sales now exceed landing fees at most airports. Southampton Airport, UK. Architects: Manser Associates.

usually greater pluralism in the approach to design, and often the employment of a wider selection of architects, designers and engineers. Where there is a split in ownership between the airport and its key buildings (as at Kennedy Airport, New York) the pattern is usually one where different airlines own specific passenger terminals. This allows them to compete with each other as integrated terminal-based services – including ticketing, baggage handling and concessionary shops – all managed by the airline company with which the passenger is flying.

How airports generate income

For the passenger, the airport is a point of arrival or departure – just another stage in the complexity of modern travel – but for the operator the airport is a means of generating income. Generally speaking, there are five ways of earning revenue:[1]

- landing fees
- concessions in terminal buildings
- leasing arrangements with airline operators
- leasing of non-airline operations such as car parks
- equipment rental (such as baggage handling).

Against these earnings. the airport owner has to set two operating expenses:

- maintenance costs (upkeep of buildings, facilities and equipment)
- operating costs (staff salaries, security, utilities costs).

The balance of revenue and expenses determines the profitability or otherwise of the airport. Contrary to expectations it is not the airlines that necessarily generate the bulk of the airport earnings. At Stansted the revenue from the car parks exceeds the landing fees paid by the airline companies, and at Heathrow the money earned through the sale or lease of concessions is one of the principal sources of income, again exceeding the landing fees.[2]

In these balances of profitability, the terminal buildings play a very large part. As an airport expands, generating more traffic flow, the percentage of income from the terminal building itself increases. The increase in throughput of passengers adds greatly to the sale of concessionary and duty-free goods, adding to the fees earned through leasing terminal space to retail and restaurant companies. Growing operational activity is therefore the main aim of the airport operator, who may reduce the fees charged to airline companies (for landing and aircraft parking etc.) in order to increase the throughput of passengers.

Generally, the larger the airport the greater the percentage of income from the passenger terminal. With small airports (serving up to about 200 000 passengers a year) the landing fees, fuel charges, hangar rentals etc. exceed the revenue from terminal areas by about 25%, but with large airports (serving over 4 million passengers a year) income from the terminal exceeds that of the landing area by 40%.[3] For the typical airport, landing fees account for about 20% of total income, but revenue generated by commercial activities of one kind or another (such as concessions in the terminal building and rents to franchising companies) can approach 50% of total income.

Looking more closely at the sources of income generated in the terminal area, evidence from the USA shows that car rentals, parking fees, restaurant leasing fees and fees from speciality shops generate about 80% of the revenue. The implications are obvious in terms of the design and management of such areas: create as much space in or around the terminal for these secondary activities, ensure that the environments formed are conducive to loitering *en route* to the plane, and (if possible) manage flight departures to maximize 'dwell time'.

Because much of the commercial revenue is the result of duty-free shopping (27% of BAA's total earnings in 1995), a recent trend has been towards providing such shops not only at the beginning of a flight (and during it) but on arrival. Although this allows the airport to exploit both departing and arriving passengers, the move has been resisted by airlines

1.4 Even regional airports such as Southampton enjoy the benefit of commuter and international travellers. Southampton Airport, UK. Architects: Manser Associates.

1.5 Airports are increasingly leisure destinations in their own right. Heathrow Terminal 3, London, UK. Architect: D.Y. Davies.

themselves, who derive considerable sales (especially with holiday charter flights) from on-board purchases. However, there is the advantage of reduced congestion and less weight on planes in transferring duty-free to the end rather than the beginning of a journey. For the operator and designer of the terminal building there are implications in re-ordering duty-free shopping. The arrivals area is one of the most congested and controlled of all zones in the terminal building, and customs staff have resisted the change. However, where arrivals duty-free shopping does occur (as at Bangkok and Singapore), the additional income for the airport can be high.

Growth in airport demand

For most of the past 20 years the world air-transport industry has seen passenger numbers grow by about 6–7% per year. From showing the characteristics of an infant industry in the 1960s and 1970s with rapid growth, fast-falling passenger-mile costs and heavy investment in infrastructure, the air transport industry has tended to stabilize in the mid-1990s, with growth closer to 3%. However, while growth rates in Europe and North America have followed this pattern, Asia and the Pacific Rim countries still show higher-than-average rates, with noticeable continuation in investment in new and expanded airports.[4] In some regions, such as western Europe, the development of alternative means of rapid transit (such as the TGV high-speed train) may further retard the growth in air transport, but for many regions travel by air remains the most viable, safe and efficient method of travelling distances over about 1000km. Also, with aircraft manufacturers developing new designs capable of carrying more passengers at less cost through lower energy levels, the cost per kilometre of air travel may again fall, fuelling further increase in demand.

Air travel is a product of four related factors: the supply of people, the need to travel, the resources available to spend, and the existence of an airline transport infrastructure. These four factors operate in different ways in different regions of the world. Whereas in the West the infrastructure exists, but an increasing percentage of people are unable to afford to travel, in the Pacific Rim and Asia more people can afford to fly but the airport infrastructure is not adequately established to serve their needs. Also, the need to travel is dependent upon the existence of an economy that requires business travel, or a tourist industry that provides holiday destinations served by air. A further factor is the characteristics of the region, especially the distribution of cities and population density.

Forecasting future demand is not simple, and changes in technology can destabilize predictive models. For example, innovation in communication technology may reduce the need to travel, and the trend towards high-speed trains and high-speed ships may further undermine the airline industry's monopoly on reduced journey time. Concerns over global warming and other adverse environmental consequences of aircraft travel may also prove a constraint on future growth.

What is an airport?

Airports are large, complex and generally highly profitable industrial enterprises. They are part of a nation's essential transportation infrastructure, which, besides providing thousands of jobs at the airport itself, supports a much wider area in social and economic terms. It has been estimated that for every job at the airport a further one is created in the region. As large industrial complexes airports consist primarily of:

- runways and taxiing areas
- air traffic control buildings
- aircraft maintenance buildings
- passenger terminals and car parks
- freight warehouses.

In the past, the airport structured these five principal activities into airside and landside zones, all enclosed within a security fence and served mainly by car or airline bus. Today, however, the trend is towards more social, commercial and tourist development at airports, with conference facilities, hotels and tourist information shops commonplace. In addition, the airport is seen as part of an integrated transport system, connected not only by car and bus but by mainline or underground railways.

1.6 Airports are major magnets of economic growth with distinctive functional territories. Lyon-Satolas Airport, France. Architects: Curtelin Ricard Bergeret/Scott Brownrigg and Turner.

Such is the expansion of facilities at airports that most today are more profitable than the airlines that use them. The major problem for the airline company is the limited services it can provide: transporting people and goods is

Table 1.1 World's top 12 airports in terms of terminal passengers

Airport	Annual passengers (millions) in 1995	Increase over previous year
Chicago O'Hare	67.3	1.2%
Atlanta	57.7	6.7%
London Heathrow	54.4	5.3%
Dallas	54.3	3.2%
Los Angeles	53.9	5.6%
Tokyo Haneda	45.8	–
Frankfurt	38.2	8.7%
San Francisco	36.3	4.7%
Miami	33.2	10.0%
Denver	31.0	−6.4%
Seoul Kimpo	30.9	14.2%
New York, Kennedy	30.3	5.3%

Source: *Flight International*, 20–26 March 1996

Table 1.2 Major European airports

Airport	Annual passengers (millions) in 1995	Increase over previous year
London Heathrow	54.4	5.3%
Frankfurt	38.2	8.7%
Paris, Charles de Gaulle	28.4	−1.1%
Paris, Orly	26.7	0.1%
Amsterdam, Schiphol	25.4	7.6%
London Gatwick	22.6	6.3%
Rome	21.1	3.8%
Madrid	19.9	7.8%
Zurich	15.4	2.0%
Düsseldorf	15.1	14.1%

Source: *Flight International*, 20–26 March 1996

not as profitable as generating revenue from rentals, concessionary arrangements with retailers or airport landing fees. Heathrow, for instance, in 1989 earned £145 million (about £4 per passenger throughput), which far exceeded the income of British Airways, the major carrier at the airport.[5] Even with no growth in aircraft movements in 1990–91, BAA, which owns 7 of Britain's major airports, reported an increase in profits of almost 10%.[6]

Airports are major transport infrastructure projects at, above and below ground. They are significant sources of pollution, and of environmental impact near and further afield, and a major concentration of energy exchange. They are also cultural, social, economic and commercial points of exchange. In many ways the airport is a microcosm of the city – a satellite that orbits at the edge of a major conurbation but which operates as an urban entity almost on its own.

There are three main groups of players at a typical airport:

* the airport company that manages the airport estate
* the airlines that use it
* the passengers.

Those who are encountered at airports are generally represented by one or other of these groups. However, as

Table 1.3 Major Asian Pacific airports

Airport	Annual passengers (millions) in 1995	Increase over previous year
Tokyo Haneda	45.8	–
Seoul Kimpo	30.9	14.2%
Hong Kong	28.0	8.1%
Tokyo	24.2	2.0%
Honolulu	23.6	2.5%
Singapore	23.2	7.2%
Bangkok	23.1	10.1%
Sydney	18.7	6.9%

Source: *Flight International*, 20–26 March 1996

The airport industry

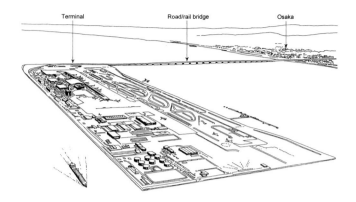

Terminal   Road/rail bridge   Osaka

1.7 Airports are concentrations of energy use, and have an enormous environmental impact. The trend is to locate airports on offshore islands. Kansai Airport, Osaka, Japan. Architects: Renzo Piano Building Workshop.

1.8 Terminals celebrate the transition from ground to air. New Doha International Airport, Qatar. Architects: Scott Brownrigg and Turner.

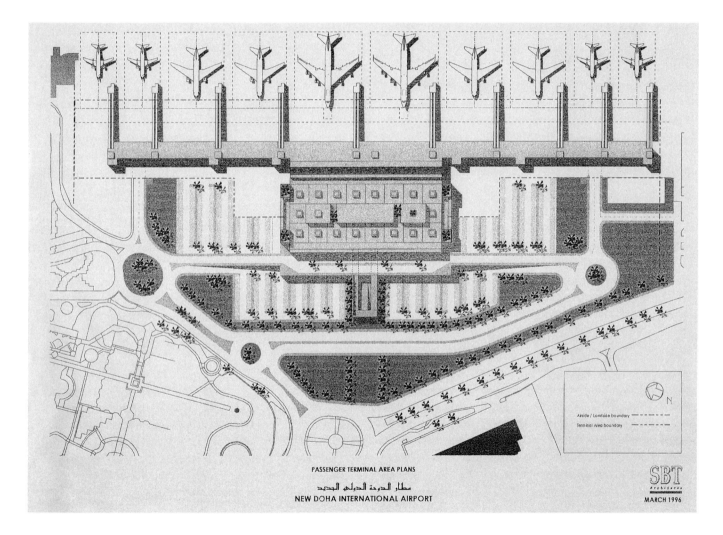

PASSENGER TERMINAL AREA PLANS

مطار الدوحة الدولي الجديد
NEW DOHA INTERNATIONAL AIRPORT

SBT
Architects

MARCH 1996

airports become more complex and more interesting as a destination in their own right, and as they take on more of the characteristics of the city they serve, there begin to emerge other user groups. Mature airports have extensive restaurant, retail and leisure facilities manned and often used by people who do not belong to the three principal groups. Also, there are security police, fire and ambulance staff. Many large airports have become leisure destina-tions, attracting people on day trips from further afield. The functional and social diversity of the modern airport leads inevitably to a blurring of the organizational clarity of the build-ings – particularly the terminal itself. In some ways a large modern airport performs like a new town. It has enormous economic impact on, and makes large demands upon, the regional infrastructure. Conceptually, an airport is structured like a town, with a centre (where the terminal buildings are

1.9 The modern terminal is really a shopping mall *en route* to the plane. North Terminal, Gatwick Airport, UK. Architects: YRM.

located), industrial areas (hangars and warehouses), an effective road system, and residential areas (hotels in the centre, motels at the edges). Many airports ape new towns in their use of public art, landmark buildings and employment of dense corridors of tree planting at their edges and along principal roads.

For the architect, the passenger terminal is the main airport building and opportunity for architectural expression. Other structures, such as hangars and control towers, are technological and structural challenges, but they do not provide the celebratory or processional potential of the terminal. Functionally, the terminal is the building that divides landside from airside: it establishes the boundary between the public realm and the private estate of the airport. This division, expressed directly in the customs and baggage control systems, allows the terminal to be the major organizational and control mechanism at the airport. To cross the line between landside and airside is symbolic of the move from the ground to the air. Ticket controls, customs and immigration barriers, baggage extraction and duty-free lounges are all part of this transition. Similarly, the means of reaching the aircraft via passenger piers or light rail systems (as at Birmingham and Stansted) is a further symptom of crossing between landside and airside.

Organizationally, the terminal building is the key element within the airport estate. It is, however, just part of an integrated system, which involves a complex interaction between airline companies, airport authorities and the traveller. The reputation of airports is, however, determined by the quality of its terminal buildings, not just as architectural imagery but in terms of customer needs. Well-designed terminal buildings enhance the reputation of the airline companies that use it, and the airport itself, and ensure that passengers enjoy a comfortable, stress-free start and end to their journey.

If an airport is a self-contained urban entity not unlike a new town at the edge of a city, the terminal buildings are its public buildings. They have much the same relationship to the airport as shopping malls and commercial buildings have to the city. The terminal building is where the travelling public congregate, exchange currency, buy snacks and gifts, use the telephone and fax machines, and savour

1.10 Retail and leisure activities can dominate the environment of the terminal. Good design consists in striking a balance between tranquillity and bustle. Terminal 3, Schiphol Airport, the Netherlands. Architects: Bentham Crouwel.

Table 1.4 Interaction between the airport system and infrastructure

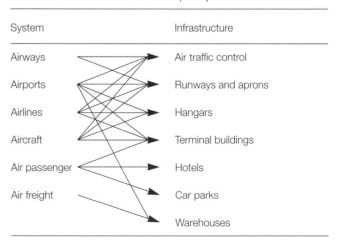

System	Infrastructure
Airways	Air traffic control
Airports	Runways and aprons
Airlines	Hangars
Aircraft	Terminal buildings
Air passenger	Hotels
Air freight	Car parks
	Warehouses

1.11 Airports, more than most building types, need to cater for unpredictable growth. Hamburg Airport, Germany. Architects: Von Gerkan, Marg & Partners.

the experience of travel. Internally, the shopping and leisure malls provide entertainment for the traveller; externally, the terminal provides the means to spectate upon the aircraft gathered on aprons outside the windows. Inside, the bustle of movement of people from different regions and at different stages of their journey provides a further spectacle. The function of terminals is to celebrate these activities, to raise the spirit, to enhance the anticipation of air travel.

How airports grow

To accommodate the growth in demand for air transportation, which has been at 6–7% per annum over the past 25 years, the infrastructure of air travel needs to grow in five distinct ways:

• More aircraft with greater carrying capacity are needed.
• Airspace and traffic control facilities need to expand.
• New and enlarged runways are needed.
• Passenger facilities need to expand, especially terminals.
• New and more efficient means of reaching the airport are needed.

At different airports, constraint upon growth may be in different areas or combinations. For example, Heathrow's expansion in the late-1990s is curtailed by lack of terminal space and by poor means of reaching the airport by public and private transport, rather than by lack of runways or airspace. In contrast, many North American airports (such as Washington) and Asian ones (such as Tokyo) have their potential expansion limited by lack of runway space.

Predicting future demand for air travel and the implications for infrastructure provision, and making better use of existing capacity, are precise arts. Part of the equation, however, relates to aircraft design. As new passenger aircraft are introduced, with shorter take-off and landing lengths, greater capacity and speedier turnaround times, the basis for prediction changes. With Boeing's introduction in 1996 of the 777 (with its greatly increased passenger-carrying capacity), and the further development of STOL (short take-off and landing) aircraft, the relationship between airline company needs and airport provision begins to change.

It has been estimated that to meet future demand some 4000–4500 extra jet aircraft are needed by the year 2000.[7] Such a level of increase puts a strain on existing provision across a broad front. Some airports grow by adding new runways (as at Manchester and Lyon), others by building new terminals (as at Heathrow and Stuttgart). However, where space is limited or access is poor there is little alternative than to build a new airport. This was the justification for the development of Stansted, the building of the new airport at Lan Tao Island in Hong Kong, Kansai Airport in Japan, and Munich Airport in Germany, and the new airport now under construction in Athens. In each of these cases the airport occupies a greenfield site (or man-made island) with, where possible, flight paths taken over water rather than land. In most of these examples, too, the airport is joined to the infrastructure of public transport at the time of construction rather than later.

Most airports expand by building new runways and new terminal buildings. Investment in both is enormous, and each makes demands upon limited space. Gatwick has expanded by a combination of new runways and new terminal buildings, though it was terminal space rather than runway space that was the greater constraint upon growth. Heathrow has seen a similar pattern (plans are afoot to build Terminal 5), but here the limiting factor is the capacity of roads, motorways and rail services to support the world's

1.13 Airports need to connect with the ground-based transportation infrastructure. Hamburg Airport, Germany. Architects: Von Gerkan, Marg & Partners.

third biggest airport and the busiest one outside North America. Where growth is more moderate it may be possible to expand the existing terminal (as happened at Marseille and Glasgow) rather than build afresh.

If the overall growth in air transport has been between 6 and 7%, the increase in international air traffic has been even more marked. In 1987 the growth here was 14%,[8] and this sector of the market has continued to expand faster than the domestic sector. International passenger traffic has been most marked in Asia and the Pacific regions, and it is here that runway capacity in particular is under most stress. International flights use bigger aircraft, make greater demands upon runway and apron capacities, and – with their larger passenger loads – put terminal buildings and baggage handling under greater strain. Hence, if airports have the capacity for international traffic, they tend also to be able to cope with national and domestic pressures.

As a general rule, the biggest constraint upon airport growth is lack of runway provision. The environmental problems associated with runways lead to lengthy planning delays, which mean that airports are often behind in their forward provision for growth. Runways cannot easily be expanded without major disruption to the operation of the

airport. New, rather than expanded, runways are generally more desirable, but overcoming community objections and meeting safety regulations can be a complex and difficult task. However, with new or expanded runway capacity, the next constraint upon growth is usually the passenger terminal. Hence there needs to be integration of provision and a phasing of expansion that allows the airport to grow in a smooth fashion. The history of Heathrow, Orly Airport in Paris and O'Hare Airport in Chicago highlights the problems created by not planning adequately for growth, particularly in the provision of terminal buildings.

The air transport industry: future trends

By the end of the 1980s the air transport industry's impact on gross world output amounted to US $700 billion, creating some 21 million jobs across the globe. By the year 2010 the economic impact is expected to exceed US $1500 billion and over 30 million jobs.[9] Growth rates in the industry, which averaged 7% in the 1970s and 6% in the 1980s, are still expected to be over 5% up to the year 2005. It is anticipated that between 1985 and 2005 the number of people travelling by air will have doubled, putting pressure on terminals, airline companies, air space and runway capacities. In Europe, IATA expects the number of passengers who travel by air to rise from 394 million per annum in 1990 to almost 1010 million by the year 2010.[10]

1.12 Terminals usually mark the growth rings of mature airports. O'Hare Airport, Chicago, USA.

World growth in air transportation will reach critical levels in terms of infrastructure provision in Europe and North America within the next decade. It is now widely admitted that the growth in aviation facilities cannot keep pace with demand. In the Pacific Rim region it was estimated that 50% of airports were constrained by capacity limitations, even by 1995.[11] In the Asia-Pacific region passenger growth of 8% per annum is the norm, with South Korea's Seoul airport achieving a 14% expansion in passengers in 1995.[12]

Aviation infrastructure consists principally of:

- airspace capacity
- airport capacity (runways and terminals)
- surface access to airports (road, rail, metro etc.).

While expansion of all three is necessary to meet future demand, it is surface access to the airport that is often the most critical and the most frequently overlooked. Links between the city, region and airport need to keep pace – in quality, comfort and convenience – with the growth in customer quality at the airport. Similarly, airspace capacity needs to be expanded (with a corresponding updating of the air traffic control system) if passenger growth increases are to be accommodated. Aircraft stacking in revolving formation above airfields while they wait for available runway space is a regular occurrence these days at the world's busier airports. Runway efficiency is also undermined by different sizes of aircraft using the runway at the same time. Commuter jets and international flights cannot use a runway simultaneously without causing difficulties for air traffic control, apron services and runway managers. Although mixed traffic causes runway-use headaches, new computer systems being developed by McDonnell Douglas and NASA seek to integrate passenger terminal area use and air traffic management.[13] Congestion in the skies and on the ground are related factors in airport planning. The three elements in the system (airspace, runways and terminals, and surface transport) need to be considered in unison if bottlenecks and inefficiencies are to be avoided.

It is estimated that 10 000 commercial aircraft operate today, carrying about 1 million passengers a day, and that a further 12 000 aeroplanes will be delivered by the year 2010.[14] A third of these will replace obsolete craft, and two-thirds will accommodate growth. The new aircraft will be larger, quieter, 'greener' and more flexible to operate than the earlier generation of aircraft. Being larger (average seating capacity of 400–500) they will ease congestion in airspace but add to that in the terminals and in surface transportation. Bigger aircraft result in sharper peaks in

1.14 The design of aircraft and loading systems tends to determine airport and terminal layout. Hamburg Airport, Germany. Architects: Von Gerkan, Marg & Partners.

1.15 Airport expansion consists in providing new links in each part of the system. Stuttgart Airport, Germany. Architects: Von Gerkan, Marg & Partners.

passenger throughput, which puts stress on interior space and public transport provision. Having a larger wingspan than earlier aircraft, the new generation of large, high-load, twin-jet aircraft (such as the Boeing 777) require greater manoeuvring space on aprons. Hence groundspace rather than airspace is put under pressure. The same will be true when Airbus Industries' A3XX plane moves into production at the turn of the century with a seating capacity of 500–650 and a range of 13 700km. These larger aircraft relieve pressure on airspace and air traffic control but shift it to ground facilities, especially apron areas, passenger terminals and the public transport infrastructure serving the airport.

Growing aircraft size is a trend discernible today. Costs, particularly energy costs and airspace congestion, mean that fewer, larger aircraft are preferable to many smaller planes. Speed, however, is another area undergoing change. The growth in the Pacific Rim market has led airlines to ask whether flights from London or New York to Tokyo, which currently take 10 or 12 hours, can be undertaken in half that time. Supersonic aircraft (known as high-speed civil aviation: HSCA) could potentially cut journey times by over a half, but the technical feasibility of carrying high passenger loads has yet to be demonstrated. Also, airport and community noise, engine emissions and seat cost remain obstacles to further development.

The future of air transport is dependent upon the provision of infrastructure (aircraft, airports, transport links) and upon airspace availability. Future growth can be met only by the expansion of all the elements in the chain of the airline journey. This means investment in aircraft design and technology, in airport runways and terminals, in airspace provision and traffic control, and in ground transportation links to airports. Satisfying customer needs means keeping the costs down for the passenger while providing comfortable, safe and fast transport. Meeting anticipated levels of growth within ever-tightening environmental regulations and reduced government subsidies is both a challenge and a massive source of employment for aircraft designers and manufacturers, airport architects and engineers, and those involved in the operational management of air transport facilities.

Limits to airport growth

As the twentieth century closes, it is apparent that the worldwide growth in air travel is outstripping the capacity of airports and air traffic control systems. The result is congestion in the air, on runways, and in terminal buildings. Growth in demand, if not met by provision, will result in delayed trips, deteriorating quality of service, unacceptable levels of overcrowding in terminal buildings, and diminishing safety in the air. For the passenger, awareness of overcrowding is most evident at the terminal, where queues and delays can undermine customer satisfaction.

The main constraints on expanding airport provision are:

- environmental factors and planning delays
- the availability of suitable land for airport construction
- the willingness of the industry to invest in expensive runway and terminal provision (particularly true with government-owned airports)
- lack of available airspace.

1.16 The terminal is at the centre of a complex system. Southampton Airport, UK. Architects: Manser Associates.

Inadequate scale of airside or landside provision can lead to bottlenecks, delay and threats to safety. Normally it is runway capacity that is the controlling element of the airport system.[15] Runway capacity is dependent upon air traffic control, characteristics of demand, environmental factors, and the number and design of runways. To increase provision one normally has to expand the number, length and orientation of runways, plus the connecting taxiways. Because there are safety criteria for the spacing of aircraft arriving or departing at an airport, the capacity of the system can be calculated. However, the weather plays a large part, and congestion can occur at times when slack exists in the system. The relationship between weather and traffic control is often more critical on a daily basis than runway capacity, until the system as a whole becomes heavily used when queuing on the ground and stacking in the air have to be employed. Predicting when the runway system is approaching capacity requires complex analytical models.

It is less easy to predict when the capacity of a terminal has been reached. Passenger needs expressed as space levels per person are not as scientifically determined as with aircraft on runways. It is evident, all the same, that many airport terminal buildings are unacceptably congested, and that the quality of journeys is suffering. Customer surveys have highlighted overcrowding of public areas and unacceptably long queues as areas of dissatisfaction with terminals, especially at check-in areas and departure lounges. Delays to passengers can lead to delays to aircraft, which puts the air traffic control system under stress.

Congestion also occurs at the interface between the runway and terminal: that is, at the terminal apron. This is where the aircraft are parked while being refuelled and serviced, and where passengers and their baggage are loaded or unloaded. Too few 'gate' or 'stand' positions on the apron can limit capacity even when runway and terminal areas are more than adequate for the level of demand. Increasing the area of the terminal apron and the number of aircraft gate positions can give the terminal extra capacity (as with the rebuilding of Heathrow's Terminal 1 with extended piers). Generally, the layout of the terminal provides gates in three recognizable geometric patterns: linear, projecting, and satellite. The clearances required for noise, blast, heat and fume protection, added to the movement characteristics of the aircraft (the angle at which it parks and its turning radius), determine the optimum layout and spacing of gate positions.

The capacity of an airport is determined by the availability of airspace, and by runway provision, apron space and terminal size. Growth in one area normally requires corresponding adjustment in another. Airports tend to carry on growing until they reach capacity, when a new airport is required. To meet the anticipated threefold increase in air traffic movements over the next 50 years airports have to adopt strategies for growth. Because the planning approval, design and construction of major airport facilities can take a decade, operators and carriers have to be alert to changing trends, and be willing to adjust future plans. The history of the airport is one of crisis management rather than the systematic analysis of growth and the expansion of provision.

References

1. Norman Ashford and Paul Wright, *Airport Engineering*, John Wiley & Sons, New York, 1991, p. 10.
2. BAA, *Shaping Up for the 21st Century*, Annual Report 1995/96, London, p. 4.
3. Extracted from Table 1.4 in Ashford and Wright, *Airport Engineering*.
4. Ashford and Wright, *Airport Engineering*, p. 25.
5. Rigas Doganis, *The Airport Business*, Routledge, London, 1992, p. 2 (see Table 1.1).
6. *Ibid.*, p. 2.
7. *Ibid.*, p. 33.
8. *Ibid.*, p. 35.
9. J. Meredith, 'Surface access to airports', in G.B.R. Fielden, A.H. Wickens and L.R. Yates (eds), *Passenger Transport After 2000 AD*, Chapman & Hall, London, 1995.
10. *Ibid.*
11. *Ibid.*, p. 52
12. Kevin O'Toole, 'Airports grow again', *Flight International*, 20–26 March 1996, p. 28.
13. Graham Warwick, 'Working to capacity', *Flight International*, 5–11 June 1996, p. 28.
14. R.A. Davis, 'From physics to customers: the Jet Age Phase II', in Fielden, Wickens and Yates, *Passenger Transport After 2000 AD*, p. 141.
15. Ashford and Wright, *Airport Engineering*, p. 185.

CHAPTER 2

The airport as a unique twentieth-century building type

The airport is the one unique building type of the latter half of the twentieth century. Like the golf course – its landscape equivalent in terms of modern origins – the airport has no direct parallels in function, scale or form. Though similar to the railway terminal in some respects, the modern airport has a size and intensity all its own. From the airport one ventures into the sky, and in a few hours to distant continents. The airport, with its runways and terminal buildings, has a huge scale, dwarfing most other urban structures. Large international airports, such as London's Heathrow, handle in a year almost the same numbers as those who live in the country. With over 55 million passengers using Heathrow each year (and 80 million predicted by 2013), the airport is a great cosmopolitan centre. As the third busiest airport in the world, Heathrow is a self-contained urban entity, with its buildings, roads and business parks serving a remarkable variety of functions. Heathrow employs more people than the city of Oxford, and has an economic impact as great as that of London Docklands. Trade alone at Heathrow amounts to £250 million per year, with 58000 direct jobs and 300000 indirect ones provided as a consequence of the airport's presence.[1] It is clearly more than just an airport; it is a city in its own right, with the terminal buildings its public landmarks. These buildings, plus the hotels, car parks, conference centres and business parks, add up to a fresh kind of twentieth-century city. Culturally, economically and socially the modern airport is a new point of exchange between people, companies and nations.

Some argue that airports are a superior kind of city. Martin Pawley, for example, claims that Heathrow is 'not only better than London, it is everything that London isn't'.[2] This assertion is based upon the convenience of airports in terms of the range of facilities provided (shops, business centres, hotels, car parks and travel modes), the feeling of security (lacking in many traditional city centres), and the sense of economic opportunity. The limits on the growth of airports (such as Heathrow and Kennedy) arise, according to Pawley, because they are not recognized as cities, which many airports clearly are in economic, physical and social terms. Large

2.1 Heathrow from the air. As a centre, Heathrow employs more people than the city of Oxford.

Heathrow Airport
① Terminal 1   ⑥ Control Tower
② Terminal 2   ⑦ Maintenance Area
③ Terminal 3   ⑧ Cargo Area
④ Terminal 4
⑤ Perry Oaks Sludge Works proposed site of Terminal 5

international airports start as airport projects and end as urban entities serving a wide range of non-airport functions. Put simply, they begin as airports and end as cities. Such expansion and change of function is not easily accommodated within an orthodox town planning paradigm.

The international airport is a modern kind of placeless city. It lacks the sense of geographical justification that is evident in most urban areas. The big, busy, multinational airport derives its logic from the distribution of world trade, the spatial pattern of international cities, and the often irrational location of national boundaries. This has led some observers to contend that the airport is a new type of city,

perhaps the most coherent of a fresh generation of post-industrial cities. In this the terminal building is its market place, cathedral and municipal town hall all rolled into one.

The architecture of airports reflects the international flavour of modern air travel. There is a sense of technological bravado balanced by national pride in airport design. Countries like to express a modern efficient image through the vehicle of national airports in general and the terminal buildings in particular. While the aircraft are the same, whether in Asia, Europe or North America, the individual terminals often retain something of local cultural identity. The

2.2 In the Middle East the terminal is less a retail mall, more a celebration of meeting and travel. King Abdulaziz Airport, Jeddah. Architects: Murphy/Jahn.

2.3 The modern airport is a new kind of city, with the terminal acting like a market hall. Munich Airport, Germany. Architects: Prof. von Busse, Blees, Kampmann & Buch.

internationalism of air transportation is invariably tempered by regional characteristics in the design of terminals themselves. This is occasionally the result of climate, and sometimes of the traditions of building in a particular area, but often of the sense that airports are great national gateways, where cultural differences have to be expressed. The comparison between London Heathrow and Paris Charles de Gaulle shows how far national characteristics can infuse airport design. While the first is a collection of disjointed terminal buildings set within an apparently haphazard masterplan, the latter is grandly conceived, beautifully executed and infused with Gallic pomp.

Different philosophies apply with regard to the nature of airports in different parts of the world. In Europe the airport is a complex interchange and a leisure destination, while in the USA the airport journey is rather akin to catching a bus. At Chicago O'Hare Airport, for instance, the typical airline passenger arrives by car, parking in a huge open car park, travels by courtesy coach to the airline terminal (not the airport), and boards the plane with generally no security, passport or customs check. Direct gate ticketing allows the passenger to proceed through the terminal without hindrance or delay. Shops, bars and duty-free facilities barely exist: the airport is a linear functional system, with the terminal – dedicated to a specific airline company – merely an enclosed space through which the passenger hurries en route to the plane.

2.4 The European terminal differs from that in the USA, where the experience can be akin to catching a bus. Munich Airport Centre, Germany. Architects: Murphy/Jahn.

In Europe, leisure activities and retail sales dominate the architecture of terminals. Airports such as Gatwick, with its separate retail floor at North Terminal sandwiched between the arrival and departure levels, and the burger-bar-dominated 'Village' in South Terminal, look and feel more like shopping malls than traditional terminals. In the Middle East and Africa the airport is normally a loss-making, though architecturally distinguished, statement of nationhood. Riyadh Airport in Saudi Arabia is typical of the rather Olympian ideal behind many airports in the Gulf States. Here retail and tourism pressures are kept to the periphery of terminals; the passenger experiences instead a grand processional sequence of public spaces – lofty, well lit and unencumbered. The terminal mirrors the aspirations, wealth and prestige of the country, not the free play of market forces (as in the UK) or ruthless airline efficiency (as in the hub airports of the USA).

The airport is the quintessential building type of the modern age. It is where human and fossil fuel energy are exchanged with greatest intensity. The floods of people arriving and departing, the similar number of greeters who assemble to celebrate the journey, and those who use the airport as a leisure or business destination in its own right, make the terminal building a great modern assembly hall. In a sense the airport is not a single functional entity but an amalgam of activities taking place simultaneously within enormously scaled buildings. To design such structures requires an appreciation of the interculturalism and inter-functionalism of modern life, and a grasp of the dramatic opportunities afforded by the sheer verve of contemporary air travel.

The approach to terminal design has changed greatly over the past generation. Writing in 1967, the then chairman of the British Airports Authority, Peter Masefield, said that 'flexible, easily put-up and easily torn-down terminals are the order of the day'.[3] Today, however, the emphasis is more upon the airport terminal as a landmark building. Certainly, it needs to be able to accommodate internal

2.5 Retaining cultural identity is important as airports become more standardized in nature. Harare Airport, Zimbabwe. Architects: Scott Brownrigg and Turner.

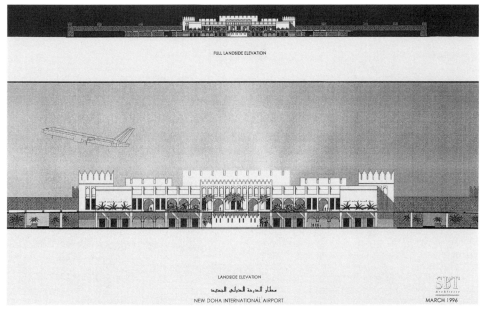

2.6 A sense of national image is required of new airports in the Middle East. New Doha International Airport, Qatar. Architects: Scott Brownrigg and Turner.

changes on a regular (and hopefully planned) basis, but architects of late have approached the design of the terminal with concepts of permanence in mind. A clearer distinction is now made between fixed parts (structural framework, broad spatial pattern and natural lighting) and the less enduring parts (partition walls, mechanical services, retail and leisure areas, baggage-handling system). It is a philosophy that allows the architect to invest heavily in the features that contribute to the character and distinctiveness of a terminal, knowing that the elements that have a shorter life can receive less of the building's budget. Many modern terminals, such as Kansai and London Stansted, notably follow this example.

The role of meaning, function and form in defining the architecture of terminals

In his *A History of Building Types*, written in 1976, Nikolaus Pevsner places the airport terminal as an adjunct to the chapter on railway stations.[4] The airport is seen as a twentieth-century postscript to the essentially nineteenth-century history of transportation buildings, of which the railway station is the prime example. To Pevsner the airport terminal is less a new building type than a development of an older, well-established typology. He does, however, refer to one unique characteristic of aerodrome buildings, as he calls them: that is, their ability to be forever growing, with

2.7 Interculturalism finds expression in many recent airport projects, as here at Seoul Airport. Transportation Centre, Seoul Airport, Korea. Architects: Terry Farrell and Partners.

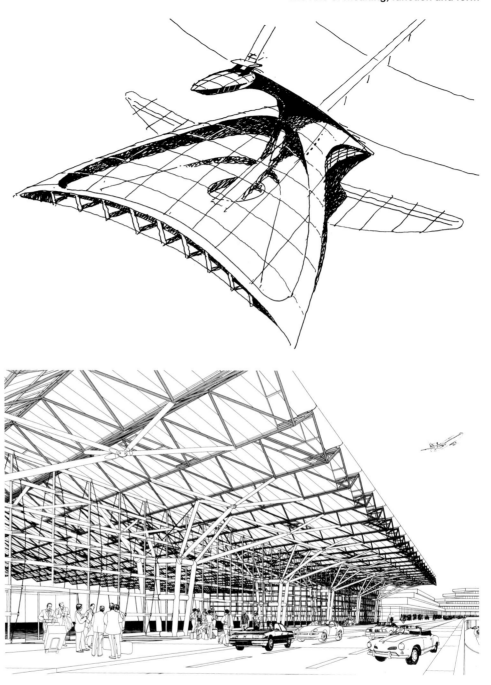

2.8 Tectonic structure is a feature of recent terminals. Cologne/Bonn Airport, Germany. Architects: Murphy/Jahn.

'cranes and scaffolding never leaving the premises'.[5] Change on its own is not, however, a feature employed by Pevsner to help define building types. Rather, distinctive building types grow from an interweaving of function, materials and styles. By such criteria Pevsner happily classifies the airport terminal along with the bus station and railway station.

More recent writers have taken a broader view of the taxonomy of building types, noting that the evolution of new types is invariably in response to fresh programmatic requirements and changing technologies. As travel has become faster, the phenomenon of mass transportation has led to the emergence of new forms, of which the modern international airport is an obvious example. Bigger buildings for

faster movement lead inevitably to the introduction of new construction techniques, which propel the evolutionary process towards a new building species. Added to this, the concept of perpetual change and dynamic growth (a feature noted by Pevsner) charges the airport building with a responsibility towards structural and spatial change, which further distances the terminal from the railway station. Whereas the station evolved to meet a relatively stable (though unfolding) new functional programme, the airport terminal is conceived as an almost temporary building, given a life of 10–15 years. The unpredictability of airports means that the functional life of the terminal is invariably shorter than the built form it houses. Though airport terminals

2.9 The geometry of space and articulation of volume is the key to establishing order in the design of terminals. King Abdulaziz Airport, Jeddah. Architects: Murphy/Jahn.

share certain similarities with the nineteenth-century railway station, they are so much part of the gestalt of late twentieth-century life that they can no longer be considered as a postscript to the former building type.

In understanding the airport terminal as a distinctive typology, it is important to grasp three main formal elements that give it shape: the plan, the design of surfaces, and the handling of light. The plan – the geometry of space, as it is sometimes described – establishes the spatial and hierarchical composition. The medium of plan and section begins the process of defining the airport as a distinctive building type. However, the design of the masses and their surfaces also plays an important part. How the materials are used, and whether the surfaces reflect the functional and socially infused meaning of the airport, are also key factors. Finally, light and the play of light in an optical sense help to distinguish the airport terminal from other related building types such as railway stations. The changing images in the complex movement through a terminal begin, as Markus puts it, to 'coalesce in the mind into a single sensation'.[6]

In defining the architectural factors that give the airport terminal its 'airportness' – its sense of typological identity – the compositional components of plan, mass and light are of fundamental importance. These combine to give the function appropriate form and meaning, which allow the terminal to be understood by its users, and which permit the terminal to be recognized as a distinctive type of building by those who have yet to enter into it.

This argument also allows function, meaning and form to have social value rather than purely aesthetic value. The term 'airport' or 'airport terminal' is exclusively a twentieth-century one; before the modern age no conception of the airport existed, and hence no preconception of the design of the terminal building had occurred in the mind of architects. By giving the airport a name one constructs a functional narrative, which allows designers to conjure up appropriate forms.[7] Without the naming of a new function there is little basis for design or public recognition of the built consequences. Hence the word 'airport' leads to spatial constructs that themselves carry social meaning. By removing

2.10   Harare Airport, Zimbabwe. Architects: Scott Brownrigg and Turner.

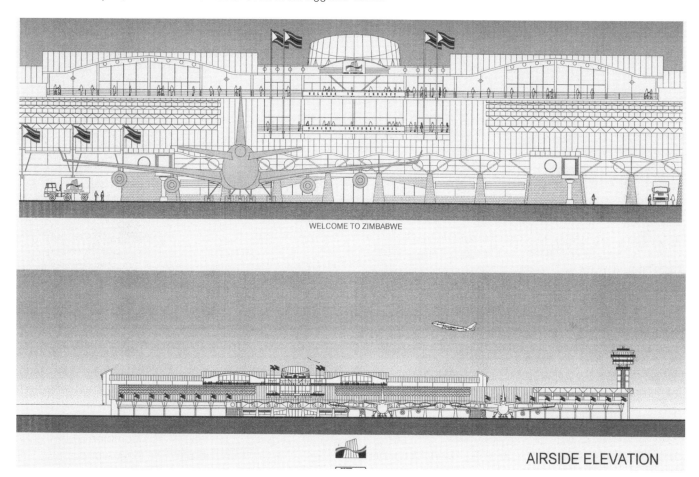

WELCOME TO ZIMBABWE

AIRSIDE ELEVATION

ambiguity through the close correspondence between function, meaning and form, there emerges a recognizable body of building types, which society at large can recognize as airports. In this sense the formal repertoire of architectural elements – plan, masses and surfaces, and light – gives meaning to the built forms. Meaning does not exist within the functional narrative unless accompanied by architectural forms; neither does meaning exist within built forms unless they carry functional legitimacy. The earliest terminal buildings, such as Eero Saarinen's TWA Terminal at New York and his Dulles Terminal at Washington (both designed around 1956), or the more Miesian terminals at O'Hare, Chicago designed at the same time by Naess and

Murphy, were important beginnings in helping to define the modern airport in a typological sense.

The maturing of airports as a building type

In the 1950s and 1960s America was the centre for airport development: here new layouts and airport patterns (such as hub airports) were developed, and the typology of the terminal was established. It was in the USA that the standard two-level departures and arrivals terminal was evolved, each level having its own deck of vehicle access. By the 1970s, however, the focus of attention had shifted to Europe, which began to develop airports integrated with

2.11 In the Pacific Rim, new airports are part of integrated transportation systems, unlike those in the USA and parts of Europe. Hong Kong's new airport at Chek Lap Kok. Architects: Foster and Partners.

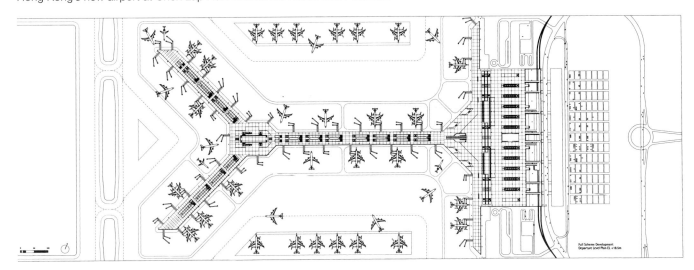

other modes of transportation. Deregulation in the 1980s opened up terminals to greater commercial pressure, and it was the UK that refined the notion of the passenger terminal as a huge open retail mall. In the 1980s also the Middle East and parts of the Far East explored the relationship between airports and nationhood, which found expression in grand civic terminals. The relatively straightforward precedent of airports represented by New York's JFK became by the early 1990s a diverse canvas of different design and management approaches. The extremes are represented by the muscular and expressive Kansai Terminal, on its huge man-made island in the Pacific, the neutral and refined Stansted Airport in the English countryside north of London, and the tented roof structure of Denver Terminal, evoking images of North American Indian tepees. In each case, though the buildings are undeniably airports, their functional meaning has been enriched by cultural differences.

As the airport has matured into a recognizably distinctive twentieth-century building type, it has also diversified into a range of formal types, whose taxonomy responds directly to different airport management systems. These inevitably reflect the values of the peoples served. Emerging nations have a different view of airports from mature nations, and where the culture of free enterprise is rife, the airport is undeniably a means of making money. What is not always recognized is the role of airports in facilitating knowledge and technology transfer between nations and within countries. New airports in undeveloped parts of the world, designed by global firms and constructed by international contractors, allow new skills and management approaches to be learned. The particular place that airports have in technology transfer and training is pertinent in Africa, which looks set to be the arena for airport development in the next century.

The flow of ideas about the nature and design of airports has moved from the New World to the Old, and from the developed parts of the Old to more distant lands. In the process of disseminating wisdom and approaches, the orthodoxy evolved at countless American airports has increasingly been challenged by different geographical and cultural factors. In Australia, Japan and China a new generation of airports is developing, based upon the airport as an element of integrated transportation. Here the role of the airport as a growth centre is recognized, not resisted, within a network of regional airports established (like Shenzhen in China) as a spur to economic, technological and social regeneration. In Australia and parts of Africa the airport is seen as part of sustainable development, bringing in eco-tourists to help preserve endangered landscapes. The environmental battles that accompanied airport expansion in the USA, Europe and Japan have been replaced in the less developed world by greater accommodation with environmental protection. Recent airports too are likely to be designed using local materials and respecting indigenous building traditions. The specifics of place, culture and climate are beginning to balance the universal standards and ideologies of IATA manuals which remain the blueprint for airport development throughout the world.

References

1. Degan Sudjic, The 100 Mile City, Flamingo, London, 1993, p. 150.
2. Martin Pawley, 'Viewpoint', The Architects' Journal, 14 December 1995, p. 18.
3. Peter Masefield, 'Closing address', Airports of the Future, Institution of Civil Engineers, London, 1967.
4. Nikolaus Pevsner, A History of Building Types, Thames & Hudson, London, 1976, pp. 225–234.
5. Ibid., p. 234.
6. Thomas A. Markus, Buildings & Power: Freedom & Control in The Origin of Modern Building Types, Routledge, London, 1993, p. 11.
7. Ibid., p. 12.

Relationship between airports, terminals and aircraft design

CHAPTER

3

With any air transport system, airports, terminals and aircraft are dependent upon each other in giving the passenger a service. The introduction of new aircraft technology, new ways of handling baggage, and new approaches to air traffic control, have implications for the operation of the airport and the design of the terminal buildings. Air transportation is a high-growth, high-cost industry, in which advances in technology are rapid and have widespread ramifications for the whole system.

The development by Boeing of the Jumbo Jet in 1970, innovations in short take-off and landing (STOL), and faster, more passenger-weight-efficient planes (such as the European Airbus) have all altered the parameters within which the aircraft industry operates. New, more energy-efficient aircraft engines, larger airframes and quicker aircraft-servicing regimes have all led to real cost savings for the passenger. Cheaper air travel is the main reason why the air transportation industry continues to expand worldwide, even in regions suffering from

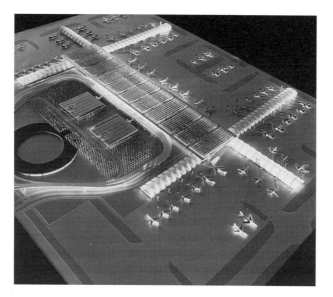

3.1 Modern terminals have a relationship to technology that is similar to that of the aircraft they serve. Bangkok Airport, Thailand. Architects: Murphy/Jahn.

general economic decline. Because about 85% of the operating costs of the entire air transport system revolves around the aircraft (including purchase price, fuel and servicing), the tendency has been to look to technology breakthroughs in aircraft design to reduce overall costs.[1] Hence the airport (runway, terminals etc.) has responded to the planes rather than vice versa.

The introduction of wide-bodied aircraft such as the Boeing 747 in the 1970s resulted not only in the lengthening of runways but also in the enlargement of terminals and access piers to accommodate the influx of passengers arriving in great waves. More recently, the growth in aircraft size has been curtailed not by technological possibility but environmental and operational factors – particularly noise in the neighbourhood of airports, and resistance from airport operators. It is feasible today to design and build aircraft capable of carrying 1000 passengers, but double-decker planes would require double-decked access piers, and greatly enlarged gate lounges and terminals. With rising construction costs and escalating land values, many airport authorities have discouraged plane makers such as Boeing from developing to the full technological potential. Instead, aircraft design in the 1990s has concentrated upon new safety levels, greater comfort, less noise and improved fuel energy performance. Such aircraft have stabilized at seating levels of about 450–550 (as in the Boeing 777) on the advice of airline companies and airport operators alike, though development is under way on the European Airbus A3XX, capable of accommodating 850 passengers and flying non-stop for 14 000km.

While airport runways were being lengthened in the 1970s to accommodate a new generation of aircraft, recently the trend has been reversed. Advances in the technology of producing high lift for take-off has had the effect of reducing the requirement for lengthy runways, particularly in the area of short- to medium-range operations. Shorter runways release land for other possible development at the perimeter of the airport (such as warehousing and hotels), and lessen the impact of aircraft noise in the vicinity of residential areas. However, for larger aircraft runways of 3km are still required, and the new generation of wide-bodied, double-decker aircraft require substantially stronger runways than in the past. A loaded A3XX will weigh 476 tonnes, which is 20% heavier than a 747, adding new stresses to runways.[2]

The interactions between aircraft design and that of the airport itself are necessarily close. The trigger for change is normally that of innovation in plane design, with airports responding (sometimes reluctantly) to new technological innovations in the aircraft industry as a whole. This affects both passenger- and freight-handling policies. Large, wide-bodied aircraft introduced extensively in the 1980s allowed operators to carry both passengers and freight. Air cargo has become a major industry alongside that of passenger transport. Although significant volumes of freight are carried in specially adapted aircraft (mostly formerly passenger aircraft), a large amount – perhaps as much as 50% – is transported in the holds of scheduled passenger services. Freight traffic is growing at a faster rate than passenger traffic, with the belly holds of wide-bodied passenger aircraft providing the capacity. The management of flight turnaround and apron services and immigration controls have all had to respond to what was originally merely the technological breakthrough of wide-bodied aircraft. As a general rule, on short- to medium-haul flights luggage and freight must be loaded and unloaded, and planes serviced and refuelled, in 100 minutes, or 120 minutes for larger aircraft on long-haul flights. The speedy disembarking of passengers is an essential component of efficient flight turnaround.

Because aircraft, airports and passengers are part of an interdependent system, we need to know which elements are critical in operational terms. Generally, limits to expansion or operational congestion occur when either

- runway capacity is exceeded, or
- terminal passenger capacity is exceeded.

What determines overcrowding of runways or terminals is dependent upon many factors. With runways it is the size of aircraft, the number of movements, and the type of aircraft: different planes have different climb and speed requirements. With terminal buildings it is not the daily flow of passengers but that at peak times, especially with the arrival of several large aircraft at about the same time. It is this that has tended to curtail the development of

3.2 Aircraft design, airport operation and the layout of terminals share a common philosophy. Southampton Airport, UK. Architects: Manser Associates.

1000-seater aircraft, though the A3XX, capable of serving larger international airports, looks set to corner a niche in the expanding air transport market, especially to the Far East.

Whereas airport capacity was limited in the 1970s by runway capacity, in the 1990s it is more likely to be constrained by passenger terminal capacity. At the terminal, capacity may be reached in terms of space per passenger (in the departure or arrivals lounge, the gate lounges and piers), baggage handling, or check-in capacity. Sudden influxes of movement – the result of larger aircraft – also put strain on immigration services and the airport road system. At airside the terminal may reach capacity with regard to apron requirements and access points for aircraft to the terminal. Hence different elements of the system may reach capacity before others, but once capacity is reached in a part the whole system is put in jeopardy.

There is greater understanding today of the nature of the interactions between aircraft design and airport operation. Future trends in plane design suggest that aircraft costs per kilometre will continue to fall in real terms. Cost savings rather than improved speed are what drive innovation in engine and airframe design. The age of the supersonic jet is coming to an end as cost and environmental factors take hold, though some predict its revival in future generations. Passenger kilometres per unit of fuel are expected to

increase by 25% by the year 2000, making air travel cheaper into the next century. Moreover, innovation in fuel-efficient turboprops means that many regional airports dependent upon the short- to medium-haul market will remain viable, and may continue to expand.[3] The airline company, airport operator, aircraft manufacturer and passenger are part of an interdependent system, in which each has profound influence upon the other.

Structure of the air transport system

The structure of air transport falls into one of three distinct models:

- a centralized system with one dominant hub (for example, Heathrow in England)
- a multi-hub system, as in the USA and Germany
- a dispersed system with only limited hub facilities, as in Italy.

The first is usually dependent upon a major capital city (London in Heathrow's case), the second upon a large country with relatively evenly distributed urban centres, and the third on decentralized air traffic at low levels of usage. Hence geography as well as politics determines the structure of air transport in a country. Where hubs are a central feature they tend to be dominated by one or two airlines (for example, British Airways at Heathrow, Air France at Paris Orly, or United Airlines at Chicago O'Hare). A dominant hub airport also leads to the 'hub and spoke' system of regional airports served mainly by the dominant airline. Consequently, to travel from New York to Newcastle in England involves a change of plane at Heathrow or Birmingham, but the connecting flight is provided by the same carrier.

The structure of the air transport system indirectly influences the structure of the airline industry. As noted, centralized hubs are usually dominated by one or two major carriers. As hub-and-spoke patterns become established, smaller airline companies – who were providers of the spoke elements – tend to be absorbed by the predatory major carrier. The effect is to encourage the growth of megacarriers at the expense of independent smaller airlines. In fact, the survival of small carriers is normally dependent upon the dispersed system of air transport with only limited hub facilities (the third of the three modes listed above).

The close relationship between large hub airports and large airline companies (such as Minneapolis St Paul Airport and North West Airlines) means that smaller airlines tend to favour smaller airports (for example, Air UK at London's Stansted). Small airports are often smaller corporate or financial entities than the airlines that use them, and as a consequence are not always able to stand up to the airlines' requirements. Under such pressures there has emerged a pattern whereby regional airports are served mainly by regional airlines and national airports by national airlines. The only exception occurs where hub-and-spoke patterns place the national carrier as the major user of a regional airport. Here a conflict may exist between national and regional airline companies, perhaps over access to terminal facilities, flight times and preferential treatment in baggage handling.

The hub airport allows the airline company responsible for its development to control the airport gates. This has obvious benefits for a particular airline, because it can establish a brand identity throughout the airport, from assembly concourse to check-in and departure gate. The disadvantage is the lack of competition that single airline control of airports entails. Where the state or airport authority controls the airport (that is, non-hub situations) the airport can offer gate positions to different airlines at fairly short notice. This encourages competition on service and price, to the benefit of passengers. At Florida's Orlando International Airport, which handled 23 million passengers in 1995, the state-owned airport attributes its growth rate (about 10% per year) and passenger appeal (voted the best airport in North America for customer appeal in 1995) to the fact that it controls the vast majority of its departure gates.[4] When a new carrier comes along (such as ValuJet in 1994), the airport can quickly offer access, thereby forcing down competitors' prices or pushing up their standard of service.

As airports have become privatized – in whole or in part – during the 1980s and 1990s, their goals have tended to be less aviation oriented. A conflict can occur between aviation objectives and non-aviation objectives, particularly within the terminal building. Non-aviation management may seek to expand retail, commercial and hotel functions that could conflict with aviation needs. Airline companies may lose their dominant position and role within the terminal, and passenger transport may become only an incidental function of the airport as a whole. Private capital, essential in the eyes of many governments as a means of reducing state subsidy, can have the effect of altering the character and management of an airport to the detriment of the passenger.

Not only are airports subject to the pressures of deregulation and privatization, but so are airline companies. In the West it is accepted that airports and airlines are principally private companies trading openly, making profits and losses for shareholders. In other parts of the world, however, both airports and airline companies are often public or quasi-public bodies. Dependent upon state subsidy, they provide a public service first and foremost. However, they too are subject to increasing pressure to generate secondary income through franchising arrangements with retailers and hotel chains. In the developing world, medium-sized semi-private airlines (such as Air Nigeria) and small private airlines operate out of public airports, with only a few services provided by the private sector. Here too the trend is towards bringing in private capital and managing the airport as a semi-public rather than totally public enterprise.

References

1. Norman Ashford and Paul Wright, *Airport Engineering*, John Wiley & Sons, New York, 1991, p. 63.
2. Mike Dash, *The Limit: Engineering on the Boundaries of Science*, BBC Books, London, 1995, p. 87.
3. Ashford and Wright, *Airport Engineering*, p. 94.
4. Graham Warwick, 'More than illusion', *Flight International*, 5–11 June 1996, p. 27.

Layout, growth and access to airports

CHAPTER 4

The layout of an airport is determined by five basic factors:

- the direction of prevailing winds (the major runway(s) being oriented to the prevailing wind with a back-up runway on a cross-wind alignment)
- the size and number of terminal buildings
- the ground transport system, especially the position of major access roads and railways
- mandatory clearance dimensions between aircraft and buildings
- topography and geology.

Small airports are usually a direct reflection of these spatial and organizational characteristics, but as airports become larger a number of secondary factors come into play, such as environmental controls, the geography of the surrounding region, and the capacity of the local road system. International airports, though their site layout is shaped primarily by wind direction, are increasingly constrained by such factors as community disturbance. As a consequence, their growth and configuration rarely permit simple planning solutions, but are compromised by influences of a regional nature.

Forecasting airport growth

Airports are planned on the basis of traffic forecasts. These are compiled on the principle not of peak demand but of average sustained demand. Many airports experience passenger or airspace overcrowding for limited periods of the year, but this is not normally taken as justifying expansion. If airports were designed to meet all peak demands then there would be excessive capacity, adding unnecessarily to operating costs. Compiling data on passenger, cargo and aircraft movements is an essential element of the master-plan process. Once the airport has begun to operate, such data need to be periodically checked to ensure that forecasts are being realized by actual volumes.

Typical of the data that need to be gathered are:[1]

- passenger statistics (international or domestic, scheduled or non-scheduled, arriving/departing or transit, weekly, daily or hourly flows)

- cargo statistics (similar breakdown as for passenger flows)
- aircraft (types, international or domestic, passenger or cargo, peak movements)
- visitors (meeters and greeters, airport visitors as non-travelling tourists, shoppers, business users).

In the interrelationship between airport masterplanning and the gathering or monitoring of statistics, three components are of principal concern: passenger traffic, cargo traffic and aircraft movements. These statistics allow the capacity of each of the major elements of the airport to be determined, such as runways, apron areas, terminal, road and railway system, and hotels. Each part, though, will require separate data gathering in order to arrive at a precise idea of usage and hence the implications for layout or design.

For the passenger terminal, operational capacity is dependent upon the performance of the following key elements:[2]

- landside access
- baggage handling
- passenger check-in capacity
- immigration control capacity
- security check capacity
- boarding gate capacity.

The relating of facilities to capacity is a necessary part of masterplanning and, at a more detailed level, of building design. Facility forecasting is normally based on statistics, justified by mathematical modelling and queuing theory employed in such complex areas as the passenger terminal. The architect does not need to know how to undertake such analysis, but it is helpful to understand the principles upon which facilities planning at airports is carried out.

Airport types

There are three main types of airport:

- international airports serving over 20 million passengers a year

- national airports serving between 2 and 20 million passengers a year
- regional airports serving up to 2 million passengers a year.

Such a classification, based upon the level of traffic flow, is a useful guide but by no means infallible. In countries such as Germany, which have a strong hub network of airports, some of the larger regional airports (Stuttgart, for example) have passenger movements that approach international dimensions. Conversely, in smaller countries with single national airports (Oslo Airport in Norway is a good example) passenger movements below the norm for the classification may still justify the inclusion of the airport in the top rank. If the level of passengers is a good general guide, other factors relevant to typological classification include:

- the split between domestic, national and international movements
- the role of the airport as an international centre for aviation or as a distribution hub
- the scale of non-airport facilities, such as other transportation modes, hotels, business and conference centres.

Taking these factors together, it is obvious that Stansted is a national not truly an international airport; that Charles de Gaulle Airport is international while Lyon is national; and that Southampton is regional while Manchester is national. Outside Europe, Kansai Airport at Osaka, John F. Kennedy, Washington Dulles, Newark, Dallas and Denver in the USA are all international, while Baltimore (with passenger levels of 16 million a year in 1996) is rather more national in character (though there are many international flights). Any classification is often confused by airport authorities and airline companies, who have the habit of 'talking up' their airport in order to raise its profile. Birmingham Airport in the UK is one such example; it is named Birmingham International in spite of levels of use of under 10 million passengers a year.

It is important to maintain, conceptually at least, the three-level classification of airport types, because the range of support facilities varies with each type. Generally speaking, the larger the airport and the greater the percentage of international passengers, the more non-airport facilities of one kind or another are needed. International airports cater disproportionately for business travellers, and they require conference and meeting rooms at the airport; they tend also to have top-quality hotels, health and fitness clubs, and perhaps a mini golf course. At the opposite extreme those using regional airports may well be commuters or holiday-makers on package holidays: their needs will be less ambitious. However, regional airports are increasingly seen as focuses for industrial or warehousing growth. In the UK, the manager of Southend Airport openly admits that it is less an airport than 'an industrial estate with a runway'.[3]

A good measure of the status of an airport is the number of alternative transport modes that support it. Both Kansai and Charles de Gaulle Airports are served by TGV or bullet trains as well as local rail and bus services, and Heathrow is busy investing in further underground railways and has plans for intercity rail links. Modern international airports currently on the drawing-board (such as Hong Kong's new airport at Chek Lap Kok, or Seoul International) are planned with integrated cross-modal transportation and such a wide range of supporting facilities that they take on the characteristics of urban areas. Even airports that are well established have to incorporate new transportation systems in order to maintain their position in airport league tables, or to enable them to move from regional to national or national to international airports. So while the earlier classification is helpful in identifying the range and scale of facilities needed, in reality few airports stand still, and most have ambitions to move up the hierarchy.

Airport types are also a clue to security risks. International terrorism tends to target major international, not minor regional airports. The damage to national prestige is greater if terrorists can successfully attack terminals of national importance. The publicity gained for such acts, even if passengers are not hurt, is more widespread and damaging to a country's economic interests if the airport attacked is the nation's principal one. Consequently, while security in the UK is equally strict at Manchester, Glasgow and Stansted Airports, it is Heathrow that is likely to be the

4.1 The classification of airports reflects passenger movements and architectural ambition. Lyon-Satolas Airport, France. Architects: Curtelin Ricard Bergeret/Scott Brownrigg and Turner.

terrorists' prime target. Airport staff, policy authorities and terrorists all realize this, with consequences for the level of security-conscious crime prevention in both the design and the management of international airports.

The development of airports is more than the satisfying of aviation needs, no matter how lucrative or demanding these may be. Airports, whether international or regional in nature, need to develop the 'total business' and this 'consists of aviation, retailing, land ownership and integrated transport opportunities.'[4] An example is the new airport at Sheffield in South Yorkshire (opened in 1997), which forms the centre of an expanded business park developed in partnership with the government-funded Sheffield Development Corporation.[5] The business park (masterplanned by Ove Arup and Partners) consists also of offices, industrial and distribution units, and is linked to a golf course, hotel and conference centre, and the national railway system.[6]

Here the new airport provides a focal point for development and, in the million or so passengers carried per year, justifies the expansion of retail facilities within the terminal. There are specific facilities for the business community: executives can jet in from different locations, have a meeting in one of the conference suites, and fly home. Business conferencing is an area of growth for regional airports, particularly those away from congested airspace locations.

Gaining access to airports

At many of the larger airports in Europe at least 50% of airline passengers arrive or depart by train. In the USA the figure is much lower. Dependence upon the private car as the main means of gaining access to airports can become self-defeating, and greatly restricts the ability of airports to expand. At busy American airports, such as Los Angeles, congestion caused by private cars means that the relatively space-efficient buses are disadvantaged. The answer adopted with growing frequency is to construct mainline train links to airports or, as in Gatwick's case, to site a new airport where existing railway investment can be utilized.

In the past, cost has been a constraint upon joint airport and railway investment. However, the environmental and social benefits of intercity train access to airports has led to the much closer integration of airport and railway construction. At London's Stansted and Lyon-Satolas new airports-cum-stations have been constructed, with the railway costs shared by the state, railway operator and airport developer. As airport usage has grown, the economics of railway links have proved attractive.

As a rule of thumb, 40–50% of airport passengers are destined for the nearby city centre, the remainder for more dispersed locations. At Gatwick, 70% of passengers arriving by plane take the train to central London, but at Heathrow the figure using the underground railway link is merely 30%. The juxtaposition of airport and station provides many benefits, but the economics of train operation require an airport handling about 12 million passengers a year before railway investment can be justified.[7] At this level of usage, capital and running costs based upon a service of about six trains per hour, each of four carriages, should break

even. With subsidy from the airport, an operator could make a small profit. Large airports such as Charles de Gaulle, Heathrow, Washington and New York have, at least in theory, the passenger capacity to build and run an efficient railway service from airport to city centre without subsidy.

Conventional railway links to airports are well able to met growing demand from rising passenger numbers (unlike roads). As demand grows, the railway operator merely needs to add additional train services or additional carriages. Increasing the number of carriages from four to eight and the frequency of trains from six to ten an hour allows the airport station to handle not 12 million passengers a year but nearly 40 million. With congested airport and motorway roads the train has obvious operational advantages for the effective management of airports. Besides moving large numbers of passengers economically and smoothly, the railway is a vital link for airport staff travelling to work, and for airline crews. As a system, railways can offer a guarantee of transit time that few other modes of transport can achieve.

To maximize the benefit of joint airport and railway construction, it is vital that both are considered at the start of the planning stage. Stations should be fully integrated into the complex fabric of airports: their infrastructure needs are, like those of the plane, heavily controlled by safety and operational requirements. Only with effective integration of different modes of transport can the needs of passengers be fully met.

Rail links to airports

If projected growth in air passenger movements is to be met, then the means of reaching airports have to be improved. The old assumption that travellers can start and finish their air journey by car, taxi or coach has proved to be flawed. The numbers using airports such as Heathrow (55 million passengers a year) mean that the road system, car parks and setting-down points are already overloaded. Rather than expand car access provision within the limited land area of an airport, it is now accepted that alternative forms of surface transport are needed. Of these, rail and underground train systems are preferred, with new railway stations

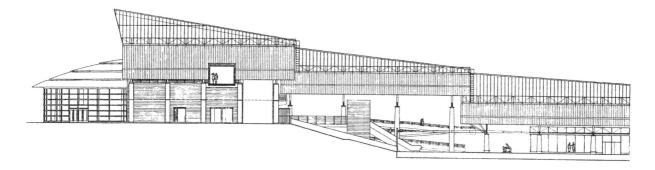

4.2 Forging new transport links to airports serves passengers and airline staff needs. Manchester Airport Station, UK. Architects: Austin: Smith-Lord.

giving direct access to passenger terminals as at Stansted and Manchester Airports.

The design of airports cannot be considered in isolation from the total journey. Surface transport to airports is a vital (and neglected) part of the chain. Compared with the fast, efficient and comfortable flight, the part of the journey at either end can be slow, frustrating and arduous. Improving links to airports means working with planning authorities, state or private railway companies and bus companies. Of the 69 airports in Europe carrying more than 2 million passengers a year, only 34 have existing or planned railway links.[8] The integration of airports into the regional and national transport infrastructure has obvious benefits for the passenger, and in the long term is the only means by which an airport can continue to expand. Bottlenecks in the sky, overcrowded runways or terminals are airport problems capable of being solved by investment, but failure to make corresponding investments in facilities outside the airport boundary can simply transfer the congestion and frustration from the air to the ground.

Improving surface access to airports requires policy coordination between airport owners and the state (central and regional government). The provision of recent TGV rail links to Paris Charles de Gaulle Airport and fast suburban services to Washington National Airport was the direct result of airport and rail operators collaborating within clear national transport policies. Failure to take account of likely traffic growth at Heathrow, in terms of both road capacity (especially the M4 and M25 motorways) and underground railway services, is an example of the way in which denationalization and deregulation have undermined provision frameworks. The Heathrow Express, with direct high-speed rail links from London Paddington to the airport, planned to open in 1998, came forward only as a result of intolerable surface transport delays. The same is true of the Navita Express in Tokyo.[9]

The Heathrow Express is planned to relieve the congestion on the existing Piccadilly Line underground railway service to the airport. With insufficient track space to provide an express service on the underground the decision was made in 1990 to construct a new high-speed service using British Rail's Great Western main line, which had surplus capacity. A new underground spur currently under construction (in 1996) running northwards from Heathrow links directly with the InterCity main line, providing the means to provide a service from city centre to airport of only 16 minutes. Looking further to the future, the new tunnel is seen as providing a link in a potential new spine of railways running right under Heathrow and joining other main line services south of the airport.

At a cost of £600 million, the undertaking is being financed by BAA with a 70% stake and British Railways Board with 30%. The Heathrow Express is scheduled to open in 1998; opening was rescheduled from 1997 after a tunnel collapse on 31 October 1994 led to extensive redesign of the tunnelling technique. Passenger levels are expected initially to be 6 million per year, increasing to 10 million when Terminal 5 opens in 2003. The service is being designed to cater for 20 trains an hour per platform, which is necessary if BAA predictions of 80 million passengers a year at Heathrow in 2016 materialize.[10]

The Stansted SkyTrain already offers a similar service. It uses specially designed trains with sliding doors for easy level access, spacious baggage storage areas, and telephones that accept credit cards, though the journey is slower, taking normally 41 minutes. The design of the station is such that passengers can take their baggage trolleys from the airport directly onto the platform, and the trains act as waiting areas, thereby dispensing with platform waiting-rooms. Served directly by lift, escalator and ramp, the model of air/rail integration at Stansted is one that travellers, according to the BAA, find particularly convenient.

Generally speaking, it can be assumed that 30–40% of air travellers will be arriving by public transport at airports serving over 2 million passengers a year and 50% at those serving over 10 million. The larger the airport, the more serious the problems of surface congestion become, and the greater the environmental pollution. Hence with very big airports the percentage of travellers arriving by train and bus increases to 50 or 60%. Passengers will be encouraged to use public transport, especially trains, if the station gives direct access to the terminal building (as at Stansted Airport in London and Schipol Airport in Amsterdam). Where more than one terminal exists this means a different station at each, or at least a transit system of terminal connection (as at London's Gatwick). It is also helpful if the airline ticket includes the rail link to the city centre with, ideally, integrated baggage handling between plane and train. Through-ticketing and baggage transfers require the airport operator, rail operator and airline to cooperate. To be successful in meeting the needs of the airport user (both passenger and airport worker), dedicated rail services need to be frequent, direct and preferably linked to high speed or intercity services.

The larger the airport, the greater is the distance between buildings and between terminals and satellites. For airport staff this means journeys that are too lengthy on foot, but which may be too congested or prohibited by car. The answer at some airports is to develop internal railway systems (people-movers), or to encourage employees and possibly passengers to use bicycles. Because most flights have provision to carry cycles, a trend is towards young people and backpackers arriving by bike, travelling by plane, and continuing their journey by bicycle at their destination. Provision of mechanical people-movers, cycle roads and cycle facilities at the terminal diversifies the access choices, and relieves congestion on the airport road system.

The life of assets at airports

Because airports are a fast evolving and rapidly changing type of development, where the life span and upgrading of elements are on different timescales, it is important to attach a notional life for the key parts of the airport estate. This is needed for accounting purposes, in order to plan maintenance programmes, and to help predict the replacement of operational elements. The life span adopted by BAA for its UK airports assumes the following timescales:[11]

- runways, taxiways and aprons: 100 years
- terminal buildings, pier and satellite structures: 50 years
- tunnels, bridges and subways: 50 years

- terminal fixtures and fittings: 20 years
- transit systems: 20–50 years
- plant and equipment (runway lighting and building plant): 5–20 years
- motor vehicles: 4–8 years
- retail units, bars and restaurants: 3–5 years
- office equipment: 5–10 years.

It is evident that runways are the one relatively permanent feature of airports, followed by the terminal buildings and other major structures. Terminal fixtures and fittings are, however, on a shorter timescale, followed by building plant and equipment, and in turn by office equipment. At a more detailed level one could include carpets, fabrics and furniture (2–5 years). For the airport architect these differing timescales create the need to design terminals that are capable of periodic upgrading without disrupting airport operations. The terminal should be able to adapt to changing and unpredictable management priorities on the one hand and to the predictable needs of building plant and furnishing improvements on the other. However, because much of the space in terminals is leased to concessionaires and retailers, their needs are also important. Retail leases at UK airports are normally on 3–5 year timescales, and this tends to be the framework for phased upgrading of shop units, bars and restaurants. Hence the airport is a complex entity, with differing and sometimes conflicting timescales for the replacement or upgrading of its elements.

The idea of asset life is both a useful accounting tool and a means of giving value to the assorted structures, fittings and components of a typical airport. The runway is as close as anything becomes to a permanent element, followed by the terminal and other large-scale structures such as bridges, underground railways and light transit systems. These are designed to have a useful life of 50 years (as against the 100 years for runways), though the moving parts (rolling stock for transit systems) are given a notional life of 20 years. Inside the terminal there are many timescales influencing the pace of replacement or upgrading. As new priorities are recognized (such as environmental concerns) the terminal will have to be changed, perhaps in a fashion not anticipated by the original designer. As other priorities are given greater weight (such as safety and security) the frequency of alterations here may increase.

The concept of fixed assets with differing timescales for internal alterations means that 'replaceability' becomes as important as flexibility. Terminals and other relatively permanent airport assets are increasingly designed using a restricted palette of parts and components. Standardization of components using a limited range of materials and as few specials as possible keeps the costs down when later changes are undertaken.[12] Two factors encourage this to occur at BAA airports:

- the adoption of best-practice techniques, whereby preselected suppliers advise on the construction details, and make a commitment to long-term quality and ease of replacement;
- the use of systematic auditing of the performance of buildings and other structures to enable the need for change or upgrading to be predicted well in advance.

BAA claims that the extra time spent on design evaluation and pre-planning leads to shorter construction periods, fewer mistakes on site, and more adaptable terminals in the future.[13]

References

1. The list is adapted from that in IATA, *Airport Terminals Reference Manual*, 7th edn, International Air Transport Association, Montreal, Canada, 1989, p. 2.2.
2. *Ibid*., p. 2.5.
3. Forbes Mutch, 'Regional forecast', *Flight International*, 5–11 June 1996, p. 24.
4. *Ibid*.
5. *Ibid*., p. 25
6. Ove Arup and Partners, *Airport Projects* (brochure), London.
7. D. McKenna, 'The rail contribution', in *Airports of the Future*, Institution of Civil Engineers, London, 1967, p. 109.
8. J. Meredith, 'Surface access to airports', in G.B.R. Fielden, A.H. Wickens and L.R. Yates (eds), *Passenger Transport After 2000 AD*, Chapman & Hall, London, 1995.
9. *Ibid*., p. 53.
10. Jackie Whitelaw (ed.), *21st Century Airports*, supplement of *New Civil Engineer/New Builder*, May 1995, p. 38.
11. BAA, *Shaping Up for the 21st Century*, Annual Report 1995/96, London.
12. *Ibid*., p. 15.
13. *Ibid*., pp. 15 and 16, and personal interview with Graham Jordon at BAA on 24 July 1996.

CHAPTER

Masterplanning airports

The role of the airport masterplan is to:

- balance the airport system with infrastructure needs
- provide a physical framework for investment
- ensure that the airport estate is effectively managed, particularly with regard to future land, financial and planning needs.

The masterplan is not simply a plan giving an outline of the physical form of the future or expanded airport, but also a description of the financial implications. Necessarily, too, it will deal with the political and environmental ramifications, particularly at the level of infrastructure demands (roads and railway access to the airport) and any planning consents needed. In an industry of rapid change and growth, masterplanning has a vital role in anticipating land, financial and infrastructural needs. It is therefore a crucial element of airport management, though one that has frequently been overlooked in the past: for example, London Gatwick's lack of forethought in runway planning in the 1970s, and Heathrow's in failing to link passenger terminal expansion with public transport provision.

Airport masterplans are usually spatial diagrams of future development options. They necessarily deal with strategic matters, leaving questions of detailed design until engineers and architects are appointed for specific projects. Masterplans need to be flexible in outlook and operation. Changes in aircraft technology, ever-stricter environmental controls, and the altering pattern of the airline industry – all have profound effects upon the airport masterplan. Hence the plan needs to offer an element of tactical flexibility within a graphic framework.

Masterplans should prescribe solutions within varying time horizons. Decisions for short-term capital improvements as well as long-term visions (say up to 15 years ahead) are both required. Plans need to address different audiences; the public has a right to know of an airport's plans, but so too do the state regulators, the local planning authority, and the financial institutions who may be asked to invest in it. The role of the masterplan is to

5.1 Conceptual clarity is the key to the airport masterplan. Anatalya Airport, Turkey. Engineers: Ove Arup and Partners.

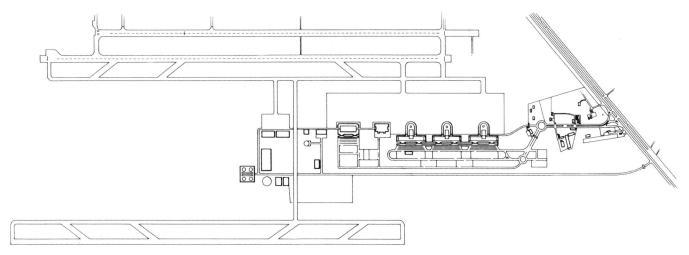

keep everybody informed, to seek a consensus for the shape and scope of future expansion, and to be flexible enough to meet reasonable objections.

As airports transfer from state to private ownership (the result of the worldwide trend towards airport deregulation and removal of government subsidies), the new owners have begun to recognize the importance of the physical masterplan in realizing the land assets at airports. Much land at the perimeter of airports has in the past been poorly used, but under new management the potential for development has tended to be seized. New non-governmental airports tend to see peripheral land as a means of raising cash to subsidize improvements elsewhere, perhaps to terminals or runways. The masterplan helps in realizing the capital tied up in the land itself by identifying surplus land and by creating the right balance of adjoining land uses and infrastructure to maximize its value. The masterplan is therefore both a technical statement of potential and a means of raising expectations and worth, which helps in increasing the valuation of land assets. BAA's and Renfrew Enterprise's use of masterplanning around Glasgow Airport is a notable example of planning-led land utilization and asset enhancement.

The development plan as a final concept will have needed to be assessed technically, politically and procedurally. The formulation of the masterplan, involving a variety of concepts and options, each subject to economic, technical,

social and environmental evaluation, will harden into a development plan for consultation. Those who compile the masterplan will, armed with surveys, facts, trends etc., be asked to justify the plan before public inquiries of one form or another. The masterplan needs to be convincing, candid in its analysis of problems, and clear in its forward vision.

Airport masterplans are continually updated documents. In an industry of rapid change, the plan should be monitored and adjusted frequently, perhaps every year. There should be regular adjustment to ensure that changing national laws (on say environmental protection) and altering government policy (on say the balance between road and rail investment) is reflected in the airport masterplan. Also, the plan needs to be adjusted in response to socio-economic conditions, to changes in national air transport policy, to the amalgamation of major airline companies, to alterations to regional land-use policies, and to changes in the design and management of aircraft themselves. As in much forward planning the parameters are subject to change, and this necessarily alters the assumptions from which the masterplan was evolved.

Intermediate plans

The masterplan is a framework for development in space and time. Within the full plan period (usually 20 or 25 years) there should be intermediate plans based upon five-yearly

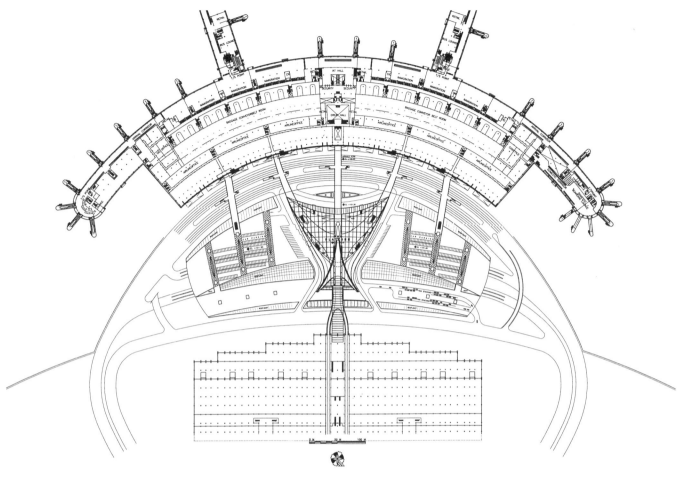

5.2 Detailed design needs to exploit the geometry of space to provide incremental growth. Transportation Centre, Seoul Airport, Korea. Architects: Terry Farrell and Partners.

increments. Major development (such as runway expansion, enlargement of a terminal or ground transport provision) should correspond with these intermediate plans, thereby allowing financial and facilities planning to proceed smoothly. The aim is to produce a long-term vision that can be implemented on the basis of well-specified incremental growth.

These intermediate plans provide both the framework for airport expansion and the means to monitor and modify the full airport scheme. Over the plan period the assumptions upon which the masterplan was based will have changed. There may, for instance, be a different pattern of passenger use, a new generation of aircraft design, and changes in government policy to air transportation. Hence the staged provision of airport facilities may need modification. The role of the masterplan and its intermediate plans is to ensure that the totality of the airport design is sufficiently flexibile to cater for the unexpected.

Compiling the masterplan

A masterplan is needed for existing and new airports. Both are subject to the same pressures, and will need to follow similar procedures in the masterplanning exercise. Generally speaking there are six stages in airport masterplanning:

1. Appoint masterplanning team and establish parameters.
2. Survey facilities and identify issues.
3. Review aviation forecasts.
4. Evolve and test concepts against environmental, financial and regulatory constraints.
5. Formulate plan and simulation (using CAD) for consultation.
6. Modify and adopt masterplan.

Often the masterplanning exercise is undertaken in order to determine whether an airport should be expanded, or whether it is preferable to build a new facility. Here, the plan needs to be concluded with a policy based upon a thorough analysis of existing conditions and forecasts. Keeping an up-to-date inventory of all the facilities and buildings at an airport is vital if the right choice is to be made between expansion and the construction of a new airport. This is an inventory not only of ground facilities but

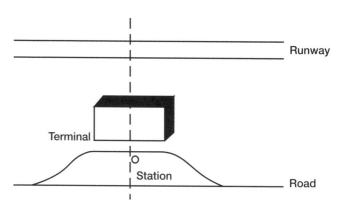

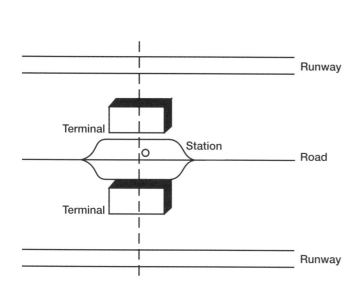

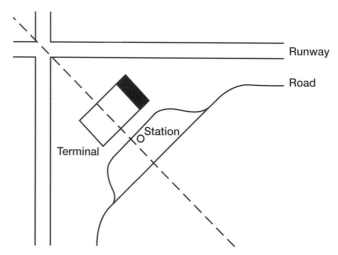

5.3 Main runway to terminal layout options.

also of airspace, air congestion and the anticipated growth in air traffic in the region over, say, the next quarter century. The survey will also need to look at buildings and urban areas outside the perimeter of the airport to see how they will be affected. Hence the inventory should contain the location, size and distance from flight paths of hospitals, schools and churches. Noise corridors and cones will need to be plotted, as will historical data on weather patterns in the area.

Existing conditions and traffic forecasts are both important areas of data gathering. Understanding the nature of demand, its profile and characteristics, allows a variety of options over different timescales to be evaluated. Once the case has been demonstrated for radical expansion of an airport or the construction of a new one, the type and scale of facilities can be determined.

Airport layout

The layout of the airport is determined by a number of related factors. As in all design exercises there are no precise rules, but rather the balancing of one factor against another

to arrive at the best compromise. The principal factors to consider, evaluate and organize spatially are:[1]

- number and orientation of runways (especially with regard to meteorology)
- number of taxiways
- size, shape and organization of aprons
- area of available land
- topography and soil conditions
- obstacles to air navigation
- number and distribution of terminal buildings, hotels and car parks
- external land uses
- phasing of development
- size and layout of airport road system
- strategy for public transport connections.

The organization of the above factors into a coherent whole then leads to the selection of preferred locations for such facilities as air traffic control tower, aircraft maintenance areas, railway or metro stations, fuel stores, rescue and fire-fighting services, and control gates. The detailed layout

5.4   Major and minor grids are often the basis for airport planning. Munich Airport, Germany. Architects: Prof. von Busse, Blees, Kampmann & Buch with Murphy/Jahn.

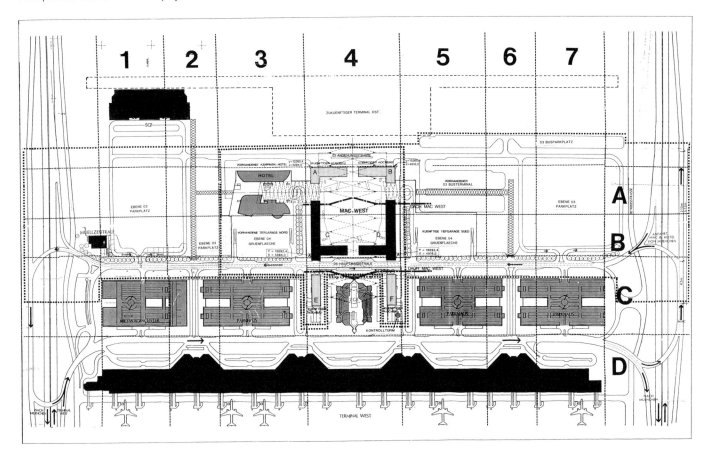

of the airport needs to balance conflicting demands, such as public access and security, air freight and passenger needs, and arrival by car or train.

In the normal planning of airports, a number of options are arrived at, evaluated and eventually rejected. The constraints – operational, financial, and in terms of development phasing – add to the complexity of airport layout design. Because airports are subject to rapid change in response to innovations in aircraft design, the masterplan needs to be able to accommodate growth. Both long-term (say 20 years) and short-term tactical flexibility (say 5–10 years) need to be provided without compromising the integrity of the whole design.

Runway layout

A key factor in the layout of the masterplan is the configuration of the runways and the relationship between runways

and the terminal building. Two main aspects of runways concern the airport designer: their length and their alignment. Length is dependent upon the type of aircraft using an airport, but for the largest planes a runway length of 2–3km is normally required. The length of the runway varies according to altitude, temperature, wind conditions and plane weight, so for a given aircraft design different runway lengths may be required at different locations. The critical length on a runway is determined by the safe take-off dimensions, not the landing dimensions, which are considerably shorter.

The capacity of runways is difficult to calculate exactly (it is dependent upon the mix and capacity of aircraft and safety regulations in operation at the time). However, as a rule most runways deal with 45–60 operations per hour in good weather and about 25% fewer in poor weather. There is clearly a correspondence between runway and terminal capacity because they both deal with the transport of the

5.5 The typology of the airport has a rational basis. Harare Airport, Zimbabwe. Architects: Scott Brownrigg and Turner.

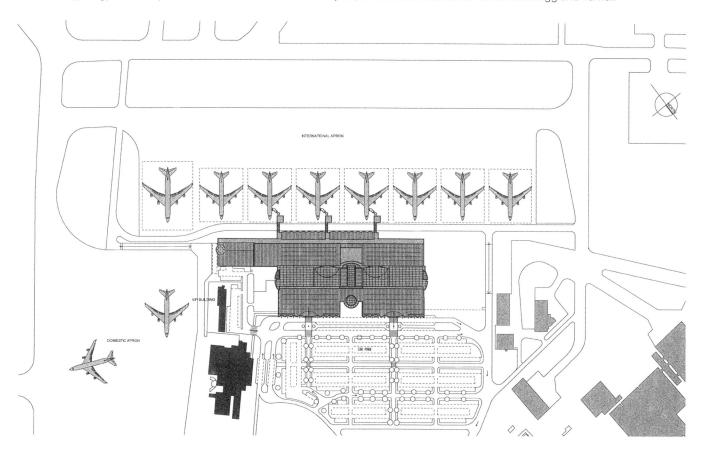

same unit of people. To increase the number of passengers handled, airport authorities often extend runways (to allow larger aircraft to land) or build additional runways. These can either be in parallel alignments or more commonly placed at an angle to each other. The advantage of the latter is the greater flexibility in maintaining operations in cross-wind conditions. Where two parallel runways are provided the terminal can straddle them, giving obvious benefit in terms of ready access and economy of airside provision. With angled runways the terminal can sit within the hinge of the runway arms (see Figure 5.3).

For safety reasons parallel runways are usually required to be at least 500m apart laterally, and with angled runways the point where they converge should obey the same dimension. Occasionally runways cross over, but generally divergent runway alignments are preferred. With modern air traffic and ground flight control, airports with two or more runways can handle up to 100 operations an hour, which

if translated into passengers (assuming 150 passengers per aircraft) means that the terminal buildings should be capable of dealing with a throughput of 15 000 per hour.

Two or more runways allow airports to cater for simultaneous landings and take-offs. High-density airports, as in the USA, sometimes employ three parallel runways, each linked to a dedicated terminal building. However, the constraint is not so much air space but taxiing space on the ground. Aircraft have to cross the path of those engaged in take-off or landing, posing the potential threat of collision.

The distance that the aircraft needs to taxi between the terminal building and the runway has a large bearing upon airline costs. Long taxi length means longer flight times, increased fuel costs, and the potential for ground traffic delay. The relationship between the location of the terminal and that of the runways (and taxiways) is crucial. Different configurations of terminal buildings, taxiways and runways affect design to a significant degree. There are complex

5.6 Masterplan for Edinburgh Airport, UK. Architects: RMJM.

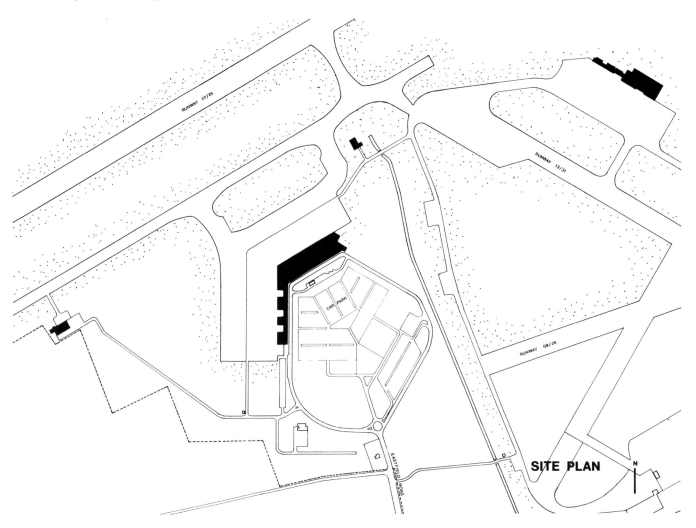

layout issues to resolve, such as airside and landside links (ensuring that smooth connections are made with public transport, for example), and internal environmental conditions to consider (such as aircraft noise, which is more objectionable with jets because of its higher frequency than with turboprops). Where the terminal is placed between parallel runways it can no longer have a clear distinction between airside and landside, because passengers are accessing aircraft on opposite faces of the building. Likewise,

taxiways that transport aircraft from the runway to the terminal building and service hangars have to be able to cater for aircraft movements in both directions simultaneously.

Physical elements of the masterplan

Airport masterplanning is a team effort, but the architect or engineer is normally responsible for the physical disposition of the parts. This involves three principal elements:

- runways and taxiways
- hangars and service aprons
- terminals

and several secondary ones:

- roads and car parks
- security enclosure
- air traffic control tower
- airport railway stations and light rail system
- hotels, conference facilities etc.
- freight warehouses.

Design is not just a question of the dimensions of the parts in plan but their height and clearance from approach slopes and the like. Similarly, runways have safety zones, and there needs to be cross-wind provision. Terminal buildings are linked to piers and gate positions, thereby determining the layout of aircraft parking and further safety clearances.

The masterplan is a spatial, logistical and three-dimensional graphic plan, which structures investment in the fourth dimension – time. It is important that the vision of the architect and engineer is reflected in the management of the airport and the needs of the airlines that use it. A number of ground rules exist to provide the operational context for the airport and to help integrate airside and landside functions. As a general rule:[2]

Runway areas

- Separate airline, general aviation and commuter traffic on apron.
- Design for efficient and flexible apron-handling operations.
- Minimize taxiing lengths.
- Locate crash and rescue services close to main runway.
- Encourage joint airline use of airside facilities.

Administration buildings

- Locate airport administration close to road and rail system.

- Centralize administration facilities with direct access to landside and airside.

Road layout

- Keep landside road system simple.
- Provide public transport at terminal kerbside and administration building.
- Locate car parks close to terminals or linked by tram system.

Terminal buildings

- Minimize walking distances.
- Facilitate inter-airline transfers of passengers.
- Separate air carrier functions (international, national, commuter) but provide easy interconnections.
- Maximize marketing and rental opportunities.
- Encourage joint airline use of facilities.
- Link terminal buildings directly to public transport.
- Link terminal buildings to hotels and short-stay car parks.

Warehouses

- Accommodate growth in air cargo.
- Ensure efficient segregation airside of passenger baggage and freight.
- Facilitate cargo transfer between airlines.

Site choice

It is assumed here that the site for the new airport has been decided, but part of the masterplan exercise often involves the selection of an area for airport expansion. Site selection for a new or greatly expanded airport is fraught with difficulties, so much so that often an ideal site does not exist and a man-made one has to be created (as at Kansai in Japan or Hong Kong's new airport at Chep Lap Kok: in both cases physical and environmental constraints were such that an artificial island had to be formed in the sea for the new airport). The site selection process should include an analysis of the following factors:[3]

5.7 The spatial pattern across the landscape reflects directly the operation of a modern airport. Notice here how planting softens the impact of the airport. Oslo Airport, Norway. Architects: Aviaplan AS.

- operational capacity: obstructions from high buildings and mountains, weather patterns and airspace considerations
- capacity potential: land availability and sustainability
- ground access: infrastructure provision (road and rail), centres of population, parking space
- development costs: land costs, soil and rock conditions, land utilization values
- environmental factors: noise, impact upon ecosystems, air and water quality, cultural impacts, endangered species
- socio-economic factors: impact upon existing communities, public service needs, changes to employment patterns
- planning issues: impact upon land uses, agriculture, forestry and transportation systems.

Balancing the above factors leads to the selection of pre-ferred locations, which can then be investigated in greater detail. Part of the analysis (sieve mapping, contouring and visual simulation) is normally undertaken using computer-aided design (CAD) techniques. Creating an image of the shape the development will take and its wider impacts helps in the final selection of a site. Interactive computer simulation also allows those affected locally to modify the proposals, thereby reducing community conflict at an early stage in the masterplanning process.

Energy and resources

It is important that the site chosen for the airport has suffi-cient supplies of electrical power and water, and adequate provision for sewage disposal for the full masterplan period: that is, 20–25 years. Airport expansion is dependent upon the ready availability of large amounts of energy and other resources. Future airports are likely also to generate some of their energy needs (by solar or wind power) and to recycle water and waste. The ecological impact of an airport is enormous, and rather than dispose of all wastes the trend will be towards recycling and energy conservation. Heat recovery from the passenger terminal plant, combined heat and power for electrical generation, and exploitation of renewable sources of energy will begin to influence future airport planning.

Within the time horizon of the masterplan it is therefore likely that the airport will begin to move towards a more sus-tainable pattern of development, with recycling loops applied to water and full life-cycle analysis of the materials used. Rather than being a development that merely consumes large amounts of energy and other finite resources, the future airport will begin to conserve and even generate its own power supplies. The openness of airports provides many opportunities for utilizing wind and solar energy (photovoltaic electrical generation is an obvious possibility), and airports near the sea could exploit wave and tidal power. The masterplan should therefore identify locations for these activities, and hence set the whole airport operation on a sounder ecological basis than in the past.

Environmental problems at airports

Of the factors that limit airport expansion, the protection of the environment is often the most critical. Five major impacts on the environment normally occur, and for each separate environmental statements or audits may be required. They are:

- noise
- air quality
- water quality
- ecosystems
- visual impact.

They are interdependent: changes in water purity from runway run-off may adversely affect local ecosystems, and noise will have consequences for wildlife disturbance. Similarly, air quality may affect rare or endangered species. The masterplan needs to address the impacts of each, and integrate protection policies into airport expansion plans.

Noise

This is a major environmental nuisance at and around airports. Aviation noise extends far beyond the boundaries of an airport in pronounced corridors several kilometres wide, which are the regular runway flight paths. Strictly speaking, outside the perimeter fence aviation noise is the responsibility of airlines, but the public generally equates the noise with airport authority responsibilities.

The impact of noise depends upon the sensitivity of affected areas and the type of aircraft involved. Noise from jet aircraft is more objectionable than that from turboprops because of its higher frequency, even at the same decibel (dB) level. Residential neighbourhoods with schools, universities and hospitals suffer more from the impact of noise than do industrial or agricultural areas. Hence, the development of an airport needs to consider noise corridors, and adjust flight paths or airport location accordingly. Because airport noise and that of approaching or exiting aircraft has become an issue of growing importance, many modern airports are constructed in positions where flight paths are taken over water rather than land.

There is a reciprocal relationship between airport noise and land-use activities. Where planning consent is granted for a new or greatly expanded airport, the aviation noise corridors (for take-off and landing) may limit land uses over a large area. Zoning regulations may be needed to ensure that development on the ground is compatible with the anticipated noise levels.

At airports where night-time flight restrictions operate, measures are taken to ensure that airlines do not violate local planning regulations. The airport authority as landlord has an important role in helping to police pilots' adherence to noise restrictions. Because noise nuisance is mainly perceived as a night-time problem, the normal practice is to restrict the number of flights during the night hours (generally defined as between 11.00pm and 6.00am) and, where night flights do occur, to ensure that quieter jets are used by imposing a noise points system.

The airport authority has an interest in keeping within noise regulations, because disturbance to local communities can prove a headache when future expansion plans are under discussion. Good public relations – an important consideration for the modern airport operator – can be easily undermined by airlines that break statutory or advisory noise limits. It is the airport authority that tends to monitor noise levels and has the power to impose fines upon airline companies that break the rules. At London Stansted a noise points system operates based upon the take-off and landing noise levels of different types of aircraft. Noisy aircraft, such as an ageing DC9, may incur a noise points score 16 times higher than that of a modern turboprop. This means that 16 quiet night flights receive the same score as a single noisy one. Airlines are given a certain noise points quota level (to meet unexpected weather or flight conditions) against which every night-time flight carries a quota count. Once the quota level has been exceeded, the airline company faces a fine, which can be as high as £1000 per violating flight. At Stansted, these fines help to fund community and environmental projects in the area.

The system at Stansted applies in modified form at all BAA airports. Local regulations define the restricted period for night flights, and set decibel levels (89dBA at Stansted) for departing flights that are unavoidably delayed. The dual system of time restriction and encouragement through the noise quota scheme to use quieter aircraft has been gradually introduced by the UK Department of Transport to all major airports. By delegating the monitoring of noise levels (mainly night-time, but increasingly also daytime where 97 dBA limits are imposed) to individual airport operators, the Department has brought greater local accountability to the issue of aircraft noise. This in turn has placed airline operators, agents and flight crews under greater scrutiny to obey noise regulations.

Noise preferential routes are the selected flight paths for each runway. Again, aircraft that fly outside the prescribed corridors are subject to fines, because facilities on the ground (such as terminals and hotels) and those in the wider neighbourhood (such as schools) will be subject to noise nuisance. Airlines that have a poor track record of obeying the regulations may find their operating licence withdrawn or conditions attached to continuing to use a particular airport. Again, referring to Stansted's experience, the prospect of gaining planning consent for a second runway is seen, in part at least, as depending upon the airport enjoying good relationships with the local community. Here noise nuisance is often the most crucial factor, and one that the airport operator, rather than the airline company, has the greater interest in avoiding.

Air quality

Airports suffer from poor air quality because of the concentrated burning of fossil fuels: aviation fuel, diesel and petroleum. The aircraft, servicing vehicles and road traffic all contribute towards a build-up of pollutants of one form or another. The combination of emissions of hydrocarbons, carbon monoxide, and oxides of nitrogen can be more damaging than the various air pollutants in isolation.

Many airports are islands of high-level pollution; the air quality is noticeably poorer than in adjoining areas. Poor air quality adversely affects human health and that of other species that exist at the airport: this is particularly noticeable in the lack of vigour displayed by trees and shrubs planted along airport estate roads.

Poor external air quality means that buildings suffer from poor internal air quality, and may stain prematurely on their outsides. With smoking still permitted (and even encouraged by the presence of duty-free shops) inside terminal buildings, the environmental conditions within buildings are far from ideal. As a consequence, most airport buildings are air-conditioned, either in whole or in part, adding at least indirectly to global health problems elsewhere through the use of CFCs.

Water quality

Airports produce a great deal of groundwater contamination, mainly through fuel spillage and run-off from runways and apron areas. Normally, treatment is required to intercept and purify the polluted water before it is allowed to enter local rivers and streams.

Water pollution occurs also with de-icing fluids and detergents used to clean aircraft at the servicing turnaround. Also, in the construction phase, soil erosion can lead to large amounts of pollution entering watercourses. As with air pollution, water quality should be embraced within the environmental statement that accompanies the masterplan. An inventory will be required of existing watercourses, their quantity and quality, and an assessment of how these will be affected by the proposed airport.

Ecosystems

Because of its physical size and environmental impact, an airport alters the ecosystems of a large area. An inventory and assessment of quality needs to be undertaken of all habitats affected. The biotic health and degree of biodiversity

5.8 Reducing the visual impact of terminals by varying the roof profile and stepping at the edge helps to absorb large buildings into the open landscape of airports. Heathrow Terminal 5, UK. Architects: Richard Rogers Partnership.

of wildlife sites should be catalogued and understood. This will then form the datum point for assessing or predicting future changes. As with other environmental factors, a distinction needs to be made between the quantitative inventory of existing conditions and the qualitative assessment of impacts at both the construction and operation stage.

Visual impact

Visual impact is an important environmental consideration. On the one hand the view of an airport identifies its location, and gives a good impression of its scale and national standing; on the other hand the appearance of the airport may jar with the open countryside in which it stands. Good design is essential if a favourable impact is to be made, and if the apparent scale of operations is to be reduced. Computer-aided graphics can help greatly in explaining the likely visual impacts and in reducing the romantic notions that often accompany artists' perspectives. CAD-generated drawings or TV monitor displays also allow interaction by the viewer with the subject, thereby permitting some detailed exploration or modification of the proposals. As the presentation drawings of Heathrow's Terminal 5 confirm, the use of advanced computer graphics can present reliable and attractive images to reviews such as public inquiries.

The visual impact of airports embraces the whole complex infrastructure, from terminal buildings to control towers, runways to hangars, and car parks to hotels. Reducing impacts may involve using one set of buildings or structures to screen another. At Terminal 5 it was decided to develop a coherent set of structures, and to give the effect of a family of designs without jarring elements. The different parts are united by design philosophy as well as constructional, surface and colour elements with the urban design relationships well developed.[4] Part of the strategy

is to conceal larger buildings behind smaller ones, thereby stepping the design composition as a whole. The intention is to reduce the visual impact of the main terminal from afar by using terraced car parking, lower buildings and landscaping as a screen, while opening up dramatic close views framed by adjoining structures.

Reducing environmental impacts: a case study of Heathrow's Terminal 5

Heathrow's Terminal 5 was subject to both an environmental impact assessment and correspondingly to a public inquiry. The latter considered the former in some detail, because the environmental consequences of the development were one of the chief grounds for objection by local authorities and community groups. At the inquiry the inspector required BAA to submit details of the design and its likely visual impact for examination, arguing that the scope and scale of the buildings were a 'material consideration'. In response BAA presented evidence explaining both the planning and design criteria for the new terminal, with 'illustrative and likely' views of what it would look like.[5] BAA was careful to hedge its bets at that time, arguing that the design by the Richard Rogers Partnership was not 'a commitment but can reasonably be used for assessment purposes'. As the inquiry has unfolded, the concept design with accompanying computer animations and sketch plans has become rather more firm with regard to appearance, scope, scale and technical performance. The effect of the inquiring has been to bring into the public arena the nature of usual impacts involved. The employment of the Rogers' office has ensured a high profile for the design which may ease planning consent difficulties.

The development of Terminal 5 consists of a core terminal building, three mini satellite terminals, maintenance hangar,

5.9 Virtual development in the form of CAD simulation has been a feature of the public inquiry into Heathrow's Terminal 5. Architects: Richard Rogers Partnership.

aprons, taxiways, car parks, office and hotel. The main terminal is rather more a transportation interchange than a traditional passenger terminal, providing links to underground and main line railways and bus services. Dimensionally it is very large, measuring 432m by 195m, and 40m high to the ridge and 29m to the eaves. The interior concourses are also lofty, with a clear height of 20m specified by BAA for the departure lounge.[6]

The materials and architectural forms have been selected to reduce visual and environmental impacts. The inclined glazing on the east and west elevations and the large overhanging canopies on the north and south elevations are intended to reduce the reflectivity of the building, especially when the sun is at low angles. An undulating roof shape has been selected to reduce light spillage at night from the large rooflights, thereby minimizing night-time sky pollution and potential hazard to pilots. In the choice of materials BAA's architects have striven to absorb the building into the

airport environment. The predominantly glazed walls, set in frames and panels of neutral greys and pale greens, allow the building to blend with the apron areas and adjoining grassland. The roof's wavy profile and soft metallic finish also apes the tones of an English sky. The colours of the terminal, car parks, office block and hotel are all in the range of off-white, grey and silver with, if the visualizations are to be trusted, touches of light green and pale blue.

To reduce the apparent scale of the collection of new buildings, a stepped profile is adopted. The visually dominating terminal has a sweeping, oscillating roof, which is lower at the outer edges giving – superficially at least – the appearance of land undulations. In addition, the different buildings nearby (such as car parks, hotel, offices and satellite terminals) are stepped in height to allow the main terminal to appear as an urban grouping with the terminal at the centre. Stylistically, there is an attempt at aesthetic integration of the different building parts by

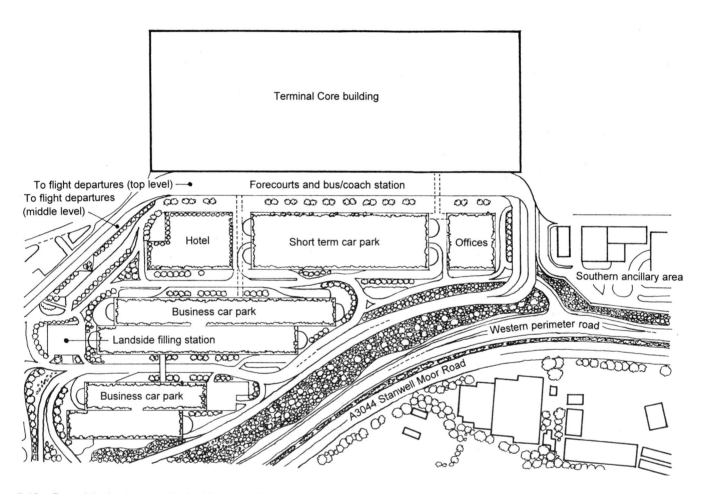

5.10 Part of the landscape plan for Heathrow Terminal 5. The terminal is to the right. Architects: Richard Rogers Partnership.

using a family of materials, construction and landscape details and a consistent design philosophy. Planting (trees, hedges, shrubs and grass banks) plays a key part in reducing the environmental impact of the whole development. The parapets of each level of the car park, as well as the hotel and office roofs, are to be planted with creepers, which tumble down the walls and clothe the concrete frames. From the landside the appearance sought will be one of greenery masking the peripheral buildings, with the predominantly glazed main terminal set within a more formal space.

Landscape is not only used to screen and soften the different buildings, it is also employed at a broader infrastructure level. Between the formal landscape associated with the buildings and the informal agricultural landscapes of Middlesex, the intention is to introduce transitional planting, which acts like layers integrating the development with the wider environment. The effect of the strategy, aided by stepped and layered buildings and planted bulbs round roads, is to allow the massive development to be absorbed into the landscape. Care has been taken with the selection of species of tree and shrub to avoid the attraction of larger birds, which can pose a hazard to air-craft. Again, to reduce the scale of the different structures, many are designed with one or two storeys beneath ground, either enclosed or hidden behind 7m high planted embankments.

The formal language of design for the different buildings embraces the play of primary shapes and geometries. The car parks are designed as cubes or rectangles with semicircular ramps 18m in diameter placed on the outsides of the buildings. These curved ramps, which provide vertical circulation for cars, are complemented by square stair towers and lifts placed on the outside of the structures. The juxtaposition of the square and circular elements gives interest to the design, and avoids the visual monotony associated with car parks. Similar plays of cubes and cylinders make up hotels and office buildings. Strong geometric forms, like large-scale planting, have been employed to reduce the apparent scale of the development.

Extent of the masterplan

It has already been noted that the impact of an airport extends far beyond its physical boundaries. Two types of masterplan are commonly encountered: that which structures the airport estate only (but with a statement of wider impacts), and that which structures both the airport and adjoining areas into an integrated development proposal. The latter is increasingly adopted as airport developers, working usually with adjoining landowners and civic authorities, recognize that integrating neighbourhood land uses with airport expansion is mutually beneficial.

An example of the wider impact of airports upon the regional infrastructure is that of Stansted. The airport's growth from its opening in 1991 with 4 million passengers a year to an expected 15 million within the decade has resulted in a planned increase in the workforce from 3500 to 14500. The increase puts pressure on roads, public transport provision, health care, education and housing. The latter is a point of particular contention in this area of still largely agricultural Essex. Essex County Council identified in its Structure Plan Review of 1994 the need for 2500 new houses to satisfy Stansted's anticipated growth. Following

a public inquiry into objections from local councils, the government inspector recommended the expansion of existing villages rather than the construction of a new town on the former American air base at Little Easton as proposed earlier. However, local people, faced with the expansion of villages such as Felsted and Takeley from about 200 houses to over 500, continue to object and, at the time of writing, have taken the issue to the High Court in London.[7] The issue illustrates how wide the economic and social impacts of major airports are, and masterplans need to plan for growth and environmental protection way outside the boundaries of the airport.

The physical and environmental planning of an airport and its hinterland should seek to ease community conflict (from problems such as noise and imbalanced local communities) and realize the potential of development alongside the airport. The growth in services such as air cargo has led to an expansion of warehousing facilities near to airports. Similarly, business parks have grown up near to major airports (for example, Stockley Park near Heathrow) because of the proximity to the transport infrastructure, and the presence of modern hotels and conference facilities. Airport expansion should therefore recognize that much growth occurs outside the perimeter fence, and that both need to be structured in time and space to ensure that infrastructure demands (water, drainage, transport) and environmental impacts are anticipated and addressed. Where the airport authority owns adjoining land, it makes great sense to maximize its development potential in tandem with airport needs.

References

1. Norman Ashford and Paul Wright, *Airport Engineering*, John Wiley & Sons, New York, 1991, p. 133. My list is an adaptation and enlargement of that cited.
2. Adapted from Ashford and Wright, *Airport Engineering*, p. 126.
3. *Ibid*., pp. 28–29.
4. Josephine Smit and Antony Oliver, 'Time for T5', in Jackie Whitelaw (ed.), *21st Century Airports*, supplement of *New Civil Engineer/New Builder*, May 1995.
5. Note for the Inquiry (Terminal 5) BAA/1786, 14 February 1996, p. 3.
6. *Ibid*., p. 7.
7. *The Guardian*, 16 April 1996.

Part two

Terminal design

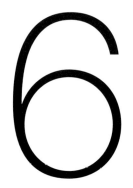

CHAPTER

6

The terminal as part of the airport system

Aircraft types and passenger terminal design

The four main scales of air transport – intercontinental, continental, regional and commuter – are each served by their own type and category of aircraft. Transport by the first is in such aircraft as the Boeing 747 (with seating for about 400), the second by say the European Airbus A310 (seating about 250), the third by the Boeing 737 (seating 150–200) and the fourth by the SAAB 340 (seating about 35). Each scale of jet has its own apron, servicing and terminal design needs. Though there are overlaps between the four main categories of aircraft, the designer of the airport knows that if each scale can be accommodated, then those planes between the capacity bands will fit comfortably into the system. As a general rule, journeys over 3000km are seen as intercontinental, between 3000 and 1500km as continental, under 1500km as regional, and under 300km as commuting.

While the intercontinental and continental market is met by jet aircraft, the lower end of the regional scale and commuter market is increasingly served by turboprops. The new generation of turboprops offer distinct advantages over jet aircraft: they are less noisy, can operate at lower altitudes, have reduced emissions, and shorter take-off and landing needs. The growth in commuter journeying by plane is being met not by small noisy jets but by relatively quiet and fuel-efficient turboprops such as the SAA 2000. In fact, while larger jet aircraft are increasingly constrained by environmental regulations of one kind or another, the new generation of turboprops with their improved performance readily meet international standards. This is further fuelling a growth in commuter journeys by plane, which changing work practices and regional politics (such as the integration of Europe) are also promoting.

The increase in commuter aircraft journeys is most marked in North America and Europe, where the majority of the 9000 commuter aircraft in the world operate. However, it has been estimated that over the next 20 years an additional 17 000 aircraft will be needed to meet demand. While this is not a large volume in financial terms (compared with growth in larger aircraft), it suggests

6.1 Key relationships at airports.

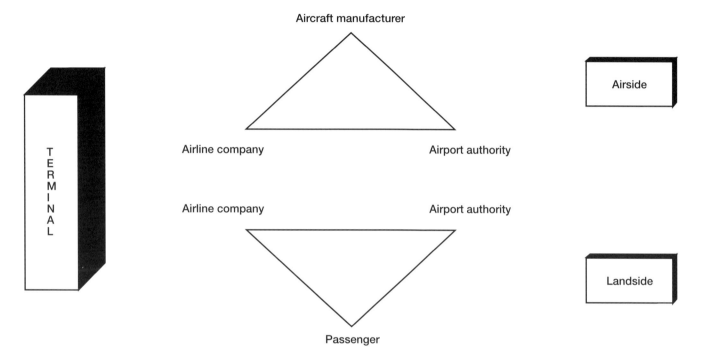

a significant increase in such traffic, which terminal design will need to accommodate. The main problem here is access from the terminal building to the plane; the usual pattern of elevated telescopic gates will not suffice. Demarcation for commuter flights is normally directly over the apron alongside the terminal or by bussing to locations further afield.

Where large numbers of commuter passengers regularly use a terminal, there needs to be provision for direct and easy access to the apron area from the departure lounge. This poses security and organization problems, because the departure lounge is normally at first-floor level. Also, because about 70% of commuter and regional traffic is provided by small independent carriers, the major airlines operating at a terminal may be reluctant to sacrifice their own operational efficiency (and security) to meet the needs of this specialized market.

The terminal building has to be capable of accommodating all four scales of commercial aircraft listed earlier. The most problematic area is normally with regard to commuter aircraft, where smallness of size, the need to take off and land quickly, and unusual aircraft design features put

terminal, gate lounge, runway and apron facilities under greatest strain. However, looking further to the future (10–20 years), a new generation of aircraft now undergoing technical investigation may require wider modification to airport design. Two trends are emerging that, if realized, will alter the assumptions under which the airline and airport industries operate. The first concerns the re-emergence of supersonic passenger aircraft. Design and technological research is being devoted to a new generation of supersonic aircraft based upon the experience of Concorde. Several manufacturers are collaborating to develop a quieter, faster, more fuel-efficient and larger-capacity supersonic jet. With business travel growth still buoyant, and the world's biggest trading nations at opposite geographical regions, aircraft designers realize that very high-speed travel has commercial advantage. The age of mass supersonic commercial air transport will probably occur well within the lifetime of airports currently being designed (that is, 50 years). The second innovation concerns very large (as against fast) aircraft, perhaps capable of carrying 1000 or more passengers. Airbus Industrie, Boeing and McDonnell Douglas are all developing prototype designs in this field. For the passenger terminal the implications for the organization and distribution of space, catering, ticketing and baggage handling will be profound. To meet such future demand, terminal design needs to be robust in concept and capable of multiple adaptation over time.

The life of an airport terminal, at about 50 years, is two or three times as long as that of the aircraft it serves, and frequently longer than the life of an airline company. In an industry of little stability, the airport is the one permanent feature. Even the airport, though, does not stand still; it evolves new runways and passenger terminals, it replaces obsolete ground transport systems, and regularly upgrades air traffic control facilities. At Heathrow there are now four terminals (with a fifth designed), while Terminal 1 has been substantially rehabilitated and extended at least twice in its 30 years of life. These changes are driven by two main factors: the increase in passenger numbers, and the evolving nature of aircraft design. Innovation in aircraft design triggers a chain reaction throughout the industry, which airline management, airport operation and passenger terminal design have then to meet. It is against this background that changes in aircraft design (the new breed of turboprops, second generation of supersonic planes, very high-capacity aircraft) and their effect upon terminals should be seen. The passenger terminal has to be capable of meeting change, but the architect is rarely able to anticipate what specific shape or direction that change will take. Flexibility, expandability and functional adaptability are the obvious design philosophies to adopt within the constraints of structural robustness and aesthetic appeal.

Energy consumption, payload and the effect upon terminal design

Energy is consumed in enormous quantities at airports. Fossil fuel is used to lift aircraft into the sky; to transport people, freight and baggage to airports; and to heat, light and ventilate airport buildings. Airports are one of the greatest energy-consuming centres per square kilometre on our planet. For every plane that travels from New York to London the amount of energy used is roughly equal to that of an ocean liner.[1] Large jet aircraft consume about 9600 litres of fuel per hour in flight, and about 2400 litres on take-off. On a long journey a typical jet burns about 40 tonnes of fuel. This leads to a great concentration of air pollution at airports, and the obvious need for extensive refuelling facilities on apron areas where spillage occurs. Pollution affects air conditioning of buildings and the choice of materials used in the construction of airports. Advanced turboprops are far more energy efficient per tonne of aircraft than turbojets, consuming about two-thirds less fuel per tonne-km. As a consequence, regional airports, which make greater use of turboprops than of jet aircraft, suffer less air pollution. In total, aviation accounts for 5% of world oil consumption and 12% of all oil used in transportation, contributing some 4–6% of the gases leading to global warming.[2]

For the airline company the factor that determines operational efficiency is not so much fuel consumption but payload. This is a factor determined by the revenue-producing load: that is, the carrying capacity in terms of passengers and freight. Jet aircraft are used where large numbers of people need to be carried. As a rule of thumb, payload represents about a fifth of the total aircraft weight. Payload and aviation fuel are the two variables in aircraft weight, and both must be carefully calculated to ensure that safety regulations are met. On long journeys fuel may account for a third of the total weight of the aircraft and payload only a sixth, but more typically fuel weight and payload are about the same (at roughly 18% each of average weight).[3]

Payload is the revenue-generating function of air transportation. But with modern aircraft design it is often not weight that is the limiting factor, but space. On passenger flights it is rare for payload weight to reach the maximum permitted under international safety regulations, because seats and aisles take up so much space. Airlines compete on quality of journey where leg-room and seat width are critical factors. As a consequence, payload limits are rarely reached except at the lower end of the market (holiday package tours, for example).

There is a relationship between aircraft carrying capacity, runway length and the design of passenger terminals. Few aircraft journeys exploit the limits of payload because of passenger space expectations. This means that most terminals have to cater for many flights slightly below their passenger-carrying capacity, rather than fewer at the weight limit. This tends to even out the peaks and troughs of aircraft movement. However, as larger and more powerful aircraft are introduced (such as the Boeing 777), the troughs are tending to be filled. Bigger aircraft mean longer runways and larger payloads. Longer runways mean modification to the design of the airport itself; larger payloads mean changes in the layout and passenger-handling methods employed at the terminal. As payloads increase (25% payload weight to aircraft weight is becoming the norm, compared with 18–20% a decade ago), check-in, baggage handling and lounge space are put under stress. Aircraft design and terminal design are directly related.

Large aircraft with heavy fuel loads and high payloads require long runways, wide apron areas and plenty of taxiing space. This means that passengers spend a lot of time on the ground in the aircraft before and after take-off. Hence the passenger arriving at the airport after a long journey is often jaded, and does not readily accept additional delays at baggage reclaim or customs clearance. Terminal design has to ensure that passengers are not unduly subjected to changes in level, long corridors, overcrowded arrival lounge areas, and disorientating movements. It also means that seats should be provided within movement flows; that interior design should relieve stress, not add to it; and that daylight and tranquillity should temper movement through the terminal.

Relationship between the mission of airport authorities and terminal design

Recognizing the value of good design has its roots in the mission statements of more progressive airport authorities. For example, the six-point mission adopted by BAA lays the foundation for the pursuit of quality in the design and management of its airports. BAA's mission can be summarized as follows:[4]

- Give safety and security the highest priority through risk auditing, and best-practice management systems.

6.2 Stansted marks the transition from first- to second-generation terminals. Stansted Airport, UK. Architects: Foster and Partners.

- Provide a good and safe working environment for employees.
- Ensure that passengers and airlines receive excellence and good value for money.
- Concentrate on the core airport business while fully developing property and retail potential.
- Encourage shareholders to believe in the company by giving them consistent growth in earnings and dividends.
- Recognize the concerns of the local (airport) communities, set challenging environmental targets, and audit performance against them.

Of the six elements of BAA's mission, three have a direct bearing upon airport design and two further influence the quality of physical development indirectly. Two strands of the mission statement are, however, worthy of special mention: safety and security, and environment. The first is crucial to successful terminal design, especially as perceived by passengers and airport managers. Without safe and secure buildings, the airport journey is fraught with potential hazard and – equally important – fear of danger, which undermines the passengers' sense of security. The expression of environmental concerns also signals changing priorities over the past decade. Airports are designed today to minimize environmental and ecological impacts, both in their design and construction and in day-to-day operations.

Because BAA is the world's biggest private airport operator, the mission of the company has more than local

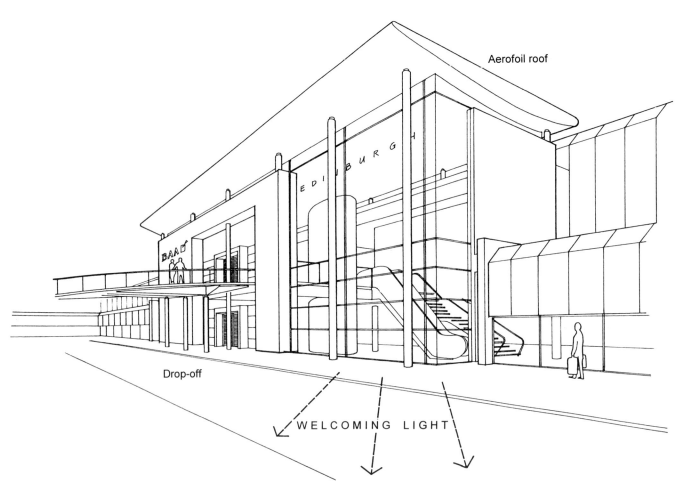

Aerofoil roof

Drop-off

WELCOMING LIGHT

6.3 Light and space are key elements of BAA design philosophy as in this proposal for extending Edinburgh Airport, UK. Architects: Parr Partnership.

relevance. The range of concerns expressed – from safety to good working environments for staff, from a culture of excellence in the provision of airport facilities to maximizing property and retail earnings – all point towards the difference between first- and second-generation airports. The sense of evolution evident say in the difference between Heathrow's Terminal 4 and the published designs for Terminal 5 can be traced to the revised mission adopted by BAA in 1992.

BAA owns and operates seven UK airports (Heathrow, Gatwick, Stansted, Glasgow, Edinburgh, Aberdeen and Southampton), as well as Melbourne, Naples and

Indianapolis Airport and the retail facilities at Pittsburgh. The company's policy is beginning to influence the culture of competitors and to raise standards generally. Also, as federally owned airports throughout the world are sold either in whole or in part to the private sector, it is BAA that is emerging as a lead contender to take them over. Hence BAA's mission of excellence, customer quality and reduced environmental impact looks set to have international application.

One can trace many recent developments at UK airports to the influence of the mission statement. The Flight Connections Centre that links Terminals 1 and 2 at Heathrow followed concerns over passenger transfer difficulties (the new Centre includes opening up views of the airport runway, showers, slumber zone and children's play area). The new international departure lounge at Terminal 1 was also in response to the pursuit of excellence in facilities expressed in the mission. Growing congestion at Terminal 1 led also to Europier (designed by the Richard Rogers Partnership), which combined expanded retail facilities with more extensive direct boarding of aircraft. Similar plans are afoot to build a three-storey extension to Heathrow's Terminal 2 (due to open in 1998), which will double the size of the departure hall. The improvements also include: modernized check-in desks; new seating areas, escalators, lifts and stairs; baggage-sorting improvements; and a new, centralized security facility.

The question of safety and security has led to many changes in the design and operation of terminals. BAA employs 3000 staff specifically in the field of airport safety and security.[5] New technologies introduced progressively at Gatwick and Glasgow Airports have speeded the electronic searching of baggage, and hand-held metal detectors for body checks now supplement traditional screening. As new safety technologies are introduced, the arrangement of security screens and waiting areas at ticket control points has had to be adapted. Physical upheaval is inevitable in an industry noted for innovation. When changes to airports are planned, either alterations to the fabric of terminals or modifications to management processes, the corresponding designs are subjected to a standardized risk assessment procedure. Designing for safety is one of the biggest differences between first- and second-generation airports.

The mission statement highlights the importance now attached to the environmental impact of airports. BAA, the Civil Aviation Authority in the UK and the Federal Aviation Authority in the USA all recognize that they have a role in reducing the damage to the environment caused by airport operations. Airports are integral parts of local communities, and those communities' concerns have been given fresh urgency. No airport can ignore the damage to local ecosystems or the visual and noise intrusion of their operations. BAA instils in its airport management the need to be environmentally responsible neighbours. The new aware-

6.4 Marseille Airport, France.

6.5 Architecture has an important role in creating well-being and marking the gateway to the sky. King Abdulaziz Airport, Jeddah, Saudi Arabia. Architects: Murphy/Jahn.

The terminal as part of the airport system

Table 6.1 Examples of airport layout concepts

Airport	Concept	Architect
Dulles International Terminal, Washington, USA	Transporter concept with 2-storey terminal	Eero Saarinen
Dulles International Terminal (Phase 2), Washington, USA	Transporter concept converted to satellite pier with enlarged terminal	Skidmore, Owings and Merrill
Fargo Airport, North Dakota, USA	$1^1/_2$-storey linear terminal	Foss Associates with Thompson Consultants
Heathrow Airport, Terminal 5, London, UK	Multistorey terminal with detached satellite piers reached by underground rail	Richard Rogers Partnership
Kansai Airport, Japan	Terminal with long parallel finger pier	Renzo Piano Building Workshop
King Khaled International Airport, Riyadh, Saudi Arabia	Triangular compact module units joined by moving walkways	Hellmuth, Obata & Kassabaum
Nashville Metropolitan Airport, USA	Radiating pier finger with multistorey terminal	Gresham, Smith and Partners and Robert Lamb Hart with Thompson Consultants
O'Hare Airport, United Terminal, Chicago, USA	2-storey linear terminal with end satellites	Murphy/Jahn with A. Epstein and Sons
San Francisco International Airport, USA	Combined radiating pier/finger with satellites	Gensler & Associates
Southampton Airport, UK	Single-storey linear terminal without piers	Manser Associates
Stansted Airport, UK	2-storey terminal with detached satellite piers reached by light rail	Foster and Partners
Tehran Airport, Iran	Radiating pier/finger with multistorey terminal	Tippetts, Abett, McCarthy, Stratton
Los Angeles Airport, Tom Bradley International Terminal, USA	Square pier/finger with multistorey terminal	Pereira, Dworsky, Sinclair Williams with Thompson Consultants

ness is expressed in the way in which airport buildings are designed to work more with nature (Terminal 5 at Heathrow is an example), the management of the wider landscape to promote ecodiversity, the development of environmentally related educational projects with local schools and colleges, and a scheme of funding noise insulation measures for houses near airports (7000 homes near Heathrow have been improved, at a cost to BAA of £10 million).[6]

Redressing the balance between passenger and airport needs

Airports are extraordinarily complex facilities – perhaps one of the most sophisticated and complicated forms of devel-

opment engineered by man. However, passengers should not be exposed to the complexity: their experience of the airport should be one of simplicity and serenity. A well-designed airport is one where routes are clear and simple to use, where the images are uplifting, even romantic, and where the jaded passenger ferried from building to plane and terminal to gate can find tranquillity and peace. Hence there are two parallel perceptions of the airport: the facilities manager wants a well-organized, finely tuned airport operation, while the typical traveller needs protection from the workings of the airport and requires instead quiet efficiency of passage. The dialectic between the two perceptions provides the basis for ordering typical airports into landside and airside facilities, into public and private routes, into openly accessible and security sterile areas, and into arrivals and departures flows. It is also the foundation for the split of passenger from baggage as near as possible to the terminal entrance, and for the undercroft of baggage and building services facilities found in most airports. It is the basis too for the use of different floor levels to accommodate cross-flows, and the logic of general retailing split from duty-free facilities.

Complexity at airports is resolved, identified and reconciled in plan and section. Airport managers and passengers need to be able to read and exploit the terminal in three dimensions: managers because of the demands made by airline companies, security staff, immigration controls and retailers; passengers because of their need to recognize the meaning and direction of places and routes within the labyrinth of a typical airport. Three-dimensional complexity is a feature of modern terminals: it derives from the scale of intermodal transport links provided today, from the extent of retailing at modern airports, and from security demands. Early terminals were relatively straightforward single- or double-level buildings, but today's airports (such as Kansai) are on four main levels, and future ones (such as Seoul International) will be on six or more levels.

If complexity is a necessary measure of size and the contemporary approach to the multifarious airport, the passenger needs some protection from its ramifications. But airports should not become dull, sanitized and neutral environments as a consequence (the problem perhaps with Stansted). The airport remains a building type with romantic overtones; its imagery requires an uplifting, technologically inspired architecture language. The crisp transparent spaces filled with sunlight and daring engineering of contemporary terminals (as at Stuttgart) allude to an airport atmosphere without subjecting passengers to the full functional paraphernalia of airport operations. The shielding of passengers from the complexity of the modern airport allows the drama and expressive possibilities of the major public terminal spaces to be exploited. The dialogue of the passenger with the concourses allows the airport architect to engage in the uplift of tired spirits, and to create legibility within intrinsically complicated and confusing buildings.

The airport designer has two distinct but parallel perceptions of quality to satisfy: the airport authority and the passenger. In the past, design manuals such as that issued by IATA emphasized functional solutions at the expense of aesthetic ones. Certainly, the modern airport needs to operate smoothly, be profitable and viable in the short and longer term. But from the passenger viewpoint, it needs to offer a great deal more. The current concern with large, theatrical interior airport spaces, with tree planting inside and outside terminals, with legibility and waymarking of routes, with natural light and ventilation, represents a shift in balance between airport and passenger priorities. Some more enlightened airport developers (such as BAA) began to put the physical and psychological needs of passengers to the fore in the early 1990s. Their example is becoming standard practice worldwide, with consequences for the whole approach to airport design. Though technical standards are still needed, they do not have the primacy of old. By putting the passenger needs alongside those of airport managers and airline companies, a new architectural culture has begun to emerge.

References

1. Robert Horonjeff, *Planning and Design of Airports*, McGraw-Hill, New York, 1962, p. 78.
2. IATA, *Airport Terminals Reference Manual*, 8th edn, International Air Transport Association, Montreal, Canada, April 1995, p. 85.
3. Horonjeff, *Planning and Design of Airports*, p. 83.
4. The list is adapted from BAA, *Shaping up for the 21st Century*, BAA Annual Report 1995/96, London, p. 1.
5. *Ibid*., p. 6.
6. *Ibid*., p. 26.

CHAPTER 7

Procurement and management of terminals

Design standards and briefing: the example of BAA

As a major provider of airport facilities in the UK, and the world's biggest airport operator, BAA has a key role to play in questions of design quality. Through its briefing instructions to architects, the method of procurement adopted, and the cost yardsticks applied, BAA has a central role in providing terminals that satisfy customer needs on the one hand, and raise architectural standards on the other. BAA spends about £400 million a year on construction services of one kind or another. This represents nearly 40% of its annual turnover.[1] In order to keep costs down, and inspired by the Latham Report of 1994, *Constructing the Team*, the BAA has set a target of achieving a 30% cost reduction per unit of construction over a three-year period.[2] Such a large reduction in unit costs, justified according to BAA Chief Executive Sir John Egan by world airport cost comparisons, is to allow BAA to compete effectively within the global economy.

How such a reduction is to be achieved is outlined in Table 7.1, but concern should perhaps be expressed over the effect of such extensive cost saving on design quality. Whereas the Latham Report promulgated a wider vision of greater teamwork, improved productivity and new working practices to reduce unnecessary litigation, all in order to achieve cost savings for the UK construction industry of 30% over a 10-year period, BAA has more immediate plans. Pointers have been identified by BAA that allow the savings to be achieved more rapidly under six headings:

- Reduce changes to design.
- Optimize specifications.
- Improve design cost-effectiveness.
- Apportion risk efficiently.
- Improve productivity.
- Reduce waste.

With the development of Heathrow's Terminal 5 by Richard Rogers on the horizon, such changes in briefing and project management have implications for architectural quality and design freedom.

Table 7.1 BAA's six pointers towards achieving a 30% cost saving on construction projects.

Reduce changes	Improve customer/market research
	Brief effectively
	Use prototypes
Optimize specification standards	Match standards to needs
	Review code standards
	Review 'institutional specifications'
Improve design cost-effectiveness	Increase use of standard designs and components
	Use 3-D design technologies to automate design and create building prototypes
	Use IT/electronic data interchange to improve communications efficiency
	Involve suppliers early in design process
	Develop supply partnering arrangements
Apportion risk efficiently	Use single project insurance
	Use industry-wide standard warranties/guarantees/bonds
	Develop a more flexible lease structure
Improve productivity	Develop off-site/on-site logistics
	Design for construction
	Use more standard designs and components
	Develop project team workflow processes
Reduce waste	Use 3-D technologies to test designs for errors, fit etc.
	Use off-site manufacturing and assembly

Source: Jackie Whitelaw (ed.), *21st Century Airports*, supplement of *New Civil Engineer/New Builder*, May 1995, p. 24

Raymond Turner, BAA's Group Design Director, has the task of coordinating design standards mainly through the issue of design guides and project briefing to consultant architects. His principal task is to ensure that new buildings fit the company's mission statement, with its emphasis upon customer satisfaction, cost competitiveness and quality of experience. Turner is anxious to standardize design solutions from concept design to detail. This is the main mechanism by which building costs can be controlled.

Table 7.2 Key elements of design management at BAA

Standardize 50% of components used in terminals

Use preselected contractors for a wide range of site and construction work

Adopt a culture of no design changes once the building is under construction

Adopt a common design management process, with BAA's project managers taking the lead

Build teams based upon the repeated use of a small number of designers, suppliers and constructors

Involve customers in design development at early stage

Develop 'framework agreements' with suppliers

Source: *Shaping Up for the 21st Century*, BAA Annual Report 1995/96, pp.15–66; and Jackie Whitelaw (ed.), *21st Century Airports*, supplement of *New Civil Engineer/New Builder*, May 1995, p. 20

It also means that replacement components can be readily obtained, and that one terminal design develops logically from the experience of another. It is partly the use of prototypes with limited developmental variations that led to the similarities between Foster's Stansted design and that by Rogers' office for Heathrow's Terminal 5.

The culture of standardization has led BAA to insist that 50% of the parts of a new terminal are made up of standardized components, provided and installed by preselected contractors under 'framework agreements'.[3] Not all products reach BAA's new standards, and one role of appointed architects is to help develop components or designs that can then become part of the standard specification. As Turner notes, not all architects are happy with the imposition of such standardization, or with the primary role of BAA's own staff in selecting finishes and products such as carpets or seats for new terminals,[4] but the avoidance of unnecessary variation is seen as essential for cost and quality control. Framework agreements also allow suppliers to develop new products without undue risk, and to enter into competition on the basis of quality standards as well as of cost.

Table 7.3 BAA's construction process

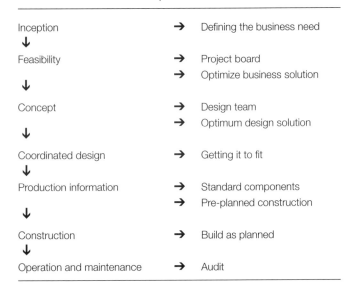

Inception	→	Defining the business need
↓		
Feasibility	→	Project board
	→	Optimize business solution
↓		
Concept	→	Design team
	→	Optimum design solution
↓		
Coordinated design	→	Getting it to fit
↓		
Production information	→	Standard components
	→	Pre-planned construction
↓		
Construction	→	Build as planned
↓		
Operation and maintenance	→	Audit

Source: *Shaping Up for the 21st Century*, BAA Annual Report 1995/96, p. 15

Having tackled common specifications, BAA is also seeking to standardize design management processes just as the Latham Report proposed. BAA's briefing guide has two parts: a common procedure for design and briefing for BAA's own staff of project managers, and standard guidelines for the appointment and briefing of external consultants. Both depend upon a universal set of design deliverables (as the BAA puts it), which are needed by certain stages so that the design can be reviewed and evaluated by BAA and potential customers before decisions become too fixed. Turner admits that the process has shifted some of the design decision-making away from designers towards project managers and contractors, adding wryly that 'design is too important to be left to the designer'.[5] Just as BAA has sought to standardize the choice of materials and specification for new terminals, it has also used its powers as client to impose a common management ethos controlling the whole design and procurement process.

The brief for Southampton illustrates the relationship between quality, cost and design standards. BAA required its new terminal (designed by Manser Associates) to 'set new standards for regional airports, both in quality of service and in cost-effectiveness'.[6] The internal layout was to be 'simple and efficient' in order to achieve the 'maximum income from the available commercial space'.[7] Hence the architect had the task of achieving design excellence in an abstract sense, and of creating a building that achieved the highest possible level of secondary income generation. Added to this, the design had to give the best 'value for money' as measured against BAA's own procurement quality standards, while also being functionally efficient within a single shell.

At a detailed level, the terminal had to be cooled to not less than '3 °C below outside ambient temperature to obviate thermal shock to users'.[8] Because aircraft engine fumes can lead to internal air pollution, the brief also required that air-chilled water coolers be of PVC-coated aluminium fins or copper coil construction to avoid corrosion.[9] Architectural design has therefore to achieve both broad operational efficiencies and detailed standards of comfort or health. The various briefing constraints shape terminals far more than is generally realized. Only with effective and enlightened briefs can truly innovative airport architecture emerge.

Managing terminals

There clearly needs to be a correspondence between the design and management strategies of airport terminals. As management approaches change, there are inevitable effects upon the use and distribution of space within terminals. As has already been noted, one of the current new directions for terminals is in the retail, leisure and conference fields, and this trend is supported by the growing use of private sector airport management companies. There has appeared recently a willingness to split the ownership of airports from the management of key services. Although certain facilities, such as baggage handling and apron services, have traditionally been carried out by specialist companies, this approach has spread to the management of the terminal itself. Today, airport authorities have begun

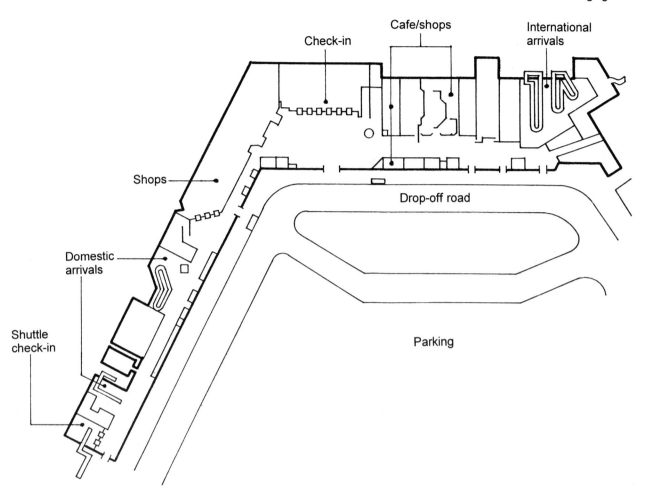

7.1 The extent of commercial floorspace often exceeds circulation areas. Edinburgh Airport, UK. Architects: RMJM.

to realize that the successful exploitation of the huge passenger flows within terminals requires the assistance of private sector companies.

One company that has begun to exploit the dialectic between ownership and management is BAA itself. Having led the retail and leisure industry expansion of UK airports in the 1980s, the company established BAA International in 1990 to take the approach and expertise further afield. By 1996 BAA International had secured contracts to manage two American airports (at Pittsburgh and Indianapolis), and had formed joint venture companies to exploit opportunities in the Asia Pacific region and in Australia. In each case, BAA working with local private sector and state partners was invited to form a joint venture to manage airports, or in the case of Melbourne, Brisbane, Adelaide and Perth airports to take over the ownership and management of the whole enterprise.

BAA's approach is to apply the lessons learnt principally at Gatwick and Heathrow to overseas airports. Working generally within 10-15 year management contracts, the company's priorities include the introduction of BAA's terminal management processes, the adoption of their Quality of Service Monitor, the implementation of a new

retail strategy, and the development of property potential inside and outside the terminal.[10] As the company's culture is adopted, the airports it manages inevitably change, creating opportunities for architects and interior designers. For example, at Pittsburgh Airport, where terminal management was taken over by BAA International in 1992, 1500m^2 of additional concession space has been created, and the money spent per passenger passing through the terminal has risen from $2.30 to $6.68. Nearer to home BAA has undertaken a detailed assessment of Naples Airport, with a view to operating the airport as it transfers from state to private ownership in 1997.

Private management of airports, either in whole or in part, opens up airports to market forces. These in turn create change and opportunity for designers of various kinds (including shop and restaurant designers, graphics and furniture designers, and facilities managers). It has also resulted in the diversification of different management cultures at airports, leading in turn to different styles of organization and design within the terminal. As Asian airports, for example, are expanded, British, American and German management skills and designers are brought in. One challenge for companies such as BAA International is

7.2 Retail sales help to justify refurbishment of older terminals. South Terminal, Gatwick Airport, UK. Architects: Chapman Taylor Partners.

how to recognize and respond to the subtle cultural differences between nations, to ensure that a standardizing management approach does not stifle regional distinctiveness at airports.

Although the pattern varies from country to country, there is growing consistency in the way in which airport authorities own and manage terminals. The key trend already

noted is the privatization of airports and the contracting out of important services, especially in the baggage handling, retail and leisure fields. Income for the airport operator at the terminal varies according to the type of service. For example, income from retailing (amounting to 44% of BAA's total profits at UK airports) is turnover related: that is, BAA takes a percentage of the retailer's sales. However, with car parking, advertising and duty-free shopping the airport operator is paid a fixed fee by the lessee irrespective of the level of sales.[11] Such contracts between the airport authority and private companies are normally on a 3- to 5-year timescale, and this in turn generates the timescale for the internal adaptation of terminal space.

High levels of retail and ancillary sales mean that airports are relatively cheap for airline companies. Airport and traffic charges for airline companies accounted for only 35% of BAA's income in 1995/96, the low rates being possible because of the £556 million generated by retail sales in the terminal itself. As a result, Heathrow and Gatwick are amongst the cheapest major airports for airline companies in the world.

Keeping abreast of expanded passenger facilities requires high levels of expenditure by the airport operator. Using BAA again as an example, the company in 1996 spent over £1 million a day on improving the quality of facilities for its passengers (over 60% of total retail earnings for the year). Quality enhancement involving physical upgrading of terminals is essential if passenger standards and revenue targets are to be met.

BAA's management strategy for terminals, initiated in 1990, has the following elements:

- using market research to establish customer needs
- increased competition in products and services
- a commitment to providing high levels of customer service
- offering value for money
- introducing international brand names to the airports
- providing a wide range of high-quality products
- creating quality retail environments
- working in partnership with retailers to meet customer needs profitably.

The management strategy, with its emphasis on retail expansion, has implications for the design and upgrading of terminals. The culture of regular market research carries the corollary that terminals will be frequently refurbished to meet the changing needs and taste of passengers. As witnessed in the upgrading of Gatwick's South Terminal to form 'The Village', and at Heathrow's Terminal 2, this entails the introduction of daylight into existing retail malls or the exploitation of new views over runways to provide tired passengers with interesting panoramas. The quality of the retail environment is an important factor in retail sales; in fact some international retailers (such as The Disney Store) require a certain standard before they will consider locating at a particular venue. Hence BAA's ambition for greater retailer growth requires investment in the physical environment of terminals to allow this to materialize.

The role of the Quality of Service Monitor (QSM)

To ensure the smooth operation of airports, BAA adopts a standard method of monitoring the performance of its terminals. Using seven main headings (cleanliness, mechanical assistance including such things as trolleys, procedures, comfort, congestion, staff helpfulness and value for money), each airport is subjected to QSM. The assessment focuses upon passenger experience but includes the monitoring of the views of other stakeholders, such as airline companies and retailers.

The surveys are undertaken without prior notice. Airport managers are encouraged to maintain vigilance and to regularly raise standards by the presence of QSM. The areas where surveying tends to concentrate are at check-in, security, baggage reclaim, immigration and departure lounges. Where low scores are achieved (the rating is 1 to 5, where 5 is excellent), this may be because of ineffective management or lack of investment in physical improvements. Regular low scores recorded at Heathrow's Terminal 1 (which handles 22 million passengers a year) led to a number of new facilities being constructed in 1995–96, such as the Flight Connections Centre, a dedicated international departures lounge, and Europier for direct flight boarding. So, while QSM is a management tool, its use

7.3 Terminals represent national values. Here at Schiphol Airport there is an air of civic provision, not the bustle of a retail mall. Schiphol Airport, the Netherlands. Architects: Bentham Crouwel.

helps to identify shortcomings, which leads to new physical investment in airports.[12]

Manipulation of space and time in the terminal

The management and, as a consequence, the design of terminals increasingly exploit space and time to increase revenue sales. They exploit space in the sense that passenger flows are interrupted by periodic banks of shops, bars, cafes, flower stalls, currency dealerships and car rental points – not just in the departure lounge but in the arrivals lounge as well. Every stage in the journey through the terminal is manipulated by commerce in one form or another. Even before reaching the check-in desks, passengers are being persuaded to part with their money, or are being exposed to sales advertising. They exploit time in the sense that airlines set extensive check-in times (up to two hours) to ensure that passengers are exposed to as much commercial distraction as possible. Boredom drives frustrated airline passengers into the shops and bars that predate

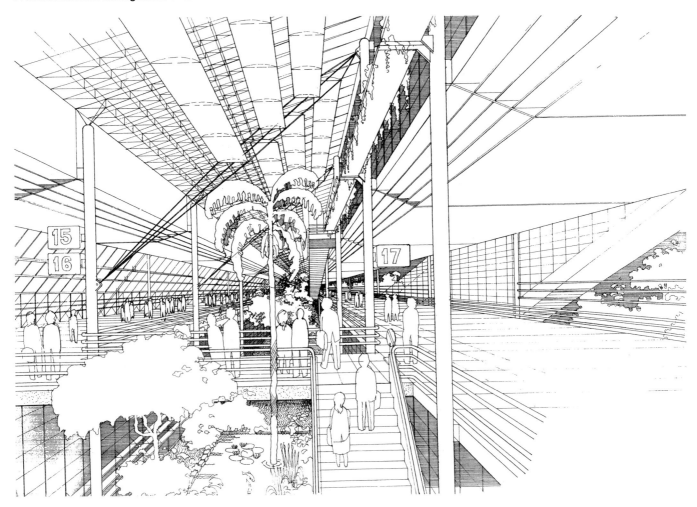

7.4 The new Bangkok Airport is seen as more than a utilitarian structure. Bangkok Airport (proposed terminal), Thailand. Architects: Scott Brownrigg and Turner.

upon their movements. Modern airports, especially in the UK and the USA, exploit time and space to extract maximum commercial advantage from the traveller. In other countries such as France and Japan, and often in the developing world, the airport terminal is seen as part of the national infrastructure – like roads and hospitals – rather than merely as a means of making money. Here commercial exploitation of the traveller, who may be isolated in the airport for long periods, is less obvious. In place of burger bars and amusement arcades one finds spacious, well-planted lounges and wide, uncluttered corridors. Although national television may be playing in the background (as it is at Lagos Airport), there is little commercial manipulation.

Terminals in the developing world

Airports are expensive undertakings – amongst the most expensive infrastructure projects for governments. Inevitably, state investment seeks to provide a service and, eventually, a profit. Normally, governments plan to earn an income from airports in 8–10 years, but with low levels of usage (as is the case in most developing countries), the state is unlikely to see a return for a much longer period, if at all. Unprofitable airports are viewed by governments in the developing world (especially Africa) as an essential public service, and also to some extent as a symbol of national prestige. Profit is not normally the prime objective; it is merely sufficient that the country has an airport able to bring in businessmen, conference delegates, international tourists and, as a last resort, to receive food aid in times of crisis.

There is a wide discrepancy between the perception of airports in the West and in emerging countries. New economic areas (such as Africa, South America and parts of Asia) see the airport as a loss-leader in purely economic terms. Hence governments are willing to subsidize airports from the national treasury, and to pay for relatively lavish terminals as a symbol of state prestige. While European and North American airports normally operate at a profit (or at least balance national subsidy with commercial earnings), in the developing world aid agencies play an increasingly big role in the provision and subsidizing of airport operations, especially in regional rather than national airports.

Table 7.4 Revenue earned by BAA at UK airports in 1995/96

Type	£m	Increase on previous year
Airport and aircraft movement charges	434	+6.1%
Retail	556	+10.5%
Property	213	+10.4%
Other revenue	50	−7.4%

Source: *Shaping Up for the 21st Century*, BAA Annual Report 1995/96, p. 29

Table 7.5 Main sources of retail revenue for BAA at UK airports in 1995/96

	£m	Increase on previous year
Duty and tax-free		
Perfume	113	+29.0%
Gifts	98	+1.4%
Liquor	91	+8.4%
Tobacco	66	+11.7%
Tax-paid retailing		
Bookshops	20	+1.7%
Catering	20	+9.6%
Bureaux de change	26	+15.5%
Specialist shops	9	+5.6%
Advertising sites	14	−4.2%
Car parks	64	+7.4%
Car rental	16	+6.0%

Source: *Shaping Up for the 21st Century*, BAA Annual Report 1995/96, p. 30; and BAA Retail Report 1996, p. 14

As a rule of thumb, airports that handle under 1 million passengers a year are unlikely to be profitable. Over 1 million passengers, the profit and loss account is likely to be neutral, but under 1 million, large losses can be expected. Most regional airports operate at a loss in the developing world, not just because of operating costs but because

Table 7.6 Percentage revenue by function earned by BAA at UK airports in 1995/96

Type	£m	% of total
Retail	556	44.4%
Airport/aircraft traffic charges	434	34.6%
Property	213	17.0%
Other (cargo subsidiaries, etc)	50	4.0%

Source: *Shaping Up for the 21st Century*, BAA Annual Report 1995/96, p. 2

there is insufficient traffic to exploit commercial revenues. In regional airports in the Third World, it is rare that 'named' food outlets are present, or that extensive duty-free shops exist. Such airports are mainly public and social facilities, there to serve a dispersed rural population in the fashion of a regional hospital or college. It is not only scale that undermines the profitability of regional airports but the nature of the traffic. With few international flights, there are not the wealthy international passengers available in numbers sufficient to generate non-aeronautical revenue. As noted earlier, airports are rarely profitable on airside operations alone; concessions, leasehold agreements, rents and parking charges are the mainstay of airport income.

References

1. Jackie Whitelaw (ed.), *21st Century Airports*, supplement of *New Civil Engineer/New Builder*, May 1995, p. 7.
2. *Ibid.*, p. 19.
3. *Ibid.*, p. 2.
4. *Ibid.*
5. *Ibid.*
6. BAA, *Southampton Eastleigh Airport Development Brief*, ref. YADR1147, 1990, p. 2.1.
7. *Ibid.*
8. *Ibid.*, p. 2.7.
9. *Ibid.*, p. 2.8.
10. BAA International, brochure, no date but probably 1995.
11. BAA Retail Report for 1996, p. 2.
12. *Ibid.*

CHAPTER

8

Flexibility and permanence in airport design

Within the functional pattern of an airport, the only basic and relatively stable element is the runways. Every other part is subject to change: the aircraft themselves, the apron areas, the piers and jetties, and not least the terminals. Hence when a new terminal is proposed (as at Heathrow with Terminal 5), every part of the airport has to adapt except the runways. Although runways may be lengthened, widened or strengthened, their basic alignment and presence do not alter. Terminals, in contrast, have to be capable of extension in all directions and their relationship to the aircraft stands has to be altered as new generations of aircraft are introduced.

The motor for change tends to be the design of aircraft. As new types, sizes and patterns of aircraft are introduced, it is the terminal that has to adapt, not the runway. New, larger aircraft impose changes on the capacity of departure lounges, airside corridors, telescopic piers and access jetties. Terminals are as a consequence designed to be as flexible in operation as possible, with internal changes as frequent as at 18-month intervals. According to Graham Jordan, BAA's head of airport planning, the speed of change at terminals will quadruple into the next century.[1] A culture of change means that airport terminals have to accommodate 'infinite flexibility', and will be designed increasingly as aggregations of modular units, whose arrangement is determined by 'long-life facility management systems'. The elements of permanence in the terminal will be the primary order of main structure and circulation routes. Even views, such as to the aircraft, and daylight may be sacrificed in the pursuit of flexibility.

The pace of change has posed a dilemma for architects. First-generation terminals were an architectural experience of some magnitude: in fact some of the world's most important twentieth-century landmarks are early airports (for example, Washington Dulles Airport of 1962, with its sweeping roofed terminal and sculpted control tower). However, managing the accelerating pace of change and expressing it in second-generation terminals has tended to erode the architectural quality of the building type. Airport terminals have become either bland but flexible Cartesian containers designed

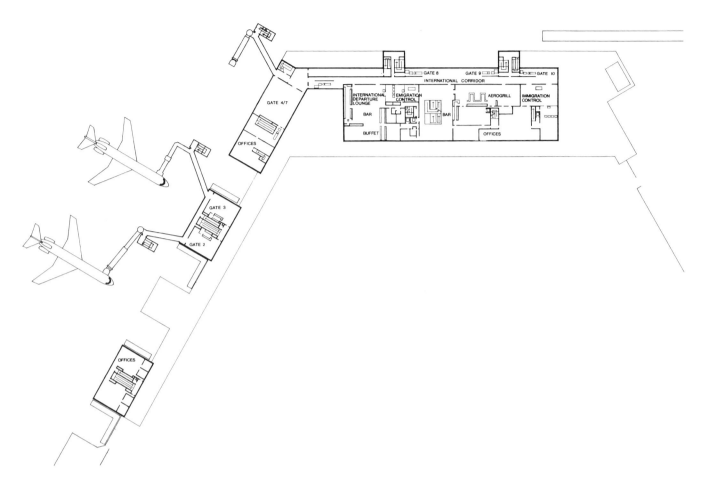

8.1 Edinburgh Airport is designed so that a matching wing can be built to the right. Flexibility and expandability are the design objectives in the modern terminal. Edinburgh Airport, UK. Architects: RMJM.

for growth, or somewhat mannered landmarks in the tradition of earlier buildings. The former – represented by Manchester's Terminal 2, the redeveloped Heathrow Terminal 3 or the United Airlines Terminal at Chicago O'Hare – are worthy and at times elegant buildings, which perform effectively in all conditions. The latter – represented by Kansai Airport, Seville Airport and Terminal 2 at Paris Charles de Gaulle – continue a heroic, if operationally more inflexible, tradition. In some recent designs – such as Heathrow Terminal 5 – which balance between the two positions, their architects have endeavoured to give the passenger a memorable experience while meeting the growing demand from airport clients for great flexibility.

Airport authorities cannot influence aircraft design. Innovation in aircraft design is driven by the big plane manufacturers, such as Boeing, European Airbus, McDonnell Douglas and SAAB. Though airports represent a bigger investment in infrastructure than the cost of the aircraft that serve them, airport owners and airline companies are forced to modify their operations when a new generation of aircraft are introduced. Change is inevitable at terminals

as long as aircraft manufacturers carry on innovating. Bigger aircraft with higher passenger capacities tend to have larger turning circles (which alter the jetty-to-apron relationships), and more demanding servicing requirements, to impose extra strain on departure lounge space, and to stretch baggage-handling systems. Terminals have to be capable of accommodating these changes perhaps as often as every 5 years while still remaining in operation. The scale and pace of change at airports are fundamentally different from those of railway stations. New stations are designed within standard track gauge and platform dimensions determined by trains whose measurements and capacity vary little over long time periods. Airports, in contrast, are subject to the unpredictable innovations of aircraft designers and their manufacturers.

Flexibility and terminal design

The terminal today is a far different building from those of a decade or two ago. Airline deregulation, the ever-present threat of international terrorism, and the need to exploit

8.2 Schematic plan of terminal building.

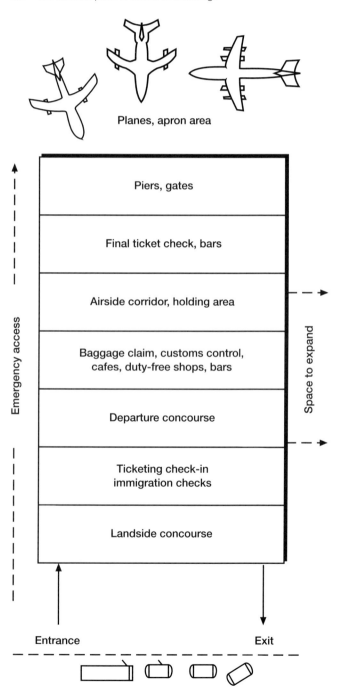

Planes, apron area

Emergency access

Piers, gates

Final ticket check, bars

Airside corridor, holding area

Space to expand

Baggage claim, customs control, cafes, duty-free shops, bars

Departure concourse

Ticketing check-in immigration checks

Landside concourse

Entrance

Exit

revenue from non-airline activities at airports, have jointly altered the assumptions upon which terminals are designed. Deregulation (introduced in the USA by the Airline Deregulation Act 1978, and in the UK by the Airports Act 1986) has had a profound impact. It has reduced the price of airline tickets, thereby spurring a growth in demand. The spirit of deregulation has encouraged airport authorities to expand income at the terminal from concessionaires and franchisees, and has reduced the scope of government controls, which were once written into design briefs. Today's airport is a loosely regulated parcel of infrastructure aimed at making the maximum of money for its private owner.

Because the airline industry is undergoing rapid management and technological change, there are few formulas for architects to use. The old assumptions upon which the design of terminals was based have been largely swept aside by industry deregulation or by advances in aircraft design. Airport terminals need to be flexible, yet capable of being worthy national landmarks in their own right. Although space standards exist (see Chapter 13), the use and distribution of space inside terminals remain static for only relatively short periods (say 10–15 years), though the structure and external enclosure may survive for 50 years. In the fluid culture of airports, architects need to be able to offer aesthetic quality and operational flexibility. Even within the terminal concept adopted (see Chapter 11), much alteration in internal layout and probably also building footprint will occur. The terminal may need to adapt to the demands of a new airline company operating out of the building, the dictates of a fresh generation of planes (which will have altered the airside relationship between terminal, apron areas and taxiway), changes in security, ticketing or baggage-handling policy, and new ideas about corporate or brand identity. Deregulation has removed boundaries and opened airports up to ideas whose origins are to be found in retail parks or the leisure industry. The architect has, on the one hand, to provide buildings of high quality to satisfy growing customer expectations and, on the other, to accommodate changes that can rarely be anticipated. Because airport buildings are subject to some abuse by the tenants who occupy the space on relatively short timescales, it is obviously important to raise the design standards as high as possible at the

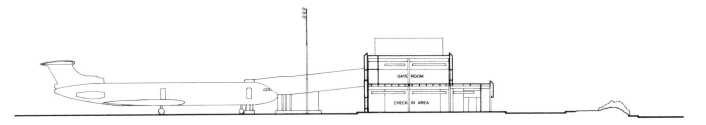

8.3 Aircraft determine layout decisions at airside just as passengers do at landside. Edinburgh Airport, UK. Architects: RMJM.

outset. The design of the terminal needs to be able to meet the demands of tenants (such as airlines and franchisees), but not by compromising the key architectural elements of space, structure, procession and light. At Stansted Airport, Sir Norman Foster's elegant design has been successively undermined by management policies apparently indifferent to the original aesthetic values.[2]

Under such pressure the architectural design of terminals is tending to distinguish between long-term elements (building structure, daylight, processional routes) and short-term alterations (such as repositioning of walls, and changes to ticket counters, shops, bars and signs). This policy allows the airport to survive as a recognizable entity yet still adapt to management changes. Making a clearer distinction between primary factors of design and secondary ones allows the terminal to meet the future without compromising the essential permanent character of the building. If this character is not present at the outset then the terminal will be less able to provide the organizational clarity and ease of orientation that passengers expect.

8.4 Changes in aircraft design trigger alterations to gate design. Munich Airport, Germany. Architects: Prof. von Busse, Blees, Kampmann & Buch.

8.5 Architectural quality at airports helps to establish national yardsticks of design. Extensions to Cologne/Bonn Airport, Germany. Architects: Murphy/Jahn.

The facilities that tend to be altered at fairly regular intervals are:

changes every 3–5 years:

• ticket counters at gate lounges
• check-in desks
• security systems
• signs and advertising
• shops, bars and restaurants;

changes every 10–15 years:

• baggage-handling systems
• building services (heating, ventilation and lighting)
• toilets and kitchens;

changes every 30–50 years:

• building structure
• building envelope
• stairs, lifts, travellators and escalators.

Hence there are three, four or five internal lifespans (and even more with finishes) for every external renewal. However,

even where the structural and perimeter frame remains static, many airports accommodate change by outward expansion (for example, Marseille by Richard Rogers Partnership). Airport terminals grow by extending lengthways, by adding additional floors, or by constructing new finger or satellite piers. Expandability, linked to internal flexibility, is the policy normally adopted. Of course, once the terminal is saturated, there is little option other than to build a new terminal, which too will mature in the same fashion.

Interactions between plane, passenger and terminal

The need for flexibility at airports is the result of the complex interaction between airline companies, aircraft design and airport authorities. This triangular 'tug of war' (Figure 8.7) explains the ever-changing parameters in which designers operate. The terminal is subject to pulls from all directions: airport authorities who want to maximize profits; airline companies that want to assert their presence or change passenger-processing arrangements; aircraft designers whose innovations make airside arrangements obsolete. The designer of the terminal has to meet all their needs, both present and anticipated.

The practice of developing hub airports and independent satellite piers allows airlines to assert their identity and control, at the expense of airport authorities. Certain plan configurations are inherently more flexible than others, but as a general rule flexibility is at the expense of architectural quality. Satellite piers and unit terminals allow a direct relationship in imagery and quality control between building fabric and airline company (hence their popularity with airlines). The arrangement leads to airports that lack a strong central design identity, because the different terminals are designed by different architects working for different clients (Chicago O'Hare is a good example). Airline companies that are successful enjoy the luxury of being able to shape the design language of their part of the airport while also taking advantage of central facilities. As the airline company prospers, it can upgrade its satellite or unit terminal, thereby attracting more passengers away from other terminals or even airports in the region. In this sense, architecture directly serves airline company ambitions, because

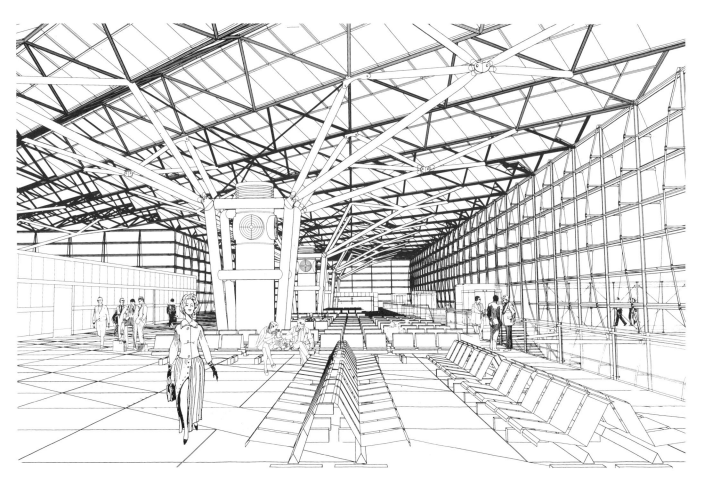

8.6 Space, light and structure are the enduring elements in terminal design. Cologne/Bonn Airport extension, Germany. Architects: Murphy/Jahn.

the satellite takes on the characteristics of an independent terminal, with its own ticketing, retail and concessionary arrangements. It also makes evident to the passenger the relationship in quality of service between the terminal experience and that in the air.

The major problem of satellite and unit terminals is the lack of facilities for transfer passengers. As the terminals become more popular they end up attracting increasing numbers of transit travellers, who – instead of ending their journeys – are merely changing planes. In the USA as many

as half the passengers at unit or hub airports are transfer passengers. Whereas the central terminal may have enough space and baggage handling for both destination and transfer needs, this may not be the case with unit and satellite terminals. Overcrowded space, congested escalators and baggage reclaim may end up reflecting poorly upon the airline company that operates out of the terminal.

In the past decade, terminal buildings have been constructed to accommodate a collection of shops, bars and duty-free outlets, but today there are new pressures. The

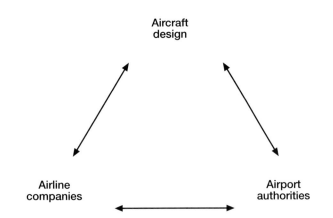

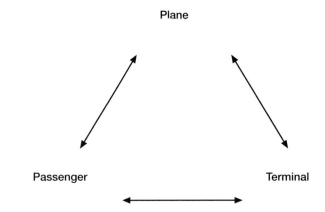

8.7   The triangular tug of war.

modern airport has become a business destination in its own right, providing conference, computing, fax and telecommunications facilities. While the 1980s saw the terminal building become a kind of shopping mall from which you could catch a plane, the 1990s have seen the emergence of the terminal as a conference venue. Today you can attend a business meeting or hold a conference at the airport, send a message on the Internet, catch up with email messages, and catch a plane home or to your next destination. As with retail changes, the terminal has had to adapt to wider changes in society.

How terminals expand

The history of the airport terminal is one of growing expansion, functional change, and increasing complexity. Terminals rarely remain static for long; the need to respond to fresh management ideas and new sources of income generation leads inevitably to internal changes, expansion at the edges and eventual rebuilding. How terminals respond to increases in passenger numbers and commercial pressure is well known. More and more floor space is given over to retail use; lofty internal volumes are sacrificed (as at Glasgow Airport) to build new floors; perimeter walls are taken down and extra bays constructed. Within time (perhaps as little as 20 years) the strain of these trends cannot be resisted without a new terminal building being constructed. At Frankfurt Airport

the old terminal was taken down in 1990 and the present one designed by Helmut Jahn built, but more commonly the earlier terminal buildings are kept and a succession of new ones built. At Heathrow plans are afoot to build Terminal 5 (to designs by the Richard Rogers Partnership) but Terminals 1–4 remain as a testament to changing technological and commercial dictates. The same pattern of a necklace of terminals surrounding a collection of runways is found at Chicago O'Hare and Los Angeles airports. The older the airport, the more passenger terminals normally exist. Space (and noise) is, however, a constraint on perpetual expansion, and in the 1990s plans are afoot to relocate some of the world's biggest airports onto greenfield sites. Again, Chicago and also Denver (both amongst the world's busiest airports) are developing plans for new airports to take the strain off existing facilities.

Airports behave like the cities they serve. They expand gradually and systematically, but are finally constrained by space and environmental factors. They then cease to grow, and expansion is met by a new airport, which (like a satellite new town) expands to its environmental limits. In its turn its expansion is limited, and again a new airport on another site is constructed. Taken together, these airports (and London is a good example) are like new cities growing, maturing and then stabilizing. They begin life as a means of facilitating movement and end up as self-contained centres of economic and social activity.

How terminals learn

Terminals, like most buildings, adapt and renew themselves in specific ways. The inexorable and accelerating march of technology expresses itself in pressure to replace obsolete windows, doors, building plant and whole structural systems. Changing management ideals create an equal momentum for internal space modification. To serve its purpose the terminal has to learn fast and adapt.

The modern terminal represents the contemporary condition whereby the internal life of a building is on a different timescale from the external life. Though certain recent terminals (Stansted for instance) have sought to ensure some sort of fit between the two by adroit design, most accept that the interior design of terminals is a world quite divorced from the architecture of their exteriors. Frequent interior revision reflects the commercial pressure that terminals are under, but the changes made on the inside mirror less visible and slower changes made to the building skin, structure and services. In fact, different parts of terminals change at different rates, and to understand the process one needs to see the building as a series of layers. The principal layers in a conceptual sense are:

technological change

- infrastructure
- building structure
- skin
- services

management change

- interior space
- finishes
- furniture.

Evidently, each layer is on a distinctive timescale, and their condition reflects both the initial capital investment and that spent on maintenance. However, one feature of terminals (as for many modern building types) is that as each layer is renewed it tends to disrupt the whole. These 'shearing

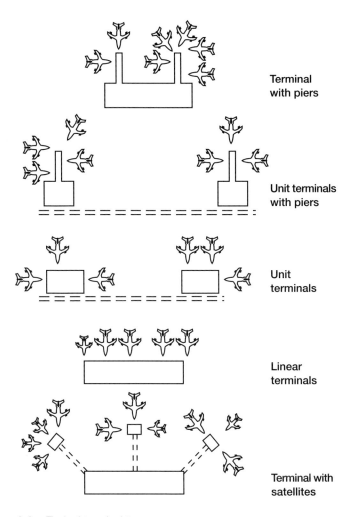

8.8 Typical terminal types.

layers of change'[3] have to be managed and anticipated by good design.

So, while the initial architecture of terminals matters, a key element in their continuing to look good is the management of the time equation. The use of terminals over time is not just a question of facilities planning but of designing terminals so that the separate layers can be renewed without undue disruption. Changes in building technology (use

8.9 Conference facilities adjacent to terminals allow the airport to serve business needs. Munich Airport Centre, Germany. Architects: Murphy/Jahn.

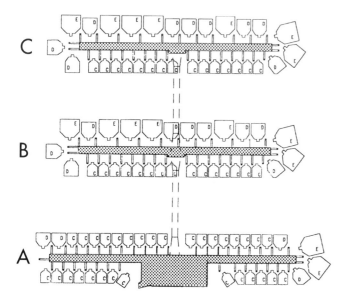

8.10 Phased growth of satellite piers at Oslo Airport, Norway. Architects: Aviaplan AS.

of energy, new materials etc.) tend to dictate alteration to the outer layers, management policy changes to the inner layers. Design therefore needs to address both the technology of terminals and airport management, especially the way in which space planning alters over time.

Terminals are functionally turbulent places: the pace of change is greater than in almost every other type of building. Architects have a responsibility to manage change by designing buildings that accommodate it from the outset. Recognizing the separate layers that make up a typical terminal allows some disconnection to be made between the parts. By keeping 'structure' free from 'skin', and 'interior space' separate from 'services', the necessary elbow-room is formed to allow the building to renew itself. The thin slice of space between structure (which has a life of 50 or 60 years) and skin (with a life of 20 years) is not just important as part of architectural expression; it facilitates change. The deliberate disjunction of the key layers allows accommodation of the inevitable changes over time. In this sense, space and time are related in the maturing of the terminal as a dynamic, interactive learning building.

76

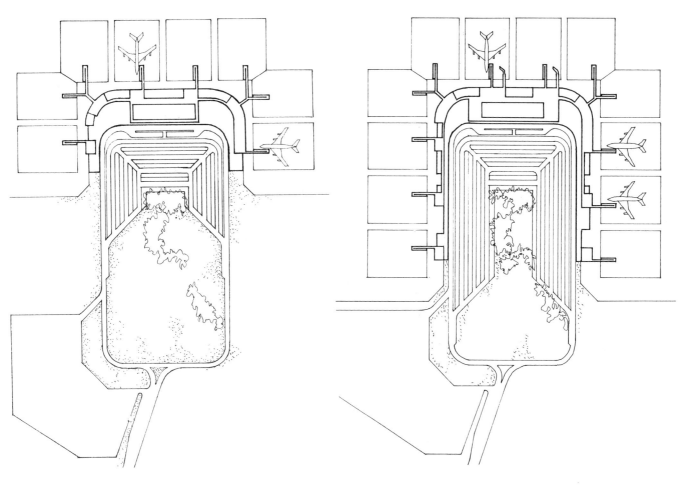

8.11 Phased linear expansion as proposed at Edinburgh Airport, UK. Architects: RMJM.

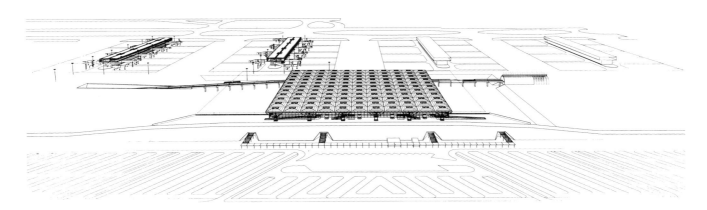

8.12 Stansted Airport, UK, with position of existing satellite piers (two more planned). Architects: Foster and Partners.

But it is evident also that the terminal has a hierarchy of change, with – generally speaking – the slow parts (site or structure) dominating those, such as finishes, that are renewed more frequently. For example, to change the layout of a departure lounge means accepting the placement of columns and the position of the terminal skin. These more senior parts of the system of layers tend to be in charge, since they are not changing as fast as the more visible junior elements.[4] There does, however, come a point when so many rapid changes are called for that the airport authority decides that a new terminal is needed, or an existing one has to be extended.

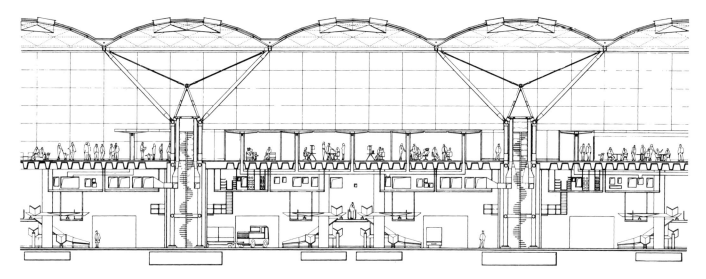

8.13 Airport terminals that distinguish between the primary and secondary layers accommodate large-scale change without undue disruption. Section through terminal, Stansted Airport, UK. Architects: Foster and Partners.

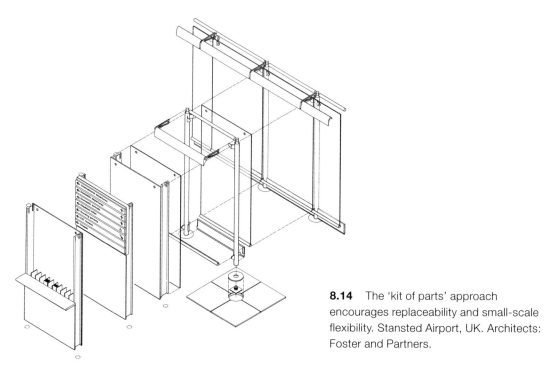

8.14 The 'kit of parts' approach encourages replaceability and small-scale flexibility. Stansted Airport, UK. Architects: Foster and Partners.

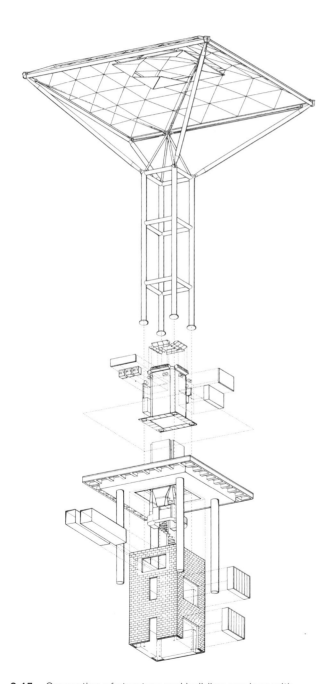

8.16 Structural separation used to define functional zones at Schiphol Airport, Amsterdam, the Netherlands. Architects: Bentham Crouwel.

Viewing the terminal as a series of layers, and the activities within it as a system, allows the designer to anticipate change even when its exact shape is not known. Terminals need to be robust in character yet resilient enough to flex with internal change. They are like arms with muscle, bone, veins and skin – each performing a distinctive function within a flexible interactive system. The immutability of some parts and the expendability of others is the basis for some recent terminal designs such as Kansai. Here, the architect Renzo Piano sought inspiration from ecosystems, with their different rates of change within balanced communities.

References

1. Personal communication with the author, 24 July 1996.
2. Kenneth Powell, 'Stansted revisited', *The Architects' Journal*, 29 August 1996, p. 26.
3. Stewart Brand, *How Buildings Learn*, Viking, New York, 1994, p. 13. Brand acknowledges Francis Duffy as the sources of his ideas on 'layers' and the variable pace of change.
4. *Ibid*., p.17.

8.15 Separation of structure and building services with an integrated system. Stansted Airport, UK. Architects: Foster and Partners.

CHAPTER 9

The terminal as a movement system

Passenger movement

Airline terminals are essentially movement systems. Two main flows occur – passengers and baggage – and both move in two opposing currents: outwards and inwards. It is important that architects recognize the imperative of movement in the allocation of space, the ordering system of structure, and the handling of light. There is increasing pressure to obstruct, deflect or slow the pace of movement in order to exploit services of one kind or another. Revenue earned from concessions and other facilities provided in the terminal should not be allowed to undermine the clear ordering of passenger concourses and other key routes. Balancing the demands of architecture and commerce requires a sharing of values between designers and airport managers. Bottlenecks in flows inevitably occur at peak times, but it is better if these are the result of security checks or immigration control rather than obstruction caused by poor design. On the journey through the terminal the passenger is more likely to accept interruptions that stem from public interest concerns than those that are caused by predatory retailers.

Movement through the terminal needs to be landmarked. There are four principal ways to achieve this: by space, by structure, by light, and by object.

Space

The definition of routes using different sizes or volumes of internal space helps the traveller to know whether a particular corridor or concourse is a major or a minor one. The hierarchy of routes through the terminal and the size of spaces need to correspond. Hence spacious internal volumes such as the landside concourse gesture towards major gathering-spaces used by all passengers passing through the terminal, while narrow corridors of single height clearly mean emergency routes or access to toilets. The orchestration of space into several recognizable hierarchies allows passengers to find their way around with the minimum of fuss.

The size and position of staircases and escalators should follow the same rules. Major routes will ideally be

9.1 Departures flow diagram.

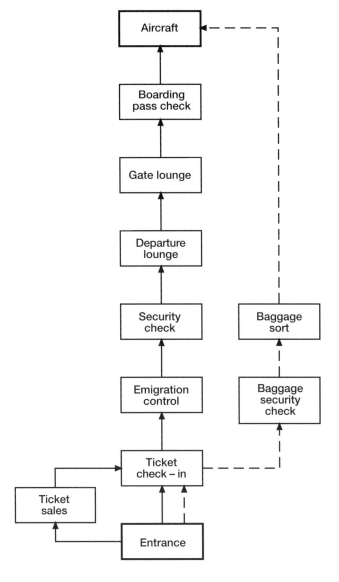

Internal space and the positioning of stairs and escalators are related factors. The correspondence between them should both direct travellers along the principal routes of a terminal and take them from one concourse level to another without confusion.

Structure

The role of the primary elements of structure – columns, walls and beams – is both to support the terminal physically and to support the perception of major routes psychologically. A row of columns in a concourse is doing more than merely holding up the roof: they are guiding passengers through a complex space. Beams too can be used to indicate a direction of flow or to provide scale in a large public area. Architectural structure is a means by which direction can be indicated and the rhythms of movement can be articulated.

The relative scale of structural elements should, like the management of interior space, reflect directly the movement or use hierarchy of that part of the terminal. Large columns obviously indicate large public spaces, small columns smaller ones. The principal route through a terminal from landside to airside should be accompanied by structural elements that, as at Kansai Airport, hint at the progression from ground to air. To exploit the aesthetic as well as structural possibilities is to see the column, beam and wall as useful elements in defining and articulating movement systems.

Light

Because they are detached buildings set in open landscapes, terminals are able to exploit light more than most building types. Light, like space and structure, is a major tactile material in its own right. Light to the terminal designer is more important than a question of lighting levels alone. Light – that is, daylight and sunlight – should be moulded, manipulated and directed with the sensitivity of a sculptor. Used in the correct fashion, light can be a solid, expressive material to guide travellers through the complex changes of direction and level encountered in a modern airline terminal.

marked by wide gracious staircases, with escalators facing the direction of flow. The angle of flights, going and width of stairs and escalators should indicate the degree of publicness or privateness of that particular route. Stairs with sharp doglegs, that are poorly lit and meanly proportioned imply minor not major airport routes.

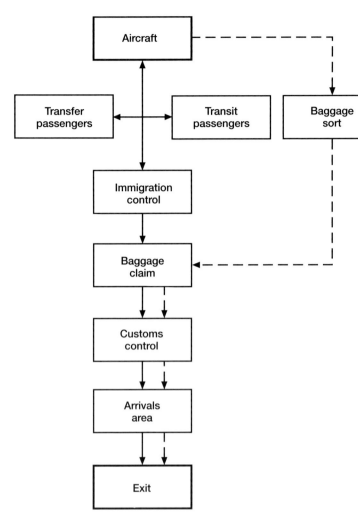

9.2 Arrivals flow diagram.

In exploiting light, the designer needs to be conscious of the path of the sun. The orientation of the terminal building should, wherever possible, allow sunlight into the core of the building. Sunlight and structure used together (as at Southampton Airport and King Khaled International in Saudi Arabia) allow the main concourse to be a central point of orientation for all those using the airport. Light helps to articulate space and animate the structural elements of a terminal, helping passengers in their perception of the building and uplifting their spirit.

The issue of hierarchy mentioned already in the context of space and structure applies equally well to light. The degree of light intensity helps to distinguish major routes from minor routes through the terminal. Daylight and sunlight can both be exploited to signal a principal staircase, the main departure lounge, or the central concourse.

Object

Object is the converse of space: the word is used to denote solid volumes within passenger terminals. Objects embrace banks of check-in counters, enclosing walls of various kinds, free-standing kiosks and lift shafts. Designers need to see 'objects' as orientating elements: solid points of reference that interrupt vistas or limit the edges of space. These solid elements contain functional space (staff offices, toilets, immigration control etc.), but their role in the terminal is also perceptual. By designing the solid parts as positive features, the architect can help passengers to understand the organization of the spaces of the terminal building. Certain key objects, for instance, can be treated as sculptural elements punctuating the free flow of space in the concourse. It may be possible, for example, to design the lift shafts as 'landmark' objects, thereby helping travellers to find the lifts and orientate themselves between different parts of the building.

Many of the principles relating to the handling of space, structure and light apply to objects. The relationship between use hierarchy and object meaning needs to correspond: major functions should be landmarked by major objects. Because airport terminals are mainly large volumes of space in which objects occur, the design of the solid elements has particular importance. Areas enclosed by walls (such as customs offices) have a function in defining the limits of concourse areas, in directing people in the desired flow, and in establishing navigation points in complex buildings.

Public art is, in many ways, a means by which object orientation can be reinforced (see Figure 9.8). The use of free-standing sculpture in concourse areas can establish a point of reference, particularly if it is located at, a crossroads in the passenger flow. Similarly, a mural attached to a wall can give that wall extra significance in the perception of interior routes. Major volumes in the terminal can be landmarked by a combination of light, structural expression and art. In combination, the elements should leave passengers in little doubt about the hierarchies of route and space in the terminal.

Integration of space, structure, light and object

The prime object of terminal design is to use all four elements together. The architect needs to orchestrate space, structure, light and object to express in the mind of the airport user the organization in plan and section of the building. The difference between Stansted and Kansai Airports, arguably two of the most important airport buildings of the past decade, is that only the latter combines these elements into a pattern that expresses the movement and space hierarchies. Stansted, in spite of its technical prowess, has a relatively uniform grid of columns and even distribution of light, which disguises rather than reinforces the pattern of passenger movement.

The proposed design of Heathrow's Terminal 5 by the Richard Rogers Partnership successfully integrates the four key elements. Here a largely glazed wave-like roof above the central concourse bathes all below in diaphanous light. The disposition of columns directs passengers through the major concourse areas. There is an eloquent dialogue of matter made up of suites of offices and shops and great voids of interior space. Three main orders of space are employed: large public volumes for people gathering, smaller but still spacious routes that connect principal functional areas together, and essentially private and utilitarian spaces expressed as small pod-like units. In such a design there is little need for directional signs: architecture alone provides the guidance.

Principles of passenger flow at large complex airports

The needs of passengers should be paramount in the design of terminal facilities. Passenger and baggage flows should be as smooth, well marked and flexible as possible. Ten design principles should be followed:

- Concourse routes should be as short and straight as possible.
- Areas used for passenger flows should not be obstructed by concessionaire, airline or government facilities.
- There should not be cross-flows.
- Routes should be capable of being used safely and comfortably by disabled travellers.
- Changes in level should be kept to a minimum but where needed should be accessed by lifts, escalators and stairs.

- All flow areas should be capable of multi-airline use unless they are dedicated terminals or piers.
- Multiple routeing should be provided to give passengers a choice of passport and customs control positions.

9.3 Terminals need to use architectural means to distinguish between major and minor routes. Hamburg Airport, Germany. Architects: Von Gerkan, Marg & Partners.

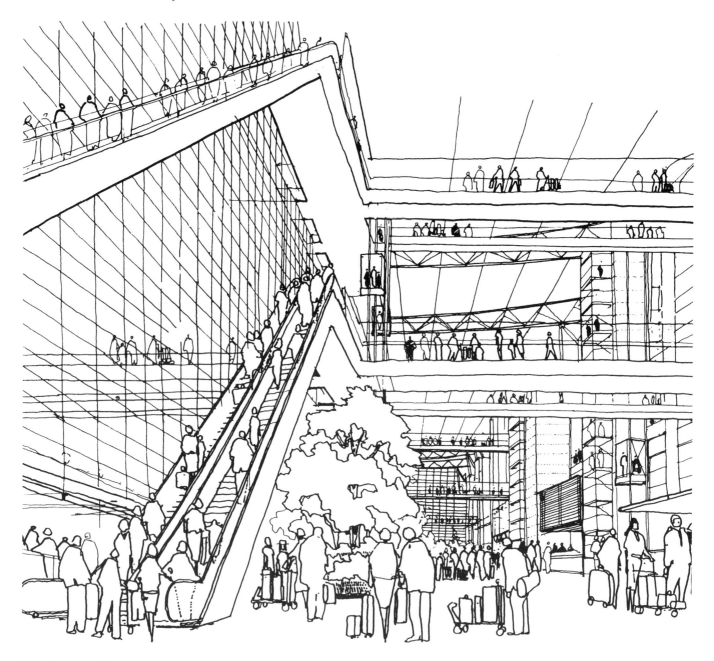

9.4 Space, volume and circulation are carefully orchestrated in this early sketch of Kansai Airport, Osaka, Japan. Architects: Renzo Piano Building Workshop.

- Flexibility of layout should be provided to cater for the unexpected.
- The design of check-in areas should allow for processing passengers individually and in groups.
- Flow routes should be capable of operating under reverse conditions.

Reasons for control

Much of the control mechanism at airports is the result of government requirements. Immigration, health and customs controls require the careful screening and routeing of passengers. Airports that cater exclusively for domestic flights do not display the same internal complexity as international terminals. The challenge for the architect is to provide clarity of route for the passenger who necessarily is herded through government control points.

On the outward journey there are two or three deliberate interruptions to the journey from land to air:

- ticket check-in (when passenger and baggage are separated)
- immigration control (outward)
- flight check-in.

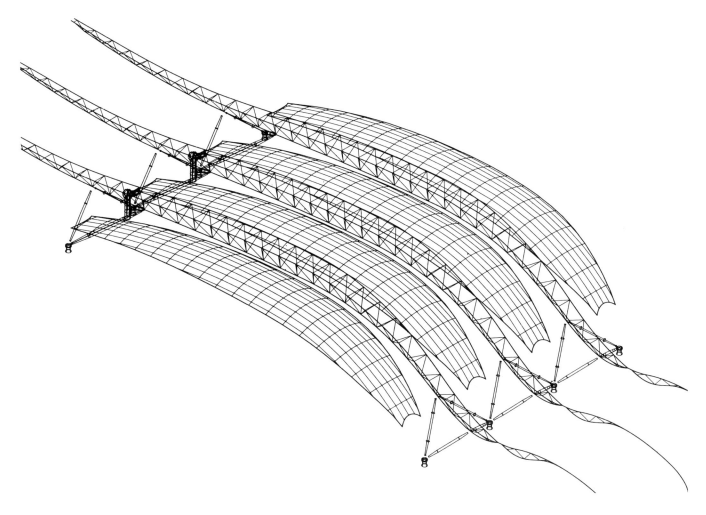

9.5 The roof structure at Kansai Airport helps to define the direction of flow. Kansai Airport, Osaka, Japan. Architects: Renzo Piano Building Workshop.

9.6 Daylight helps to orientate passengers in the confusing environment of modern terminals. Zurich Airport 2000, Switzerland. Architects: Nicholas Grimshaw & Partners.

9.7   Sunlight helps to animate structure and route. Glasgow Airport extension, UK. Architects: Parr Partnership.

9.8   Sculpture used aid orientation in the terminal interior. Terminal 3, Schiphol Airport, the Netherlands. Architects: Bentham Crouwel.

On the inward journey there are three interruptions for international flights, and one usually for domestic:

- immigration control (inward)
- baggage reclaim (optional)
- customs control.

As a consequence, the smooth flow of passengers becomes a series of filter points where those travelling are segregated from terminal visitors, domestic and international passengers are channelled into separate streams, those with baggage are divided from those without, and those of national origin are split from non-nationals. How these filters and physical barriers are designed greatly influences the smooth running of an airport and how the passenger feels about the experience. Lengthy delays may be the result of a poorly managed airport, but the frustration can be alleviated by well-designed waiting areas and concourses.

Because the filter points often contain bottlenecks it is important that areas adjacent to them be provided with seating for tired travellers, the elderly and those with young children. Such areas should be attractively proportioned, well lit and restfully designed. Ideally, those waiting at baggage reclaim, check-in and immigration control should

9.9 Stretched canopies, structural steelwork and pools of sunlight combine to create a vivid image of the new Terminal 5 at Heathrow, UK. Architects: Richard Rogers Partnership.

be provided with pockets of space away from the thrust of airport flows that are scaled for family groups rather than the individual.

Location of barriers

Where the segregation occurs is clearly important. At arrival, international and domestic passengers should be separated at the airside of the terminal, often by the use of a segregated airside corridor. For security reasons, arriving and departing passengers are also normally separated on airside of the immigration control barrier. The need to introduce physical segregation is translated by many terminals into different floor levels. The requirement for government controls at airports (immigration, health, customs) and the need for operational flexibility are often in conflict. Over-rigid regulations can lead to compartmentalized terminal buildings, which lack architectural qualities. The interpenetration of large volumes of space, views and plenty of daylight is often compromised at terminals by the rigidity of government regulation. Here, the management's need for flexibility and the designer's aspiration for an open democratic terminal are in conflict with security policy.

Assisted passenger flow

As a general rule, passenger flows should be as straight and short as possible. Cross-flows of movement, lengthy and tortuous routes, and many changes in level should be avoided. Main passenger flow routes should also be landmarked or waymarked using architectural means.

However, with certain passenger terminal layouts (such as finger piers, satellite piers and multi-terminal airports) long walking distances are inevitable. Under such conditions the airport designer needs to consider how to assist the passenger. According to IATA manuals 300m is the accepted maximum walking distance between the point of check-in and aircraft boarding without some form of mechanical assistance. People-mover systems, whether by travellator, light rail or airport buses, are expensive to provide and maintain. Compact terminals that require no assistance to be provided to horizontal movement are preferred. Assisted vertical movement is, of course, commonplace whether by escalator or by lift. With both horizontal and vertical assisted passenger movement, the designer needs to know whether baggage needs to be transported as well. If so, the facilities provided should be capable of catering for passengers and trolleys together.

Two main systems of horizontal assisted movement are found within terminals and between terminals and gate lounges.

Travellator

This consists of a deck of moving pavement set at about the speed of brisk walking. Travellators are normally wide enough to allow two passengers with their trolleys to pass side by side (hence the width is about 1.4m). The width of

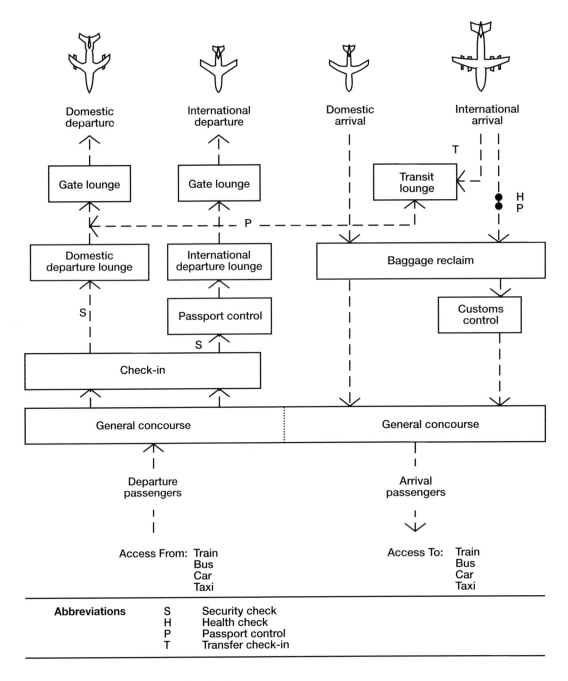

9.10 Baggage and passenger flow at a typical terminal.

the travellator is, however, dependent upon the volume of traffic. The length of the travellator is determined by safety and maintenance factors (these normally result in a length of about 60m). Hence long routes consist of several units of travellator divided by short lengths of static floor space.

Travellators are moving walkways, which carry passengers over longish distances and up or down shallow inclines (up to about 1:15). Travellators come in single, double or triple widths and in varying lengths. They are normally designed to suit the layout of the airport using manufacturers'

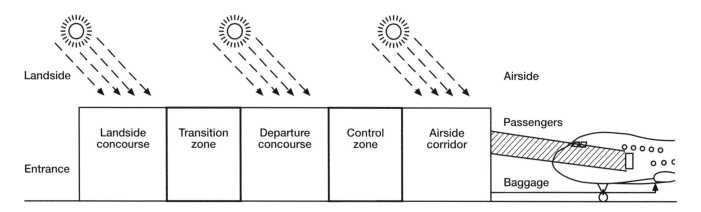

9.11 Typical section of terminal. Notice how sunlight can be used to help define the concourse areas from control zones, providing an alternating sequence of light and dark areas *en route* to the plane.

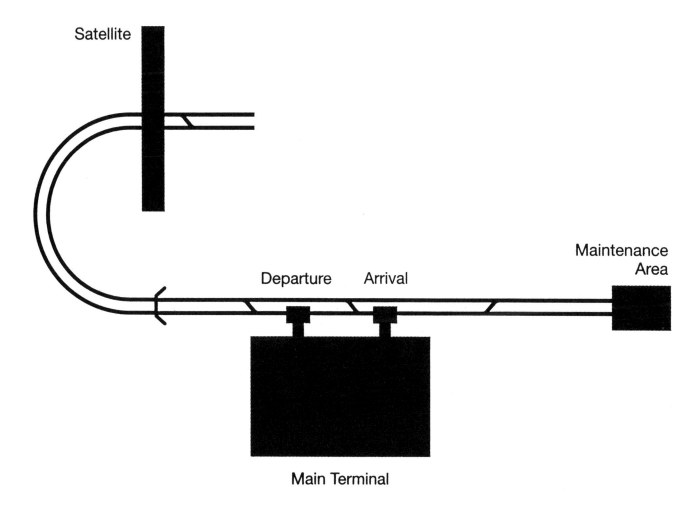

9.12 Diagram of rapid people-mover at Stansted Airport, UK. Architects: Foster and Partners.

9.13 AEG Westinghouse light rail system at Stansted Airport, UK. Architects: Foster and Partners.

standard dimensions. Because travellators move people relatively slowly and in the same direction of flow they would have taken walking, passengers are rarely disorientated. However, as the speed is gentle it is important to provide visual stimulation either in the form of visibility over the apron areas or by advertising or public art provided nearer at hand.

Walking lengths over 1200m should not be met by the provision of travellators. The time factor is limiting: passengers become bored and flights are unduly delayed. Above this distance some form of fast mechanical transport is required, such as the light rail systems used at Stansted and Birmingham Airports. Light rail or bus transport between terminal building and gate pier allows the airport to exploit the benefit of lateral dispersal. Consequently, with such a system the terminal is normally designed upon the basis of distant satellites (as at Stansted) or of apron boarding of aircraft. A combination of travellators and rail systems frequently occurs as well, especially at large airports (such as Gatwick).

There is clearly a relationship between the design strategy for the airport and the means chosen to move passengers and their baggage. Small simple terminals at regional airports can dispense with people-movers, but large international airports cannot function without them. As aircraft become larger and air travel becomes cheaper, the more airports will have to adapt their terminals to mechanical forms of moving passengers.

Rapid people-movers

The limiting factor in the provision of travellator-type movement systems is time and effort. Beyond distances of about 1200m faster forms of people-mover are needed. These consist of various types of micro-transportation (known as personal rapid transit, PRT), from light rail to minibus and air-cushioned train systems. Between about 1 and 4km PRTs are required. The system adopted is usually dependent upon cost (capital and revenue), the number of passenger journeys required, and capacity. Minibus systems are fine for small groups of up to 15 passengers, but for large airports the capacity of each train should approach that of the bigger aircraft (about 300 people). Light rail systems with two or three carriages, each carrying up to 100 passengers, begin to approach this figure. A recent example is at Kansai Airport, where each gate wing (in total about 2km in length) is served by a light rail system with six stations.

With light rail and other tram systems the provision needs to be at departure floor level. This allows a smooth transition between airport terminal and the gate pier or jetty giving access to the plane. Changing levels along the journey should be avoided. Some systems, however, operate beneath ground level, thereby leaving apron and terminal airside areas free for service vehicles, baggage trolleys and parked aircraft. Elevated rail systems have the advantage of leaving the apron level free for service vehicles, and because they are at the height of airport doors, passengers do not have to undergo disorientating changes in level.

Passenger-loading bridges

Passenger-loading bridges (or jetties as they are sometimes called) provide elevated access directly from the terminal building to the aircraft. Depending upon the terminal layout, they give direct access from the airside corridor or departure gate lounge to the aircraft standing on the apron.

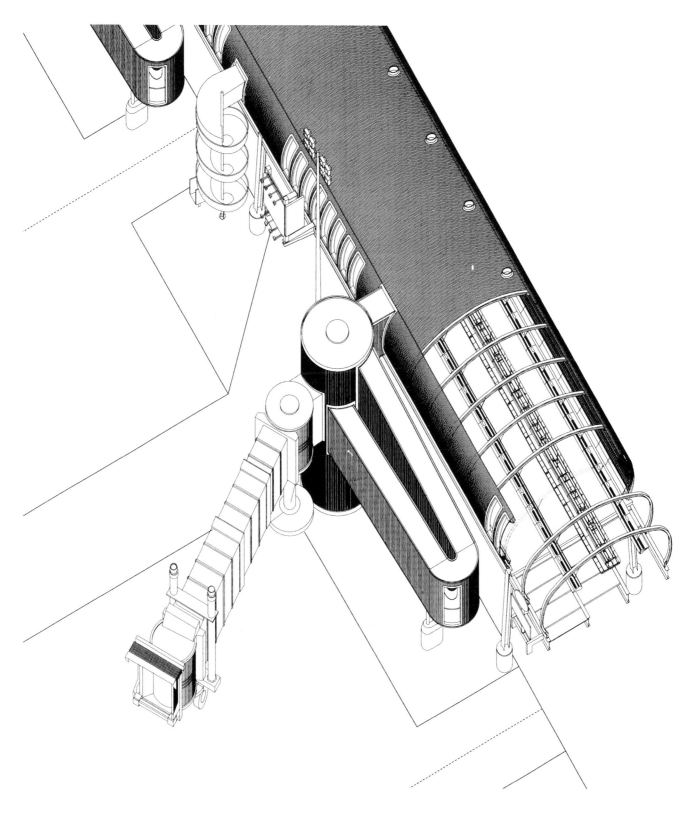

9.14 Pier 4 at Heathrow, UK. Architects: Nicholas Grimshaw & Partners.

Passenger-loading bridges add greatly to the comfort and convenience of passengers, and avoid the need to use mobile apron stairs. For the airline company, direct loading via enclosed bridges is faster, smoother and more secure than the use of apron vehicles or apron stairs. For the airport operator, passenger-loading bridges allow quicker turnaround of aircraft and hence potentially higher earnings. The more extreme the weather at a particular airport, and the greater the passenger turnaround, the more likely it is that loading bridges will be employed.

Because aircraft come in different sizes with varying height of passenger door, loading bridges need to be capable of elevational and directional flexibility. They work upon pneumatic telescopic principles, with clearly defined docking points for different types of aircraft. Two main forms of loading bridge exist: fixed and mobile. The former consist of a bridge in a permanent position relative to the apron, with a flexible, telescopic nose capable of limited vertical and horizontal movement to suit different heights and positions of aircraft door. The latter consist of wheeled loading bridges anchored at the terminal end but still capable of fairly large rotational as well as vertical movement. Mobile loading bridges are more expensive to build and maintain, but offer greater operational flexibility. Some loading bridges have two or three lengths to allow for the large level changes needed in segregated airside corridors.

With both mobile and fixed bridges the accuracy of aircraft docking and the relative tolerance of the loading bridge system need to correspond. Aircraft docking guidance, aircraft parking, the mating of loading bridges and apron servicing (refuelling etc.) need to be considered as an integrated operation. Normally, a single loading bridge is sufficient for aircraft as large as the Boeing 747, but at busy airports where turnaround time is critical two loading bridges may be needed. Certainly two or even three will be required when aircraft capable of transporting 1000 passengers come into operation around 2005. Corridors linking the loading bridge to the terminal should be at least 2m wide, and 3m where two bridges converge into a single corridor.

Table 9.1 Some aircraft passenger door sill heights

Aircraft type	Aircraft passenger door sill height (m)
Airbus A310	4.48 (average)
Airbus A320	3.41
Boeing 737-300	2.70 (average)
Boeing 747-400	5.00 (average)
Boeing 777-200	4.71
British Aerospace 146-300	1.88
McDonnell Douglas DC-8	3.32 (average)
McDonnell Douglas MD-90	2.30 (average)
Tupolev TU-154	3.26 (average)

Source: Christopher J. Blow, *Airport Terminals*, 2nd edn, Butterworth-Heinemann, Oxford, 1996, pp. 208–211.

Baggage handling

One of the principal reasons why terminals are multilevel is to deal with the complexity of baggage movement. Baggage is loaded onto aircraft at apron level via baggage holds, while the passengers board the aircraft at nearly 4m above apron level. The difference in height between the aircraft passenger door and the baggage hold requires all but the most simple terminals to split passenger levels from baggage levels soon after check-in. Quite how and when the segregation occurs varies according to the layout of the terminal, the proportion of destination and transit passengers expected, the balance between domestic and international flights, and how passengers arrive at the terminal – air, train, coach, mini-bus etc. Also, the needs of arrival and departure passengers vary: those arriving tend to enter the terminal in large groups, those departing singly or in small groups. Baggage handling is one of the most complex and, in terms of passenger perception, most critical factors in the success of a terminal.

The passenger load factor (the passenger flows that result from the number, size and frequency of aircraft) determines the baggage-handling capacity required. Not all passengers are terminating, however. Many, especially at hub airports, are merely transferring to another flight. Their baggage should transfer from one aircraft to another as smoothly as the passengers. Large aircraft mean large surges in baggage-handling needs. Hence even with existing terminals there is often periodic upgrading of baggage facilities to match innovations in aircraft design, or changes in security arrangements.

Baggage handling is an integral part of passenger terminal operation. Though rarely seen by the passenger after check-in, baggage movement is one of the processes that order the interior spaces and distribution of floor levels at the terminal. Different baggage-handling systems exist, from fully automated computer-controlled systems using driverless electronic carts to simple conveyor belt systems. The terminal layout and the needs of baggage handling should be integrated at the design concept stage. Baggage movement is not a bolt-on after the terminal has been designed, but a central ordering system as important as passenger flows.

10.1 Typical section through a smaller split-level terminal. Edinburgh Airport, UK. Architects: RMJM.

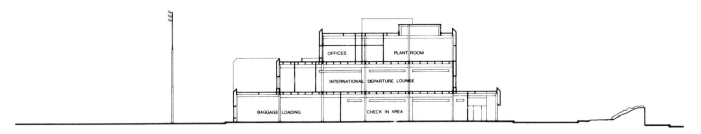

Six guiding principles should be adopted in baggage handling:

- Minimize the number of handling operations.
- Ensure that the baggage-handling system is consistent with the characteristics of aircraft movement (type of passenger, size of aircraft, frequency of flights).
- Avoid turns and level changes.
- Ensure that conveyor belt slopes do not exceed 15°.
- Avoid baggage flow crossing passenger flows, aircraft flows and air freight flows.
- Place baggage-sorting areas adjacent to the apron.

Baggage flow, unlike passenger flow, should be as rapid, direct and simple as possible. Whereas passengers are encouraged to loiter, shop and stop in bars en route to the plane, speed is of the essence with baggage handling. Because many passengers are likely to be transferring, baggage systems need to be flexible and reliable to ensure that passenger and baggage arrive together at their destination. Baggage movement is a two-way process. While with departing passengers there may be a longish period (up to 2 hours) between check-in and flight departure, with arrivals the passenger expects to be reunited with baggage in a matter of minutes (in 14 minutes with Manchester Airport's quality assurance scheme).

Baggage needs to be planned on a linear flow basis. Baggage and passengers are parallel currents, which pass through the terminal in a disciplined logical order. The two flow systems (passenger and baggage) are related but operate on parallel paths, separating at ticket check-in and reuniting at baggage claim at the end of the journey. Because it is a flow system, abrupt changes in direction or level should be avoided. Normally a conveyor belt transports baggage from the passenger check-in to be sorted in the departure baggage area. Here it is loaded onto baggage carts or small containers for transporting by electric or diesel vehicles to the holds of aircraft waiting nearby on the apron. Baggage flow, like passenger flow, is critical in terms of time. Any baggage-handling system needs to be capable of catering for peak as well as normal flows, for interruptions due to adverse weather, for security checks, for equipment breakdown, and for last-minute passengers reporting directly to gate positions.

Arriving baggage has different characteristics from those of departing baggage. Customs clearance requires incoming passengers and baggage to pass through control mechanisms together. Passengers need quick reacquaintance with their baggage if they are carrying duty-free goods purchased on the plane, and transfer baggage needs to be sorted from arrival baggage before the baggage claim area. Speed and clarity of operation are key factors in meeting passenger and airline needs.

Between the aircraft and baggage claim conveyor belt there is normally a baggage-sorting area. It is here that the baggage of transfer and arrival passengers is separated. Because transfer baggage is likely to be destined for a number of different locations, sorting needs to be done efficiently and speedily, especially where transfers are between airline companies. At 'hub' airports such as Heathrow, where 30% of the 54 million passengers a year are transfers, the logistics of baggage handling require sophisticated solutions. Normally, the procedures for handling baggage are jointly devised between airport authorities, specialist handling companies such as ServisAir, and airline companies, with the airport facilities manager

10.2 The movement of baggage is a major factor in the layout of terminals. Terminal 4, Heathrow Airport, UK. Architects: Scott Brownrigg and Turner.

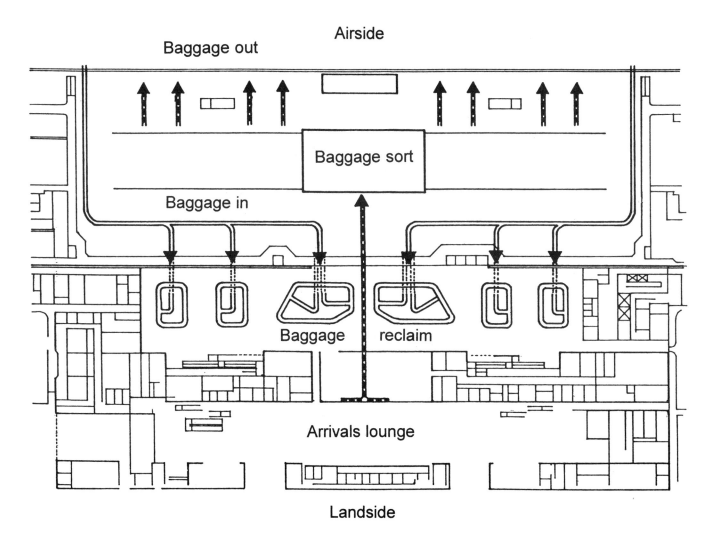

translating the system into briefing instructions to the architect. Because the life of baggage-handling systems (and customs regulations) is normally far less than that of the terminal itself, periodic upgrading is the norm. This of course has implications for apron procedures on the one hand, and for terminal design on the other.

The baggage-handling system

Baggage handling is normally a service provided at the terminal by the airport authority or subcontractors rather than the airline company. With unit terminals or dedicated satellites, however, greater airline control of the baggage-handling system occurs. Normally, the airport authority provides a shared service for a number of airline companies with, occasionally, private baggage-handling contractors operating part or all

of the system. Where contractors are employed this may consist of baggage sorting or more frequently baggage transportation across apron areas to the aircraft.

The choice of baggage-handling system (and its subsequent upgrading on a 5–10 year timescale) is normally decided by the airport authority in collaboration with the airline companies operating out of a terminal. Most airports use a shared system, rather than an airline-dedicated system linked to a quality assurance guarantee. Baggage handling is an increasingly automated computer-controlled system, using bar-coded tag identification (common in supermarkets). Breakdowns due to failure of the mechanical conveyor system or power supplies can bring the operation of the airport to a standstill. Most terminals are designed with a bypass capability to allow manual handling of baggage in emergencies.

Over the past three years BAA has invested £42 million at Heathrow in a new baggage-handling system. Using a system tested initially at Dallas Airport, the baggage at Heathrow travels the 1.4km between terminals 1 and 4 in a specially constructed tunnel 4.5m in diameter and 20m underground. Special carts transport baggage at a rate of 42 bags per minute at a speed that allows transfer baggage to move from terminal to terminal in a maximum of 18 minutes.[1] Because British Airways is the main beneficiary of the new system (BA operates 90% of flights from Terminal 4) it contributed towards the construction costs, and has taken a lease on the new facility over a 10-year period. Hitherto baggage was transported between terminals by road, taking as long as an hour and frequently delaying the departure of flights.

The normal method of baggage handling is by means of conveyor belts in the terminal, linked to container or trolley transportation of baggage across the apron. The conveyor belt system is usually designed on the basis of a belt 0.9m wide with a headroom clearance of 1m.[2] Mechanical deflection (usually tilt operated) of the baggage is also needed to allow checked-in baggage to move from one belt system to another depending upon the destination flight. Special provision is needed at bends in the conveyor belt and at changes in level. Bends, which consist of double conveyor belts, require the inner belt to be set at a slightly lower speed to avoid baggage snagging. Level changes are best accommodated by setting the belts at shallow angles (up 5°) rather than by using escalators, lifts or metal chutes.

The system employed needs to be able to cater for peak demand, not just typical flow levels. It also requires a capability to distinguish baggage between airlines, flight number, destination and class of passenger. The system also requires the ability to handle abnormal baggage such as bicycles, surfboards, skis, golf clubs and pets. Normally such items are segregated at flight check-in with special containers or trolleys used.

The departure baggage area is where the sorting and loading into baggage containers occurs. Up to this point most baggage will have been transported by conveyor belt directly from the check-in desk; beyond this point baggage is placed in containers or on trolleys for transportation to the aircraft. The process is a movement flow, with each transfer point capable of dealing with peak demand in order to avoid bottlenecks. The critical parts are normally baggage check-in, baggage sorting, baggage loading, and aircraft loading. The degree of automation present normally reflects the volume of baggage to be handled. In modern sophisticated systems baggage sorting and baggage loading is a combined operation where bar-coded baggage is mechanically directed (via computer-controlled deflectors) to designated carts, trolleys or containers.

The baggage make-up area is a vital part of the baggage departure area: it is here that containers or carts are loaded for transportation across the apron to waiting aircraft. Separate entry and exit points are required for the electric or diesel-driven vehicles, which tow usually three or four carts at a time. Detailed design is important: the conveyor belt should be at a comfortable working height, lighting should be high and of an even standard to allow staff to read the tags readily, ventilation should be provided to disperse vehicle fumes or those from battery recharging areas, and flooring needs to be non-slip (when wet and dry) yet able to provide non-skid conditions for wheeled transport without tyre noise. Dimensional clearances required are 3.2m height and 3m width for baggage carts or containers.[3] In operational terms it is advisable for departure baggage make-up areas and arrivals baggage breakdown areas to be practically side by side, thereby permitting the easy transfer of containers and carts. The usual plan is to have two lanes of baggage carts (an offload lane and a bypass lane) each 3m wide and separated from the conveyor belt by a work area 0.9m wide.

Baggage handling requires staff to be fully informed of airline and apron operations, and airline operators to be equally informed of the minute-by-minute flow of baggage through make-up and breakdown areas. Closed-circuit television in baggage-handling areas ensures that airport management staff and airline operators have up-to-date information on the state of baggage operations. This leads to early recognition of problems, and helps with the security of baggage. Flight information boards, large clocks, telephones and intercom are also required in the baggage-handling areas.

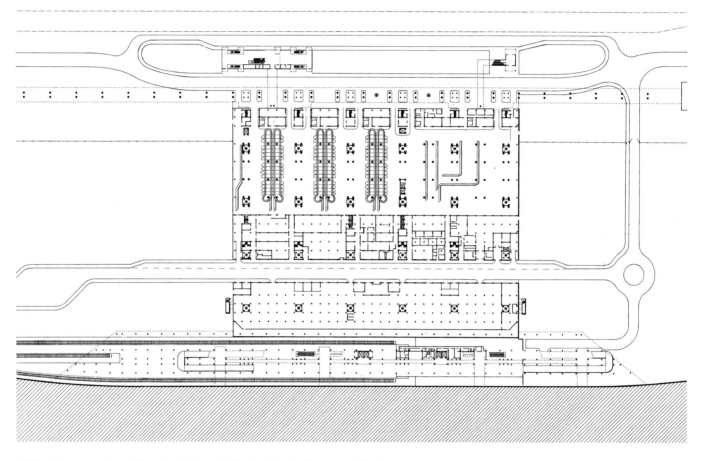

10.3 Baggage plan at Stansted Airport, UK. Architects: Foster and Partners.

The design of the baggage system and that of the terminal are closely related. Centralized terminals require different baggage-handling systems from decentralized and satellite arrangements. Similarly, hub airports have different baggage characteristics from mainly destination airports. As a rule of thumb it is better to keep baggage-handling systems as simple as possible, with manual sorting and cart loading preferable to expensive and vulnerable fully automated systems. However, beyond certain baggage-handling capacities mechanical systems are unavoidable, but again manual back-up is required in order to keep the airport operational in the event of system breakdown.

Security controls and baggage handling

All baggage, domestic or international, has to pass through a security check before entering the aircraft hold. This normally consists of an X-ray examination, manual checking of suspect baggage, and additional spot checks on certain high-risk flights (such as Dublin to London). After clearance, baggage enters a sterile area, where any contact with non-secure personnel or non-screened baggage must be avoided. Like a hospital, the airport operates with sterile and non-sterile zones where physical interaction can put at risk passengers, airport personnel and the aircraft themselves. Just as contact between security-screened and non-screened passengers is not permitted, so too with baggage. Because suspect baggage may prove to contain a bomb or incendiary device, there needs to be a secure storage area where it can be placed before being made safe.

One important safety principle of baggage handling is that of ensuring that both passenger and baggage travel on the same flight. Baggage must not be allowed to enter the aircraft hold without an accompanying passenger on board. After the Lockerbie bomb in December 1988, security has tightened in this regard. The difficulty is greatest with transferring passengers: here there is the risk that a passenger will deliberately miss the flight connection on which his or her baggage (possibly filled with explosives) has already been loaded. To avoid this, baggage and passengers are paired on computers held at check-in, baggage sorting, gate check-in, and baggage aircraft loading. By using an electronic bar-code on the passenger boarding pass and baggage tag, there is little possibility that baggage will go astray or travel unaccompanied. Also, laser bar-coding of baggage speeds up operations, allowing up to 60 bags per minute to be sorted without loss of security.

Before the bringing down of Pan Am flight 103 over Lockerbie with the loss of over 300 passengers, baggage transfer from connecting flights was assumed to have been checked at the original airport. Because not all airports operated the same security standards, the Lockerbie bomber was able to exploit poor security at one airport to place a bomb on a plane flying out of another. The subsequent policy change to screen all baggage prior to departure, including that transferring between flights and airlines, placed a considerable burden on busy airports such as Heathrow, where over a quarter of passengers are transferring between flights. After Lockerbie the US scanning equipment specialist Vivid Technologies developed a system for BAA that detects explosives, drugs, weapons and currency without direct visual contact.[4] Using advanced X-ray techniques, the system identifies 'suspect' baggage for further scans and direct visual examination by a member of the security staff. The system has the capacity to examine 1200 bags per hour, second-level scanning for suspect baggage takes a further 10 seconds, and for

the less than 1% of baggage that is still suspect, manual inspection can be undertaken (always with the owner of the baggage present) in a couple of minutes. From a terminal design point of view, the new system requires additional space for equipment and conveyor belts, as well as rooms for the temporary storage of suspect baggage. Though largely invisible to the passenger, the expensive new security checks have led to safer air travel, but they add to the cost and complexity of baggage-handling procedures.

Baggage reclaim

Once the aircraft has arrived, baggage is dispersed via cart, trolley or container to the breakdown area, where it is divided between destination and transfer. The operation is largely manual, with airport staff unloading carts or containers and placing baggage upon the appropriate conveyor belt. Up to four carts can normally be parked alongside a work area, which is served by a conveyor belt that takes baggage via a loop system to the baggage claim area. Four carts or containers would normally contain the baggage for about 80–100 passengers, so for a large aircraft two or three conveyor belts are needed for each arriving flight. The plan arrangement consists of a sequence of baggage claim peninsulas (normally about 10–15m apart) served by offload areas with bypass lanes for vehicle access.

The passenger reclaims baggage in the baggage claim area. A variety of methods are used to allow passengers to spot and then retrieve their baggage within the general mêlée of such areas. The plan shape of the conveyor belt can be linear or circular, or a combination. With recirculating baggage claim the passenger can remain stationary, but in smaller airports the baggage is deposited in one place (normally a long low counter), and the passenger moves along until the appropriate bags are located.

Baggage claim belts should be at a convenient height for passengers (0.45m for a sloping belt and 0.35m for a flat belt[5]) and operated at a speed of 23m/min. As with departures, baggage provision should be made for manual handling of bulky baggage (such as folded bicycles). Once the passengers have retrieved their baggage they

10.4 Typical baggage belt in reclaim area at Glasgow Airport, UK. Architects: Foster and Partners.

require ready access to personal baggage trolleys. These need to be stored near to the conveyor belts in staging areas. Two complications often occur. First, not all baggage is claimed, and secure storage areas are needed nearby for unclaimed (or suspect) baggage. Second, transfer baggage may arrive by mistake in the baggage reclaim area. Facilities need to exist to identify and rectify the mistake so that subsequent flights are not delayed.

Once passengers and baggage are united they may proceed to customs control or, if on a domestic flight, directly to the arrivals lounge.

References

1. Antony Oliver, 'A case for speed', in Jackie Whitelaw (ed.), *21st Century Airports*, supplement of *New Civil Engineer/New Builder*, May 1995, p. 66.
2. IATA, *Airport Terminals Reference Manual*, 7th edn, International Air Transport Association, Montreal, Canada, 1989, pp. 3.51.
3. Christopher J. Blow, *Airport Terminals*, 2nd edn, Butterworth-Heinemann, Oxford, 1996, p. 152.
4. Oliver, *op.cit.* p. 68.
5. *Airport Terminals Reference Manual*, p. 3.58.

CHAPTER

11

Terminal design concepts

The terminal building contains the various facilities that passengers and their baggage need between landside and airside, and for those transferring between aircraft. The transition is in two directions (arriving and departing), with an equal number of passengers involved in each flow. Hence the terminal building should provide a welcoming approach from both landside and airside.

Because the terminal building is part of a larger system of airport elements (including roads, apron areas and aircraft taxiways), its position is determined precisely by the masterplan. This will prescribe a specific location, the means by which connections are made to other facilities, and the extent of the footprint and height of the passenger terminal building. The geometry of the terminal building reflects in a direct fashion the wider geometry of the airport: a point that designers need to bear in mind if passengers are not to become disorientated.

Six basic criteria should be observed in the design of passenger movement in the terminal building:[1]

- easy orientation for the travelling public
- shortest possible walking distances
- minimum level changes
- avoidance of passenger cross-flows
- built-in flexibility
- separation of arriving and departing passengers.

Two basic philosophies have been adopted for terminals in the past. In the centralized concept all the major elements are grouped together into a single multilevel building; in the dispersed system the functions are spread into a number of buildings, each often under the control of a separate company or airline. Hence in the first philosophy passenger and baggage handling, aircraft stands, car parking and railway station are housed in a megastructure (as at Kansai Airport, Japan); in the second the various facilities are decentralized and dispersed geographically across the airport (as at Manchester Airport). However, the design concept is the result of many factors, including: the nature of traffic demand; the number of participating airlines; the traffic split between international and domestic, charter and

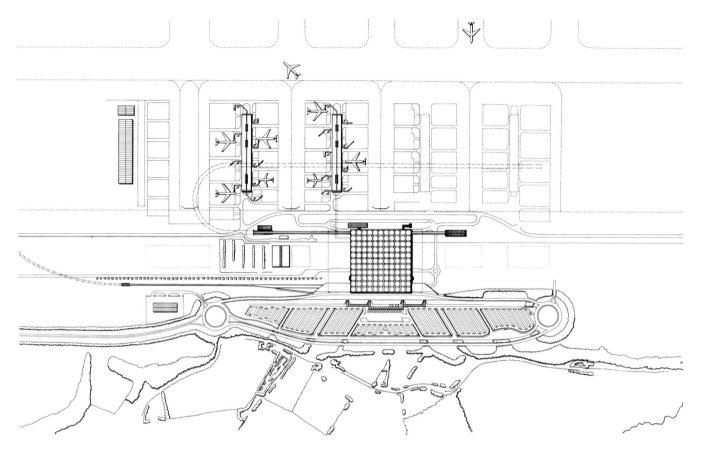

11.1   Rational orthogonal planning based upon major and minor grids at Stansted Airport, UK. Architects: Foster and Partners.

scheduled flights; site characteristics; access modes; and financial arrangements.[2]

Alternative terminal design layouts

Five distinct terminal and pier concepts exist, each with its own advantages, and each appropriate for different situations:[3]

- central terminal with pier/finger (centralized terminal)
- open apron or linear (semi-centralized or decentralized terminal)
- remote apron or transporter (centralized terminal)
- central terminal with remote satellites (centralized terminal)
- unit terminal (semi-centralized or decentralized terminal).

The facilities manager and designer of the passenger terminal will select the system that best suits the airport in question, but if the airport is being expanded (rather than developed from scratch) the choice is often less open. For instance,

if a terminal is facing periodic enlargement it is likely that an open apron or linear concept will be adopted, or a unit terminal. The central terminal with pier/finger, though it is popular with airport authorities, airlines and government authorities, and is the most numerous configuration, is inherently inflexible when it comes to future expansion.

Central terminal with pier/finger

This is a much employed layout (e.g. Amsterdam Schiphol Airport, Kansai Airport), with a central terminal serving a radiating, orthogonal or linear group of gate piers that give direct access to aircraft. The main advantages are the centralization of facilities (shops, duty free, restaurants, immigration control, check-in) and the clear, visible relationship between terminal and departure piers. Because the terminal serves a large number of piers, it can be an economic arrangement in terms of building and apron costs. The disadvantages, however, include congestion in the terminal at peak times, lack of car parking space at the terminal entrance (for the number of passengers), long walking distances from terminal to gate, reduced

11.2 Linked terminals at Lyon-Satolas Airport, France.
Architects: Curtelin Ricard Bergeret/Scott Brownrigg and Turner.

manoeuvring space for aircraft alongside gates, and the need to separate arriving and departing passengers on different levels. In addition, this arrangement involves extensive baggage conveying and (normally) the need to provide travellators. Also, the geometry of the layout makes expansion difficult. To overcome congestion in the terminal, a variation involves constructing a mini-satellite at the end of each pier, with its own restaurant, retail and direct check-in facilities for domestic flights.

Open apron or linear

This consists of a long terminal with semi-centralized groups of check-in counters forming nodes within a linear building. A recent example is the new Munich Airport (1992), which has four international departure units.[4] Aircraft park directly alongside the terminal (on the opposite side to the landside

entrance), usually without the construction of piers. An airside corridor provides access along the full length of the building to the departure (and arrival) gates. The main advantages are: the short walking distance between the terminal and gate, and the correspondingly short journey for baggage handling; simple separation of arriving and departing passengers (can be via an airside corridor rather than different levels); easy passenger orientation (aircraft can be seen on arrival at the terminal); and long kerb lengths, which allow plenty of space for setting down and picking up passengers. The disadvantages are: the duplication of facilities and services (check-in, shops, restaurants, immigration control, flight information boards, etc.); long walking distances for transfer passengers; high capital and building running costs; and lack of flexibility for catering for different aircraft designs.

Remote apron or transporter

This system consists of a centralized terminal with dispersed aircraft-loading positions on the apron. An example can be seen at Mirabel International Airport, Montreal. The

11.3 Linear gate pier linked to a central terminal at Kansai Airport, Osaka, Japan. Architects: Renzo Piano Building Workshop.

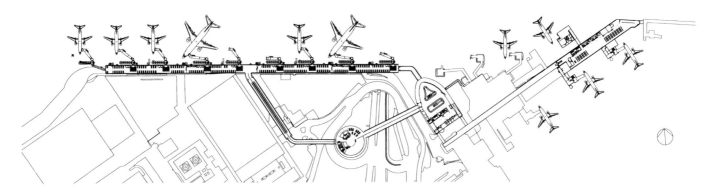

11.4   Pier 4A at Heathrow's Terminal 4, UK. Architects: Nicholas Grimshaw & Partners.

aircraft are parked on the open apron and reached by transporters, which serve as mobile lounges and gate hold rooms. Baggage too is transported to the aircraft on separate mobile apron equipment. The main advantages are flexibility of operation, reduced costs of the terminal building, ease of separating arriving and departing passengers, and reduced walking distances. However, this system has serious disadvantages: vehicle breakdowns or lack of mobile equipment can lead to poor levels of service in aircraft loading or unloading; maintenance and operating costs are high; the system is vulnerable in industrial disputes, and slow in transporting passengers from terminal to aircraft; and there is a need for additional airline and security staff.

Central terminal with remote satellites

The layout here consists of a central terminal building and a number of satellites around which aircraft are parked for receiving passengers. An example is Stansted Airport, where the satellites are reached by a rapid transit system. The terminal and satellites are joined above or below ground by travellators. Baggage is separated from the passenger at the central check-in and transported usually by vehicles operating across the apron. The main advantage of the concept is the centralization of facilities and services, though further shops or duty-free outlets are often provided in each satellite. It has the added advantage that security checks can easily be carried out at the entrance to each satellite.

The system also allows further satellites to be constructed without causing great disruption, if demand grows. Usually, a single airline company is responsible for each satellite, thereby reinforcing a sense of brand identity and allowing passengers to change planes without having to pass through the terminal. The disadvantages are: high capital, running and operating costs (the configuration is relatively expensive compared with, say, the open apron or linear concept, travellator costs are high, baggage handling is expensive, and staff costs are high); limited expansion of the terminal (as against satellites); and long distances, necessitating early check-in times, and making transfers between airlines difficult (though not between planes at the same satellite). However, the arrangement is considered sufficiently attractive to be the basis of Heathrow's new Terminal 5.

Unit terminal

This concept is based upon a number of terminals linked by the airport road system, underground railway or pedestrian travellator. A particularly good example is J F Kennedy, New York, where there are nine terminals, each managed by a different airline. Each terminal provides integrated passenger and baggage facilities, with flight stand and gate check-in close by or incorporated into a single service. It is an arrangement that allows airports to grow incrementally, with different airline companies taking a major stake in each terminal. The main advantages are the short

11.11   Airports increasingly support a range of activities beyond that of air transportation. Here at Cologne/Bonn Airport, Germany, there are hotels, conference centres and leisure facilities placed as satellites around the terminal. Architects: Murphy/Jahn.

airline can 'adopt' a terminal, further units can be added without greatly disrupting the life of the airport, and parking can be accommodated directly alongside the terminal. In contrast, centralized terminals with satellites or piers allow the terminal building to provide plenty of space for retail, leisure and business functions, which have the advantage of supplementing an airport authority's income.

Choosing between single-level and multilevel terminals

The main function of level changes at terminals is to improve the operational efficiency of passenger and baggage movement. There are four main factors to consider in deciding between single, double and multilevel terminals:

• the volume of passenger flow

• the mix between destination and transfer passengers, and between domestic and international
• the relationship between walking distances and airport capacity
• the type and size of aircraft using a terminal.

Two-level terminals reduce the distance that passengers need to travel, and allow direct access from the upper floor to the aircraft door. Because the aircraft door is normally 4m above the ground, most airports use this figure or slightly more (5 or 6m) for the height between ground and first-floor level.

The smooth movement of passengers and their baggage is the main factor determining the sectional profile of the terminal. Structural elements, such as columns, windows and walls, contribute to the aesthetic appearance and help to define the flow patterns through the terminal.

1   Dramatic pedestrian walkway at
Munich Airport Germany. Architects:
Murphy/Jahn and Prof. von Busse,
Blees, Kampmann & Buch

2   CAD is a useful means of
anticipating visual impact and
encouraging public debate. Valladolid
Airport, Spain. Architects: Llewelyn -
Davies

3 Large terminals are analogous with the shopping malls of new towns. O' Hare Airport, Chicago, USA. Architects: Murphy/Jahn

4 Southampton Airport. The interior helps establish BAA's brand identity. Southampton Airport, UK. Architects: Manser Associates

5 Southampton Airport represents well the culture of design excellence at BAA based upon teamwork between client, designer and contractor. Southampton Airport, UK. Architects: Manser Associates

6 The baggage reclaim areas at Stansted Airport. Architects: Foster and Partners

7 Stansted Airport is an elegant pavilion set in the flat English landscape. Architects: Foster and Partners

8 The new generation of airport buildings shows higher regard for environmental design than in the past. Munich Airport Centre, Germany. Architects: Murphy/Jahn

9 Terminals have become leisure destinations in their own right. Stuttgart Airport, Germany. Architects: von Gerkan, Marg & Partners

10 Terminals are buildings where structural forms define functional and spatial patterns. Bangkok Airport, Thailand. Architects: Murphy/Jahn

11 The airport is increasingly a conference and business centre. This exhibition hall is part of the Munich Airport Centre and stands alongside the terminal hotel. Architects: Murphy/Jahn

12 The rather earthy canyon at Kansai contrasts pleasantly with the airy departure lounges. Kansai Airport, Osaka, Japan. Architects: Renzo Piano Building Workshop

13 Kansai marks the emergence of the 21st century airport in its attempt to reduce environmental impact by geographical isolation. Kansai Airport, Osaka, Japan. Architects: Renzo Piano Building Workshop

14 Terminals need to strike a balance between retail revenue and tranquil space for weary airline travellers. Hamburg Airport, Germany. Architects: von Gerkan, Marg & Partners

Space and facilities for the general public should be subordinate to passenger space and passenger facilities.[7] The interaction between passenger flow, terminal space and structure is an important one. The organization of the building in plan and section is the primary factor that determines all other decisions. Design and the method of construction need to support the passenger's perception of the flows through the building. They also need to support the organization of the building in terms of airline staff. The functional path followed by passengers at ground- or first-floor level and baggage on the same or a different level is a system reinforced, not impeded, by architectural design.

Because multilevel terminals are by their nature confusing buildings, the task of design is to establish efficient movement patterns and give a sense of orientation. Design should encourage passengers to use architectural clues to find their way around. This means exploiting daylight and sunlight as navigation aids, using the main structural elements to gesture the presence of major routes and concourses, and using the design of interior volumes to signal the flow patterns. Critical points in the flow, such as main entrances, ticket check-in and customs control, should be marked by changes in design. The choice of materials, colour, texture and profile of surfaces needs to signal the presence of important events in the movement through the terminal.

References

1. Adapted from IATA, *Airport Terminals Reference Manual*, 7th edn, International Air Transport Association, Montreal, Canada, 1989, p. 3.26.
2. Norman Ashford and Paul Wright, *Airport Engineering*, John Wiley & Sons, New York, 1991, p. 293.
3. Adapted from Ashford and Wright, *Airport Engineering*, and IATA, *Airport Terminals Reference Manual*.
4. Christopher J. Blow, *Airport Terminals*, 2nd edn, Butterworth-Heinemann, Oxford, 1996, pp. 96-97.
5. *Ibid.*, pp. 105–106.
6. These and other examples are taken from *Progressive Architecture*, 3.87, pp. 96–104.
7. IATA, *Airport Terminals Reference Manual*, p. 3.32.

CHAPTER 12

Function and meaning in the design of terminals

Design characteristics of passenger terminals

Airport terminals need to be outstanding, satisfying and memorable buildings, which benefit all users or stakeholders:[1]

- passengers
- airport staff
- airport authorities
- airline companies
- the country in general.

As a functional and building planning exercise, terminals are an organizational, logistical, resource and architectural challenge. Because they are particularly complex building types their design needs to eliminate ambiguity and confusion, addressing instead questions of clarity of use, functional legibility and route identification. To remove stress (one of the biggest complaints about modern airports) terminals should provide:

- calmness and tranquillity
- the presence of nature in public areas
- natural finishes and materials wherever possible
- spatial and organizational clarity
- structure and light that express the patterns of use and functional hierarchies.

Because airport terminals are subject to much internal change and external growth they should also:

- be designed for operational flexibility
- be extendible in part and in whole, preferably in more than one direction
- be designed so that the major spaces and activities can be changed without compromising the operation of the whole
- address safety and security in a flexible manner.

In order to meet these constraints the typical passenger terminal normally consists of three main parts or elements, each with its own form and pattern of uses:

12.1 Stress reduction through design is a growing feature of terminal design. Oslo Airport, Norway. Architects: Aviaplan AS.

- the main terminal
- piers that give access to aircraft
- ancillary buildings such as railway stations, control towers, car parks and hotels.

Factors that tend to distinguish the present generation of airport terminals are:

- design for flexibility and extendibility
- passenger and user friendliness
- safety and security by design, surveillance and electronic means
- an environmentally friendly approach to the selection of materials and means of providing building services

- architectural quality that addresses the management and perception of value
- cost efficiency through the standardization of finishes, materials and components.

The four key functions of the terminal

The functional design and architectural design of terminals need clearly to correspond. In simple terms the passenger terminal performs four main functions:[2]

- It facilitates a change of transport mode (from train to plane, from car to plane, etc.).
- It processes passengers (ticket check, customs clearance, immigration control).
- It provides passenger services of various kinds (shopping, toilets, eating, meeting and greeting, business and conference).
- It organizes and groups passengers into discrete batches ready for journeys by plane.

Table 12.1 Functional areas and activities in terminal

Movement	Activities	Space
Departures	Check-in	
	Commercial areas	Departure concourse
	Customs	
	Security	
	Shopping	Departure lounge
	Eating	
	Gate check-in	Gate lounge
Arrivals	Immigration	Arrivals waiting area
	Security	
	Baggage claim	Baggage hall
	Customs	Customs hall
	Meeting	Arrivals concourse
	Refreshment	
Transfers	Security	
	Customs	Departure lounge/
	Immigration	Transfer lounge

113

12.2 Clarity of circulation is an important aspect of terminal design. Oslo Airport, Norway. Architects: Aviaplan AS.

These four functions interconnect and interchange. Because the terminal handles movement in opposing currents the space allocated has, to a degree, to be capable of working in reverse. This is particularly true in the gate lounges.

Taking these four primary functions together it is evident that the passenger terminal has to provide space and clarity of use for circulation, processing, secondary services of various kinds, and gathering. In fact the extent of circulation and gathering is such that the typical airport consists mainly of space, not rooms. This means that space is used for a variety of functions (processing, gathering, servicing passenger needs, batching of passengers into flight grouping) with the consequence that the architect has to give particular areas of space the necessary cues to allow passengers to understand the intended purpose. Although open space exceeds enclosed volume, the terminal has to define by design means how an area of space is to be used. Rooms can have nameplates to distinguish their function, but this

12.3   Tectonic structure, large interior volume and light provide the means of creating airport atmosphere. Extension to Cologne/Bonn Airport, Germany. Architects: Murphy/Jahn.

is less easy with space. Hence the terminal designer has to give functional meaning to the interior volumes, and here the size of the space, the gesturing of structure, the handling of light and 'atmosphere' have all to be exploited.

The four primary functions need to be capable of operating smoothly throughout the total design life of a terminal: that is, 50 years. The trend is for the secondary functions (such as security) to increase at the expense of the primary ones. Also, within the four primary functional orders, passenger services (retail, banking or conference, for example)

tends to expand at the expense of processing efficiency. As the balance of importance changes, the use of space in the terminal alters too. Hence, while the terminal must be capable of meeting current functional patterns, it must also be able to adapt to future ones without putting the operation of the airport in jeopardy. Whereas the terminals of old catered exclusively for passengers, the current generation of terminals are designed to attract non-travellers to airport facilities. This too compromises the simple functional pattern outlined earlier.

12.4   At Seoul Airport the proposed transportation centre sits between the two terminals. Transportation Centre, Seoul Airport, Korea. Architects: Terry Farrell and Partners.

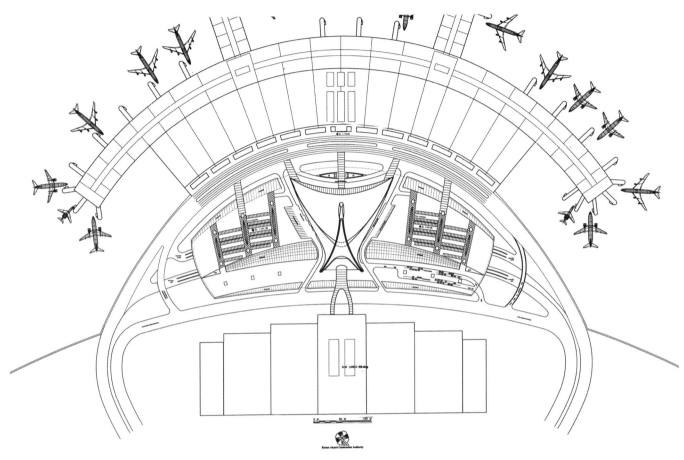

Change of transport mode

This function is of growing importance as modern terminals seek to accommodate a wide range of public transport access provision. Architects are increasingly required to provide convenient and legible connection at terminals to rail, metro, bus and private car access. The integration of airports with the regional and national transport infrastructure places particular strain upon the terminal building itself. Some recent terminals (such as that proposed for the new Seoul International Airport) give prominence to the intermodal function, relegating the terminal proper to a secondary role. At Seoul a huge triangular transportation centre serves two terminals attached one at the apex and the other at the base of the triangle.

Processing passengers

The processing of passengers involves airline staff in baggage and ticket checking, and government officials in security, health and immigration controls. While ticketing is

becoming easier as the airline companies introduce smoother passage through check-in controls, the governmental controls are tending to become stricter. The rise in international terrorism, in drug trafficking, the spread of disease, and the increase in political refugees, all mean that ever-tighter controls are needed. Generally, the processing function consists of:

airline function

• ticket check-in
• baggage handling
• gate check

governmental function

• health control
• passport control
• immigration control
• customs control
• security check.

12.5 Directing and grouping passengers is a function of the terminal. O'Hare Airport, Chicago, USA.

Passenger services

There has been a marked increase in the range and scale of passenger services over the past decade. Generally speaking the terminal may need to provide the following passenger facilities or services:

- retail sales, including duty-free
- restaurants and bars
- banks, post office and currency exchange shops
- business and conference support
- leisure and tourist information
- amusement arcades
- museum (of flight)
- information points, especially for disabled travellers
- health club
- VIP facilities.

The need to provide these facilities should be balanced by the legitimate demands of other passengers for tranquil spaces away from the noisy bustle of retail malls.

Organizing and grouping passengers

Part of the function of the terminal is to organize passengers into logical flows. This consists in segregating them into arriving and departing currents, in distinguishing physically between passengers and non-travelling visitors, in forming holding areas, and in distinguishing between airside and landside movements. The architecture of the terminal plays an important part in defining the organization of movement. Space, enclosure and barrier are essential ingredients in functional differentiation. The typical terminal contains the following key holding spaces:

- passenger lounges, including general concourse, departure, arrivals and gate lounges
- airside corridor or lounge
- observation deck or lounge
- baggage reclaim area.

The areas are usually served by restaurants, bars and shops of various kinds, arranged as perimeter attractions, galleries or islands.

12.6 Diagrammatic structure of retail facilities at terminal for departure passengers.

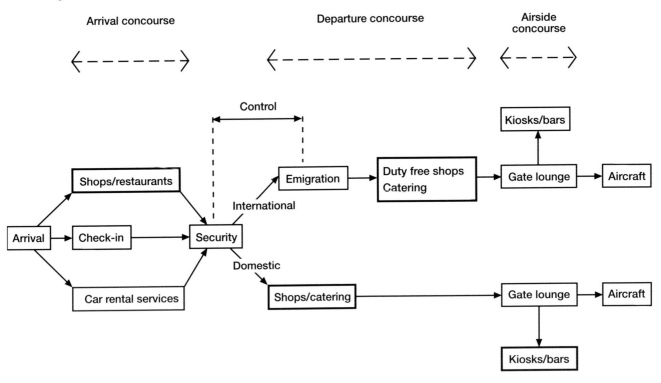

Functional elements of the terminal building

The basic organization of a terminal can be separated into two parallel functional patterns of passenger and baggage movement: departures and arrivals. Both shape the profile in plan and section of the terminal. In addition, there are private facilities that support or regulate the public passenger flows relating to airport, airline and government functions. Their offices and facilities play an important but minor role in shaping the design of terminals.

The terminal consists of two main public spaces: the departures concourse and the arrivals concourse. Each is a key spatial element, which needs to be separately identified. Although the departures and arrivals concourse may coalesce at the airside corridor, the two concourses should not meet after kerbside. There may, however, have to be provision for crossover to serve the needs of transit passengers, and the possibility of either being used in reverse flow.

The departures concourse consists of:

- circulation areas
- waiting areas, including departure lounge
- shops, bars and restaurants
- telephones, fax and business facilities
- information points
- toilets, rest-rooms and first aid
- ticket sales
- passenger and baggage check-in
- immigration control.

The flow relationship, with retail facilities highlighted, is shown in Figure 12.6.

The arrivals concourse consists of:

- circulation areas
- waiting areas, including arrivals lounge
- limited shops and bars
- telephones and toilets
- baggage claim
- customs, health and immigration control.

The flow relationship, again with retail facilities highlighted, is shown in Figure 12.7.

In addition, the terminal building may contain passenger accommodation and facilities that are shared between the departure and arrivals concourses. This includes:

- a common kerbside lounge or concourse (known sometimes as assembly, entrance or general concourse)
- an airside corridor or concourse
- common, transit lounge.

Terminals also contain a wide range of offices or facilities devoted to the passenger movement function, such as:

- airport offices
- airline offices
- customs offices
- immigration and health offices
- baggage-handling services.

12.7   Diagrammatic structure of facilities at terminal for arrivals passengers.

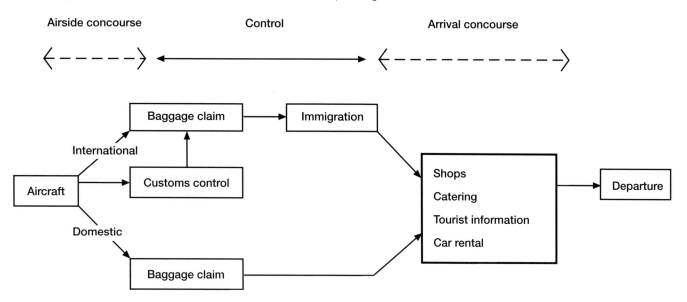

The terminal building can be seen as containing three broad functional groupings of accommodation, devoted to departures, arrivals and shared facilities respectively. The triangular relationship between the three – exploited occasionally in triangular-shaped terminals such as King Khaled International Airport at Riyadh, Saudi Arabia – leads also to three-level terminals where offices and baggage handling occupy an interstitial level between the departures and arrivals floor. Such terminals provide a clear split in accommodation between public and private facilities, and between governmental ones and those of airline companies.

The terminal designer has the task of giving form to these functional divisions. The airport is a complex play of organizational systems, and the architect has the prime responsibility of shaping and providing meaning to the various parts.

Within each subdivision of accommodation there are a number of variables and options available, depending upon the size and operational characteristics of a particular airport. Planning solutions that work well in one terminal building may not function so smoothly in another. Some of the more complex design issues are listed below.

Circulation areas

The major circulation area occurs between the landside facade and the ticket check-in area. This normally consists of a parallel concourse immediately behind the glazed front of the passenger terminal. Known sometimes as the 'landside concourse' or 'assembly concourse' this area is shared by the general public and the travelling public, and in some layouts by departure and arrivals passengers. Because shops, car rental outlets, bars and restaurants, and ticket sales are found in this area, as well as meeters and greeters and those accompanying departing passengers, there are

many flows involved. The circulation areas need to be wide enough to accommodate the various activities, yet of dimensions and shape that guide passengers in the direction of flow.

Facilities such as toilets and flight information boards intended for those travelling should be arranged to prevent the general public from obstructing routes or visibility. Space utilization in the landside and departure concourse should promote efficient and uniform use of the circulation areas, bearing in mind the uneven flows of use that stem from flight departure times. Zoning facilities, and making a clear distinction in the design of space between public and private, and between passenger needs and those of the non-travelling public, can greatly promote the smooth use of concourse areas. Similarly, ticket sales for those who intend to fly but have not purchased a ticket should be provided near to the passenger flow route but should not obstruct it. This is particularly important where, as in much of the USA, self-service ticket machines are provided.

Passenger check-in

The check-in counters and adjoining queuing area are, for the airline company, a crucial zone in the departure concourse. The area is normally part of the shared landside and departure concourse, though on occasions the two areas are partially split (as at Manchester Airport Terminal 2). Check-in is where passengers are allocated a seat and their baggage is transferred to an automated handling system. After check-in, the passenger can idle through the concourse relieved of baggage trolleys, and proceed to customs and flight security checks.

The check-in facility consists of a number of counters arranged as either frontal or island types. Frontal types are made up of a long bank of check-in positions spaced to allow

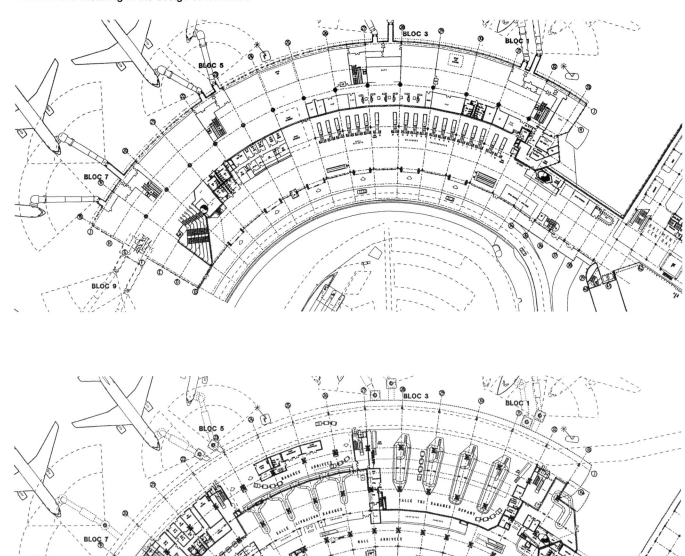

12.8   Detail floor plan for extension to Lyon-Satolas Airport, France. Architects: Curtelin Ricard Bergeret with Scott Brownrigg and Turner.

passengers to pass between the counters after check-in. As such, the frontal type arrangement helps to form the barrier between the public departure concourse and the departure lounge devoted specifically for those travelling. Island-type counters consist of banks of check-in points arranged usually along the flow of the departure concourse. There is no attempt to limit access at this point to the departure lounge, where separate control points based upon boarding cards exist. Island counters are useful where centralized check-in occurs (the passenger can proceed straight to the gate lounge, as in commuting flights). Normally, island counters have about 15 check-in positions with the islands spaced 20–25m apart, and perhaps staggered in plan.

With both systems (frontal or island) it is important that the distance from kerbside or railway station to the check-in counter is as short as possible. Where lengthy journeys are encountered, assisted-movement systems should be provided such as travellators or monorail. Clearly, space is needed for passengers and for personal baggage trolleys.

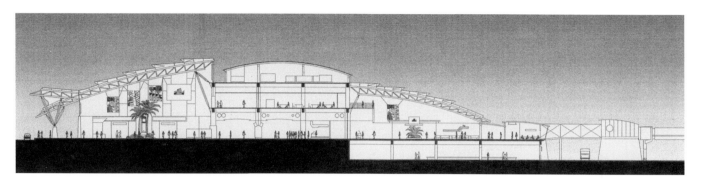

12.9   Section through proposed Harare Airport, Zimbabwe. Notice how the change in ground level is exploited to smooth lateral movement from road to plane. Architects: Scott Brownrigg and Turner.

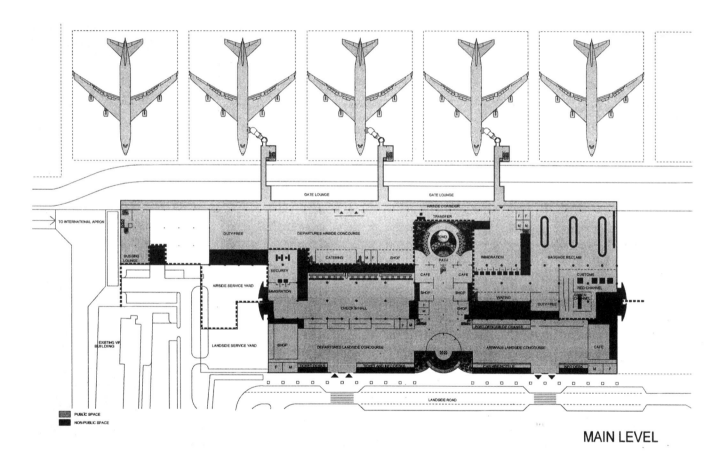

12.10   Plan of Harare Airport, Zimbabwe. Architects: Scott Brownrigg and Turner.

It is also important that passengers without baggage to check in have the facility to go directly to gate check-in.

Check-in facilities under any system should be designed so that an airline company can influence the character and layout of the facility. At check-in, the customer comes into contact with the airline for the first time on the journey. It is here that perceptions of quality can be communicated.

References

1. The objectives are taken from Aviaplan AS (brochure), Oslo, 1995.
2. The list is an expansion of those quoted by Norman Ashford and Paul Wright in *Airport Engineering*, John Wiley & Sons, New York, 1991, pp. 286–287. The authors acknowledge only three functions, relegating 'passenger services' to a subfunction of 'processing'. Another useful source is IATA, *Airport Terminals Reference Manual*, 8th edn, International Air Transport Association, Montreal, Canada, 1995, pp. 110–112.

CHAPTER

13

Passenger types, space standards and territories

The terminal is the interface between landside and airside, between the customs-controlled and duty-free world and that of the public concourse, and between being on the ground and in the air. As a building the airline terminal is a crucial and symbolic structure on every airline passenger's journey. It is both gateway to the air and, in the opposite direction, a gateway to a country. One progresses through the terminal, moving between a series of controls and temptations from terminal entrance via the exit gate to the aircraft.

Principal terminal territories

Most terminal buildings consist of six distinct territories on departure:

- entrance concourse
- flight check-in and information
- shops, bars, restaurants, cinemas etc.
- passport control
- departure lounge and duty-free shops
- pier and gate to plane

and four territories on arrival:

- arrivals lounge
- baggage reclaim
- customs and immigration control
- exit hall.

Generally, the division between arrivals and departure is split (at least in larger airports) between different levels, with the majority adopting first floor for departures and ground floor for arrivals. Also, the entrance concourse and exit hall are usually the same space, perhaps zoned laterally to avoid conflict of movement.

Early generations of terminal buildings (such as Heathrow Terminal 1) placed few temptations between the passengers' arrival in the building and check-in, or between the departure lounge and gate lounge. However, with greater commercial pressure and the need to achieve higher profits, the modern terminal has a sequence of

13.1 CAD perspective of concourse interior at Hong Kong's new airport at Chek Lap Kok. Architects: Foster and Partners.

shops, cafes and bars placed conspicuously between the essential elements of the journey. Now upon entering a terminal building the passenger is more likely to be faced not by a bank of flight check-in desks but by burger bars, newspaper stalls and gift shops. These have to be negotiated before eye contact can be made with the airline company's desk. A similar pattern of interrupted movement through the terminal occurs after baggage check-in. Again, with less baggage, the traveller is vulnerable to the pull of

dwell-time, and here more commercial outlets will be found, especially close to passenger flows. This sequence continues until the passenger boards the plane and, to a lesser extent, returns when he arrives at the destination. The design of the terminal building is as much shaped by the needs of duty-free and tax-paid shopping, refreshment and leisure as by the logistical path from taxi to plane.

The revenue generated at terminals is determined partly by the nature of flights handled, and partly by the split

13.2 Retail plan at departure lounge. Gatwick North Terminal, UK. Architects: YRM.

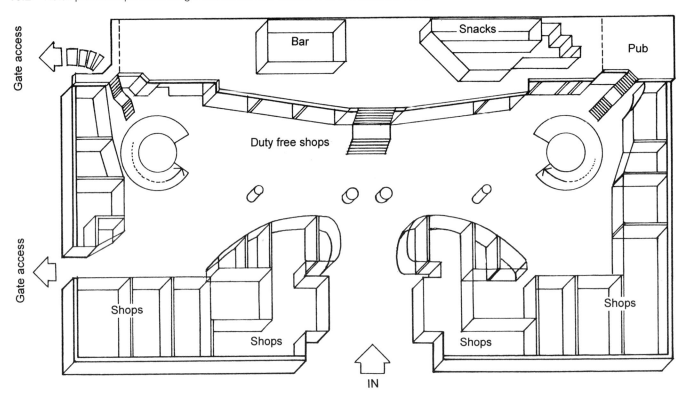

13.3 Passenger movement is a key function of the modern terminal. Dallas/Fort Worth Airport, USA. Architects: Hellmuth, Obata & Kassabaum

between passengers, airport workers and visitors. Passengers are the most lucrative source of income, especially long-haul holiday and charter passengers. The latter in particular tend to spend longer in terminals than other passengers, and the special characteristics of charter holidays tend to encourage a spending spree at airports. Business travellers, though they may use conference, health club and restaurant facilities, tend to be frequent users of terminals, and pass through without loitering in shopping areas. Business trips do not attract 'meeters and greeters', so there is less income generated here as well. The design of a terminal needs to reflect the passenger mix: where charter and scheduled flights share a terminal the range of facilities (and of opportunities to spend money) is greater than in a terminal catering almost exclusively for domestic business travel. The trend towards the commercialization of terminals is fuelled by a combination of airport privatization and the growth in relatively high-spending charter passengers.

A good example of the favourable environment at terminals from the point of view of retailers is the toy store

Hamleys. Besides the company's headquarters store in London's Regent Street, it has outlets at Heathrow and Schipol Airport and also a store at the Channel Tunnel terminus near Folkestone. Hamleys recognizes that modern transportation buildings provide locations as favourable to trade as traditional high streets. Similarly, Mappin & Webb's shop at Heathrow's Terminal 4 is the biggest-selling outlet for Rolex watches in the UK.[1] Besides retailing, some airports are beginning to introduce museum facilities into terminals. At Gatwick an attraction known as Skyview provides a museum on the theme of flight. There are sections on aviation history and on how the airport works on a daily basis, a chance to sit in a De Havilland Comet cockpit, a simulation ride in a Harrier jump-jet, and a fine panoramic viewing gallery. The shift from retail to leisure is one of the defining elements of late twentieth-century terminals.

Passenger types

Passengers at terminals come in a variety of types, and each has its own needs. There are often whole families, heavily laden and travelling at a slow pace in comparison with business passengers armed only with a briefcase and generally rather in a hurry. Long-haul passengers tend to carry the most baggage, and are usually tired from long flights, leading to frequent stops, often for refreshments. Transferring passengers are often racing through the terminal in order to catch connecting flights. Elderly travellers, perhaps in wheelchairs, also form a clear group, as do young mothers with small children. The diversity of passenger types places facilities under different pressures. The design of the terminal should therefore be such that all categories of passenger are successfully catered for: in fact, passenger loyalty depends as much upon the experience of the terminal as on that of the flight itself. One source of particular frustration is that of queuing. Queues are wasteful of space, pose a threat in the event of fires, create a poor impression of the airport, and use space that could be exploited for retail sales. The eradication or reduction of queuing requires attention to architectural design and airport management. For example, queues often build up near to congested exits, escalators or lifts owing to lack of

provision for peak demand. Queues are also the result of ineffective management: a lack of airline staff frequently leads to long lines of people at check-in desks (this is a particular problem with charter flights). Innovations in central ticketing, which allow check-in at airport stations and car parks, offer future solutions. As a general rule passengers should be relieved of their baggage immediately upon entering the terminal, and ideally before they reach the building.

Types of terminal user other than passengers

Terminal buildings do not of course cater only for passengers. Although passengers may be numerically the largest component of terminal users there are at least five other groups of users:

- airport employees (airline staff, airport staff, shop and restaurant staff, customs officials)
- meeters and greeters (who often buy souvenirs)
- leisure visitors (who use the airport as a tourist attraction)
- local residents (who use the terminal as a convenient point to shop)
- business people (who use the airport's conference facilities).

13.5 Spacious check-in concourse at Manchester's Terminal 2 provides a welcoming entrance to the airport. Manchester Airport, UK. Architects: Scott Brownrigg and Turner.

Catering for the needs of all these groups requires careful planning of airport terminal facilities, perhaps assisted by computer queue-modelling systems. There are obvious conflicts to resolve in the allocation and distribution of terminal space. Ensuring that airline passengers receive clear guidance and information on their journey through a busy terminal is a priority that should not be jeopardized by commercial pressure. In some airports, such as Gatwick and Frankfurt, the passengers' smooth movement through the functional zones of the terminal appears at times to be impeded by shops, bars and souvenir shops. When fires occur (as at Dusseldorf Airport in 1996) it is important that passengers' perception of escape routes remain clear.

Passenger space standards

The growing commercial pressure at terminals should not be at the expense of space standards for users. IATA recommends the following average standards of space per airport passenger:

- check-in queue area: $1.4m^2$
- waiting and circulation: $1.9m^2$
- hold area: $1m^2$
- baggage reclaim area: $1.6m^2$
- government inspection: $1m^2$.

Taking all the space needs together, it has been calculated that the gross area of a terminal is $14m^2$ per peak-hour passenger for domestic operations and $24m^2$ for international.[3] Modern safety needs may increase these figures by 20% where total separation of departure and arrival passengers is needed at airside, and where special security baggage-handling systems are demanded. The total floor area per passenger may then approach $29m^2$.

Terminal facilities

The terminal building provides services of various kinds, including shopping, banking, hairdressing, entertainment, business facilities, car hire, and shoe cleaning. There are also services beyond that of retail or commercial sales: some, such as lost persons points and chaplaincy support, have a distinct social purpose. With 54 million passengers a year using Heathrow Airport, the throughput of people begins to approach that of the whole population of Britain. Viewed in such terms terminal buildings are more than just retail malls en route to the plane.

The non-retail services provided in terminal buildings at larger airports may include:

- banks
- foreign exchange shops
- information on land-based travel (trains, buses)
- car rental
- tourist information
- showers
- rest areas (with short-stay beds)
- laundry and dry cleaning
- beauty salon
- hairdressing
- medical services
- conference and business facilities
- spiritual support (chapel or mosque)
- cinemas and video area
- amusement arcade
- health centre
- business club
- swimming pool
- VIP lounge.

Some of the facilities and services may be provided in an adjoining building (such as a hotel) but most are contained within the terminal itself.

The Federal Aviation Authority (FAA) recommends the terminal design space standards listed in Table 13.1, which supplement the passenger space standards listed earlier. Because space standards are a reflection of levels of use

Table 13.1 Terminal space standards

Area	Space per peak hour passenger (m²)
Ticket lobby	0.95
Waiting areas (departure lounge etc.)	1.8
Eating and shopping areas	2.1
Visitor waiting areas (arrivals concourse etc.)	1.5
Baggage claim	1.0
Toilets	0.3
Customs	3.3
Immigration	1.0
Public health	1.5
Circulation, building plant, walls etc.	19.1
Airline operational	4.8

Source: FAA Terminal Space Design Standards

on the one hand, and of efficiency of space utilization on the other, the standards are not absolute but merely recommended. Also, congestion is a measure of peak demand overcrowding, and not of the terminal under normal working conditions. Hence terms like 'typical peak hour passenger' and 'standard busy rate' are employed to distinguish between peak and normal operation.

The table confirms that terminals are buildings primarily of circulation space; areas of specific function and enclosure are of secondary importance in terms of total floor area.

Commercial versus facilities management

The design and layout of the terminal building highlight the dilemma between the concept of the terminal as a means of generating income for the airport and that of the building as a public and social facility. The relative balance between the two positions directly influences the character of the terminal. With terminals designed to generate the maximum of income, passengers are faced by banks of shops, bars, car rental offices and duty-free areas, with the travelling element such as check-in desks having a minor role. In contrast, in terminals such as Saarinen's TWA building at Kennedy Airport, New York, which have more of a public service role, the uncluttered space and uncrowded concourse areas give priority to the needs of passengers. Here check-in desks, staircases and travel information provide for those travelling rather than those visiting to purchase goods.

The trend at terminals is, however, to exploit 'dwell-time' by providing a range of facilities and entertainments to distract the traveller between arrival at the airport and departure on the plane. Commercial needs rather than social ones are normally given priority at the design briefing stage. The layout, organization and design of passenger terminals have increasingly to accept the demands of income generation. In fact, BAA earns over £450 million per year from retail-type activities at its UK airports, which exceeds by £50 million the amount of money that the company spends each year on building operations of various kinds. Viewed in this way retail revenues pay for terminals without the additional income from landing fees. Airport managers and finance directors of airline companies understand how to exploit passenger flows to generate revenue. Terminal design therefore often directly reflects the need to maximize concession revenues. This means placing as many retail activities and as much commercial space between entrance and plane as possible. It also means putting these activities (shops, bars, restaurants, duty-free concessions, car rental offices) directly in the line of passenger movement. Where concourses are split between arrivals and departure levels, it means placing commercial space on each floor level, thereby generating income from both departing and arriving passengers. Under such pressure it is easy to see modern passenger terminals as retail malls through which passengers pass – not to the supermarket check-out but to the airport check-in or departure lounge. It also explains the pressure to upgrade and expand earlier generations of terminals (such as Gatwick's North Terminal) in order to earn more from retail sales.

The location of retail space is of crucial importance to the ability of franchises to generate income. Direct contact by passengers with commercial areas (say within 10m and on the same level) on their passage through the terminal is ideal.

13.6 Retail and catering facilities can enliven concourse areas. Terminal 2, Manchester Airport, UK. Architects: Scott Brownrigg and Turner.

Locations out of the line of movement or out of eye-shot are less favoured, and tend to be used for specialist services such as hairdressing, cinemas or health clubs.

In 1993/94 retailing revenues at UK airports exceeded for the first time those from charging airlines for the use of the facilities. Landing fees, which provided the bulk of income hitherto, now provide less income for BAA than retail or car parking revenue generation. Such is the growth in retail and leisure activities at airports that BAA has set a target of doubling the retail space at its airports by the end of the century. This puts pressure on public concourses and on the openness and legibility of interior routes, and poses additional fire and security threats. It is no coincidence that the fire at Dusseldorf Airport in April 1996, which killed 16 people, began in the shopping area of the terminal. Detecting fires and organising escape becomes more difficult as terminals become more multi-functional in nature.

Types of shop and their location

The characteristics of shops in different terminals reflect the type and destination of the passengers present. For example, Far Eastern passengers at Heathrow's Terminal 4 lead to shops such as Harrods, Selfridges and Austin Reed, which tend to sell classic fashion goods and high-quality accessories, while at Terminal 2, which is served by Air France and Alitalia, most sales are of traditional English goods. The types of shop reflect the type of people at a particular terminal. Where there are plenty of package holiday-makers using a terminal, one would expect more bars, restaurants and shops selling leisure and sporting wear. For some retailers, the objective of having shops at airports is not simply one of sales but of ensuring that foreign visitors see the company's name as soon as they arrive in the country. Terminal shopping is often profitable for the retailer: BAA's research has shown that landside concourse shops earn twice as much per square metre as do high street shops, and airside shops (where goods are tax free) nearly three times as much.[4]

Normally, with separate arrivals and departure floors retail activities are concentrated on both, but some terminals (such as at Gatwick) place an intermediate commercial floor between the two. This has the advantage of removing some of the clutter from the principal floors and allowing larger retail units to locate in the terminal. As a consequence the North Terminal at Gatwick has many household name stores within the complex. For the traveller, there is the choice of avoiding the retail areas altogether or of shopping in stores where price and quality are more competitive than with more traditional layouts.

13.7 Terminals linked to hotels greatly expand the commercial potential of airports. Munich Airport Centre, Germany. Architects: Murphy/Jahn.

It is normally considered a disadvantage for retailers if passengers have to move up or down a level to use shops or catering facilities. Where shopping at airports is successful with changing levels it is normally because many purchases are not undertaken by those about to travel but by casual visitors, airport staff and greeters. Where large glazed lifts and plenty of escalators are provided, some of the disincentive to change level is overcome, but evidence from Frankfurt Airport suggests that even with such measures turnover is down by 40% with multilevel terminal shopping.[5]

The design and layout of terminals are driven by the need to generate as much secondary income as possible. Although in American airports the car rental business provides the biggest income (by way of rents and leasehold arrangements) for the terminal, in European and Asian airports it is that from shops, bars and particularly duty-free outlets. Because terminal income often exceeds that of airside income (such as landing fees and aircraft parking) there is much pressure to improve the performance of existing airports where space for commercial activities may be

13.8 Materials that maintain their appearance and are easily cleaned are a feature of circulation areas. Manchester Airport Link, UK. Architects: Aukett Associates.

limited by out-of-date designs. As a consequence there is currently a trend towards expanding existing terminals to create extra commercial space (for example, the recent enlargement of Marseille Airport by the Richard Rogers Partnership).

The distinction between the retail zones of a terminal building needs to be defined by the choice of finishes and lighting, though it is tending to be eroded by commercial pressures. The passenger and leisure visitor are both potential customers of franchisers; the departing and arriving passenger is also targeted, as is the airport and airline employee. To some extent the distinction between airside and landside is being weakened, with many retail outlets now placed beyond the immigration control barrier. The clearly defined distinction between flow areas and commercial areas is a casualty of changing design and management philosophies. In the older generation of terminals (such as Heathrow's Terminal 1 or Paris Orly) large volumes of movement space were provided without the competition of retail units, flower stalls and advertising hoardings. However, today's terminal is based upon the concept of avoiding the physical separation of passenger flows from other activities. What is now sought is a kind of integration in space planning where passengers are deliberately routed through commercial areas and encouraged to linger by long check-in times.

Other sources of commercial revenue

Besides direct sales, the passengers' presence also generates income from advertising. Large, often changing signs are an increasing feature of the international terminal building. Their presence needs to be designed into the fabric of the terminal rather than (as is normally the case) added as an ill-fitting afterthought. The best locations for advertising hoardings and free-standing boards are close to passenger traffic routes within and outside the terminal. For those that let advertising space, a site at right angles to flow generates a great deal more income than one placed parallel to movement. On long routes, such as access corridors leading to gate lounges, well-designed advertising displays can enliven a dull journey, but too much advertising may annoy jaded passengers.

Another source of income at or adjacent to terminals is from hotels. It has been estimated that a throughput of 1 million passengers per annum generates the demand for a 100-bed hotel (that is, a 50-room hotel).[6] As with retail space, the hotel can be run by the airport authority itself, or more likely by a hotel franchiser who pays for the lease of land or rental of part of the terminal building. At Charles de Gaulle Airport in Paris, the hotel is placed in the centre of a combined airport station and terminal complex, providing ready access between the various facilities and modes of travel. Normally with such close integration the airport generates income both through the leasehold of land and through a levy on the hotel's turnover. Because hotels often provide conference facilities, the presence of a hotel can generate additional income in the terminal through extra passenger use and non-travelling person use.

The choice of materials and finishes

The functional territories of a terminal need to be defined by the choice of finishes, the method of lighting and the level of sound insulation. Although there is a trend towards the homogenized interior, design should help the passenger to distinguish the main sequence of spaces and their intended use. Finishes play an important role in imparting a

13.9 Daylight and artificial light need to define routes and important areas such as check-in desks. Stansted Airport, UK. Architects: Foster and Partners.

sense of place and purpose within the terminal building. The main gathering areas, such as the departure lounge, need to have a different character from that of the check-in concourse or the mall. Similarly, customs control and baggage claim areas have their own distinctive technical standards to meet and qualities to impart.

The choice of materials is therefore an aesthetic and practical one. Terminals are demanding places for materials: wall and floor finishes should continue to look good in spite of high levels of use and the wear and tear of baggage trolleys. The main thoroughfares and adjacent lower levels of walls need particularly to retain a good appearance if the image of the terminal is to be maintained. In selecting materials the architect should consider the importance of the interior space in terms of functional hierarchy, the way it is going to be used (areas where snacks or burgers are eaten pose particular problems), and the level of usage. Generally, the heaviest wear areas are given terrazzo, polished granite or ceramic tile finishes on floors, and walls are protected from trolleys, cleaning machines and wheel-chairs by splayed skirtings and reinforced corners. With panel systems, the walls need to be robust, protected perhaps by stainless steel handrails and trolley guards, and capable of being readily replaced in the event of damage. With all finishes, replaceability without excessive cost and disruption of the operation of the terminal is a key consideration.

Less trafficked areas are normally carpeted. Carpets, normally specially designed for the airport, provide a quiet, soft and relatively cheap finish. Patterned carpets, though tiring on the eye, allow spills and damage to occur without spoiling the overall appearance. As with harder floor finishes, carpets can be readily renewed in areas subject to greater wear simply by patching.

The different territories of modern terminals are normally expressed in the choice of materials. Shopping malls subject to great wear normally have terrazzo flooring, with refreshment areas or shops choosing their own finishes depending upon technical requirements: for example, ceramic tiles in fast food outlets, or carpeted flooring in bookshops. The customs, immigration and security check zones, too, are usually defined with different materials for desks, screens and floors.

The choice of materials influences the acoustic performance of different areas. The selection of carpeting, for instance, helps to attenuate noise in the departure lounge, which may stem from aircraft taking off on nearby runways. The desirability of offering interesting airport views from lounges and airside concourses carries the problem of dealing with aircraft noise. Normally, a combination of double or triple glazing, carpeting and soft furnishing to seats can achieve the standards laid down in BS 2750. Aircraft sound, however, which is part of the passengers' expectation of journeying by plane,

may be quite unacceptable in customs control areas or airline offices. A good rule of thumb for such areas is to achieve a dBA of 40 – a standard that may require extensive noise attenuation in offices or control areas overlooking runways.[7]

Lighting is part of the establishment of character in different parts of the terminal. Daylight should be present in the core areas of the terminal as a matter of course. Deep-plan buildings need to be subdivided by grids of sky-lights, or opened to the outside by folds in the roof. Light, both daylight and sunlight, is vital in guiding passengers through complex terminals. Artificial light is also vital in determining ambience, comfort and safety. Light levels need to vary according to the functional status of each part of the terminal. Main thoroughfares require higher levels of lighting than do quiet sitting areas, and immigration control needs sharp lighting for obvious reasons. Lighting, whether by ceiling or by wall-mounted fittings, or by spot or diffused sources, gives character and sparkle to different areas. Certain reflective materials, such as polished terrazzo, benefit from the radiance of artificial light, and with stain-less steel, glass or marble stairs, integral strip lighting can enhance the design effect.

The departure lounge

Depending upon the size and complexity of the airport, the departure lounge may consist of three separate areas:

- common departure lounge
- gate lounge
- transfer lounge

or all three combined into a single envelope. The departure lounge serves three distinct types of passenger: those departing from the airport, those transferring from one flight to another, and those transiting on the same flight. In terms of airport operations the last two groups of passengers should remain on airside, and those departing directly (the first group) should not be allowed to pass back to landside.

It is preferable, both architecturally and organizational-ly, to combine the three lounges into a single concourse where local circumstances allow. This avoids duplication of space and manpower, and allows shops and restaurants to serve all those travelling. The gate lounge is the forward assembly point, where passengers gather before boarding the aircraft. It normally overlooks the airport apron, and passengers are held here for relatively short periods. It is usually a carpeted area with seats and a few concessionary outlets. As a rule of thumb, a square metre of space should be provided for every passenger: hence for aircraft seating 400 a space of 400m^2 is required in the gate lounge.[8]

The common departure lounge is where most travelling passengers congregate after clearing passport control, including those who are transferring between flights. Segregation may occur within the overall space to define gate lounges, but generally the departure lounge is a wide, spacious and leisurely concourse served by a mixture of shops, bars, cafes, duty-free areas, banks, business facilities, toilets and health clubs. Because some passengers may wait here for a few hours there is more space than in the gate lounge (normally 2m^2 per passenger); there are good views over the airport, plenty of natural light, and perhaps entertainment for children. Many flight information points are also required, and airline transfer desks.

The transit lounge is a space where passengers wait while flights are serviced on long-haul journeys, but normally it is simply part of the common departures lounge. The transfer lounge exists alongside the arrivals concourse for passengers who are transferring from one flight to another. Another directly connected but discrete area is the VIP lounge set aside for first class or business class passengers. With space per passenger of 3 or 4m^2, this area is normally designed to resemble an exclusive club.

The airside corridor either sits between the departure lounge and the aircraft gate positions or is a part of their overall space. It has the function of allowing linear circulation between the main departure lounge, a number of gate lounges and aircraft boarding positions. The airside corridor is in effect a walkway along the airside face of the terminal, which connects the different lounges with the aircraft boarding gate. Depending upon the nature of the terminal, the airside corridor needs to accommodate departing and arriving passengers without undue congestion. A great deal of

13.10 Light and views across the airport apron help to give the departure lounge interest and tranquillity. Terminal 2, Manchester Airport, UK. Architects: Scott Brownrigg and Turner.

information is needed here about flights, gate positions and exit routes. When airside corridors are over 300m long consideration should be given to travellators. Because all passengers will need to pass through the airside corridor, enough space should be provided for wheelchair users, passengers with baggage trolleys and those with visual impairment. Light, colour and texture should all be employed to aid passenger movement at this critical point in their journey through the terminal.

First class, business class and VIP passengers

With the growth in holiday package tours and casual leisure use of terminals, airport authorities have introduced fast-track routes for first and business class travellers. These extend from specially designated car parks close to the terminal to special check-in counters, fast routes through security and passport control, and preferential check-outs at duty-free shops. At airports such as Heathrow and Gatwick, first and business class travellers are given a Fast Track pass, which bypasses many of the queuing bottlenecks. The need to provide for these additional routes in a secure and discrete fashion is normally written into briefs

13.11 Generous provision of lifts and escalators benefits both able and disabled passengers. Terminal 2, Manchester Airport, UK. Architects: Scott Brownrigg and Turner.

issued to architects by airport authorities. At Gatwick the Fast Track route cuts, according to BAA, up to 30 minutes off the journey through the terminal.

Fast-track routeing through the terminal is generally related to VIP facilities. First and business class passengers have their own waiting lounges normally provided by the airline with which they are flying rather than by the airport authority. Such waiting lounges consist of de luxe suites of rooms and bars, dedicated facilities such as fax machines, and occasionally direct access to secretarial services. Special rooms for VIPs (as against first or business class passengers) are provided at larger airports, with direct access by car from both landside and airside. Sometimes security, customs and passport control is provided adjacent to the VIP suite.

Provision for disabled passengers

Airports in general and passenger terminals in particular need to cater for the needs of able-bodied and disabled people alike. All stages in the journey should provide facilities for the disabled passenger in a fashion that does not hint at social discrimination. As a matter of principle disabled people should not be separated physically, but should share in the circulation provision provided for all. Hence lifts that

allow ambulant passengers with baggage trolleys to move between levels should be of such a design that wheelchair users can also use them.

The routes from railway station, bus stop and car park to terminal, the routes through the terminal to the aircraft, and any rapid transit system between terminals, should all be designed with disabled people in mind. Physical impairment is relatively common (affecting 1 in about 50 passengers at UK airports), and others have varying degrees of psychological problems, which may influence their choice of routes in various ways. Good design consists of anticipating these problems and providing alternative access provision wherever possible. Lifts pose particular problems: the physical enclosure triggers panic attacks in some, and high overhanging balconies tend to destabilize others.

Most airports provide preferential treatment for disabled passengers. This commonly consists of special parking areas close to the terminal, designated zones near lifts or travellators at long-stay car parks, and concessionary fares on buses or taxis for those with proof of Mobility Allowance. Also, courtesy telephones are commonly provided for disabled passengers, with specially trained staff on hand to provide assistance through the terminal. British Airways, which carries 65 000 incapacitated passengers annually (two-thirds of whom use wheelchairs), provides a member of staff to take disabled passengers through the various controls and onto the aircraft.

Catering for physical and psychological problems is a question of design and management of terminals. Those with impaired sight or hearing provide a particular problem at airports, because flight information and route are vital passenger needs. Signs and flight information boards need to be easily read and understood, especially in airports where voice announcements are not made. Partially sighted passengers may need a combination of information provided by electronic screens close at hand and large lettered signs further afield. It is better to provide a variety of types of signs and information panels, rather than rely upon a single means of communication. Those who are deaf or hard of hearing should be provided with induction loops to assist hearing aids. At many airports a special

13.12 Signage needs to be clear, to have a sense of information hierarchy, and to be positioned well. North Terminal, Gatwick Airport, UK. Architects: YRM.

information desk is provided to assist such travellers, and (as at Gatwick's South Terminal) this may be equipped with Minicom Supertel telephones.

The term 'disabled traveller' normally covers passengers who:[9]

- use wheelchairs
- are deaf or blind
- are elderly and find walking difficult
- have physical or sensory disabilities that necessitate some special assistance.

However, in designing terminals for disabled passengers, it is important that a broad definition of impairment is adopted. With an ageing population, many travellers have various degrees of restricted mobility, and most would object to being classified as 'disabled passengers'. A simple rule is to provide for the greatest quality and variety of access and information provision, because this will benefit both able and disabled passengers. Hence lifts, escalators, travellators, ramps and stairs of generous dimensions are all needed; signs of various kinds and sizes, and information available in different forms, all help those who use airports. Designers need to cater for the full spectrum of disabilities by providing, on the one hand, Braille facilities at lifts and, on the other hand, signing that takes account of colour blindness. Special seating at queuing points may be required too, because elderly people require more frequent rest.

Disabled access has both a physical and a psychological dimension. Space must be provided for wheelchair users, but – equally important – those with disability do not wish to be given special routes but to be allowed use of the normal flow areas. Segregation of disabled passengers is, except in the worst cases, an undesirable solution. Good design should ensure that corridors and concourses are free of steps, narrow doorways and bottlenecks at shops or control points. At changes in level there should be ramps (maximum rise 1 in 15), escalators and lifts. Doorways should be wide enough for wheelchairs and stretcher trolleys. Special parking bays for disabled use should be provided adjacent to the terminal door. Because many disabled passengers are accompanied by a relative or carer, space sufficient for two people to pass unimpeded should be the norm.

As a matter of course, there needs to be adequate provision of disabled toilets (preferably unisex and with space for helpers), and special low-level check-in desks for wheelchair users. Because dignity is a dimension to the disabled outlook, it is important wherever possible for the disabled passenger to be able to negotiate the journey through the airport without special assistance. Although airline staff may be on hand to provide assistance, many passengers with physical, visual, hearing or speech impairment prefer to remain independent. Where special information desks for disabled passengers are provided, some of these should be unattended and merely self-contained information booths (known as Communicaid II) as at Vancouver International Airport.[10]

References

1. Nick Barrett, 'Retailer made', in Jackie Whitelaw (ed.), *21st Century Airports*, supplement of *New Civil Engineer/New Builder*, May 1995, p. 42.
2. IATA, *Airport Terminals Reference Manual*, 8th edn, International Air Transport Association, Montreal, Canada, 1995, p. 105.
3. Norman Ashford and Paul Wright, *Airport Engineering*, John Wiley & Sons, New York, 1991, p. 304.
4. Barrett, 'Retailer made', p. 43.
5. Rigas Doganis, *The Airport Business*, Routledge, London, 1992, p. 139.
6. *Ibid.*, p. 142.
7. Christopher J. Blow, *Airport Terminals*, 2nd edn, Butterworth-Heinemann, Oxford, 1996, p. 158.
8. IATA, *Airport Terminals Reference Manual*, 7th edn, International Air Transport Association, Montreal, Canada, 1989, p. 3.61.
9. The definition is based upon that of the UK Air Transport Users' Committee, 1992.
10. Christopher J. Blow, *Airport Terminals*, 1st edn, Butterworth-Heinemann, Oxford, 1991, p. 127.

CHAPTER 14

Technical standards

Fire safety and airport design

Airport terminals are hazardous buildings in terms of fire. Their deep plans and enclosed volumes mean that smoke extraction is a priority; the concessionary areas (shops, restaurants and bars) pose high fire risk; the number of people milling around mean that should a fire break out, many will inevitably be affected; and there are often long escape distances. However, terminals are also well-managed places with orderly routes and disciplined people, and because they are mainly open buildings, passengers can readily move away from the seat of a fire. Also, airports have their own on-site fire brigades and well-drilled staff, and should a fire break out the response time is quicker than in conventional situations.

Designing for fire safety consists of:

- determining the relative risk in different areas of the terminal
- establishing likely smoke patterns and spread of fire
- making assumptions about levels of occupancy
- determining the extent of fire containment by compartmentation and the fire loads involved
- using the 'islands' approach to smoke extraction and sprinkler systems
- determining the position of fire alarm and smoke detection systems
- making assumptions about fire brigade and airport staff response times
- determining the likely structural response of the building in the event of a fire.

The traditional method of rigid compartmentation has given way to the 'islands of risk approach', whereby much greater openness is permitted, and smoke extraction is encouraged by interior height. Large internal volumes divided by a combination of fire compartments and smoke extraction and sprinkler systems above the high-risk areas are replacing the earlier emphasis upon compartmentation alone.[1]

Most recent airport buildings have abandoned rigid fire compartmentation, because it tends to obstruct

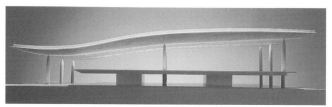

14.1 Openness and height have replaced the gloomy low ceilings of first-generation airports. Oslo Airport, Norway. Architects: Aviaplan AS.

movement essential for the smooth passage of people and baggage from landside to airside. Not only do fire partitions and self-closing doors physically interrupt movement, they also obscure the legibility of routes at a perceptual level. Today terminals tend to be designed on the principle of openness, with islands of greater fire risk (such as shops, bars, seating areas and check-in desks) protected by sprinklers (some using partial foam deluge systems) and smoke extraction hoods. Elsewhere interior volume and building height are encouraged, because smoke can be naturally extracted by windows in the roof, and as smoke not flame is the killer in most fires, large volumes mean that the density and hence the toxicity of smoke is reduced.

Identifying islands of potential hazard and spacing them sufficiently apart to prevent fire spread from one to another is the approach at Kansai.[2] At each high-risk island, containment of the fire by smoke extraction and sprinkler systems is preferred to an approach whereby the whole of the terminal is treated equally. Having identified the fire-risk islands, each is evaluated according to level of hazard, and the choice of materials, sprinkler system and method of smoke extraction modified accordingly. The fire at Frankfurt Airport in 1996 spread because no such island containment policy applied: at Frankfurt, as at most traditional terminals, there was an overall sprinkler and smoke extraction system, which did not discriminate in terms of level of risk.

Because smoke and heat rise in the event of a fire it is possible to modify the ceiling profile to draw toxic chemicals out of the building. Again, the openness and interior transparency at Kansai meant that even in a building of 15 million m³ it was possible to design for fire safety without physical subdivision of the terminal. The design approach, which encourages natural extraction, also supports passenger orientation in the event of a fire. As long as the exits, routes and stairs can be readily comprehended, large open volumes underpin, not inhibit, smoke evacuation in the event of a fire. Identifying risk islands and forming containment around them leads to a new approach to fire engineering. It means, for instance, that minimum distances need to be established between islands; that voids between floors are needed to allow smoke to rise to the roof; and that subsequent changes in the distribution and density of shops, bars and check-in desks need corresponding changes to sprinkler and smoke hood systems.

Many fires are started deliberately, and to avoid opportunities most airport authorities have introduced a policy of avoiding concealment sites. Hence modern terminals tend not to have litter bins, left luggage areas or unlocked cupboards. Preventing an arsonist from starting a fire or a terrorist from planting a bomb, by designing for openness and visibility of all public areas, tends to be the practice today. Where concealment sites are inevitable for other reasons (as in toilet cubicles) their design must seek in the choice of materials the containment of a fire or blast.

As most modern terminals are constructed of structural steelwork, this needs to be protected from fire. The usual standard is for the frame of a terminal to have a fire rating of 1½ hours in public areas and 1 hour in offices. The steelwork needs to be encased (by, for instance, glass-reinforced cement) to a height above floor level of 4 or 5m;

14.2   Visibility, permeability and lofty volumes are a feature of today's terminals. Cologne/Bonn Airport, Germany. Architects: Murphy/Jahn.

the remaining exposed structural steelwork must be painted with intumescent paint; and concealed structure must be lined with dry boarding. While smoke is the main killer for humans, it is flames that do the most damage to the structure of airports. Where risk of flame spread is high (as in baggage areas) there need to be masonry fire walls separating these areas from public concourses.

Lighting

Much has already been said about light as part of the essential architectural experience of terminals, but light is also an important technical consideration. The artificial lighting of terminals is normally the chief source of energy use (exceeding that of heating or cooling), and the means of lighting, the lamp sources used etc. have great impact upon comfort, safety and general ambience. The trend towards greater natural lighting in terminals is a means of saving energy, of reducing the build-up of heat from artificial sources, and of helping with passenger orientation. But the balance in energy use between natural and artificial lighting is complex, and much depends upon local conditions. The heat loss through windows has to be made up by energy released from other sources, and this generally entails fossil fuel. For any

14.3   The cross-section of the terminal is shaped by the needs of fire containment and smoke extraction. Harare Airport, Zimbabwe. Architects: Scott Brownrigg and Turner.

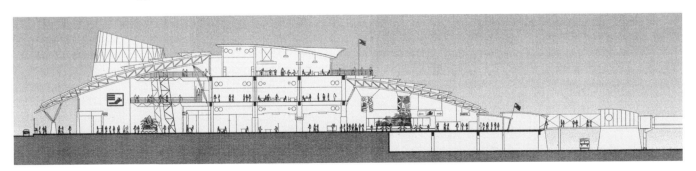

14.4 The external envelope of the terminal has to balance light penetration against solar gain, and the designer needs to alter window design according to orientation. Bangkok Airport, Thailand. Architects: Murphy/Jahn.

given terminal there is an 'optimum glass area which depends on the climate and orientation of glass'.[3] Given that light levels in terminals are normally similar to that in offices (especially where tickets have to be read, and where security is important), designers need to calculate carefully the relationship between window area, orientation and subsequent fabric heat loss.

The working light level in terminals is normally 200 lux, but this standard varies according to the degree of security or tranquillity of space. Such a figure suggests an upper daylight factor of about 4%, which invalidates the totally glazed facade at a stroke. Where large areas of wall or roof glazing are used (as at Stansted or Kansai) it is angled, shaded, screened and treated in a fashion to reduce daylight (and particularly sunlight) penetration. At Stansted, for example, the 11m rooflights over the concourse sit above a perforated metal shade, which reduces the light transmission by 50%.[4]

Few terminals are designed without natural lighting and electric lighting being considered from an architectural point of view in tandem. It is important to maintain a similar pattern of lighting by day and by night so that passenger perceptions of route and volume do not vary. This means that some electric light is used in the day even if not justified by external light levels. A common pattern is to design for a natural lighting daylight factor in concourses of 1 or 2% in combination with electric lighting design of about 500 lux.[5] The result is that while electric lighting overwhelms natural lighting, there is still a sense of 'daylight'. Where daylight alone is used to light concourses, on overcast days the lack of sparkle can make for dull interiors.

The close juxtaposition of natural and artificial sources of light means that the designer can feel confident that the architectural experience remains much the same throughout 24 hours. Again, referring to Stansted, the system uses 400 watt lamps clustered at each structural tree shining upwards so that the light is reflected off the roof adjacent to the skylight.[6] The result is that both natural light through the roof and artificial light are concentrated immediately above the structural tree, giving them visual emphasis within the terminal. Light therefore draws attention to the structural concept, which – being uniformly applied – helps

14.5 Architect's sketches for the component design at Bangkok Airport, Thailand. Architects: Murphy/Jahn.

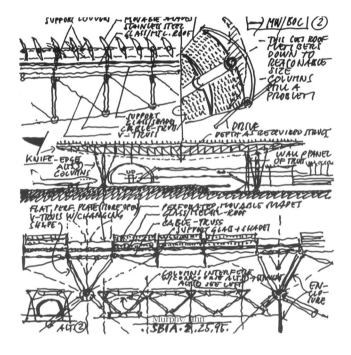

passengers to understand the logic and organization of the building. A similar philosophy prevails at Kansai Airport, where the rooflit canyon (or central street) has artificial light sources concentrated along its length. Because of the crucial question of passenger orientation, it is vital that architectural design and lighting design (both natural and artificial means) share the same approach.

Similar principles apply to wall lighting. A vertical window admits only about 40% of the daylight of a horizontal rooflight, but with a low sun glare can be a problem through windows. Sunlight penetration through vertical windows brings the adjoining interior spaces alive, but direct sunlight can lead to discomfort, especially for people sitting or working directly in its rays. As a result, wall glazing needs to be screened (either externally or internally), or the angle of glass tilted (as proposed at Heathrow Terminal 5) or curved (as at Kansai). As a rule, glare tends to be a problem associated with wall not roof glazing.

A combination of external screening, roof overhangs and surface treatment of the glass can deal effectively with glare while also allowing good levels of daylight penetration. Except for the deepest planned terminals, natural light from wall and roof glazing can be adequate for daylight hours. There is the need, however, to increase general light levels at key points in the building: ticket check-in, baggage areas, passport control and around shops and restaurants. Here the pattern tends to be to intensify light levels by artificial not natural means. So while general concourse areas are mainly naturally lit (and in some cases ventilated) there are pools of brighter electric light and specific task lighting (as at check-in desks). These more brightly lit areas, often located near the centre of the building, lead to high levels of energy use and consequent heat build-up. Lighting and heating design then need to be considered together, with building management systems employed that recycle the heat from lights in cold weather.

Many modern terminals are designed as passive solar buildings: the transparency helps with energy conservation, security of the building itself, and general appearance. But excessive glazing, added to lack of thermal capacity in the fabric, can lead to great heat loss in the winter and heat gain in the summer. Largely glazed terminals, though they save on artificial lighting, lead inevitably to partial or complete air-conditioning (often requiring the use of ozone-damaging CFCs).

Heating

Heating, lighting, the thermal capacity of the terminal, occupancy levels and the transparency of the envelope are related factors. Most terminals of any size rely upon air-conditioning for part or all of the year, and part or all of the building. Most systems use circulating air as the means of heat or cooling distribution. The profile of the building aids the circulation of air: for instance, the undulating and curvaceous forms of Kansai and Heathrow's Terminal 5 are a direct response to air circulation. Typically, air-conditioning circulates cooled air in the summer and warmed air in the winter. Air is normally blown into the concourse spaces horizontally and rises or falls depending upon its temperature. The shape of the space is an important factor in the degree of penetration of the blown air, and the patterns of

14.6 The Futurist imagery of modern airports is based upon the expression of architectural structure, movement and walls of light. Bangkok Airport, Thailand. Architects: Murphy/Jahn.

air movement established. It is not architectural fashion but air-conditioning that determines the curved undulating roof shapes of many recent terminals. The natural curve of a jet of blown air at a set temperature and velocity produces its own distinctive profile. Combining this with structural and spatial geometry leads inevitably to the distinctive new generation of terminals seen today.

Because air rises or falls according to temperature, the angle of discharge of air-conditioning nozzles needs to be capable of adjustment. At Kansai, nozzles positioned immediately beneath the roof distribute air at different angles according to specific need, with air drawn back in via planting boxes on the floor. The angle of nozzles can be adjusted electronically according to the season.

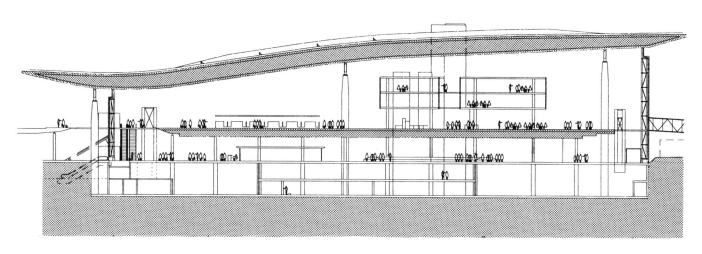

14.7 The profile of roofs is often determined by the flow of air released under pressure at low level and extracted at high level. Oslo Airport, Norway. Architects: Aviaplan AS.

Most airports have macro and micro systems for heating. The former provide background heat (or cooled air) to the whole terminal, the latter to specific areas such as the arrivals walkway. In good building services design the micro installations often use recycled heat from the macro system. Fabric canopies as at Kansai and Denver, are sometimes used to deflect recirculating air or provide solar screening.[7]

Because terminals are lofty structures it is usually possible to exploit the 'stack effect' to encourage natural ventilation and to establish circulating air currents. Also, height means that the level of occupation (the lower 3m zone) can have different characteristics from those of the remainder of the interior volume. Hence it is only really necessary to heat or cool the levels that passengers use; the other spaces can have quite different temperature characteristics. With large volumes it is also possible to exploit the principle of night-time cooling whereby air at say 16°C is circulated through the building at a sufficient rate to cool the fabric, which then maintains an acceptable temperature during the day. Heating systems that rely upon circulating air allow this to happen, and if the equipment is integrated into the structure then it does so with coherence and elegance.[8]

Most terminals rely upon heat extraction systems to recover the heat from extirpated air or water in order to increase the temperature of the fresh air. At Stansted a central refrigeration plant extracts heat from the chilled water to keep it cool and then discharges the heat into a water circulating system at around 40–50°C.[9] This heat is then used for the main air-handling system. During most of the year the heating load can be met by heat extraction, but in particularly cold weather (below 5°C) boilers provide back-up.

Safety and security

The trend in terminal design towards greater transparency and openness is partly the result of increasing concern over airport security. Large glazed malls allow security staff to monitor what is happening both inside and outside the terminal, and the natural light that flows through glazed rather than solid walls improves the effectiveness of CCTV. High levels of natural light give greater definition to the images on security screens and, in particular, allow facial features to be discerned. Designing for maximum transparency is the norm, because it allows police and airport security staff to see everything that is going on.

As designs for airports are being generated, the layouts are subjected to risk analysis by the airport authority and police. Overcoming security risks by good design is a growing aspect of design monitoring prior to construction. While the trend towards greater openness and transparency in terminals is driven partly by passenger wayfinding needs, the avoidance of obstruction or walls behind which terrorists can hide (or place bombs) is of equal importance. Of the six elements that form BAA's Mission Statement, the first is 'safety and security', thereby confirming the highest priority given to this aspect of airport management.

There are three distinct approaches to effective security design: surveillance, space syntax and territoriality.

Surveillance

The effective surveillance of the interior of terminals and key exterior points is crucial in the creation of a safe and secure environment. The airport lounges, shopping areas, toilets and entrance points are particularly at risk, and require surveillance directly by security staff and indirectly via CCTV cameras. Places where cars are allowed to drop off or pick up passengers adjacent to terminals pose special risks, and here management policy towards parking has to be especially vigilant.

Surveillance is most effective in terminals that are spacious and open. Well-placed cameras and patrolling police can monitor behaviour more effectively in such areas. Where physical enclosure is needed (such as around shops, bars and toilets) there needs to be extra surveillance provision, which is often provided by additional cameras placed in strategic locations. Crime prevention and airport security are mutually beneficial concerns, and cameras or security staff can detect either form of anti-social behaviour.

Surveillance is normally undertaken by uniformed security staff, police and plain-clothes detectives, and via conspicuous or hidden cameras. The range of personal and visual monitoring of terminal spaces is aimed at combating many types of crime, from pocket-picking to drug couriers, and from terrorists to baggage thieves. Airport design has a part to play in crime prevention by providing areas, routes and entrances that can be readily overlooked.

Space syntax

This is a measure of the number of people using an area of terminal space at any particular time. Safe places are those that are occupied at an optimum level: under-occupation of space poses a potential threat, as does over-occupation. At levels of over one person per square metre there are dangers, and at under one person per 20m^2 there are also risks. High levels of human density make visual surveillance difficult, and the bumping and colliding of people and trolleys pose a danger from petty thieves as well as from risks of physical injury. Low levels of space occupation, particularly in corridors or smaller spaces, expose passengers to attack, armed robbery or mugging.

Space syntax is not an easy balance to achieve. In large spaces, such as airport lounges, low levels of occupation are restful, but the same density of occupation in more confined spaces (perhaps when there are only two people per length of corridor) can pose a threat. There are age and gender issues involved as well. Female users of terminals feel safer in buildings that are relatively heavily used, and fear unused spaces, especially late at night (perhaps after

14.8 The level of human usage is a factor in giving terminals a sense of security. Overused and underused areas both feel dangerous to vulnerable travellers. North Terminal, Gatwick Airport, UK. Architects: YRM.

14.9 Design that gives passengers a feeling of well-being in busy public areas reflects well upon the airport authorities. Chicago O'Hare Airport, USA. Architects: Group One Design/Perkins & Will.

a delayed flight). Ageing passengers too fear lack of human contact, especially where their reduced mobility may place them behind other passengers.

It is by no means easy to design terminals at optimum levels of space syntax. The erratic pattern of use of airports means that terminal spaces change during the day from being heavily crowded to being sparsely populated. What architects can do, however, is avoid short lengths and dog-legs of passageway, lifts that are rarely used, and remote airport lounges that cannot be seen from public areas. Space syntax is a measure of occupation and the relative distance between points of human density (departure concourse, check-in, etc.). Because well-used airports tend to be safer (and feel safer) than poorly used ones, there is a need for design policy and management of the terminal to be in step.

Space syntax is a useful density guide: it is to do with the characteristics of space and distance between people. Linear space (corridors) has different safety and security characteristics from those of wide space (lounges). People feel safe when there are others nearby, but cease to feel happy when strangers violate their immediate personal space. The level of background noise is also a factor: noisy places mean that cries for help cannot be heard, and hence the safety margins come down.

Territoriality

In the design of terminals, architects should seek to ensure that all the users (including passengers, airline staff and retailers) assume a territorial attitude to the space they are occupying at that moment. This is by no means easy, either psychologically or practically, in a public building. However, if users and stakeholders at terminals assumed a territorial attitude then anti-social behaviour would be challenged, thereby benefiting all. Designing terminals to generate territoriality means using physical and psychological means to define areas of space over which users would exercise certain safety or security rights. For the passenger it may mean grouping seats into small but casual enclosures where several families could exercise control over behaviour. A person here who leaves a bag unattended or drops litter will be either challenged by the group or will feel too embarrassed to undertake such behaviour in the first place. The geometry of the seating arrangement and the presence of planting tubs or tables may help to create this sense of territory.

Retailers too need to take charge of their parcel of terminal space. The design of a shop and the adjacent public area should be such that the shop assistants feel encouraged to challenge anti-social behaviour, to check quickly upon an unattended bag, and to clear rubbish before it poses a fire threat. The way in which shops, restaurants and bars form subterritories within large modern terminals helps with stimulating a sense of safety and security within units of the terminal. In fact, the more distinctive the retail unit is the more effectively it challenges the anonymity and lack of sense of territory in the terminal itself.

The same is true of the space in terminals occupied by airline companies. It is important that staff here exercise a territorial attitude over the space, and that design helps to define the limits of the space. By the use of different colours of carpet, upholstery, distinctive signage and custom-designed furniture, a piece of territorial space can be described and recognized by potential burglars, terrorists and the public at large. Airline staff will not only be able to recognize 'their' space but will feel encouraged to exercise surveillance over it. Those intent upon anti-social behaviour will recognize this and be deterred.

The three main elements of safety and security by design – surveillance, space syntax and territoriality – need to be integrated. Defining territories and subterritories within large terminals is by no means easy, but it is essential. Once territory is defined, opportunities should be provided to exercise physical and electronic surveillance over it, and this to some measure involves ensuring that the space is occupied at optimum levels – not overcrowded or deserted. It is also important through design and management to create a feeling of safety and security: good design is not just a case of preventing crime but of reducing the fear of crime.

In addition to designing for safety and security at a broad level there are a number of specific measures that can be taken according to the perceived level of risk. These include:[10]

- ensuring the physical separation of arriving and departing passengers on airside
- spot checking of security at gate lounges (in addition to centralized security combs of passengers and baggage)
- prohibition of visitors to airside, even with domestic flights
- isolation of piers by fast-acting drop grilles in the event of terrorist activity
- provision of extra space for security checks and dedicated check-in areas for high-risk flights or destinations
- ensuring that airside is security sterile by limiting (or preventing) commercial concessions on the airside
- removal of car parking or set-down adjacent to terminal at times of high terrorist activity

- prohibition of left luggage areas in the terminal
- prohibition of rubbish bins in the terminal
- avoidance of open mezzanine or gallery floors overlooking passenger areas
- closure of observation decks overlooking apron areas and runways
- construction of buildings to include materials that can absorb blast damage.

Because many existing terminals were constructed before terrorism became a problem, much attention has been focused recently upon upgrading security measures. These have led to ad hoc alterations that, although they improve the level of safety, do not usually form comprehensive and well coordinated measures. Older terminals necessarily have to accept poor security, but in new terminals design for safety and security (of people, baggage and buildings) is amongst the highest priorities.

References

1. P. Beever, 'Burning questions', *Architecture Today*, March 1995 (No 56), pp. 45–46.
2. Peter Buchanan, 'Kansai', *The Architectural Review*, November 1994, p. 76.
3. Max Fordham, 'Servicing the spaces', *The Architectural Review*, May 1991, p. 78.
4. *Ibid.*
5. *Ibid.*
6. *Ibid.*, p. 79.
7. Peter Buchanan, 'Services and fire', *The Architectural Review*, November 1994, p. 75.
8. These two words were used by Max Fordham, op. cit., with regard to Stansted Airport.
9. Fordham, 'Servicing the spaces', p. 80.
10. Adapted from Norman Ashford and Paul Wright, *Airport Engineering*, John Wiley & Sons, New York, 1991, p. 292.

CHAPTER 15

Major international airport terminals

Kansai Airport, Osaka, Japan

The new airport at Kansai, designed by the Renzo Piano Building Workshop and opened in 1994, displays with greater authority than any other the emergence of a new generation of airport architecture. The characteristics that make it important are scale, complexity, engineering prowess and technological splendour. Kansai was the first airport of any size to be developed entirely upon a man-made island, to exploit open curvaceous forms in order to reduce ecological impacts, to manipulate light and structure to waymark the passenger routes through the terminal, to give the skin of the buildings the qualities of those of the planes, and to develop a multi-modal transportation centre rather than merely an airport. Conceived in the 1980s, and designed and constructed in the early 1990s, Kansai Airport is generally regarded as the model for the twenty-first century. The imagery is appropriate for the next century: the emphasis upon public transport access to the airport, the efforts devoted to passenger legibility and the approach to environmental design – all signal a new approach to airport development in the widest sense.

Piano's design was engineered by Ove Arup and Partners, and the approach to structure gives the terminal and the ancillary buildings a powerful order. Of all recent airport buildings, Kansai is the closest to one where the architecture of space and light, and the design of structure and constructional details, seem to push at the frontiers of the tectonic experience. Anyone who experiences the passenger terminal at Kansai will be impressed by the fusion of structural and architectural design. The sense of structure evident in the enormous curved beams and braced columns is not a hollow gesture, but is designed to give clarity and order to the terminal. Columns, beams, lattice girders and sweeping lantern lights are guiding elements that direct, deflect and assemble weary passengers. In a passenger terminal 1.6km long (it is claimed to be the longest building in the world) light and structure are the elements that punctuate interior volume and give it meaning. Piano's design rejects neutral space and minimal expression: at Kansai

15.1 The section of Kansai Airport terminal is clearly influenced by the aeroplanes themselves. Kansai Airport, Osaka, Japan. Architects: Renzo Piano Building Workshop.

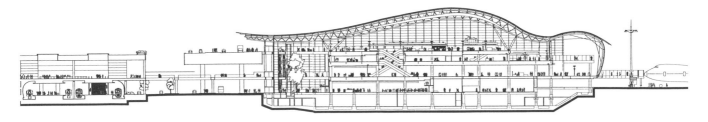

the approach to design is one of animating the key routes through the terminal with a different form of structural and spatial articulation at each zone, employed to suggest hierarchies of use.

If one examines the plan and section of the airport the correspondence between form, function and meaning becomes evident. The design splits into four related parts, each subscribing to the same geometric and structural logic. The first, and most dominant, is the terminal itself; the second is the long airside boarding wing; the third is the railway station; and the fourth is the multi-storey car parks. The composition has a strict order – rationalism tempered by processional clarity, especially in the routes from car parks and station to terminal and thence to the boarding wing. The axis of movement, interrupted at various points by roads, concourses and a massive public canyon at the landside of the terminal, merely defines stages in the passengers' journey. For a building of such dimensions and level of use (25 million passengers a year) there is a remarkable sense of direction. This derives in part from the orderly nature of the plan and the way in which different spaces have been fashioned in distinctive ways. For example, the public canyon is solid and earthy – its colours and monumentality refer to traditional loadbearing architecture – while the departures lounge and airside wing are lightweight and expressive of high technology with distinct aeronautical overtones.

Part of Kansai's clarity derives from the handling of the cross-section of the airport. The terminal has an undulating roof, whose wave-like profile rises and falls to reflect the importance of the accommodation inside. This symbolism is needed because the terminal departs from the orthodox pattern of separating international from domestic movements into separate terminals. Instead, a single building

handles all flights, with the organizational complexity handled not by separate buildings but by using four different floor levels in the terminal, and by lateral zoning of the long airside boarding and arrivals wing. To help resolve the confusion that the use of a single multifunctional terminal entails, the design places particular emphasis on a large lofty public concourse known at Kansai as the 'canyon'. With the proportions of a four-storey city street, the ochre-coloured canyon is a magnificent thoroughfare nearly 250m long. All passengers have to cross the canyon, and most do so at high level via first-floor bridges, which serve mainly those arriving on domestic flights, and at third-floor level for those departing. At ground-floor level the canyon is crossed by international arrivals who experience this spectacular space immediately after customs clearance. It is a worthy gateway to a nation.

The canyon is a public street within the airport, but it is not a shopping mall. It serves mainly as a means to give passengers a sense of place within a building type noted for placelessness. The canyon organizes people and airport functions; it provides information; and it is a location for 'meeters and greeters' to join up. Shopping and business suites are provided on decks partly overlooking the canyon and partly in the body of the terminal beneath the undulating roof.

At the airside, the terminal has another grand lofty space known as the 'departures lounge'. Whereas the canyon is urban, vertical and rectangular in quality, the departure lounge is wide and rounded, and has detailing that evokes that of the aircraft outside on the apron. Also, while the canyon is mainly rooflit, the lounge is lit by curved windows, which look out across the runways and downwards to the aircraft being prepared for take-off. The different

15.3 The section of Terminal 1 at Charles de Gaulle Airport resembles a flying saucer. Architects: Paul Andreu, Aéroports de Paris.

island, and lateral movement, which occurs in earthquakes. Rather than design a single connected structure, Ove Arup and Partners chose a double loosely tied structure where pin-joints rather than rigid connection predominate. This allows[2] for beam movements of 0.5m and landside glazing movement of 150m.

Ecology is the inspiration for the strategy behind the air-conditioning, the landscaping of the 4.37 by 1.25km man-made island, and the incorporation of planting into the terminal. The basic shape of the building derives from

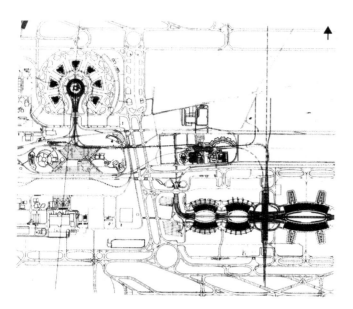

15.4 Geometric clarity and grand gestures are features of French airports. Charles de Gaulle Airport, masterplan. Architects: Paul Andreu, Aéroports de Paris.

nature's own profiling of shapes into undulating sand-dunes at the ocean edge. The Building Workshop sought in its initial investigation of the design that of 'technology emulating, and in harmony, with nature'.[3] This is most evident in the relationship of the roof profile to the 'natural curve of a jet of air blown into the departures hall from the land side'.[4] By adjusting the building profile to the natural flow of air currents, there is no need to provide suspended ducts, which disfigure rectangular, flat-roofed terminals. The approach to air-conditioning (and to smoke venting) alludes to conditions outdoors rather than indoors, just as the masterplan seeks to create an island forest rather than merely rows of trees, and in the terminal itself a sense of a winter garden. There are limits to working with nature, though the design pushes at these frontiers to the benefit of later terminal designs such as Heathrow's Terminal 5 by Richard Rogers. At Kansai the ecologically inspired macro-system of natural ventilation is tempered locally by micro-systems that heat or cool specific locations by more conventional means.

Although Kansai was a team effort, involving principally the Renzo Piano Building Workshop, Ove Arup and Partners and the local practice of Nikken Sekkei, the airport is a considerable achievement and displays remarkable consistency. It is one of the greatest engineering feats of the modern age, yet in the principles adopted it points towards a new contract between man and nature. At a fundamental level, the airport at Kansai begins to respond, protect and add to local ecosystems: it seeks a harmonious relationship with the ocean, climate and vegetation of this part of Asia. That the airport, arguably the least sustainable of all modern urban structures, should try to emulate natural systems is perhaps Kansai's main claim to be a precursor for the design of terminals into the next century.

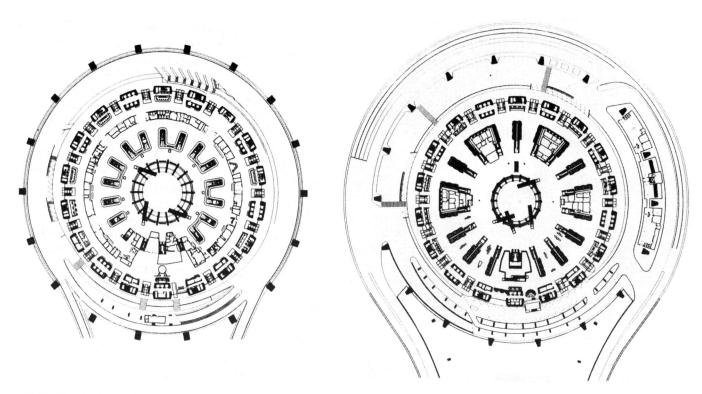

15.5 Circular forms give close proximity to aircraft, but they can be disconcerting. Terminal 1, Charles de Gaulle Airport, France. Architects: Paul Andreu, Aéroports de Paris.

Charles de Gaulle Airport, Paris, France

Unlike London Heathrow with its four terminals and New York's John F. Kennedy with nine terminals, Charles de Gaulle Airport, north of Paris, has only two terminals. The first, constructed in 1974, is a grand circular building in the French Rationalist tradition; the second (near completion) is linear in form, with flattened linked terminals placed on either side of a new railway station. Charles de Gaulle handles less than half the passengers that Heathrow handles, and yet the architecture and scale of public transport facilities are more generous in spirit. Both Terminals 1 and 2 were designed by Paul Andreu, who has become one of the world's leading architectural consultants on airport design, and who played a major part in shaping the design philosophy at Kansai Airport.[5]

Terminal 1 adopts the circle as an organizing principle (just as Nicholas Grimshaw did at the Venice Biennale exhibition design, described later in this chapter). It is a hollow-centred circle, heroic in form, with a scale and geometric clarity befitting the airport age. The movement systems revolve around the central core, which is criss-crossed by elevators and transparent passenger tubes. There are five main levels, each similar in plan, with offices or control points forming a ring outside the circular concourse areas. The arrivals lounge is on level 5, the departures lounge on level 3, shopping on level 2, and (though abandoned for security reasons) car parking on the roof. Outside these, circular roads and ramps revolve within a perimeter structural system of great concrete columns, which fork as they rise.

The imagery is powerful and sculptural. From the outside the circular concrete drum recalls a flying saucer (especially

15.6 Elegant conception in Terminal 2 (left) and proposed third terminal (right) astride Roissy Station (centre). Charles de Gaulle Airport, France. Architects: Paul Andreu, Aéroports de Paris.

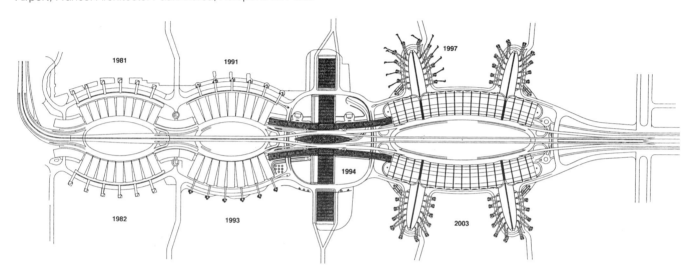

with its angled walls); from the inside there is a sense of space and grandeur. In its way Terminal 1 gives air travel an appropriate sense of drama and futurist imagery, but the concept is flawed from two perspectives. First, because the terminal is circular it has not proved easy to extend, and second, because each floor is much like the one above or below, it is difficult to gain a sense of relative level or direction. The attempted reconciliation of linear progression within a circular form undermines the clarity of the design. Terminals are necessarily a progression through ticket controls and security checks, and when these are placed in a centralized circular megastructure the functional organization and plan form begin to disconnect. However, the circular form does mean that passengers can gain access to aircraft more directly than in linear terminals, and close proximity to aircraft (which are parked on the apron almost immediately outside the circumference of the terminal) does give passengers interesting airport views.

Terminal 1 is based upon the dual concepts of close proximity to aircraft and dense mixed-use terminal design.[6] Andreu developed the idea from the perspective of reducing the time taken to pass through the terminal by simply reducing travel distances. Close interaction with the aircraft before boarding is said to enhance the anticipation of air travel, and the compression of activities in the terminal

adds to the sense of excitement. In many fundamental ways the design is opposed to current o.rthodoxy with its emphasis upon clarity of route, avoidance of cross-flowrws, juxtaposition of lounges and retail floors, and the emphasis now placed upon security.

Entry from the terminal to the aircraft is via seven satellites, which are arranged with geometric regularity around the circular building. Again, just as the circular terminal does not give a sense of direction, so too with the satellites, which are themselves five-sided structures of identical form. Rationalist and heroic in inspiration, Terminal 1 seems to have abandoned the human dimension, favouring instead the grand scale of modern aircraft and the abstract, placeless geometries of airport masterplans.

Terminal 1 adopts a distinctive, rather French approach to airport design. The powerful circular imagery of the design, especially the use of rough brutal concrete inside and out, sets the terminal outside the framework of taste fashioned by more cautious clients (such as BAA). Yet there are lessons in the design: Terminal 1 approaches airport design from the precept of the values of the city, not those of the airport. The building is a great dense mixed-use chamber with a lofty atrium in the centre. Building structure and services are not concealed behind suspended and false walls (as in many terminals) but exposed to view. In

15.7   Model of Hong Kong's new airport at Chek Lap Kok. Architects: Foster and Partners.

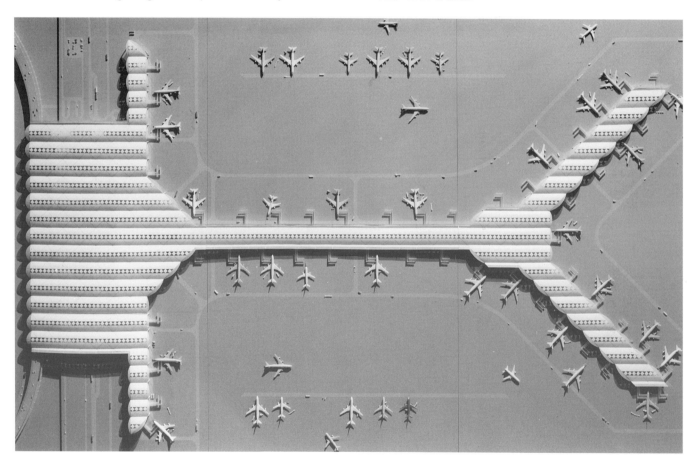

fact, architectural structure is the main means by which scale is imparted and direction imposed.

Terminal 2 can be seen as an adjustment to Terminal 1. It shares a sense of geometric order and heroic uncompromising scale, but now the circular shape is compressed into three flattened ellipses. Each is essentially a linear progression, with an axis placed at right angles to that of the underground TGV railway line. Where the two axes intersect, a great circular railway station (known as Roissy) is placed, with a hotel built as a bridge above the station roof. Hence the dense vertical integration of activities at Terminal 1 is replaced by low horizontal spread at Terminal 2. Also, while Terminal 1 is a shared facility between airline

companies, Terminal 2 is dedicated almost entirely to Air France. With an expected capacity of 20 million passengers a year (as against 10 million at Terminal 1), the design has evolved on the basis of modular linear expansion. The three linked subterminals of the present design can readily be extended in either direction, and should Air France contract, the separate subterminals could each be managed by a different airline.

Terminal 2 is closer in spirit to practice elsewhere. The integration laterally of airport terminal, railway station and other land uses (e.g. hotel) recalls the pattern at, say, Kansai, and the disaggregation of the terminal into linear parts is not unlike American unit terminals. Perhaps the

15.8 Section through concourse at Hong Kong's new airport at Chek Lap Kok. Notice the typological distinction between function elements (gate spine to left, concourse centre and car park and roads to right). Architects: Foster and Partners.

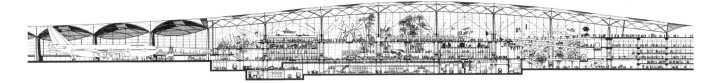

most important lesson of Charles de Gaulle Airport is the need to maintain clarity in the masterplan – both spatial and organizational – and then to express this in powerful architectural forms: for airport architecture is about giving the airport environment a sense of place and uplifting the spirit of those who travel by air.[7]

Hong Kong's new airport at Chek Lap Kok

The new airport on the man-made Chek Lap Kok island in Hong Kong Bay is the centrepiece of a large infrastructure project involving also new railways, roads, bridges and causeways. The airport, intended to meet Hong Kong's economic needs into the twenty-first century, is planned to cater for 35 million passengers a year when the airport opens in 1997, growing to 87 million in 2040.

Designed by Sir Norman Foster and Partners, the concept extends the architectural language of Stansted, but now translated into a much grander multilevel terminal. Unlike Stansted, the roof is a gentle arch, and at Chek Lap Kok the satellites are united with the main terminal by lengthy gate spines served by both pedestrian and light rail movements. In plan the design recalls the footprint of a primitive aeroplane, with angled wings, a tailpiece and fuselage. Here however the analogy ends, for in section and detail the design speaks the language of transport architecture, not flight.

The main terminal concourse consists of three main levels – baggage handling on ground, arrivals on first, and departures on second floor – and extends beneath a wide gentle arch from a five-storey car park on landside to satellite piers and waiting aircraft on airside. Structural design (by Ove Arup and Partners) inevitably plays a large part in determining the character and quality of the terminal. Such are the dimensions of the terminal (it will be the size of

John F. Kennedy at New York and London Heathrow Terminal 5 put together) that the spacing of columns and the grid of roof beams have a primary role in articulating interior space and making it understandable to travellers. Over 4 million ft^2 (40 000m^2) of terminal will be enclosed by the delicate curvaceous roof, and according to Foster's office the baggage hall beneath will be the size of Wembley Stadium. With interior volumes on this scale, structure is more than an exercise in supporting floors and roofs: it is the main means by which directional legibility and internal order are provided.

The design and brief have been developed with BAA International (also the client body at Shenzhen Airport in China), who have had a long-standing relationship with both architect and engineer. BAA, having successfully undertaken airport expansion in the UK, has recently taken its expertise in project management, site feasibility and cost control to other parts of the world, often employing UK designers and engineers in the process. The new terminal at Hong Kong also reflects the changing function of airports. Besides handing passengers, the airport is also expected to store and re-transit over 1.3 million tonnes of cargo a year, and within the terminal itself about 10% of the floor area is given over to business and conference facilities. No longer can terminals be viewed as a singular activity: they inevitably engage in the social and business life of the city they serve.

Foster's Hong Kong office, established to produce the 30 000 contract drawings needed to bring the terminal to fruition, has paid considerable attention to the standardization of parts. Elements of construction have been designed to avoid variation, and (in tune with BAA ethos) the design has matured in collaboration with component manufacturers and suppliers. This inevitably has given Chek Lap Kok an air of repetitive order, especially in the design

15.9 Roof design at Chek Lap Kok, Hong Kong. Unlike the roof at Stansted, here Foster and Partners' design alludes to the direction of movement and aircraft imagery.

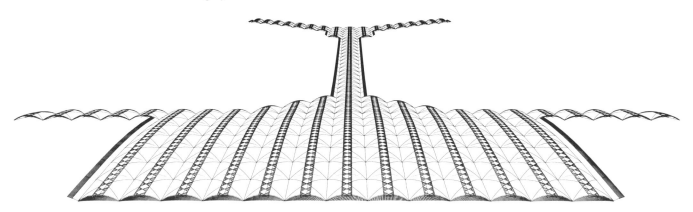

of roof elements and principal facades. A major 36m square structural grid breaks progressively down into 12m and 9m planning grids, which lead in turn to component and partition grids of 1500mm. The hierarchy of grids from structural frames to constructional units allows components, assemblies and panels to be produced relatively economically. The sense of a rectangular order in plan and refined curved forms in section provide a robust discipline throughout both terminal and satellite areas. In this sense the design is a logical development of the precedent of Stansted, confirming that terminal's continuing relevance to airport architecture.

Airport Design: Fifth International Biennale of Architecture, Venice 1991

As a generic design proposal, that by Nicholas Grimshaw & Partners for an international airport at the Venice Biennale of 1991 has had influence on the development of ideas surrounding terminal design. Grimshaw's design consisted of an integrated airport and railway station based upon an oval plan. The relative simplicity of the spatial geometry, which involved only two radii, and the clarity of the routes through the proposed terminal made the building memorable as an architectural concept when exhibited at the Biennale. *Its influence* is perhaps to be seen as far apart as Richard Rogers' competition entry for Heathrow's Terminal 5 and Aviaplan's design for Oslo Airport. Both extend the language of huge-scale muscular-framed pylons

with extensive internal landscaping between elements of the building, and plenty of daylight flooding through breaks or folds in the roof.

Grimshaw's terminal design was also one of the first to be conceived deliberately as a landmark structure within the openness of a typical international airport. The oval footprint and the elegantly curved roof created a sense that the terminal was the focal point architecturally within the vast collection of buildings that constitute the modern airport. From the outside the terminal consisted of an elliptical bubble of translucent roofs traversed by great deep lattices supported by angled columns. The building was nearly all roof, which swept down like the petals of an enormous flower, each fold or segment separately expressed. From the inside of the terminal, the experience would have been akin to walking through a giant doughnut with a great elliptical glazed atrium in the centre. This space, filled with forest-sized trees, marked the barrier between arrivals and departures, celebrating the transition with rare aplomb.

The exaggerated attention given in the design to questions of light, planting, directional understanding and architectural space signalled a new direction in 1991 for airport design. Hitherto (Stansted is a good example) terminals were conceived as elegant but rational structures: large flexible boxes able to accommodate changes in airport planning without being compromised by excessive architectural ambition. Grimshaw's design turned such concepts on their head; the role of design was now to exert a presence, to give legibility to users confused by the changes of level and direction of a typical airport, to uplift the spirit, and to provide a celebratory gateway to the country that the airport served. Instead of a flat-roofed, Cartesian conception, Grimshaw provided at the Venice Biennale a modern cathedral of flight.

The section is a simple one: all the services and facilities needed are placed in a great market hall, mainly at one level. Trains deliver passengers to this deck, who process through check-in, restaurants, shops etc., all at the same level (with obvious advantage for disabled passengers). The central atrium is a giant green space to overlook from cafes and galleries around its edge, rather in the way that houses face onto a leafy square in central London. The trees, earth banks and shrubs located here are not designed to be entered but to be looked upon. Hence landscape and nature are used to relieve the stress of modern airline travel, not to screen an offensive object. Baggage is handled beneath the main deck, where air-conditioning equipment is also housed. Fresh air, admitted at low level, is drawn through the terminal by the thermal currents generated by people and equipment. It is extracted at roof level through vents that also provide smoke extraction in the event of a fire. With similar economy, the air intake points at lower level double up as fire escapes in an emergency.

The physics of air movement supports the oval-shaped terminal plan and the curved section. It combines also to create an architectural space that gives presence and dignity to mass modern air travel. The concept design is based upon an anticipated aircraft movement every two minutes (or up to 14 000 passengers per hour), with 68 parking stands for aircraft ranging from 120 to 800 seats in size. This approximates to 30 million passenger movements a year, roughly the capacity of Terminal 5.

The terminal and piers are physically separated: passengers travel between the two on underground railways in the fashion of Stansted. The piers (or airbridges as the design calls them) are detached structures laid out as two parallel arms crossing the airport apron. Trains running every two or three minutes would each carry 150 passengers to the different aircraft gates along each pier.

Inevitably, Grimshaw's concept design at the Venice Biennale and his competition entry for the design of Heathrow's Terminal 5 have much in common. Although the arrangement of piers changed, there is little difference in fundamental thinking. Both designs feature a large central glazed space – essential for orientation and the creation of interior scale. In both too the expression of massive structural members is the primary aesthetic element, and in each design curvaceous volumes and daylight suppress the tendency of commercial activity to reduce internal spaces to second-rate shopping malls. Although the practice has yet to construct a major new airport, the ideas put about in exhibition and competition entry have helped shape the thinking of others.

Terminal 5, Heathrow, London

Terminal 5 at Heathrow promises to take one step further the new approach to airport design witnessed already at Stansted and Kansai. If the proposals by the Richard Rogers Partnership emerge relatively unaltered, the new terminal will on completion in 2003 confirm the arrival of a fresh generation of airport architecture. Whereas the first wave of airport terminals were largely characterless, orthogonal, poorly lit and often labyrinthine structures, more recent terminals – of which the embryonic design for Terminal 5 is a prime example – exploit natural light, spaciousness and curvaceous forms to reduce the stress of air travel, and to provide greater clarity of route. The design commission, awarded to Rogers in a limited competition in 1991, which included Renzo Piano and Michael Manser as assessors, also represents a move towards combating the trend whereby terminals look the same the world over.

Terminal 5 combines two principal technical elements – new rapid baggage handling and assisted people-movement systems – with the design of space and structure, which draws upon a combination of ecological and urban metaphors. The rationality of movement is tempered by great tranquil spaces, where the variegations of light, shade, solid and void are meant to recall the pattern of streets and parks in a city. The juxtaposition of invisible mechanical systems, which move baggage with unprecedented

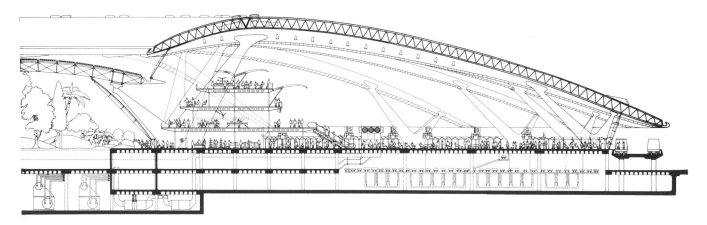

15.10 Proposal by Nicholas Grimshaw & Partners for Terminal 5 at Heathrow based upon the design for an international airport exhibited at the Venice Biennale in 1991.

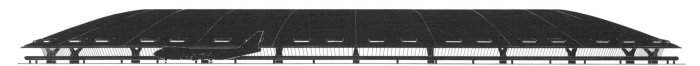

15.11 Elevation of Grimshaw's design for Terminal 5. The concept owes something to Andreu's circular forms employed at Charles de Gaulle Airport, though here modified by the need for natural ventilation and greenery.

speed and efficiency, with sensuous tent-like shelters and almost floating ceilings supported by branching columns gives Terminal 5 an altogether different character from Heathrow's earlier buildings. The patterns of light, structure and diaphanous material are intended by the architects to give passengers a 'positive memorable experience'.[8]

In some regards Terminal 5 represents a new appreciation of the commercial value of good design on behalf of BAA. The brief instructed Richard Rogers' office to develop a design that was unmistakably of the UK, and which would act as a prestigious front door to the country. Coordinated by Raymond Turner, BAA's design director, the building will fail, he claims, if it is not an exceptional experience for the passenger and fails to promote the customer-oriented ethos of BAA.[9] In order to help integrate the different buildings and structures into a coherent whole, the brief required that all the principal buildings (T5 is more than a single

terminal) should share a common architectural style, with the Rogers' office being 'the guardian of design principles'.[10] According to the BAA, the quality of the environment is the main means by which customer perceptions are shaped. Large spaces beneath an undulating and unfolding roof, plenty of natural light, and a structural system that is reminiscent of trees in a park achieve a distinctiveness that may help to set Terminal 5 apart from other major world airport terminals.

The building is rectangular in plan and, like Stansted, extends a bay of roof outwards to protect the landside approach road and the airside access jetties. Hence - passengers are sheltered at the car and bus drop-off point on one side of the terminal and at the point where planes are boarded on the other. The sheltering roofs are not canopies attached to the side of the building but part of a single undulating roof, which rises and falls to mirror the

157

15.12 The Richard Rogers Partnership design for Terminal 5 at Heathrow uses technology as a metaphor for contemporary culture. In its absorption of ecological principles the design strikes a new balance between the airport and nature.

activities inside the terminal. At its highest point the roof glides over six-storey interior spaces created by three linear ridges of retail and office accommodation. The sequence of atria and accommodation islands helps to define the functional progression through the terminal. The principal public areas, marked by lofty atria, contain the four main concourses: assembly and check-in; shopping; customs and departures; and airside aisle.

The progression through the building is steered by natural light: successive bands of daylight signal the next stage in

the journey through the terminal. Immediately beneath each line of rooflights stand the branched columns that support the roof. Consequently, the columns and their radiating arms are picked out in light, adding a further element to passenger orientation. Two types of natural light are employed: direct light, which enters the centre of the building, and a softer, diffused light, which filters through the complex roof structure.[11] Because artificial light is the principal element of bought-in energy (accounting for about 40% of building running costs), the design seeks to optimise natural sources.

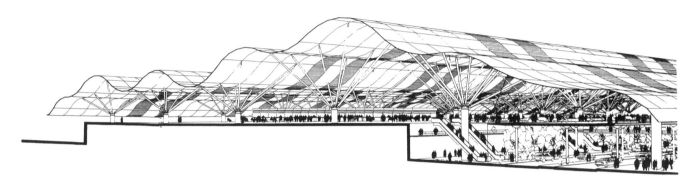

15.13 Sectional perspective of Heathrow Terminal 5. Architects: Richard Rogers Partnership.

Roof glazing allows daylight penetration into the core of the building, where major offices (for airline, customs and immigration staff) and concourses (duty-free shopping etc.) are located. The undulating roof is also intended to reduce (by deflection) light spillage into the night sky: a potential hazard for pilots and a source of community annoyance.

Terminal 5 owes its geometric simplicity and structural elegance to the precedent set by Stansted, yet it takes Stansted's tree-like columns and islands of rooflights a step further forward. The undulating roof gives interest and direction, whereas Stansted's flat ceilings are without a sense of hierarchy or progression. While Terminal 5 and Stansted may share similarities in plan and structural arrangement, the cross-sections of the two buildings are quite different. Terminal 5 is a multilevel terminal with departures above arrivals in the traditional arrangement, but split to allow diagonal daylight penetration. A central bank of elevated shops and bars allows the baggage reclaim hall to flow beneath, and gives justification for the roof to rise in the middle. The irregular elevation given to the roof not only enlivens the building from the outside (particularly, one anticipates, with views from the air); it also gives meaning to the interior progression inside. In this respect it is a hybrid between the exuberant, structurally muscular Kansai Airport and the neutral yet refined flat-roofed Englishness of Foster's design at Stansted.

The roof is a major defining element in the design. Its wave-like form extends the precedent of Kansai in two important ways. Whereas Renzo Piano's roof has a double asymmetrical shallow and abrupt curve, the design of Terminal 5 consists of five symmetrical waves of varying height. The effect is not one of a single wave but of a series of ripples peaked in the centre. The other significant departure from Kansai concerns the construction of the roof. Kansai is beefy and vigorous in its structure and detail, with several layers of roof construction each individually expressed. Rogers' roof design is 'a single-layer skin', which passengers perceive as a delicate cover that is supple and that shapes the space.[12] It is free of services, so that the elegance of the structure is not compromised. Again, following the example of Stansted, the height of the roof allows smoke venting by natural means. In some ways the architecture of Terminal 5 is softer than in many recent airports, and its engineering is understated and poetic rather than posturing. This is to achieve what John Young (a partner in Rogers' office) describes as an 'ambience of calm and visual clarity'.[13]

Some principles of the construction have already been fixed. To speed site operations it has been decided to use steel for the superstructure, concrete on pad (not pile) foundations for the substructure, and lightweight cladding. With little space for the storage of materials on site, and complex beneath-ground conditions (because of airport services, underground railways etc.), the need to reduce weight and maximize prefabrication has emerged as an important discipline. The building will not be air-conditioned throughout its area or throughout the day. The intention is to use mixed-mode ventilation maximizing the thermal

15.14 Bands of light penetrate the roof of Heathrow Terminal 5, which rises and falls in response to the accommodation inside. Architects: Richard Rogers Partnership.

currents inside, which flow from the interesting roof shape. Natural light, and ventilation are all part of the environmental strategy, aimed not just at energy conservation but at the health and psychological welfare of workers and passengers.

The design combines the detached satellite terminal arrangement with the idea of a core terminal served directly by aircraft parked on the apron. It dispenses with long elevated piers, preferring to use instead relatively short lengths of underground passageways with travellators and rapid transit systems. These serve the two independent satellite terminals (a third one is planned for the future) but access from the extended Picadilly Line and Heathrow Express stations is possible only via the main terminal. The arrangement allows aircraft to park close to the buildings in a 'toastrack' plan, thereby maximizing apron and taxiing areas. The compact layout also reduces travel distances for passengers, and provides ease of transportation

160

15.15 Direction of progress indicated by light and roof undulation. Architects: Richard Rogers Partnership.

interchange. The satellite buildings (or mini-terminals) are designed as smaller versions of the core terminal. They share its folded curved roofs, which allow light to penetrate to the centre. The simple repetitive plan form repeats the arrangement elsewhere, though there is less need to orientate the passenger where proximity to views outwards across the airport runways suffices.

It is evident that in the design of Terminal 5 effort has been made to learn from earlier airport designs – mainly Kansai, Stansted and Stuttgart. The BAA's policy of prototype development, evaluation and subsequent refinement allows the sources and influences at Terminal 5 to be identified. However, the design promises to have that sense of occasion that Rogers rightly identifies as a feature of great nineteenth century railway stations[14]. Both architect and client share

an ambition to create a 'light, airy, stress-free environment' in what is rather more a massive passenger transport interchange than merely a terminal building in the traditional sense. As with Victorian railway termini, the engineer has played a large part in shaping the architecture as well as the structural design of the building. Inevitably, Ove Arup and Partners have been the engineering collaborators working with Rogers' office since their commission in 1991, just as they did earlier with Foster at Stansted and Piano at Kansai.

When Terminal 5 is completed in 2004 it will handle 30 million passengers a year, nearly half of Heathrow's predicted total at that time. This compares with 90–100 million expected at Seoul Airport by 2000 (whose principal terminal is being designed by Terry Farrell and Partners), 25 million at

15.16 The proposed new airport at Bangkok is evidence that tectonic architecture and regional traditions can be reconciled. Architects: Murphy/Jahn.

Kansai, and 10 million at Stansted. With such numbers, architecture is the main vehicle available to uplift the spirits and provide a spectacle in the tradition of the great stations of the past. Light appears, from the published plans, to be the key to the architectural experience and the means of navigating such a complex, multi-level building. Light and hierarchies of space are also used to define the major processional routes through the terminal. Because natural light is exploited to the full, problems of glare and solar gain have had to be overcome using louvres, angled walls and eaves overhangs. The expressed environmental controls provide a measure of complexity and detailed richness to the design, especially theprovision of fabric canopies so conspicuous in the published interior views. Angled walls, required to reduce solar gain, have the advantage also of reducing radar reflectivity.

The passenger needs of comfort, stress-free travel, legibility and excitement, which were BAA's prime concerns, have been translated into an elegant design. As Turner notes, Terminal 5 represents an 'inside out' approach to design.[15] It is not a classical modernist pavilion in a verdant park (the model of Stansted), but a building shaped by environmental factors, site planning factors, the need for passenger orientation, and current thought on the relationship between architectural quality and corporate mission. That BAA should value design as a marketing tool and a means of promoting company loyalty represents a departure from earlier practice in the 1960s and 1970s. Though the design

of Terminal 5 is by no means fixed, and will have to adjust to planning conditions that flow from the current (in 1996) public inquiry, there is an elegant robustness to what Rogers' office calls a 'seamless unity of space, structure and natural light'.[16]

New procurement guidelines for Terminal 5

Besides the new design approaches outlined, Terminal 5 is the first major UK airport to be evolved within BAA's construction, procurement and project management guidelines of 1995 (see Chapter 7). The architects and engineers have generated the design within a kit of parts that, once developed and tested, will be manufactured with life-cycle quality, ease of assembly and replaceability in mind. Prefabrication and standardization are key concepts: both are considered essential in cost control, in speed of construction and in terms of reliability. Added to this, many products (because of site access and storage constraints) will be flown in, thereby exposing UK suppliers to international competition – another BAA tenet.

Prefabrication limits the freedom of design but, as Rogers notes, 'good architecture is about rhythm and continuity',[17] both of which stem from a limited palette of components. At an estimated cost of £1.25 billion, the role of the architect is seen by BAA as primarily that of ensuring 'value for money', with the philosophy of value engineering providing the discipline to judge design decisions against

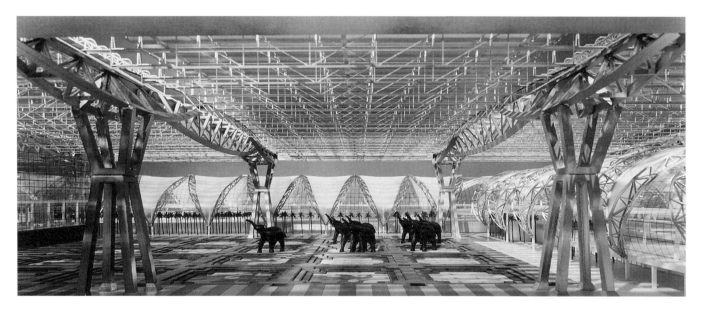

15.17 The central concourse at Bangkok Airport is intended as a great gathering place, not unlike the booking halls of nineteenth-century railway stations. Architects: Murphy/Jahn.

measurable benefits. In fact the airport authority intends to construct Terminal 5 at a cost of £1000 per m² as against the usual £1600 per m². Davies (of Rogers' office) had some trepidation initially, and still thinks the design team should at times have taken a firmer line, but he concedes that defending the integrity of the scheme is not undermined by questions of value for money. The aim is to have 50% of the detailed design completed before construction starts, with 'framework agreements' providing the basis for fine tuning on site.[18]

Second Bangkok International Airport, Thailand

The new Bangkok International Airport will be built on a large vacant site outside Bangkok, and is due to open in 1998. Designed by Murphy/Jahn to cater for 30 million passengers a year, the concept places emphasis upon passenger rather than aircraft movement. With an expected flow per hour of 5000 international and 2000 domestic passengers, there are to be 50 gates arranged alongside a lengthy U-shaped terminal with two main landside entrances (domestic and international).

The terminal will have an area of 0.5 million m², and is broken down into separate parts in order to provide relief and legibility. The concept is simple: a series of large modular terminals, each served by wings of airside corridor with aircraft gates on either side. The main terminal sits beneath a giant roof trellis, which unifies the various elements and provides shelter from solar radiation. The trellis is constructed of steel and concrete, and arches over the access road on landside and a courtyard of palm groves on airside.

The terminal itself is curved with full-height windows, providing views across the apron area. These enormous triangular openings also provide the spatial framework for aircraft gates and the adjoining gate lounges.

Murphy/Jahn have developed a particular tectonic language for their terminals. Here, they suspend the ticketing area from the structural trellis, and exploit the visual dynamics of the interpenetration of the tubular concourses with rectangular and cylindrical rotundas. The result is a design of great structural daring and interesting arrangements for the introduction of natural lighting into the core of the building.

The internal arrangement in the terminal, with its curved lattice beams and stretched rounded roof, is complemented by the approach to the design of the outdoor spaces. These are seen as landscaped courtyards with trees, sculpture and pavement patterns. Because they are the first areas of Thailand seen by arriving passengers, there are cultural artefacts such as sculpted elephants placed amongst the planting. Hence the high-tech architectural language of the terminal itself is counter-balanced by traditional features in the spaces between the buildings, just as in the design for the new Seoul International Airport the tempering of modernity by tradition is seen as important in giving the new generation of airports a sense of place.

References

1. Peter Buchanan, 'Kansai', *The Architectural Review*, November 1994, p. 68.
2. *Ibid.*
3. *Ibid.*, p. 46.
4. *Ibid.*, p. 74.
5. Dan Cruikshank, 'Charles de Gaulle Airport, Paris, 1967–1996', *RIBA Journal*, January 1996, p. 41.
6. *Ibid.*, p. 43.
7. The argument is made by Serge Salat and Francoise Labbe, *Paul Andreu*: *Between Silence and Light*, Hachette, Hong Kong, 1990.
8. Josephine Smit & Antony Oliver, 'Time for T5', in Jackie Whitelaw (ed.), *21st Century Airports*, supplement of *New Civil Engineer/New Builder,* May 1995, p. 10.
9. *Ibid*.
10. *Note for the Inquiry* (Terminal 5), BAA/1786, 14 February 1996, p. 11.
11. *Ibid*., p.12.
12. Smit and Oliver, 'Time for T5', p.14.
13. *The Architects' Journal,* 27 June 1996, p. 8.
14. Smit and Oliver, 'Time for T5', p. 12.
15. *Ibid.,* p. 14.
16. *The Architects' Journal,* 27 June 1996, p. 9.
17. Smit and Oliver, 'Time for T5', p. 14.
18. Barrie Evans, 'Integrating project teams', *The Architects' Journal*, 17 October 1996, p. 40.

National airport terminals   CHAPTER

16

Stansted Airport, UK

Stansted Airport has two particular interests for the terminal designer: it is essentially a single-level building (contrary to the orthodoxy outlined in Chapter 11), and the evenly spaced grid of columns does not gesture to the direction of passenger flow. Sir Norman Foster's concept design, evolved between 1982 and 1984, was based upon the idea of an elegant and directionally neutral terminal with detached satellites set in a spacious English landscape. There is a classical simplicity and an aesthetic calm in the work, as a result not only of the graceful cube-like buildings placed within flat green fields, but of the ordered discipline of the buildings themselves. Each is primarily a felicitous composition of expressed columns and roof structure, which order shops, booths and ticket points in pools of natural light, with walls and floors in various shades of grey.

The approach at Stansted is a far cry from other recent terminals, where colour, the interconnection of interior levels and dramatic directional structure (such as at Kansai and Terminal 2 at Charles de Gaulle) lead passengers from landside to airside. The detailed brief at Stansted issued to Foster's office instructed the architect to create:

- a convenient, safe terminal
- an adaptable terminal capable of phased construction
- a modern terminal able to accommodate the largest aircraft of the foreseeable future (up to 800 seats)
- an economical terminal, at least 10% cheaper than other recent BAA buildings.

It was a brief that tended to encourage a single-storey solution, in terms of cost, flexibility, passenger convenience and incremental development. The brief also gave Foster's office a central role. His practice was to design a total terminal, from building services to ticket counters, telephone booths and signage. A single concept was to permeate the whole design in the heroic modernist manner, but the integrity of this totality has

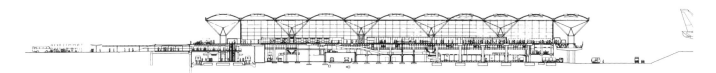

16.1 Section of Stansted Airport, UK. Notice how the main structure extends beyond the limits of the terminal, creating shelter at the edge. Architects: Foster and Partners.

16.2 Light rail trams are used to transport passengers from the terminal to the satellites at Stansted Airport, UK. Each AEG Westinghouse tram cost £1 million. Architects: Foster and Partners.

proved difficult to defend even in the first five years of operation.

The choice of a single-storey building sets the terminal at Stansted apart from other larger airports. Whereas single-level buildings are often the preferred choice for smaller regional airports (such as Southampton), the complexity of international airports leads invariably to two- or three-level passenger terminals. At Stansted, both Sir Norman Payne, the chairman of BAA at the time, and Foster favoured a one-level terminal. Payne said that BAA had 'known for years that the ideal airport terminal was a large open space on one level – like the Olympia Exhibition Hall'.[1] This provided the economy of construction, flexibility and maximizing of retail revenue that BAA required, and for Foster provided the justification for a calm, elegant and transparent pavilion set in an uncluttered landscape. Moreover, the openness of Stansted (nearly 1000ha of developable space) provided the means to spread laterally rather than build vertically, which tends to be dictated elsewhere by site restrictions (as at Gatwick, Manchester and Heathrow).

Stansted is a pavilion-like terminal six bays by six, with each column (or cluster of four) on an orthogonal grid of 36m. In its single-storey, rather rectangular simplicity, the design owes something to the terminal at O'Hare Airport, Chicago designed by Naess and Murphy (later to become Murphy/ Jahn) in 1962. Both Stansted and O'Hare share the Miesian architectural model of crisp cubes of accommodation within large sheets of glazing set behind a disciplined structural framework. It is perhaps no coincidence that both Payne and Foster share a respect for the undemonstrative example of O'Hare's early terminals.

The decision at Stansted to separate the main passenger terminal from the satellites used for boarding the planes was a departure from previous UK practice. Hitherto it was more common to have radiating finger piers, which took passengers, often along lengthy high-level walkways, to the aircraft gate. Similarly, the practice common in the USA of using unit terminals serving major airline companies was rejected. Instead, BAA opted for a hybrid system whereby passengers travel by electrically powered trams (a form of light rapid transit) from within the terminal building to two (later to become four) satellites built out on the apron.

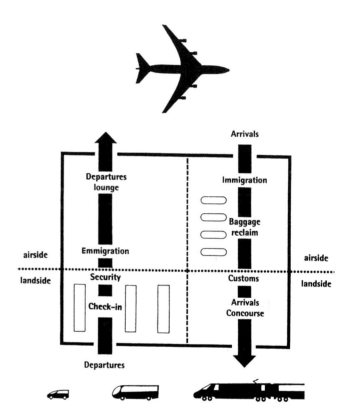

16.3 Concept plan for Stansted Airport, UK. The rational basis for the plan has an undeniable logic. Architects: Foster and Partners.

Following Gatwick's example, Stansted employed rapid transit people-movers (each of the five Westinghouse shuttle trams cost £1 million), thereby adding to the sense of innovation that is a recurring feature of the design.

BAA was anxious to build adaptability into the design at the outset. While the brief called for operational flexibility, Payne and his colleagues were conscious particularly of the retail opportunities that modern airports provide. Though Foster voiced disdain for this aspect of terminals, describing them as 'discount shopping centres on a grand scale, with an emphasis on emptying your pockets, rather than charging you with the thrill of travel',[2] the brief gave little direct instruction about the need to accommodate the

16.4 The sophistication of the constructional detailing at Stansted gives the building appeal at many levels. Stansted Airport, UK. Architects: Foster and Partners.

retail revolution then under way. Design evolution at Stansted unfolded against a background where the large internal volumes required by BAA and elegantly provided by Foster's office gradually became seen as potential floorspace for highly profitable retailers. Inevitably, soon after the building had opened, the purity of the original concept was compromised. Rather than place shops, bars and duty-free on a separate floor (as at the North Terminal at Gatwick) or split the terminal into a departures level complete with shops and a less cluttered arrivals level (as at Manchester Terminal 2 or in Rogers' design for Heathrow's Terminal 5), the single-storey solution at Stansted proved vulnerable to the very success of airports as a popular building type in which to loiter and shop for fashion and leisure goods. It has also suffered from growing concern over international terrorism, resulting in the installation of additional opaque security screens and barriers, which undermine the building's essential transparency.

The large internal spaces at Stansted exist mainly as a base course of bars, shops and customs control areas, which form the day-to-day life of the passenger terminal. The architect's original sketches showed the possibility of

seeing directly through the terminal from landside to waiting aircraft on the apron. The visual link between landside and airside was a central goal of design philosophy, which served to justify the lofty internal volumes, the elaborate tree-like columns, and the pools of sunlight that were intended to articulate the interior routes. In fact, the choice of a single-storey building was largely fashioned by the idea of a unifying airport ground plan zoned between landside and airside, with the terminal straddling the two.

If the simplicity and elegance of Stansted have proved vulnerable to changes in the management and use of interior space, this should not detract from the airport's considerable aesthetic and practical qualities. Much survives of Foster's original concept: the linear progression through the building without changes in level or direction; the openness, which allows views to be had across the runways and, internally, along the major public concourses; the use of light (especially sunlight) to animate interior spaces and define routes; and finally the exploitation of architectural structure to give scale and presence to the building. Notwithstanding the encroachment by fast-food shops, free-standing market stalls, and the glitter of bars, the building's underlying order

16.5 Diffused dappled light is a major part of the aesthetic experience at Stansted Airport, UK. Architects: Foster and Partner.

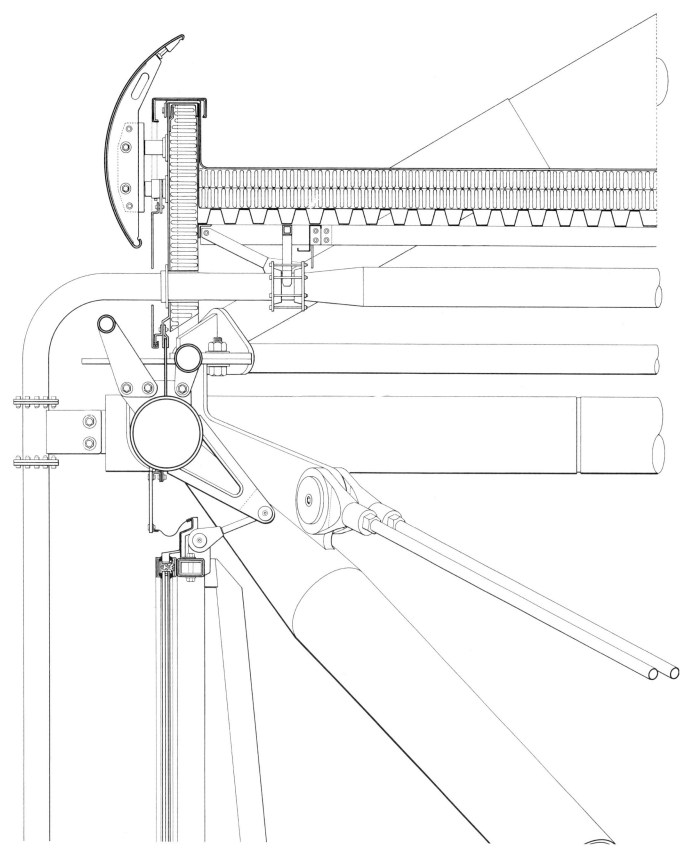

16.6 Eaves detail at Stansted. The airfoil deals effectively with wind loading. Notice how space between the components allows access to the various elements and ready replacement of parts. Stansted Airport, UK. Architects: Foster and Partners.

and simplicity shine through. At the edges of the building, particularly, the Miesian logic of the glazing and framing details, the use of an enormous porte-cochère of free-standing columns at the road edge, and the corresponding arrangement through which the shuttle passes, all testify to thoughtful design.

Adaptability and phased construction, required of the BAA brief, have been met largely in two ways. The terminal, though square in plan, can be extended sideways. The lateral expansion does not require any modification to the roadside or rail approach, nor to the airside shuttle system. Additional bays allow for the construction of extra baggage-handling facilities, and increased space for departures and arrivals lounges, but without upsetting the operation of the airport. Both sides of the terminal can be expanded by two bays, thereby nearly doubling the building's capacity. The other way in which expansion can be met is by constructing additional satellites. Two of the four originally planned have been built, but by increasing the number of shuttle trams from five to eight, they can readily serve the four independent satellites designed for the full 15 million passenger projection.

The architecture of Stansted is noteworthy because of Foster's skilful manipulation of architectural volumes, structure and daylight. The volumes are not complex and interconnected but regular and serene in the manner of the Sainsbury Centre at the University of East Anglia. By adopting an unusually high ceiling level (justified partly as a means of smoke control) the sense of interior space is heightened. Whereas BAA terminals elsewhere have ceiling heights of 6–10m, at Stansted the height is 12m. Cleverly, the design exploits the perception of the high ceiling by creating square pools of natural light within a roof structure not unlike interconnected umbrellas. The grids of squares of light in both directions set against the angular steelwork of the columns, and the general luminescence of the space, give Stansted a quality quite unlike modern terminals elsewhere. It is an architecture of frame, panel and light – not of walls, weight and heavy engineering. Only in the baggage undercroft and in the British Rail station does heaviness rather than a sense of lightness prevail.

Terminals have to accommodate a great deal of clutter, and adapt during their life in unexpected ways. The approach at Stansted seeks to use the space within the four separate supports that make up each major column as a services and information zone. Pipes, ducts, kiosks and booths are provided within these regular bays (each 3m square) and hence are evenly distributed throughout the terminal. By using the space within each cluster of four columns for air handling and light fittings, both light and fresh air are manipulated to enhance the passenger experience. Up-lighters placed within the column zone highlight the branches of the roof space, helping to create legibility and a sense of linear direction in public spaces – increasingly encroached upon by retail activities of various kinds. While the bases of the tree columns are often lost in the whirl of lower-level activities, the diagonal branches of the trees remain visible and picked out in light. Similarly, fresh clean air is dissipated through the trunks of the columns, metaphorically referring to the trees as health-giving elements in the design of the terminal.

The attempt at Stansted to create 'clarity and transparency' was specifically in order to help travellers to orientate themselves. Foster exploits views of aircraft, runways and landscape to help explain visually where 'you are actually going'.[3] This is evident in the three key parts of the journey – through the terminal itself, the shuttle trams, and at the satellites. Each is mainly a glazed structure where views out are largely unobstructed, and where the passenger moves logically in the direction of perceived flow from landside to airside. Only in the terminal itself, where the even spacing of columns suggests a more neutral directional bias, do the architectural cues have an element of ambiguity. Here, as *Progressive Architecture* notes, the breadth and depth of the space have become excessively obstructed by encroaching shops, bars, kiosks, check-in, security, customs and baggage claim facilities, which undermine the passengers' sense of direction.[4]

Being single storey, highly glazed and rooflit, Stansted can claim to be a relatively low-energy terminal. There is balance struck between lighting and heating energy demands, with much of the heat provided by solar and casual gains (that is, from heat provided by artificial

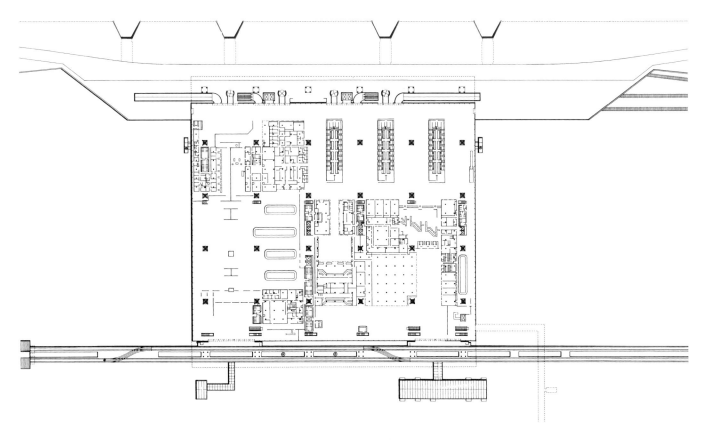

16.7 Concourse plan at Stansted. The shuttle trams are at the bottom. Stansted Airport, UK. Architects: Foster and Partners.

lighting and equipment). Because the building is largely naturally lit, daylight and sunlight become part of the aesthetic experience. By avoiding the levels of artificial lighting common to other terminals, Stansted not only saves energy (about half a million kilowatts of electricity a year),[5] but is relatively economical to run, because lighting at terminals is responsible for about 40% of total bought-in energy. Also, with lower levels of artificial lighting, the problem of excessive heat build-up in the summer months is reduced, thereby minimizing the size of mechanical ventilation plant. The main problem at Stansted is one of glare: direct sunlight, especially through wall glazing, can be uncomfortable at times in spite of the fritting of the glass.

In terms of UK airport design, Stansted, as *The Architectural Review* notes, sets a 'standard in being logical, customer-orientated and elegant':[6]

- logical in the sense of a clearly articulated linear progression from landside to airside, in the structural clarity, and in the adept handling of light
- customer-orientated in the lack of stairs, changes in direction and disorientating internal corridors, the scale of internal spaces, and the integration of rail and air
- elegant in the graceful well-proportioned lines, the sense of calm and repose.

16.8   Landside elevation of Stansted terminal. Architects: Foster and Partners.

Notwithstanding the seemingly inevitable compromises forced upon the building by changes in management ideology (especially with regard to retail expansion and advertising), the terminal represents an interesting new direction in airport design. With hindsight, perhaps the controlling hand of one designer cannot determine every detail, and should not attempt to do so within an industry noted for its flux. Perhaps all the terminal architect can expect to shape are the essentials of good architecture – space, structure and light – leaving many details to be determined by others and freely altered on short timescales. If there is a single lesson to be learned from Stansted, it is the need to split the signature spaces and architectural elements from the lesser details, allowing the former to have lasting qualities and the latter to adapt more readily to market needs. As *Progressive Architecture* warns, the design at Stansted 'imposes an elegant but possibly vulnerable order on the chaotic activities of airports'.[7]

Stuttgart Airport, Germany

Designed by the German practice Von Gerkan, Marg & Partners (GMP), the terminal at Stuttgart Airport serves a metropolitan area of 4 million. It is one of six busy regional airports providing, in an integrated fashion, the needs of the unified Germany of the 1990s. The form of the terminal consists of two separately expressed rectangles: the first houses the check-in, arrivals and departures concourses; the second a three-storey airside concourse facing across the runways. In plan the two rectangles, both expressed boldly in elemental shapes, slide into and through each other. Whereas the block housing the main public concourses is mainly glazed and transparent, the other – providing direct access to the aircraft – is more solid, with apertures cut crisply from panelled impervious walls. Architecturally, too, the two elements of accommodation are

given distinction in the cross-section shapes adopted: a triangle for the transparent block and a trapezoidal form for the airside block.

Von Gerkan, the partner responsible for the design, chose a language that, in its play of shapes and transparencies, helped to give passengers a sense of arrival and thence a feeling of direction en route to or from the plane. The section of the terminal rises upwards as one moves from landside to airside, hinting metaphorically at the transition from ground to flight (see also Munich Airport, Chapter 18). The rising ceiling, expressed also in the growing height of tree-like branching columns, allows passengers after check-in to move towards greater light and interior volume. However, the airside concourse cuts across the space, providing terraces and viewing ledges to look both backwards into the public concourses and outwards to the aircraft waiting on apron areas. The relative solidity of the airside concourse seems at odds with the spirit of the whole, though it is justified by the balances of solidity and transparency sought by the architect. The argument draws in part upon the need to reduce noise from aircraft within the terminal, and to provide an architectural framework for the airline offices, bars and duty-free shops found in such areas. Where the triangular-sectioned concourse block faces the runways, noise attenuation devices in the form of expressed louvres provide further animation to the airside facade.

Inside the main concourse block, architectural structure and rooflighting help to articulate the complex patterns of movement within the public areas. As at Stansted, columns and beams create such a powerful visual order that different activities within the spaces below are contained fairly happily. The bands of rooflights on a two-way grid help to express the structural bays of the columns, also helping to reinforce the fundamental spatial order of the interior. The progression of different concourses within this space and

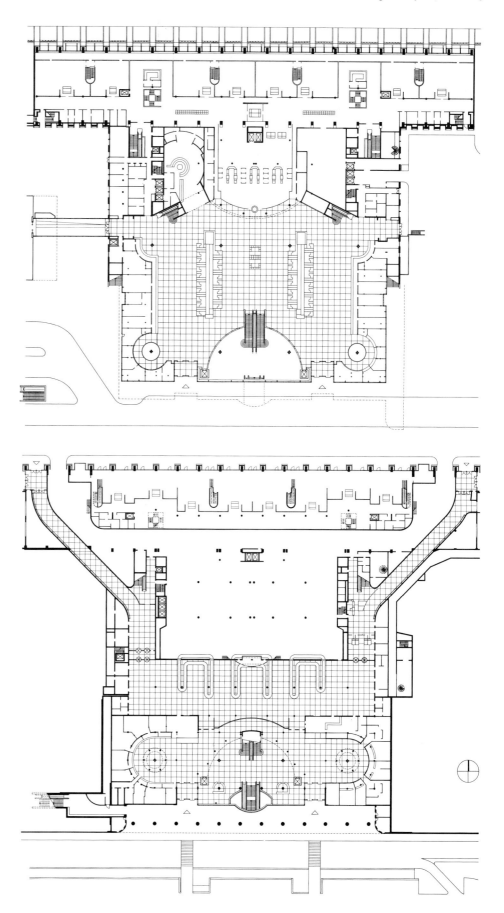

16.9 Arrivals and departures
levels at Stuttgart Airport,
Germany. Architects: Von Gerkan,
Marg & Partners.

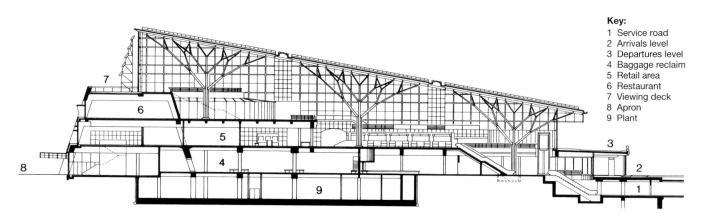

Key:
1 Service road
2 Arrivals level
3 Departures level
4 Baggage reclaim
5 Retail area
6 Restaurant
7 Viewing deck
8 Apron
9 Plant

16.10   Section through Stuttgart Airport, Germany: the terminal rises towards airside. Architects: Von Gerkan, Marg & Partners.

the linking staircases and escalators all obey the structural logic and gesturing of the columns. Because the movement through the terminal from landside to airside is both linear and upward, diagonal views are important. Here again the design seeks to exploit these, with projections into the space for restaurants, bars and viewing areas providing dramatic angled views through the branching columns.

16.11   Departures concourse at Stuttgart Airport, Germany. Architects: Von Gerkan, Marg & Partners.

Such is the complexity of the structural arrangement that a single column splits into 48 branches before it reaches the ceiling.

Stuttgart Airport shares affinities with Stansted (it was designed after Foster's proposals had been published), and helps to point towards the growing subtlety of terminals such as Heathrow's Terminal 5. Stuttgart can be seen as a tilted version of Stansted, and one that exploits the traditional arrangement of the departure lounge above the arrivals lounge (Stansted is a single-level terminal). However, in the orchestration of progression, architectural space and structure, Stuttgart has a refinement lacking in Stansted and which the design by the same architects for Munich Airport effectively extends.

Hamburg Airport, Germany

The rebuilding of the terminal at Hamburg Airport has resulted in a building that is a useful model for larger regional airports. Designed by Von Gerkan, Marg & Partners (GMP) and constructed in 1994, the terminal handles about 8 million passengers a year, many on charter holiday flights. Roughly comparable in capacity to London's Stansted, the building is on two main levels, with departures above arrivals in orthodox fashion. The section of the building splits the incoming and departing passengers, subjecting those arriving from flights to a lower level largely devoid of natural light or spatial drama. As a compensation, however, the departures hall is a grand expansive space. Here elegant curved trusses, lines of lantern lights and branching columns not only articulate the space but, in the incline of the ceiling, hint at the direction of flow and allude to the transition from ground to air.

The new Hamburg Airport is a model of integrated facilities with the terminal at its centre. Two blocks of offices sit as book-ends on either side of the main terminal, and a circular car park to the south-east completes the composition. Taken together these building elements and others planned (such as a circular atriumed hotel) form an urban whole, and help to shield the terminal from external noise and unwanted solar gains. The two rationally composed office blocks placed against the gables of the terminal contrast pleasantly with the structurally expressive and transparent terminal and, being so close, allow office workers to take advantage of the facilities provided for passengers. At Hamburg, the terminal is not an isolated building but the focus of a fairly dense composition of different land uses and architectural forms grafted onto an existing airport. In this regard it represents different thinking from that in the UK, where at Southampton and Manchester Airports the terminal is largely for passengers, not a centre for integrated regional development.

The design of the new terminal at Hamburg represents a refinement of the precedent at Stuttgart, designed in 1991 by the same architects. Like Stuttgart, Hamburg is a split-level terminal with a grand double-height departure hall sitting above a ground floor used for arrivals, baggage handling and mechanical plant. Emphasis is placed spatially and architecturally upon the departure hall: it is more a public gathering space than a mere concourse. Sensibly, the shops and restaurants that disfigure other terminals are at Hamburg kept mainly to elevated galleries overlooking the hall. Twin scissor-shaped staircases and escalators lead to these galleries, which in their openness and position help to animate the space with activity. Beyond this double-height bank of commerce stands the airside corridor (here called the departure pier), which serves not only the new terminal but older terminals that survive from earlier periods.

16.12 Acoustic and solar shading at Stuttgart Airport, Germany. The walls are angled to deflect sound. Architects: Von Gerkan, Marg & Partners.

16.13 Hamburg Airport, Germany. Architects: Von Gerkan, Marg & Partners.

16.14 Hamburg Airport, Germany. Architects: Von Gerkan, Marg & Partners.

The departure pier is an important element of the design, and provides commendable open views both into the departure hall and outwards to aircraft standing on the apron. The pier is almost entirely glazed, each structural bay being divided by three large sheets of fritted glass set in minimal frames. To reduce glare and solar gains, there is a large skirt of expressed aluminium panels held on diagonal struts, which follow the gentle curve of the pier. The view from airside is inviting; the transparency of the pier and the constructional finesse of the air jetties make the journey from the plane as welcoming as that in the opposite direction from car, bus or train.

GMP bring a structural and organizational sophistication to their airports. The practice combines rational planning with bold cross-sections and strong formal geometries. As a result their terminals are clear to use, with routes marked by the direction of structural members and expressed in the flow of light, both counterbalanced by pure architectural forms. At Hamburg seven large triangular trusses describe a gentle inclined curve across the ceiling, with each truss also defining the dimensions of lines of skylights. Hence the passenger can follow the pull of these aesthetic forces towards the departure gate, and by implication upwards to the departure pier. Even passengers using the almost subterranean arrivals hall are welcomed by a pool of light and crescent of shops at the end of their journey from the baggage reclaim area. Here too cafes and bars are provided

en route to the car park and bus stops. It is a pattern that allows those waiting for arriving passengers to enjoy a cup of coffee while enduring the frustration of delayed flights. Again, sectional geometries are well used, with the arrivals concourse placed beneath the raised road.

It has been suggested that both Hamburg and Stuttgart airports represent important steps towards the emergence of a clear typology for the smaller regional terminal. The assertion is based upon the clarity, simplicity and directness of circulation patterns, and the grandeur and drama of the main spaces.[8] Certainly, compared with many larger terminals, the architects for Hamburg have established a pattern of uses inside the terminal and land uses outside that supports passenger needs in a clear and attractive fashion. The design also expresses the excitement and sheer thrill of air travel – an exhilaration found mainly in the curved wing-like section and the seven crescents of lantern lights over the departures hall. Because the terminal is highly glazed (but protected by oversailing roofs and *brise soleil*), it glows at night in a welcoming fashion, and provides few dark corners to worry security staff. The very transparency of the building contrasts pleasantly with the relative solidity of treatment of the related buildings in the complex – the two office blocks, circular hotel and car parks. As an urban grouping, therefore, the play of architectural transparency and volume helps to define the function of each part and reinforce functional hierarchies. As the airport is developed to its full capacity (three such terminals are proposed placed side by side) this sense of a civic dimension will increase. Just as Terminal 5 at Heathrow is seeking to give that airport more the qualities of a city, so too but on a smaller scale at Hamburg.

Cologne/Bonn Airport, Germany

The extension to Cologne/Bonn Airport demonstrates how existing terminals can be enlarged without destroying the original design concept. Designed by Murphy/Jahn, the extensions consist of two wings that extend the present terminal with, in addition, a new terminal built alongside one of the wings. Whereas the original terminal was built of powerful concrete forms, which stepped to create a

16.15 Cologne/Bonn Airport, Germany: model. Architects: Murphy/Jahn.

distinctive profile, the new buildings are mainly glazed, with steel frames and lightweight roofs.

Structural elegance and rational planning, features of Murphy/Jahn's airport architecture elsewhere, find particular expression at Cologne/Bonn. The functional problem of creating a large extension (it roughly doubles existing provision) without destroying the coherence of the original has been solved by reinforcing the existing footprint of splayed wings. These are constructed about the wedge-shaped road system, creating an extended 'wall' of terminals with set-down points evenly spaced. The height of the new buildings is deliberately kept lower than that of the original terminal in order to maintain the functional hierarchy.

Within the new terminal a double-height roadside concourse distributes passengers into departures at high level

16.18   Seville Airport, Spain: section. Architect: Rafael Moneo.

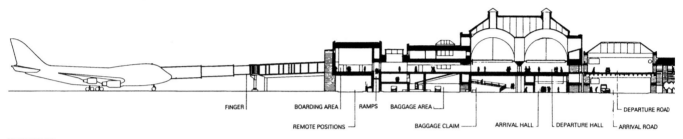

FINGER | BOARDING AREA | RAMPS | BAGGAGE AREA | DEPARTURE ROAD

REMOTE POSITIONS | BAGGAGE CLAIM | ARRIVAL HALL | DEPARTURE HALL | ARRIVAL ROAD

CROSS SECTION

steps are used as defining gestures. Again, with the boarding area a slot of space and light defines this zone from the customs and control region. Within a language of unifying elements, Moneo ensures a degree of structural independence for the principal parts in order to guide passenger perceptions.[9] Within these tight and contrived independent spaces, the architect skilfully inserts stairs, ramps and lifts, thereby adding to their significance.

Seville is remarkable for the reversal in thinking behind the design. The exterior is solid and mainly impervious (not transparent and lightweight); the interior spaces are inward and contemplative (not airy spacious shopping malls); the car parks are walled – almost medieval – gardens (not random expanses of asphalt). Gravity rather than weightlessness determines the architectural gestures of the main terminal spaces. Colour too is used with purpose: strong blues, yellows and white replace the neutral silver greys of other airports. Even with a relatively orthodox two-level terminal (departures above arrivals with a two-level entrance roadway) Moneo has shown that the modern terminal can absorb local architectural traditions to enhance the dialectic between international and regional cultural traditions.

Sondica Airport, Bilbao, Spain

Designed in 1990 by Santiago Calatrava's office in Zurich, the new terminal building is part of the comprehensive redevelopment of Bilbao's principal airport. Rather than construct a new airport on a fresh site, the authorities chose the logistically more difficult task of rebuilding and restructuring the airport around the existing infrastructure of runways and hangars. Bilbao, like many regional airports in Europe, has had to adapt over the past decade to an un-

expected rise in passenger movements. The city of Bilbao has proved particularly successful at attracting new investment, and this in turn has placed pressure on its airport.

Calatrava's design provides the powerful architectural vision and consistent structural language necessary to accommodate future growth. The brief required of the architect a framework whereby future extensions and increases in traffic could be housed without destroying the clarity of the concept. The airport at Bilbao has also had to cater for a big increase in international flights, with the new terminal accommodating regional, national and also international movements.

The concept places great emphasis upon a spacious departure concourse. This lofty and expansive central volume, clad predominantly in glass, orders all other functions about itself. It rises from an almost triangular plan to a prow high above the airside corridor. The beak-like prow hangs above the aircraft standing at their gates, reminiscent of a giant bird of prey. From the ridged spine of the departure lounge roof runs a fan of beams and angled columns that supports the glass roof. It is a design of characteristic Calatrava bravado, which derives its authority from the way in which the departure lounge gestures towards the act of flying, with the airside concourse hinting at the aircraft wings. Irrespective of the appropriateness of the bird metaphor there is no denying the way in which the design clearly articulates the principal public areas, and distinguishes them formally from the aisles or gate spine that give access to the aircraft. Unlike many airports, the car park too is closely related, and shares in the architectural language. It is axially located on the central route through the terminal, with a hanging canopy suspended over four floors marking the car park entrance.

16.19 Sondica Airport, Bilbao, Spain. Notice how in Calatrava's design the passenger is directed by the angle of walls and positioning structure. Architects: Calatrava Valls.

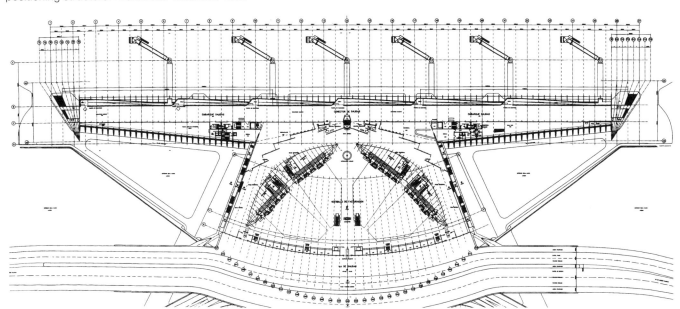

Rather than separate the arrivals and departures lounges laterally, Calatrava places them both in a great central space. They are merely at different levels one above the other, not diagonally staggered as at Stuttgart, Kansai and in the design for Terminal 5. All ancillary accommodation (customs, airline offices and airport administration) is housed in the arms (or wings) overlooking the aircraft parking areas.

Sondica Airport terminal owes a great deal in its spatial and structural concepts to Lyon-Satolas Station, also by Calatrava. Both feature a large, sculptural – rather zoomorphic – central form with wings that give access to trains or planes. Where one uses a departures aisle the other uses platforms, but the concept remains much the same. As at Satolas also, the structural materials move from concrete at or below the ground to steel in the air. Both structural materials at Sondica will be covered in metal panels rather than left exposed in the polluted airport atmosphere.

Sondica Airport is remarkable for the application of a consistent – yet sculpturally expressive – architectural syntax. Calatrava's uses of structure and internal volume are not empty gestures but the main means by which functional meaning and organizational hierarchies are communicated to the airport traveller. The terminal is due to open in 1998.

King Abdulaziz International Airport, Jeddah, Saudi Arabia

Designed by Murphy/Jahn of Chicago, the new airport for Jeddah consists of a central rooflit terminal and two curving arms of airside corridor giving direct access to gate lounges. The layout is based upon a square of runways and taxiing areas in which the terminal is centrally located. Access roads pass beneath the aircraft-taxiing ways, and reach the terminal at basement level. As a consequence, vertical movement through the building is as important as horizontal movement, and to make this as enjoyable as possible natural light is taken through a series of internal courtyards to the lowest level.

The concept has an elegant simplicity. The central terminal is lozenge shaped, with a central glazed street that accommodates vertical movement and distributes functions laterally about the spine. In the centre there is a small temple for worship.

The curved lightweight roof gives the terminal a tented character, which befits a terminal designed mainly for

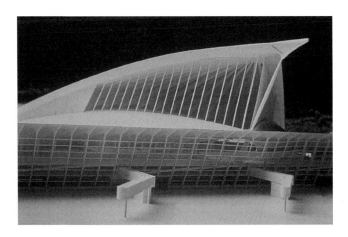

16.20 Sondica Airport, Bilbao, Spain: model. Architects: Calatrava Valls.

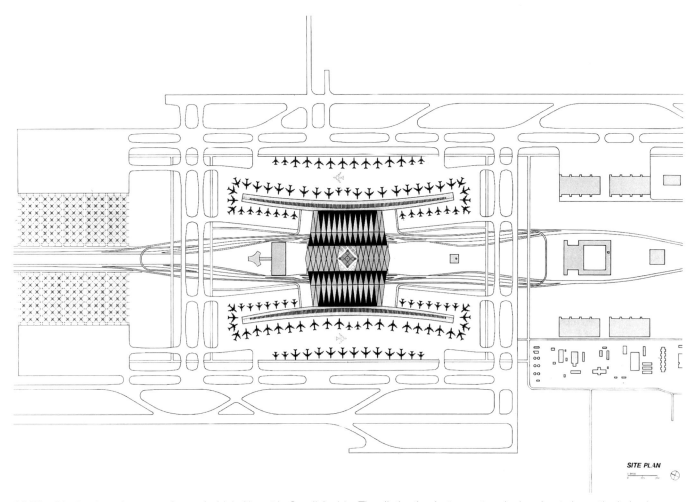

16.21 Masterplan of proposed new Jeddah Airport in Saudi Arabia. The distinction between terminal and gate is particularly clear, as is that between the central concourse and check-in areas. A mosque is proposed in the centre. King Abdulaziz Airport, Jeddah. Architects: Murphy/Jahn.

pilgrims. However, between each facet of roof a line of glazing brings light into the building, creating a diamond-shaped grid of daylight. Angled columns on the lower level and tree-shaped columns and beams on the upper level reinforce the lightweight, almost nomadic, quality of the terminal.

Functionally, the split between a central terminal where ticket check-in, passport control and shopping occurs, and the slender angled wings of the airside concourses, gives the building a form that is easily grasped. The layout adopted can also be readily extended by constructing satellites along each pier.

Shenzhen Airport, China

The design for the second terminal at Shenzhen Airport in China (only some 30km north of Hong Kong) was won in competition by the UK practice Llewelyn-Davies in collaboration with BAA International in 1995. It is planned to handle 12 million passengers a year, and scheduled to

open in 1998. Shenzhen Airport is one of ten regional airports designated as centres for economic development by the Chinese government in 1990. Although opened only in 1991 it had by 1995 become the country's fifth busiest airport, with the first terminal handling nearly 4 million passengers a year.

The concept behind the design for the second terminal is one of logical and legible routes through the building, an emphasis upon customer quality in the concourse areas, and elegance in the handling of space and structure. While the design had to adopt the building footprint imposed by the airport masterplan, the use of architectural means such as transparency, large column-free spans, an undulating roof, and clear spatial progression of interior volumes, gives the building lightness of touch. The published computer-generated views suggest a terminal not unlike Stansted in plan, with its prominently single-storey section and columns that branch just above head level. The wavy roof, suggestive of a hybrid between Southampton and T5, lifts at the landside access road to provide a lofty welcoming shelter.

16.22 Shenzhen Airport, China. A new airport to serve one of China's fastest-growing regions. Architects: Llewelyn-Davies.

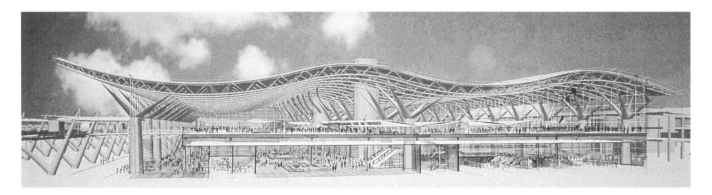

16.23 Shenzhen Airport, China. Architects: Llewelyn-Davies.

The need to bring daylight without heat gain into the core of the terminal has resulted in narrow bands of roof glazing integral with external solar screening. The roof canopy extends on all sides over the line of walls in order to provide further solar protection.

References

1. Norman Payne is quoted in Kenneth Powell, *Stansted: Norman Foster and the Architecture of Flight*, Blueprint Monograph, London, 1992, p. 21.

2. *Ibid.*, p. 23.
3. *Ibid.*, p. 35.
4. Thomas Fisher, 'Against entropy', *Progressive Architecture*, December 1991, p. 55.
5. *Ibid.*, p. 66.
6. Peter Davey, 'Airports come of age', *The Architectural Review*, May 1991, p. 37.
7. Fisher, *Progressive Architecture*, p. 54.
8. John Mark, 'Aerial drama', *The Architectural Review*, February 1995, p. 59.
9. John Morris Dixon, 'Welcome to Seville', *Progressive Architecture*, 7.92, p. 82.

CHAPTER 17

Regional airport terminals

Southampton Airport, UK

Designed in 1990 by the London architects Manser Associates, the new terminal at Southampton Airport was one of the first to fold and undulate the roof to bring daylight into the core of the building. Southampton is a small regional airport, all on one level in terms of passenger concourses, with a three-storey spine of offices for airport, airline and immigration staff through the centre. Between the central offices and the arrivals and departures concourses – arranged as aisles on either side – are two wide bands of rooflights, which bring light into the public areas. Functionally, the generous rooflights lead to a relatively energy-efficient building by saving on the cost of artificial lighting, but perceptually the juxtaposition of the roof glazing, diagonal roof structure and the elevated wall of offices creates a sense of place and direction within the terminal.

There is a simple articulation of the main architectural elements in both plan and section. The simplicity, coupled with relatively uncluttered interior spaces and a bird-like form externally, gives Southampton Airport a rare elegance for the genre. The projection of the central spine of office accommodation towards the runway in order to house flight control offices adds to the avian outline. Externally, it is relatively easy to read the major elements of accommodation: the transparency of the building envelope and the logic of the arrangement together add up to a building with functional clarity. Inside, too, the progression of spaces and routes for the passenger is clearly marked in terms of volume, spatial sequences and light. Architecture seems deliberately to overcome the sense of disorientation and alienation found in other airports. Admittedly, this is in part a product of size; Southampton handles less than a million passenger movements a year. But Manser has used openness, transparency (both upwards and outwards) and structural refinement to calm and guide the airline traveller.

The plan is commendably rational, and owes something to Stansted's geometric simplicity. Like Stansted, this is a single-level terminal, nearly square in plan, with

17.1 Southampton Airport, UK. The exterior marks the skilful resolution of a complex programme. Architects: Manser Associates.

oversailing roofs that protect the external walls from solar gain and interior spaces from glare. The two main concourses – arrivals and departures – are rather more two atria. The first on landside receives passengers, then processes them through ticket check and passport control. Here a few cafes, shops and bars are located, but the rising curve of the roof and the expansive angled rooflight put commerce in its place.

The second, on airside, is a similarly proportioned space, with duty-free shops and bars having views out at the gable over aircraft waiting on the apron. Because all aircraft are boarded on foot or by apron bus, the usual arrangement of jetty and gate piers is absent. This not only adds to the elegance of the terminal but means that passengers can engage more directly in the experience of air travel.

Structurally, the terminal has marked simplicity of form and detail. By using the walls of the central spine of offices as part of the building's main supporting structure, there is no need for secondary columns. Southampton is column free, with wide span loads taken on a series of diagonal struts. The central spine orders the terminal perceptually and also in terms of constructional logic. Without columns the spaces have a greater sense of size, and for retailers and facilities managers the lack of columns provides operational flexibility. Under these conditions walls and daylight take on extra significance, and here the design exploits the walls' ability to define territory and restrict access. The route through the central spine is clearly expressed, with big square openings cut into the off-white panelled walls.

The middle floor of the three-storey spine contains the building services, including air-conditioning. However, its location right in the centre of the terminal means that no secondary ducts are needed: air can be taken directly into the public concourses on either side and above the airline offices and below to the customs and baggage areas. Without roof-mounted ducting the public concourses retain their structural simplicity.

Part of the philosophy behind the design is an ambition to express the workings and construction of the building. Manser has sought to make explicit the means by which the building is supported, how it performs as a working terminal, and how the parts are assembled. It is an approach to design with a certain spartanness, yet at Southampton (as at Stansted) there is not the utilitarian feeling experienced in some other regional airports. This is due to the use of beams bent into concave curves with assemblies held apart to allow space and light to bounce off the surfaces. There is a sense of order that pervades the whole and the parts: a rigour that may prove vulnerable in time as the airport is used and adapted.

Being simple in concept, the terminal can readily be extended. It is designed to allow for linear growth in either direction. The structural bays are not ended with solid walls, but merely stop where current passenger demand requires. The brief required extendibility, and the external finishes – mainly silver polyester-coated aluminium panels and clear glazing – can readily be demounted.

Southampton has met BAA's demands for a relatively cheap (it cost £23 million in 1994), elegant but adaptable regional terminal. It has become a model for other countries, with interest in the building being expressed from as far apart as Australia, Russia and Malaysia.[1] Part of the value of the terminal lies in the relative economy of the design and the way in which the money used has been directed at achieving greatest benefit for the passenger. Southampton Airport cost £800/m^2 as against £1250/m^2 at Stansted and half the amount for a typical multi-storey terminal.[2]

Two Australian airports: Brisbane and Rockhampton

Regional airports have the opportunity to provide clarity of route that is often denied to larger airports. Two good examples are the airports at Brisbane and Rockhampton, both in Queensland, Australia. The first is by far the larger, catering for nearly 1 million passengers a year; the second is much smaller, with traffic flows only about a tenth of that figure. In scale Brisbane is roughly analogous with Edinburgh and Rockhampton with Southampton.

Unlike bigger airports, which are really mini cities, regional airports have to mediate between the human scale and that of aircraft within the limited dimensions of fairly small termini. The typical regional airport is a long, shallow building with a road on landside and aircraft parked alongside the terminal (without lengthy piers) at airside. This is certainly the form at Rockhampton, where all aircraft are boarded directly from the apron, and in modified form at Brisbane, where in addition there are three satellites. However, the typology is relatively simple: a two-storey terminal with departures on upper level and arrivals below, and a roof-glazed concourse parallel to the road.

This basic form lends itself to local variation, and is readily capable of being expanded should demand increase. At Brisbane it is bent into a huge crescent, which forms an embrace for the car park and points the three satellite piers in different directions towards the runway. The terminal itself has a central vaulted rooflit spine, which elegantly divides the public concourse (where check-in is located) from

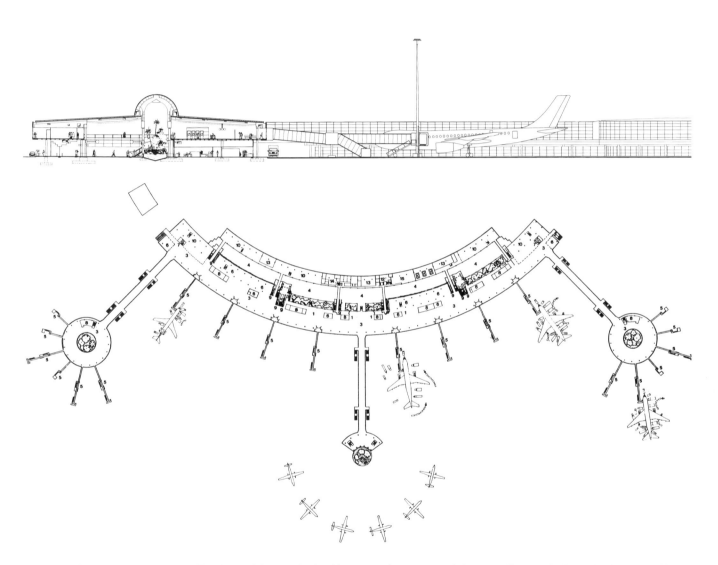

17.2 Brisbane Airport, Australia. The form of the terminal, with a sweeping curve and three satellites, articulates the function with particular clarity. Architects: Bligh Voller Architect.

the departure lounge. The spine is lofty, filled with interior planting and expressed in concrete barrel vaults. Being on a shallow curve it provides a point of orientation for those entering from either landside or airside – the sunlit double-height space contrasts pleasantly with the more utilitarian spaces on either side. The slender concrete columns and palms evoke the mood of a tropical garden right in the centre of the terminus, and provide a moment of tranquillity for the traveller.

One advantage of slender curved terminals is that they can readily be extended. Expansion at regional airports tends to be by linear extension of existing buildings, while

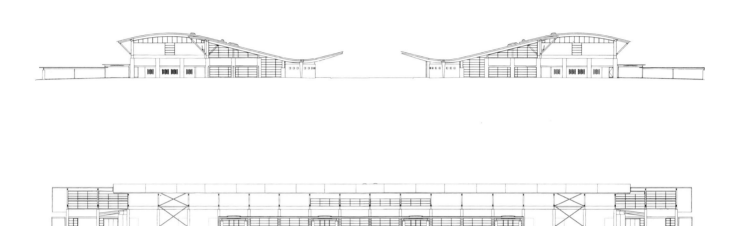

17.3   Rockhampton Airport, Australia: elevation and section of terminal. Architects: Bligh Voller Architect.

at international airports expansion is normally via the construction of whole new termini (as at Heathrow and John F. Kennedy). The shallow curve at Brisbane is ended with temporary gables, and all internal routes are designed so that they can be extended later without operational disruption.

Designed by Bligh Voller Architect, the Brisbane terminal has remarkable clarity of organization, which results, at least in part, from a 'calmly understated minimalist grid'.[3] The grid, like that at Stansted, is a lightweight steel frame developed to support an aluminium and glass cladding system. From both the inside and the outside the rectilinear lines of the silicone and neoprene extruded joints contrast pleasantly with the expressed concrete portals of the entrance canopies and the internal mall.

A similar well-organized approach is found at Rockhampton Airport by the same architects. Again its basic form and architectural language derive from articulating the interior routes and bringing daylight into the centre of the terminal. At Rockhampton, however, an undulating roof is adopted, partly as a reference to the profile of the modern aircraft fuselage but also to help protect the building from wind pressure. As in many recent terminals, the ends of the roof project to protect the landside drop-off point and the airside access routes.

The roof at Rockhampton rises towards the aircraft, gesturing at the enhanced scale on airside. At its highest point the roof is glazed, allowing the presence of the sky to penetrate to the interior lounges. Although designed for vertical segregation (of departing and arriving passengers), it currently operates as a single-level terminal. As with Southampton Airport, the undulating roof is both an internal means of articulating route and an external gesture towards flight.[4]

References

1. Martin Spring, 'Air waves', *Building,* 9 December 1994, p. 32.
2. *Ibid.,* p. 34.
3. Michael Keniger, 'Queensland drama', *The Architectural Review,* December 1989, p. 7.
4. *Ibid.,* p. 63.

Other airport structures

CHAPTER

18

Transportation Centre at the new International Airport at Inchon, Seoul, South Korea

The new Inchon International Airport at Seoul in South Korea confirms the important place that the Asia Pacific region is currently playing in the development of a new approach to airport design. Designed by the UK practice of Terry Farrell and Partners, Seoul International Airport continues the new and largely invigorated approach already seen at Kansai and evident too in the design of Hong Kong's new airport at Chek Lap Kok and the second Bangkok International Airport in Thailand. These are all essentially large-scale infrastructure projects, which act as intermodal transportation centres and urban development nodes, rather than simply as airports. As international, national and regional transportation centres they perform many functions, besides providing access to the air. Linked to high-speed train and local train and bus services, they will see many travellers pass through the airport en route to other destinations. As a result these new Asian airports (of which Seoul is perhaps the best example to date) require a fresh approach to form, organization and function. The role of design is primarily that of providing clarity and orietation while also meeting the needs of flexibility and operational flexibility.

According to Terry Farrell and Partners, the main factors that determined the design of the new airport at Seoul were the requirements to:

• provide a gateway to South Korea, and signify in symbolic fashion a reunified nation
• provide a focal point for international and inter-Asia trade activities (that is, more than just air movement)
• provide a transportation centre embracing a wide range of intermodal systems
• exploit design possibilities to provide user legibility through the airport.

The masterplan at Seoul is capable of being implemented in phased units over a 20-year timescale. The project is, however, more than just the construction of

18.1 Seoul Airport, Korea: proposed Transportation Centre with the 'Great Hall' as a fan-shaped focus. Architects: Terry Farrell and Partners.

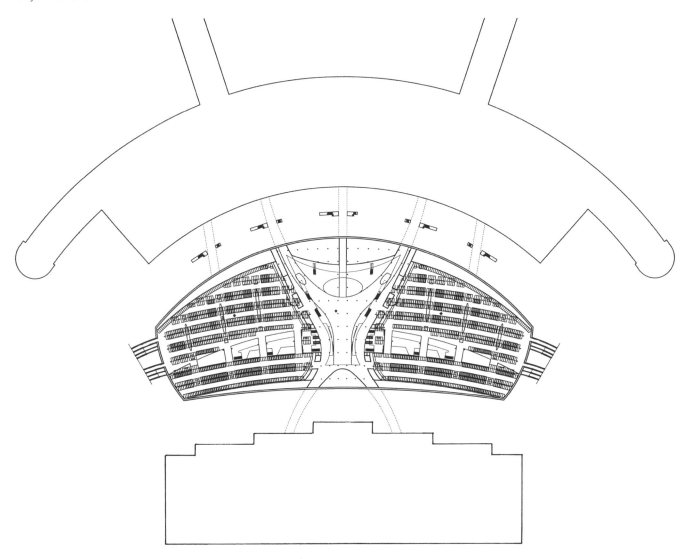

an airport: it includes the development of reclaimed land between Yong Jong and Yong Yu islands just east of the airport site, the construction of an eight-lane expressway, double track railroad, double-deck suspension bridge, underwater road tunnel, high-speed ferry service and helicopter routes. Not all parts are designed by Farrell's office, but the masterplan provides the spatial and investment framework whereby over time the various elements can be provided in a well-organized fashion.

The airport consists of a Transportation Centre sitting between a crescent-shaped Terminal 1 and a rectangular Terminal 2. The Centre is the visually dominant part: it towers over the two terminals and establishes axes through them. Both terminals are key aesthetic parts (hence the

18.2 The Transportation Centre combines Western technology with a respect for Korean traditions. Seoul Airport, Korea. Architects: Terry Farrell and Partners.

use of crescent and rectangular forms), visually recognizable in plan and section but subservient to the Centre. The latter sits astride the parallel tracks of the railway, which – like the runways – are the main parameters in determining the site layout.

The Centre is a complex and expressive structure: it signals in dramatic fashion the presence of the airport, and hints towards the passengers' contact with Korean culture. The decision to locate the control tower within the Centre (as against an isolated structure as in most airports) gives the means to project a great prow above the Centre's roof. The angled control tower, sitting on double legs and counterbalanced both structurally and visually by the curved steel walls of the Centre, promises to provide a memorable bird-like image for weary passengers. There is an undeniable hint of Calatrava in the concept design, but Farrell's office has been developing along similar lines in other infrastructure projects for some time (for example, the CrossRail bridge over the River Thames of 1993).

A central axis unites the Centre in direct fashion with Terminals 1 and 2. The axis is defined by various means: the huge curving triangular roof, elevated banks of escalators, the spreading from a central point of secondary routes, and double-height volumes. The Centre is a separate structure between the terminals and between multi-storey car parks, which flank either wing. Light, gardens and space are taken between each part, thereby providing identity for the major elements. The effect of the deliberate differences in expression between the key parts of the airport, the parcels of garden space between them, and the exuberant triangular form of the Centre are all intended to allude to the flamboyant and colourful Korean architectural tradition. The roof of the Great Hall of the Centre is, according to the architect, a direct reference to 'a bird in flight' and a symbolic gesture towards Korean culture expressed in local Buddhist temples.

Normally, the passenger terminal building dominates an airport, and is the main architectural experience for travellers. At Seoul, however, the Transportation Centre is the primary element: it is the largest structure, and the one through which all passengers pass en route to or from either terminal. The justification for the Centre's prominence is the scale and

extent of intermodal transport facilities at Seoul. Farrell's design celebrates in an unprecedented fashion the mainly public means of reaching the airport (rail, metro, bus) at the expense of the private car. Inside the Centre the four-platform railway station exists as an identifiable element with its own glazed roof, sitting within the curved atrium space of the Great Hall of the main building. At the station, passengers can check in their baggage before proceeding at a more leisurely pace to Terminals 1 and 2.

Natural light is admitted via the enormous glazed atrium to all six levels of the Centre. At high level (on level 4) a people-mover system is proposed to take passengers via an elevated light railway to either terminal. Placed high up within the Great Hall, the light railway will have its own station served by lifts and escalators. The Centre and its radiating connections to Terminal 1 are, according to Farrell, symbolic of the Korean fan, yet the metaphor is steeped also in Western futurist imagery.

The grand glazed roof of the Centre's Great Hall will be a spectacle from the air, especially with the neck of the air traffic control tower angled dramatically above the roof. The tower shares the structural logic of the remainder of the Centre from which it grows, and has a deliberate totem-like quality in its detailed treatment. The way in which the Centre nestles into the curve of Terminal 1 and extends arms to

18.3 Air traffic control towers give airports an essential vertical dimension. They need to be designed as landmarks. Schiphol Airport, Amsterdam, the Netherlands. Architects: Bentham Crouwel.

Hall the ambience of a temple surrounded by quasi-public space. This will help to reinforce in passengers' minds the role of the Centre as a symbolic pavilion and gateway – to the airport and to Korean culture.

Geometry, openness and light are the main characteristics of the design. Triangular geometry is the driving force that orders the principal spaces in plan, and it is used again to structure the interior volumes. The symbolic roof is both a metaphor and the means by which legibility and land-marking are provided. In what is thought to be the largest intermodal transportation centre in the world, Farrell's design exploits with particular potency the idea of bold expressive structural form to provide functional clarity. Yet it is boldness that combines the Western rationalist approach to airport design with respect for Korean cultural traditions in their widest sense. The combination of rationalism and romanticism at Seoul represents a valuable search for place-specific airports in an increasingly standardized world culture.

Air traffic control towers

Air traffic control towers are one of the most distinctive and architecturally prominent structures at airports. Within the wide open landscapes of a typical airport, the control tower represents a vertical point of reference, which can do much to enhance the image and aesthetic profile of an airport. Being shaped by demanding functional programmes, such towers are also often highly sculpted three-dimensional structures. Their main function is that of controlling the movement of aircraft in the air and the movement of service vehicles and planes on the ground. The need to have visual surveillance over both results in buildings that are often isolated structures some way apart from the remainder of the airport buildings. However, because the operation of the passenger terminal and that of the aircraft are necessarily related, control towers are sometimes constructed as rooftop extensions to the main terminal or more frequently loosely affiliated structures.

Control towers direct and coordinate aircraft movements in the vicinity of the airport. Air traffic control staff monitor aircraft movement on apron areas, taxiways, runways and

Terminal 2 suggests a controlled composition rather than incremental growth, which is the pattern at most international airports. There are no Cartesian grids at Seoul, and little evident opportunity for subsequent linear expansion. Farrell's design is a grand statement in the tradition of a fine nineteenth-century railway terminal. This is evident too in the treatment of spaces between the principal buildings. The Transportation Centre is constructed (for safety reasons) partly below ground, and only the curved roof of the Great Hall breaks the skyline. On either side of the glazed roof, however, gardens are proposed, which will give the Great

18.4 Proposed air traffic control tower at Oslo International Airport, Norway. Architects: Aviaplan AS.

18.5 Control tower at Sydney Airport, Australia. Architects: Ancher/Mortlock/Wooley.

in the air. Clear visibility is crucial, and sightlines dictate the positioning of the tower relative to other structures such as hangars, terminals and piers. From the tower itself it is vital that views are unobstructed by columns, that glare does not occur or interfere with display screens, and that visibility angles are maintained. The angle and configuration of the glazing need to provide safe and comfortable working

conditions under both sunny and cloudy skies, during the day and night. Ergonomics is one of the main design constraints in control towers.

Because control towers are physically divorced from the ground and are placed in high fire-risk locations, the means of escape in emergency is an important factor. The escape stairs add to the formal composition and complement the

18.6 Strikingly planted roof of car park at Munich Airport Centre, Germany. Architects: Murphy/Jahn.

lifts normally used in gaining access. In some control towers, such as at Sydney Airport, the escape stair plots a different geometry from that of the main shaft of the tower, thereby enhancing the design as a three-dimensional composition.

Another novel control tower is at O'Hare International Airport, Chicago, designed by Murphy/Jahn Architects in 1990. It is grander than the example at Sydney but shares its sculptural complexity. The core of the tower is a hollow concrete column, which contains elevator, cables and technical equipment, with the escape staircase wrapping around it.[1] The concrete core supports a steel-framed faceted glass curtain of ancillary and office accommodation. The swelling and contracting of the glass wall reflects the internal planning, with its control room at the upper level. During the day the three-dimensional tower provides a welcome point of orientation at the airport: at night it glows, giving the tower depth and luminosity and adding to its symbolic significance.

Control towers normally consist of mainly large, open, column-free working space overlooking runway and sky. Air traffic control staff monitor aircraft movements visually and on electronic screens. The navigational installations require periodic upgrading of the electronic and mechanical equipment, creating a need to design such towers with replaceability in mind. The life of air traffic control systems is generally under 10 years, requiring three or four complete refits in the life of a typical control tower. As with the design of passenger terminals, the life of the outer structure and of the internal arrangement are on two quite different timescales.

Munich Airport Centre, Germany

The Munich Airport Centre reflects the growing role of airports in providing conference, business, office and hotel facilities. The Centre, designed by Murphy/Jahn, serves both the airport and the Munich region. With direct access on the one hand to the airport and on the other to the S-Bahn railway system, the Munich Airport Centre is able to attract custom from both directions.

The concept is relatively simple: a grid of hotels, offices, shops, restaurants, conference centre and clubs, located parallel to the main terminal building. Between the two, the existing road system provides ready access to the airport terminal on one side and the new Centre on the other. With gridded layouts of buildings the streets and malls take on particular significance. Here they alternate between access roads and glazed walkways, which in turn lead off giant sheltering glazed canopies.

The presence of a planned new railway station within the complex opens the development to non-travelling uses. There are leisure and conference facilities spread between leafy courtyards constructed on the roofs of subterranean car parks. The new Centre has also been designed to provide direct check-in and baggage claim facilities in the hotels and conference centre, thereby allowing the new facility to relieve pressure within the existing terminal.

The architectural concept developed by Murphy/Jahn breaks down the rigid division between the inside and the outside of the terminal building. Canopy-sheltered courtyards and streets allow the various buildings to merge with each other, creating a sense of urban village. Exterior planting plays a key part: it softens the interiors of buildings and their facades, tempering the harsh lines of the tectonic airport architecture. The combination of building and landscape design, and airport and conference centre buildings, has allowed Munich Airport to become a good example of the airport as a self-contained, economically diverse urban entity.

References

1. Werner Blaser (ed.), *Helmut Jahn Airports,* Birkhäuser Verlag, Berlin 1991, p. 94.

Part three

The airport of the future

CHAPTER

19

Characteristics of twenty-first-century

The question is sometimes asked: What is likely to distinguish twenty-first-century airports from those of the twentieth century? The airport is one of the very few thoroughly modern building types. There are no precedents for the airport or its principal building – the passenger terminal. The airport evolved just before the Second World War from largely temporary structural beginnings: tents, marquees and Nissen huts in the case of Heathrow. By the 1960s the airport had matured into a distinctive and immediately recognizable group of buildings and engineering works. The passenger terminal was a large usually rectangular building, sometimes with a two-level road system on landside and long glazed piers giving direct access to aircraft on airside. The control tower was a separate structure overlooking the runways and apron areas. Hangars, aircraft service areas, car parks, hotels and office buildings for airlines or airport authority made up the supporting entourage.

By the close of the century, however, the airport began one of those shifts of form that mark the maturing of a building type. Just as species evolve and settle into recognizable forms in response to changing conditions, so too the airport (and particularly the passenger terminal) started to develop new characteristics. Whereas the first generation of airports were relatively simple entities serving the fairly straightforward function of supporting air transportation for a wealthy minority, the later terminals became part of mass transportation, partly in response to the unexpected growth in global tourism. Inevitably, the airport has had to respond to these changing conditions, and in the process has evolved into a mature species. No longer is the airport a rather grand railway station served by cars on one side and planes on the other: today the airport is a complex, dynamic, multifunctional entity mirroring the cultural richness and diversity of modern life. As a consequence the modern airport is a regional growth centre having no respect for green belts or the traditional values of the small communities nearby.

Not all airports have evolved yet to this level of typological sophistication, but it is possible to identify the key elements that distinguish the twenty-first-century airport

19.1 Airports start as one or two terminal buildings and finish up as new towns. This example is Stuttgart Airport, Germany.

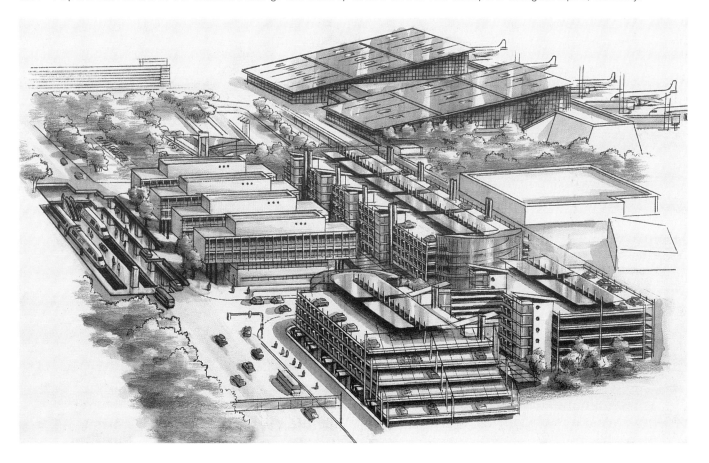

from that of the twentieth century. Three determining factors are involved:

- land-use diversity
- intermodal transport integration
- environmental sensitivity

which together help to define second-generation airports and give them their distinctive architectural form.

Land-use diversity

As airports have matured they have become major economic centres. Modern airports are now business centres that operate quite independently of air travel; they are locations for conferences; they contain hotels used by local people, and shopping malls that serve regional retail needs; and they are important warehousing centres. As Gatwick has matured, the number of people using the various facilities from air museum to retail mall has risen. At Heathrow, the chapels, gym, business centres and hairdressers cater for the 55,000 airport staff as well as the 55 million who pass through the terminals each year. At the smaller scale, some regional airports are less airports in the traditional sense and more industrial estates with a runway through the centre.

The loss of functional simplicity is expressed in the diversity of buildings and land uses encountered at a modern

19.2 Airports are developing into two types: those that are integrated into the urban structure (such as Munich) and those that are separate entities, often built on man-made islands (such as Kansai). Munich Airport Centre, Germany. Architects: Murphy/Jahn.

airport. Early photographs of airports show simply a runway, terminal and large open car park – the prime elements connected by single-level two-way roads. By the 1960s car parks had become multistorey, and roads two-level and one-way; terminals had complex split sections; and two or three runways were commonplace. A similar shift in complexity and intensity began to occur in the 1990s: airports had become regional or even national centres for economic growth with conference, business, leisure and retail pressures within the airport proper and in the hinterland. Rather than seek to control these pressures, most governments have accepted the economic and social advantages of airport-led growth, and had by the 1990s begun to plan for the changes to the regional infrastructure. What started as an airport had (again Gatwick is a good example) become a major magnet for development, influencing the pattern of land uses, transportation systems and employment distribution within a 20km radius.

Looking at London's airports – Heathrow, Gatwick and Stansted – it is clear that all have become new towns, attracting people and jobs from other areas. Without official recognition Gatwick has become the Milton Keynes of the south side of London, and Stansted looks set to be the same for the north-east quadrant. Orthodox town planning cannot control the pressures brought about by airport expansion: what steps are taken are mainly token, and in preserving one parcel of land from development government controls merely transfer the pressure elsewhere. Just as new towns evolved from relatively simple beginnings (especially the plantation towns of Ireland, France or America) so the airport new town started life with a straightforward brief. With time and success the typical twentieth-century airport has grown into a sizeable town with the airport runway and passenger terminal at its centre. Looking further ahead into the mid-twenty-first century one can imagine airports such as Heathrow having their own university, hospital, and maybe even professional soccer team – all characteristics of mature cities. Even today one does not talk of Heathrow Airport but merely Heathrow; the place has clearly outgrown its original justification.

Given the apparent inevitability of growth, one needs to question airports constructed on man-made islands (such as Kansai and Chek Lap Kok in Hong Kong). Islands in the ocean can accommodate airport functions, but they cannot provide the space needed for the expansion of the regional economy. The choice of physical separation (such as Kansai Airport) or integration into the regional infrastructure of development (such as Chicago Midway) is one that airport authorities and governments need to consider carefully.

Airports change into complex beings over time. Piecemeal development or wholesale redevelopment (the two means by which growth and complexity are accommodated) lead remorselessly towards functional multiplicity. The result is a collection of buildings approaching an urban whole, with the same formal intricacy and hierarchical relationships as are encountered in a mature town. Heathrow, Charles de Gaulle and Kennedy airports all display these characteristics. The twenty-first-century airport, however, if built from scratch (as in Hong Kong's Chek Lap Kok or Seoul International) can house the land-use diversity within a structure that accepts the changing nature of airports. Foster's design for Chek Lap Kok provides an urban concept from the outset: the majestic plan with great wings and

terraces is mildly suggestive of an ambitious eighteenth-century new town such as Bath. Accommodating growth and diversity within a plan of robustness and clarity is a characteristic of the twenty-first-century airport.

Intermodal transport integration

Modern airports are becoming large and complex transportation interchanges, where you can move freely between car, bus, rail, metro and aircraft. It is the integration, often within a single building, of transportation modes that distinguishes twenty-first-century airports from those of the twentieth century. In fact, such are the level and variety of transport systems at some modern airports that many passengers pass through them or change at them without the intention of using the airport at all. Berlin (ICE), Charles de Gaulle and Schiphol airports are as much interchanges for all kinds of transportation services as they are airports. Here some passengers transfer from metro to regional or high-speed railway services, or from car to rail, and do not venture into the airport departure lounge at any part of the journey.

In many ways the changes in the distribution and complexity of land uses at airports and the growing integration at them of other forms of transportation are related factors. For an airport to serve effectively as a conference venue it needs local as well as regional and international transport links. Similarly, if an airport is to become a leisure or transit venue in its own right, it requires efficient bus, underground or mainline rail services. One trend in airport development noticeably evident at present is the extension of rail services to airport terminals (Manchester and Lyon Satolas are good examples). A better mix of transport facilities allows different types of people with different needs and diverse income levels to use the full range of facilities present at modern airports. If an airport is to serve its regional population effectively then intermodal transportation is essential.

It is true to say that the effective integration at airports of various types of rail, bus and private transport distinguishes the contemporary airport. This helps airline passengers to reach the airport with reduced frustration, it avoids travel delays for airport or airline staff, and it encourages

19.3 The new Oslo Airport is well connected to the road and rail network (notice station at bottom). Architects: Aviaplan AS.

the airport to grow as a business or leisure centre. Many large airports such as Heathrow cannot legitimately claim that they are airports of the twenty-first century (as BAA does) until a better balance is struck between public and private means of getting there.

The integration of the full repertoire of public transport facilities into airport buildings adds greatly to the complexity and difficulty of designing terminals. At some airports the terminal and other forms of transportation are physically embraced within an enormous interchange (those designed for Bilbao and Seoul airports are good examples); in others (such as Kansai or Manchester airports) the bus and rail terminals are separate structures within the estate of airport buildings. At Charles de Gaulle, itself a model of effective transportation integration, the five levels of the terminal allow road, rail and plane connection to be achieved with remarkable clarity. If the physical integration within a large terminal interchange of various kinds of public transport represents the high point of modern airport engineering, then the architect has the task of maintaining legibility through the maze of levels and structures involved. Intermodal transportation not only helps us to define the twenty-first-century airport, it establishes a modified typology for the building type.

Environmental sensitivity

To call modern airports 'environmentally' benign is to engage in relative, not absolute terms. Transportation by plane and all the supporting infrastructure of the contemporary airport is one of the most ecologically damaging human endeavours. However, the twenty-first-century airport recognizes the environmental problem while the twentieth-century airport ignored it or fought to disclaim damage with the help of lawyers. What characterizes recent airport development and contemporary airport management is the open recognition of the scale and complexity of adverse environmental impacts. This has led to airport designers having to address environmental and ecological issues at the outset, and to airport managers responding more effectively to airlines that break noise, pollution or public safety standards.

The new environmental consciousness that has emerged as a feature of the twenty-first-century airport finds expression in five distinct ways:

- Airports are designed to respond to, rather than resist, climate, ecology and nature.
- Terminals are designed to reduce the use of energy.
- Terminals employ materials of low toxicity, and maximize natural sources of light and ventilation.
- Planting forms an important air purification and spiritual function in and around terminals.
- The airport authorities and local communities cooperate on environmental action.

These five points are not separate but related expressions of the new environmental awareness. The neighbourhood of an airport is seen not as a battleground between community groups and those who manage the airport but as a hinterland of common interest. Macro-level environmental action involving partnership between airport authorities, local councils, schools and wildlife groups is becoming more commonplace. As BAA recognizes, airports can grow only if the whole community, not just the airport managers, share a common goal, and in this the reduction of environmental impacts is a key element.

The airport of the future looks set to exploit the forces of nature to make travel less fatiguing and buildings less energy consuming. Designs such as that for Heathrow's Terminal 5 and the new international terminal at Oslo point in new ecological directions. At Terminal 5 the sectional profile of the building exploits air currents to promote natural ventilation and the extraction of smoke in the event of a fire. Here too interior planting purifies the air and provides an air of tranquillity, and exterior planting helps to baffle aircraft noise, sifts out pollutants, and modifies surface drainage by ecological means. At Oslo the terminal – designed by Aviaplan AS architects – uses local timber and stone in the structure and finishes in order to reduce the toxicity of the building and limit the importation of materials from across the world. As in many recent airport designs natural light is maximized to reduce the need to consume energy generated by non-renewable means. Solar gain and interior glare are combated by external grilles, with daylight shelves used to increase the penetration of natural light into the depths of the terminal.

Unlike an earlier generation of airports, many recent masterplans provide a necklace of tree belts, pockets of wildlife habitat and earth banks to both screen terminal buildings and encourage the absorption of the airport into the wider landscape. At both Gatwick and Heathrow recent landscape plans attempt to bring the agricultural or woodland countryside up to the terminal buildings, car parks and hotels. Through the selection of plant species, and in the choice of colours for the buildings, airport and environment seek a happier compromise than in the past.

These characteristics are increasingly features of world airports. The ecology movement finds sharper expression today than in the past. Kansai Airport is one of the more environmentally benign of major recent airports. The design of the terminal and the choice of planting mitigate to a degree the intrusion of a man-made island and the removal of a mountain on the Japanese coast to construct it. Similarly, in the USA the new hub airport at Denver borrows the tent-ed metaphor of the local indigenous people as a sop to environmental concerns. At Seoul International Airport, the design by Terry Farrell and Partners creates oriental gardens inside the terminal, and dense planted squares between it and adjacent buildings.

The twenty-first-century airport is a microcosm of the twenty-first-century city where work, leisure, travel and ecological systems melt into one. The challenge for architects and engineers is to match more equitably the industrial and organizational system of the airport with the natural systems and cultural priorities of the region that it serves. This means a better balance between airport design and nature in its widest sense: a correspondence between building engineering, human values and ecological principles. The idea of a flexible environmentally friendly terminal, where few parts are fixed and much is evolved on the principle of renewable modules, begins to give the modern airport the underlying order of an ecosystem. The twenty-first-century airport and its region will take on the features of a mature ecosystem where resources are used locally, where the minimum of materials are used to create the maximum social and environmental benefit, and where the airport is at the centre of a sustainable pattern of development.

The terminal of the future CHAPTER 20

As the airport takes on a distinctively different form at the close of the twentieth century from that in the middle, so too the passenger terminal is evolving in distinctive ways. The future terminal will be quite different from that experienced at most airports today – differences that reflect social and technological trends in the world at large, and specific changes in the management of airports. The modern airport, and certainly the airport of the twenty-first century, is a huge, complex and noisy theatre. It is a focus for a wide diversity of human activity – from travel to leisure, from shopping to health clubs, from plane-spotting to conferences, and from family reunions to church outings. Airports have become travel theme parks, where up to half the people present are not about to fly at all. Such functional ambiguity has undermined the simplicity of the airport and given it characteristics similar to those of cities. The 'vast, diversified and noisy theatre' of the typical modern airport reflects directly the chaotic, complex, multicultural and fragmented contemporary urban condition.

The airport as a new type of city

Arguably, big airports such as London Heathrow are a vision of the city of the twenty-first century – urban areas made up primarily of information systems, of complicated multilevelled movement, of individuals who with their mobile phones and fax machines are self-contained workstations travelling around the world without offices or even homes. Airports are increasingly places where time is as important as money, where business people meet and strike deals, and where buying and eating become the prime leisure activities for weary travellers. Heathrow is a worrying but challenging vision, which architects have to address if their designs for terminals are to have any contemporary relevance in the widest sense.

Modern terminals such as Kansai – claimed to be the biggest building in the world – are so large that they have invalidated the Modern Movement's fixation with the singular architectural object. Size and internal complexity have made the terminal of the future (the design

20.1 Airports are becoming urban assemblies offering architectural quality and civic values. Zurich Airport redevelopment. Architects: Nicholas Grimshaw & Partners.

for Heathrow Terminal 5 is a good example) into megastructures, where activities inside are housed as self-contained villages surrounded by open space. The large international terminal of the twenty-first century looks set to take on the characteristics of traditional urban areas, not just in their functional and human multiplicity, but in the formal language employed. Big modern terminals are arranged in plan with streets and squares, gardens and towers, districts and neighbourhoods. When a building becomes as large and diversified as a small town (Heathrow alone employs 55 000 people) then it is inevitable that the prime buildings take on civic characteristics.

The repertoire of streets, malls, squares, villages and landmarks that characterizes the design of some of the more ambitious airport terminals currently on the drawing board (such as Seoul International, or Chek Lap Kok at Hong Kong) reflect the changing life of airports. When 54 million or more passengers pass through an airport in a single year (in Heathrow's case more than the population of the country it serves), there are ramifications for design. Terminals cannot be conceived as solitary, singular, high-

technology enclosures any more; they need to form urban assemblies, with neighbouring buildings such as hotels and car parks playing subsidiary roles in an architectural sense. Internally there is the need to create route legibility and a sense of place in public areas. Psychologically the modern terminal needs to provide stimulation for some and tranquillity for others.

The vast complexity of passenger terminals, with their great intermodal transport connections and electronic communication webs, provides a possible model for life in the twenty-first century. Evidence suggests that the single sublime object represented by Stansted Airport does not provide the model for the cultural, human and commercial richness of contemporary life. Instead, the passenger terminal that accepts the messy, noisy competitive world, and resolves the sometimes uncomfortable demands into a building of richness, complexity and nobility, serves management and passenger needs more effectively. The obvious precedents are the medieval cloth halls and the great expansive nineteenth-century corn exchanges or railway terminals of many European towns. They functioned as

20.2 Kansai Airport is the personification of tectonic perfection. It is an architecture that defies gravity, just like the aircraft that the terminal serves. The swaying angled lines of the structure and the rhythms of light provide a memorable experience. It is a gateway both to the sky and to Japanese culture. Kansai Airport, Osaka, Japan. Architects: Renzo Piano Building Workshop.

heroic places of financial or transport exchange, but they were also centres for social interchange, for gossip and meeting unrelated to trade or movement. The halls, exchanges and stations were magnificent urban landmarks – some based upon circular or elliptical shapes – with internal malls for trade or refreshment set apart from public gathering spaces. Interior galleries and lofty rooflit halls provided a dramatic and imposing backcloth for both commerce and town life.

The search for place in terminal design

Modern airport terminals are so large that they cannot be readily comprehended. The use of streets, malls and gardens inside the terminal allows the passenger to grasp the sense of direction or location. But formal and spatial geometries are not enough: the volumes created need to be expressed and articulated. Here structure plays a part. Columns, beams, arches and lintels bring the space alive, and allow the traveller to grasp the sense of direction, the

speed of movement through the terminal, and the functional hierarchies present. Again Kansai is a good example: the departure lounge with its oversailing curved steel lattices and the flowing textile canopies signals significance beyond that of constructional need. The modern terminal uses structure and construction to communicate meaning and function in the messy, noisy theatre of airport life.

Space and structure together form important components in the design of terminals, but light – especially the white light of sunlight and the dappled play of daylight – provides a further element in the designer's repertoire. The terminal of the future will use light as a tactile material, moulded and shafted to guide passengers and to help define sitting areas or shopping malls. The single feature that distinguishes first-generation from second-generation terminals is the introduction of natural light into the centre of the buildings. As terminals have become larger light has assumed greater importance. Light is now used to draw passengers in the direction of flow from landside to airside, to define in the opposite direction baggage reclaim or exit

20.3 For the terminal designer light is a tactile material, which can be moulded and manipulated like any other. Light mixed with structure and interior space is the essence of the architectural experience. Hong Kong's new airport at Chek Lap Kok.
Architects: Foster and Partners.

routes. Light is also used to distinguish public from private routes, noisy from quiet areas, and festive from tranquil spaces. Sunlight is employed to provide sparkle, to animate structure, and to bring alive the exhilarating and lofty volumes of modern airport terminals.

In conjunction with light, roofs have changed their shape or form. The important role of interior volume in accommodating the functional diversity of modern terminals is complemented by great wavy roofs, which open and fold to bring in daylight. Light, both sunlight and diffused daylight,

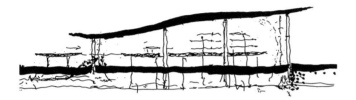

20.4 Section through Oslo Airport showing how differential height is a feature of modern terminals. Oslo Airport, Norway. Architects: Aviaplan AS.

is used to penetrate to dark cores of the terminal building, allowing interior planted gardens to become the norm and giving justification to the construction of shopping malls and retail villages within the huge megastructures of modern terminals. Taken to its logical conclusion the terminal of the future becomes a great doughnut-shaped building with an enormous atrium above a tree-planted winter garden at the heart of the building. In Nicholas Grimshaw's prototype design for the terminal of the twenty-first century, exhibited at the Venice Biennale in 1991, the vision extended to a naturally ventilated elliptical botanical garden around which passengers circulate left or right. Instead of arrivals and departures being differentiated by moving up or down a level, Grimshaw rotates them around a huge green garden in the centre. The roof is curved and depressed in the middle – not flat as in earlier terminals – with the space between the terminal and garden roof used to promote ventilation and smoke extraction on solar principles.

Modern terminals are increasingly engaging with the twentieth century's fascination with the vertical dimension. Early terminals were single- or double-storey buildings, but today's terminals are four storeys high (Kansai, for example), and future terminals are set to become nearly twice that height (such as Heathrow Terminal 5 and Seoul). Airports have always exploited the vertical dimension – flight itself is its ultimate manifestation – but the passenger terminal has only recently explored height and the spatial dynamics of multilevel. Technical and safety criteria limit the height of terminals, but that has not prevented designers from setting their buildings some way below ground in order to balance the vertical dimension with the horizontal. Superimposed levels expressed as daring bridges, flying escalators and interpenetrating lifts now connect the main floor levels of the modern terminal with secondary galleries. As retail floors are slotted between the principal departures and arrivals levels (as at Gatwick North Terminal) or form dramatic cliffside galleries overlooking the departure lounge (as at Stuttgart), the more the sense of vertical movement and interpenetrability of upward space is exploited. Multistorey terminals now replace the single- or double-deck terminals of old, adding to the complexity and drama of the modern terminal. This in turn has led architects to approach the design of terminals as exercises in cross-sectional manipulation as much as in plan. The sheer scale of the modern terminal demands the use of the vertical dimension in order to prevent terminals from becoming endless ground-capturing structures.

20.5 The vertical dimension exploited at Stuttgart Airport, Germany. Architects: Von Gerkan, Marg & Partners.

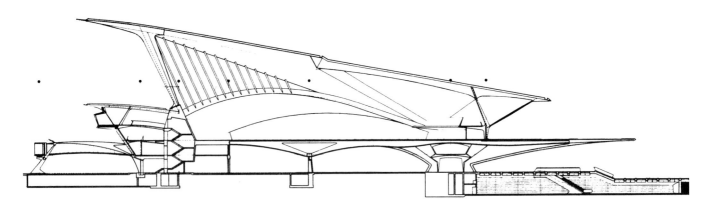

20.6 Curved expressive lines based upon zoomorphic shapes are replacing the Cartesian boxes of earlier terminals. Sondica Airport, Bilbao, Spain. Architect: Santiago Calatrava.

20.7 Glider wing profile proposed at Zurich Airport, Switzerland. Architects: Nicholas Grimshaw & Partners.

Culture and meaning through design

The architectural potential of the modern terminal is developing in all directions. The possibilities in space and height are being exploited: the dynamics of the horizontal and vertical plane, and the juxtaposition of the flat and undulating line. The serpentine curve of many recent terminals is a reflection of the sense of adventure and liberation from modernist design orthodoxy. Where once Cartesian two-way grids predominated (as at Bahrain International or Montreal Mirabel), the modern terminal is angular, directional, curved, exuberant and expressive. Rationality is in retreat; the romanticism and expressionism of the very earliest airports are in the ascendancy. Part of this is spurred on by the fear that the modern airport is becoming standardized, with little to distinguish one terminal from another. The serpentine line, the oval, the crescent, the angular and the fan-shaped terminal allow their designers to explore the dialectic between the international and the regional – to balance the tried and tested layouts dictated by IATA design

manuals with the distinctive cultural traditions of different parts of the world. The terminal of the twenty-first century will be a building of diversity and cultural richness whereas the terminal of the twentieth century was mainly a building of orthodoxy, repetition and standardization.

Another manifestation of the terminal of the future is the formal distinction made between key parts of the building. Early terminals made little architectural differentiation between the main check-in concourse, the departure lounge and the gate lounge. Neither did earlier terminals distinguish between the terminal and the transportation interchange that served it. However, as intermodal links become more extensive, and as the functional clarity between passengers actually flying and visitors to the airport becomes less clear, the terminal itself has tended to split into three recognizable elements: the transportation centre, the public concourse of the airport, and the gate lounge. The first now contains trains, buses and trams; the second retail malls, cinemas and business facilities; and the third bars and duty-free shops for those actually flying. The more the functions

20.8 Spatial separation of the parts gives the terminal greater formal strength. King Abdulaziz Airport, Jeddah, Saudi Arabia. Architects: Murphy/Jahn.

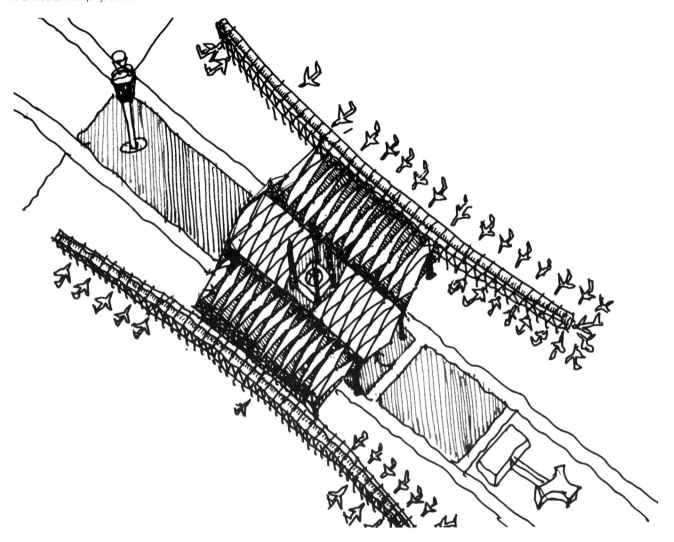

diversify, the greater is the need to accommodate each within its own building or sub-building rather than in a form-less, confusing megastructure.

Reconciling technology with ecology

The final expression of the terminal of the future is in the balances struck between nature and technology. The terminal of the twenty-first century will work with ecology

not against it: environmental systems and building systems operating largely in tune. This means, for instance, that the terminal will not be entirely sealed against the forces of climate, but will flex and respond to wind, rain and sun. The laws of nature and physics will determine in direct fashion the shape and operation of the building. The undulating roofs and angled walls of many recent airport terminals are a reflection of heightened ecological awareness, not a mere fashion. The folded wavy roof allows the natural air currents

20.9   The laws of nature and physics are coming together in fresh ways in modern terminals. Bangkok Airport, Thailand. Architects: Murphy/Jahn.

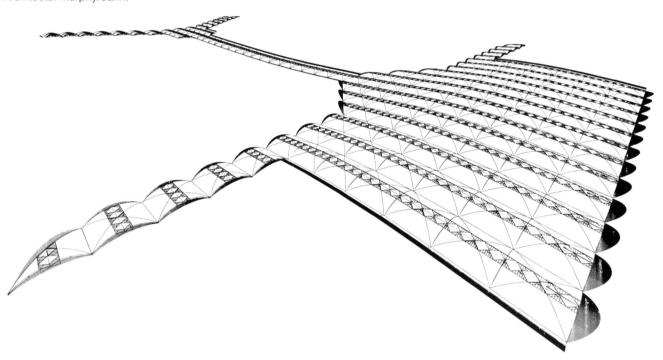

20.10   The roof at Hong Kong's new airport at Chek Lap Kok, has a sense of weightlessness that allows it almost to take off. Architects: Foster and Partners.

to ventilate the building without the use of climate-destroying air-conditioning; it facilitates smoke venting in the event of a fire; and it allows the terminal building to slip through the turbulent air currents of a typhoon. Interior planting too provides important air purification and humidity control. Both interior and exterior tree planting help to filter out sunlight, and provide the necessary tranquillity to overcome stress. The terminal of the future will live, move and breath like a giant living organism, stretching out tentacles of life and recycled impacts into the wider environment.

Terminals and tectonic expression

Because airport terminals engage more directly than most other building types in questions of structure and the poetics of construction, they approach tectonic perfection. A tectonic architecture is one of weightless effects, where the 'eurythmy of its parts and the articulation of its joints'[1] become the main means of expression. The best terminals combine in rare and splendid form the tectonic ideal: it is this symbiosis of spatial and technological expression that helps us to define the airport terminal.

Certain terminals, such as Stansted or Stuttgart, put greater weight upon tectonic than other forms of expression. Terminal 1 at Charles de Gaulle is muscular in its construction but hardly tectonic. A tectonic architecture is one in which structure and construction aspire to undermine the apparent weight of the building, reducing gravity to an almost floating unearthly state. Joints, lines, ties and slender members replace the heavyweight wall and column;

20.11 At Shenzhen Airport, China, the technology of construction hints at the cultural revolution currently being experienced in China. Architects: Llewelyn-Davies.

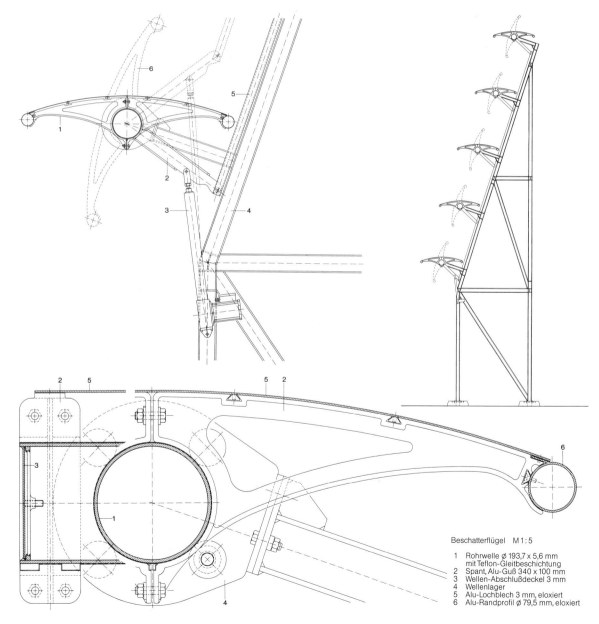

Beschatterflügel   M 1 : 5

1 Rohrwelle ⌀ 193,7 x 5,6 mm
   mit Teflon-Gleitbeschichtung
2 Spant, Alu-Guß 340 x 100 mm
3 Wellen-Abschlußdeckel 3 mm
4 Wellenlager
5 Alu-Lochblech 3 mm, eloxiert
6 Alu-Randprofil ⌀ 79,5 mm, eloxiert

20.12   The articulation of the joints and panels gives the terminal its tectonic interest at a detailed level. These drawings were prepared for Stuttgart Airport by Von Gerkan, Marg & Partners.

20.13 The section through the satellite spine at Chek Lap Kok, Hong Kong, shows how the technology of construction approaches that of the aircraft. Architects: Foster and Partners.

20.14 Stuttgart Airport, Germany, roof plan and section; the roof engages in tectonic discourse almost from the ground up. Architects: Von Gerkan, Marg & Partners.

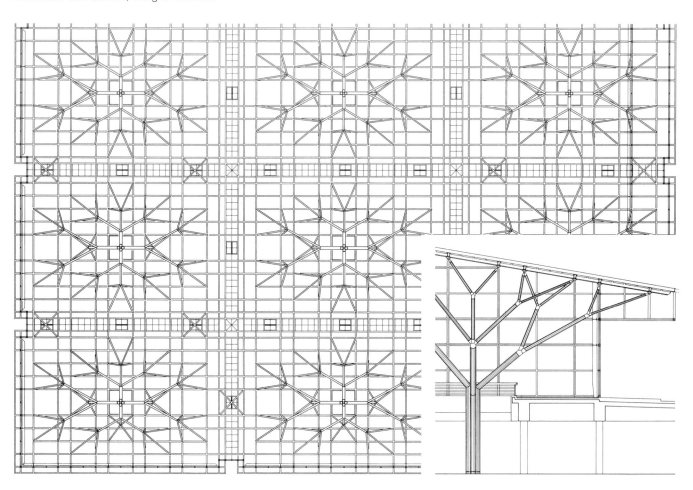

corners are understated or eroded; ceilings float; floors are thin horizontal planes.[2] The tectonic is becoming a quasi-autonomous force stamped upon modern terminals throughout the world. The reason is obvious: terminals are like the aircraft they serve – part of the topographical technology of modern life. For many architects the tectonic is the Gestalt of the age, and the terminal is the perfect vehicle for its expression.

Through technology, terminals are transformed into buildings of beauty and tranquillity. It is evident in the case studies of real and projected terminals that a particular approach to a tectonic architecture is unfolding. There are four identifiable elements in the terminal of the future:

- the search for weightlessness
- the poetic expression of the separate parts in space
- the articulation of the process of movement
- a preference for thinness over thickness.

Integrated with other design dictates, such as space management and ecology, there emerges a formal technological language for the creation of the modern terminal. In this the tectonic plays a greater or lesser part: it can shape the whole architectural concept (as in the design proposal for Heathrow Terminal 5) or merely the expression of elements (as in the roof at Kansai). Many architects see the question of technology and its expression as a spiritual mission; here the airport environment is a perfect testbed for their ideals. Where the constructional process as well as the overall concept is embraced within the tectonic discourse, there emerges an elegance befitting the airport age.

References

1. Kenneth Frampton, *Studies in Tectonic Culture: The Poetics of Construction in Nineteenth and Twentieth Century Architecture*, MIT Press, Cambridge, MA, 1995, p. 20.
2. *Ibid.*, p. 22.

Glossary

aircraft gate position
An aircraft stand close to a terminal and identified by a specific gate.

aircraft movement
An aircraft take-off or landing.

aircraft stand
Area on apron where aircraft is parked for servicing, loading etc.

airport
An area of land (including buildings, runways and control towers) for the arrival or departure of aircraft.

airport roads
Network of public and private roads providing access to airport buildings and areas.

airside
Area under government or airport control providing access to aircraft, and prohibited to non-travelling public.

apron
Paved area on airside where aircraft are parked for loading.

arriving passenger
A passenger arriving at terminal by air.

automated people-mover (travellator)
A transportation system for moving large numbers of people travelling distances too great on foot.

baggage
The personal property of a passenger.

carousel
Rotating baggage-claim device.

channel
Route for passengers through terminal.

CIP lounge
Special airport lounge for commercially important passengers.

closed-circuit television (CCTV)
Television primarily for security surveillance.

concessions
Passenger amenities provided by retail, food services etc.

concourse
Open space or hall in passenger terminal, used for circulation or waiting.

customs area
Part of terminal building under control of customs authorities.

departing passenger
A passenger departing from a terminal by air.

domestic flight
Flight within a single country not involving government controls.

dwell time
Time that a passenger spends in a terminal.

flight information board
Electronic signage board showing flight details.

gate
Point of passenger access to aircraft.

gate lounge
Waiting area adjacent to gate.

government controls
Checkpoints for government, health and immigration control.

hub airport
Airport designed primarily as a transfer facility, normally under the control of a single airline.

international flight
A flight between two or more countries, and subject to government controls.

landside
Area of airport or terminal to which non-travelling public has access.

loading bridge
Adjustable corridor bridging terminal and aircraft door.

meeting point
Defined area for rendezvous, normally in arrival concourse.

pier
A protruding extension to a terminal building giving access to aircraft gate.

satellite
Building surrounded by aircraft gate positions, normally separate from terminal building.

screening
Security checking by personal or electronic means of passengers and airport staff.

sterile area
Area of terminal building to which only security-cleared passengers and staff have access.

terminal building
A building between landside and airside where passenger and baggage processing takes place.

transit lounge
Area set aside for passenger who has arrived by plane but is not terminating at airport.

visitor
Non-passenger and non-employee using terminal building.

Bibliography

Books

Ashford, N.J., Stanton, H.P.M. and Moore, C.A. *Airport Operations*, Pitman, London, 1991.

Ashford, N.J. and Wright, P. *Airport Engineering*, John Wiley & Sons, New York, 1991.

Blow, C.J.. *Airport Terminals*, 2nd edn, Butterworth-Heinemann, Oxford, 1996.

Dash, M. *The Limit: Engineering on the Boundaries of Science*, BBC Books, London, 1995.

Doganis, R. *The Airport Business*, Routledge, London, 1992.

Frampton, K. *Studies in Tectonic Culture: The Poetics of Construction in Nineteenth and Twentieth Century Architecture*, MIT Press, Cambridge, MA, 1995.

Hart, W. *The Airport Passenger Terminal*, John Wiley & Sons, New York, 1986.

Horonjeff, R. *Planning and Design of Airports*, McGraw-Hill, New York, 1962; 4th edn, 1992.

Whitelaw, J. (ed.) *Airports of the 21st Century*, Thomas Telford Publications, London, 1995.

Wickens, A.H. and Yates, L.R. (eds) *Passenger Transport after 2000 AD*, Chapman & Hall, London, 1995.

Wright, A.J. *World Airports*, Ian Allan, London, 1991.

Journals

Many have been employed, but the reader is directed particularly to *The Architectural Review*, *Progressive Architecture* and *Flight International*.

Reports

Many have been cited in text, but see particularly Civil Aviation Authority Annual Reports, Design Guides and Accounts; BAA Annual Reports, Retail Reports, Briefing Manuals; BA Annual Reports.

Note: The bibliography refers to principal sources employed: further references can be found at the end of each chapter.

Illustration acknowledgements

The author and publisher would like to thank the following individuals and organizations for permission to reproduce material. We have made every effort to contact and acknowledge copyright holders, but if any errors have been made we would be happy to correct them at a later printing.

Photographers

Richard Davies 15.7, **7**
Dennis Gilbert 10.4, 13.9, 15.2, 16.5, **6**
Ken Kirkwood 16.4
Michael Penner 1.12, 1.15, 9.3, 16.13, 16.14, 16.15, **14**
Mario Renzi 1.6, 4.1, 11.2
Peter Schulz 1.13, **3**
Lee Taylor 13.1
Morley von Sternburg 3.2, 17.1
Nigel Young 18.2

Individuals and organizations

Adtranz 9.13, 16.2
Austin: Smith-Lord 4.2
Aviaplan AS 8.9, 12.1, 12.2, 14.1, 14.7, 18.4, 20.4
British Airport Authority 1.3, 1.5, 1.9, 1.17, 2.1, 5.8, 5.9, 6.2, 9.9, 15.13, 15.14, 15.15

Dallas/Fort Worth International Airport 13.3
Flughafen Hamburg GmbH 1.14
Foster and Partners 2.11, 8.12, 8.13, 8.14, 8.15, 10.3, 11.1, 15.9, 16.1, 16.6, 16.7, 16.8, 20.3, 20.10, 20.13
Kansai International Airport Co Ltd 1.2, 1.7, 11.3, 20.2, **12, 13**
Llewelyn Davies **2**
Manser Associates **4, 5**
Aéroport Marseille, Provence 6.4
Munich Airport 2.3, 5.4, 8.4
Murphy/Jahn 2.2, 2.4, 2.8, 2.9, 3.1, 6.5, 8.5, 8.6, 8.9, 11.11, 12.3, 13.7, 14.2, 14.4, 14.5, 14.6, 15.16, 15.17, 16.16, 16.21, 18.6, 19.2, 20.8, 20.9, **1, 8, 10, 11**
Nicholas Grimshaw & Partners 15.10, 15.11, 20.1, 20.7
NV Luchthaven Schiphol 1.10, 7.3, 8.16, 9.8, 18.3
Ove Arup and Partners 5.1
Parr Partnership 6.3
Renzo Piano Building Workshop 9.4, 9.5
Richard Rogers Partnership 5.10, 6.4, 11.6, 15.12
Scott Brownrigg and Turner 2.5, 2.6, 2.10, 5.5, 7.4, 11.10, 14.3
Stuttgart Airport Authority 1.16, 16.11, 20.5, **9**
Terry Farrell and Partners 2.7, 18.1

Figure numbers in **bold** indicate colour illustrations.

Index

JAZZ IMPROVISATION

VOLUME IV

Contemporary Piano Styles

John Mehegan

Watson-Guptill Publications/New York

Amsco Publications
New York/London/Sydney

To my family: Gay, Tara,

Sean, Sophie and Bronson

Copyright © 1965 by Watson-Guptill Publications,
a division of Billboard Publications, Inc.,
1515 Broadway, New York, NY 10036

Exclusive distributors to the

Music Sales Corporation
257 Park Avenue South
New York, NY 10010

Music Sales Limited
8/9 Frith Street
London W1V 5TZ, England

Music Sales Pty. Limited
120 Rothschild Street
Rosebery
Sydney, NSW 2018, Australia

Library of Congress Catalog Card Number: 58-13525

ISBN 0-8230-2574-8

Manufactured in U.S.A.

15 16 17 18 19/99 98 97 96 95

PREFACE

For twenty years or more, I have spent most of my working time as a singer of folksongs. But I have never been able to withstand my fascination with all music, so that at times I have written popular songs, composed orchestral scores for films and T.V., played tuba and bass fiddle as a young man in bands and orchestras, sung in church choirs and madrigal groups — and in between, listened hard to music from pre-Gregorian chant to post-Stravinsky.

It behooved me some years ago to take another musical busman's holiday and study jazz piano with Johnny Mehegan. My ears sprang up almost literally; I had been listening to jazz, I discovered, without hearing it. I found out why I really didn't get too moved by its most important element: improvisation. It is one thing to like the singing of, say, Billie Holiday; it is something else entirely to understand what the musicians behind her are doing with the underlying melodic, harmonic and rhythmic structure, without which there would be no musical Billie Holiday. It is this structure which is jazz, no matter how pretty Peggy Lee is, or how many teeth Louis Armstrong shows when he grins, or how tricky the acrobatics of Gene Krupa or how many prizes awarded by jazz magazines.

Johnny Mehegan has built a unique musical monument. History remembers with exceptional honor those men gifted enough to sift and winnow the complex variables, of human knowledge into a Code of Law. This Johnny has done with these melodic, harmonic and rhythmic laws of consonant jazz improvisation, and, in four books, has given it, at long last, a "habitation and a name."

Tom Glazer
May, 1965

CONTENTS

SECTION II

SECTION III

INTRODUCTION

The aspiring jazz musician — and jazz pianist in particular — has been long faced with the dilemma of the lack of any clearly organized field of thought which is true to tradition, comprehensive, and yet presents the materials that he desires without stylistic constriction.

As one of those who was forced to wade into this vast area in order to select, sort, and organize these materials so that I would have the tools to be a developing musician I can testify to the frustrations and discouragements that this task entails.

Yet, unless one is to be a slave to vogue, and dependent on the questionable rewards of mimicry, one must know in some clearly organized way about the materials which one wishes to use in improvisation. It is only through thorough understanding of these materials and the principles involved in their use that increasing degrees of freedom in performance are gained (or won).

The more clearly one understands the fundamentals, the more encompassing can be the generalization — and thus the more true freedom is won (attained).

It is my opinion that the presentation of materials to be found in John Mehegan's books on improvisation are the most concise, thorough and comprehensive, and will offer the talented pianist a priceless saving of time, and the benefit of a concept which will not impose style, and therefore will allow his individual treatment to develop.

Bill Evans
May, 1965

INTRODUCTION

The history of jazz piano from 1950 to the present has been an intense struggle between the forces of the present and those of the past to create an amalgam of both which can inherit the future. These forces are represented by individuals who fall roughly into the following groups: the traditionalists, the moderates and the avant-garde. This volume will deal mainly with the efforts of the first two groups with some commentary on the avant-garde which at this writing appears to be embattled with the age-old problem of the artist's relationship to freedom on the one hand and discipline on the other.

The following outline illustrates the major (indicated by *) and minor figures in this turbulent period:

THE TRADITIONALISTS
        Oscar Peterson*
        Les McCann
        Gene Harris
        Barry Harris
        Eddie Costa

THE MODERATES
        Bill Evans*
        Wynton Kelly
        Ahmad Jamal
        Horace Silver
        Bobby Timmons
        Red Garland
        McCoy Tyner

THE AVANT-GARDE
        Don Friedman
        Claire Fisher
        Bob James
        Herbie Hancock
        Andrew Hill
        Cecil Taylor

THE TRADITIONALISTS

The traditionalists are sometimes referred to as the "funk" school, which is a reference to the presence of blues and gospel idioms in their playing. McCann and Gene Harris are definitely in the "funk" school. Barry Harris is probably the outstanding exponent of the traditions of style and idiom established by Bud Powell. The late Eddie Costa was a successor to the "hard bop" idioms of Horace Silver, expressed through the aggressive mallet technique employed by vibraphonists.

Peterson is the major figure in the present struggle to preserve the vast repository of style and idiom extending back to the Mid-Thirties. In an unheralded Carnegie Hall concert in 1949, this Canadian pianist established himself as the major consolidating figure of the Fifties and, simultaneously, one of the central figures in the contemporary scene.

This was indeed fortunate, since in the course of the tumultuous years of the Forties, much had been overlooked, prematurely discarded or overemphasized, to the general detriment of jazz piano. More important, Peterson, almost single-handedly, rescued jazz piano from the secondary accompaning role it had assumed, and re-established it as a major voice in the noble jazz tradition of Hines, Waller, Wilson and Tatum.

Many neglected innovations introduced by such keyboard figures as Art Tatum, Nat Cole, Jimmy Jones, Bud Powell, Erroll Garner, Nat Jaffe, Lennie Tristano, Thelonious Monk, Horace Silver, Cy Walter, George Shearing, Jess Stacy, Dodo Marmarosa, Tad Dammeron and Ellis Larkins, plus a host of horn men from Benny Carter and Coleman Hawkins through Lester Young, Dizzy Gillespie, Charlie Parker and Miles Davis — this vast amalgam of sound — were added to Peterson's personal genius to forge one of the most persuasive keyboard styles of the Fifties and early Sixties.

Despite this seemingly eclectic background, Peterson has made important innovations in areas equally as vital as those altered by Powell and Silver. First, Peterson, by virtue of his vast technique and knowledge, can swing "harder" than any other pianist in the contemporary jazz scene. He possesses a sense of form and dynamics sadly missing in many present-day pianists. Above all, he displays the ability to communicate his intentions to an audience with the sureness of an experienced concert artist. He is a *pianist* in the entire connotation of that term.

An important aspect of Peterson's genius is his ability to play "horn lines" — ideas accessible on the saxophone or trumpet, but generally "unpianistic" when applied to the keyboard. This ability has endowed Peterson with a melodic quality in his improvised lines generally lacking in jazz pianists. This ability, translated into practical pianistic terms, signifies that Peterson seems to possess the ability to "pre-hear" any succession of intervals and simultaneously to translate these steps into finger strokes — something even the most skilled jazz pianist will find difficult. Most jazz pianists content themselves by playing easily accessible lines through manual mechanics rather than attempting "unpianistic horn lines" that are more melodic. Unlike his contemporaries, Peterson possesses the ability to play these inaccessible horn lines — a part of his distinguished sound.

Figure 1 illustrates the contrast between a pianistic phrase and a relatively unpianistic phrase by Peterson.

Fig. 1.

For some years Peterson used a guitar-bass accompaniment. This strong harmonic underpinning has seriously altered the role of the left hand as a supporting structure for the "horn line" in the right hand.

The basis of the Peterson "sound" lies in a marvelously fluid right hand supported by a modernized version of the Tatum scale-tone tenth-chord system (*Jazz Improvisation*, Vol. III, Section II). This sound first appeared in the Nat Cole trio of the early Forties, but was properly mounted as a major keyboard style by Peterson in the early Fifties. This sound was a reaction against the arid "shell" style of Powell and Silver.

This style, as presented in the Peterson trio, was a signal for the return of "vertical" harmony, which had languished through the "horizontal" period of the Forties. At the same time, it made clear to all jazz pianists that the prevailing shell style was no longer tolerable, and, regardless of hand span, that some other solution must be evolved to meet the growing resurgence of vertical harmony in the emerging keyboard image. Although Peterson, himself, played no active role in the emerging image of the new pianism, his re-statement of the past both in beauty of line and effortless performance will remain a permanent document in the history of jazz piano.

THE MODERATES

The first indications of a general move away from both tenth and shell formations in the left hand appeared in the Mid-Fifties. Initially heard in recordings of "Red" Garland and Wynton Kelly and later in popularized versions by Ahmad Jamal, the new "sound" gradually emerged in the form of left-hand voicings, or ornamental structures employing various componants of ninths, elevenths and thirteenths. However, this style remained in a fallow state until the turn of the decade and the appearance of Bill Evans. Much as Peterson had captured the best of the Forties, Evans immediately established himself as a sensitive consolidator of the harmonic explorations of the Fifties and, in addition, brought this incipient style to its fruition through his personal genius. Evans' achievement was multi-faceted in that the previous concepts of rhythm, harmony and melody were subjected to a searching analysis, and many previously revered ideas were either abandoned or seriously modified.

This stylistic sound, which is adaptable to the left hand for supporting a "blowing line" or to the right-hand for " 'comping," (accompanying) purposes, will be treated thoroughly in this volume.

Since any organization of musical sound derives its final character from the rhythmic crucible which surrounds it, Evans' innovation in the time factor of jazz simultaneously altered the prevailing harmonic and melodic values. First, the previous tenet of a hard, percussive, unpedaled line was abandoned in favor of a legato, pedaled attack in which the marcato eighth note was replaced by a filigree of sixteenths and thirty-seconds, interspersed with highly syncopated clusters of chords. In Evans' work with bass and drums (especially with Paul Motian and the late Scott LaFarro), time values were even more modified to such a point that the underlying quarter-note pulse was perceptable only to the most acute listener. As in contemporary painting, Evans did much to destroy the photographic image and to create a delicate world of the abstract and the surreal.

In the previous period there had been some general exploration of the harmonic idioms of French Impressionism, but under the direct influence of Miles Davis and arranger Gil Evans, pianist Bill Evans extracted an entirely new body of idiom from the early Twentieth-Century Spanish composers, Albeniz, de Falla, and Granados, as well as the French Impressionists. In general Twentieth-Century Spanish music is, on the one hand, more introspective than its French counterpart and, on the other hand, is infused with the rhythmic vitality of the Spanish temperament, which is closely akin to our own pulsating energy. The essence of this style, to a large extent, can be described as the use of a highly selective group of "textures" or "voicings" which are capable of conveying chord values with great definition, although, in most cases, the tones of the structure have been totally rearranged and the root completely deleted from the total sound. The term "voicing" is usually applied to a chord in which one or more of its basic components (root, third, fifth, seventh) has been reassigned to an entirely different register of the keyboard or transferred to another instrument — usually the string bass.

The melodic factor in jazz is usually to be found in the improvised line. In this area, Evans introduced many startling innovations. Aside from the previously mentioned introduction of the pedaled, legato touch, the older concept of "target" tones, also known as the Parker "hinges" (see Vol. I, pp. 127 - 131), were to some extent abandoned in favor of "vertical" lines moving in long, extended phrases without any particular horizontal connections. Furthermore, previous concepts of the memorable melodic line, as evinced by Peterson, were largely abandoned. Unheard of structures, such as unmodified scales and modes (displaced scales), appeared as part of a revolutionary attack upon the traditional, improvised line.

THE AVANT-GARDE

What these various innovations will come to mean to the future of jazz piano is difficult to evaluate at this writing. First, it should be pointed out that a small segment of the jazz-piano Establishment has been slow to accept these innovations, which represent a major assault upon time-worn concepts. Many pianists have remained within the "funk" school; others have remained loyal to the enduring Powell idiom, which dates back to the early Forties. The innovations of Evans and the avant-garde have raised serious problems regarding both the essence of the jazz art and its future as the music approaches the vanishing point of both tonality and the rhythmic symmetry that sent the image of jazz to the far reaches of the earth. Even at this writing, it is apparent that jazz has already lost the enormous periphery of its audience; jazz clubs are closing or changing their policies to the major recipiant of the "floater" sections of the jazz audience, the folk musicians. Perhaps jazz is about to go "underground," as it did in 1940, to begin another painful transition. If this is true, the present struggle will be possibly a struggle for actual survival, since the contemporary terms are much more severe than those of the

Forties; this time the conflict is not between two levels of tonality or two images of the jazz beat, the conflict is between tonality and atonality on the one hand and the classic symmetry of the jazz beat and the free form of serious contemporary music on the other. It may very well be that the future of jazz will be decided in this musical Armageddon.

The avant-garde has challenged this sound barrier, armed with the "freedom" of free form, but, at the same time, held captive by the very lack of freedom which, in the past, had made the jazz musician free. In the past, the jazz pianist had evolved an intensely expressive idiom based in part upon a fierce premise of what *was to be played* joined by an equally fierce premise of what *was not to be played*. This privilege of choosing the "best of both worlds" no longer exists for the jazz musician. At the same time, an art form must go on to its own personal destiny, whatever that destiny may be.

There are many factors here: the painful need for acceptance, the desire to escape from the night-club "entertainment" atmosphere and, above all, the aspiration to transform the art form from a parochial craft into a major art. The freedom and status of the serious musician is a constant reminder to the jazzman of the monetary and psychic rewards that await the successful practitioner in a "high" art. There is a double burden here for the Negro musician, who sees both himself and his art held in either silent contempt or distant admiration.

For this reason, in recent years many leading Negro figures in jazz have increasingly appeared to use the art form as a forum to project a variety of personal and social angers. This is an inevitable step since, if the Negro people can rightfully claim an art form, it is certainly jazz. The use of art as a social platform is not new; in fact, there is a compelling argument maintaining that all great art is the result of dramatizing social injustice. There is a strange poetry here, for jazz certainly began as a form of protest against the social injustice of the Reconstruction period in the South. Eventually, it became an important facet of American popular culture serving as entertainment for those millions of people throughout the world who recognized the charm of the symbol while, at the same time, forgot the pain of the reality that created the symbol.

Perhaps jazz must momentarily return to its womb of protest in order to revitalize the joy and affirmation that has always been its personal testament.

John Mehegan
May 15, 1965
New York City

18

Oscar Peterson's

JOY SPRING

JOY SPRING

Oscar Peterson

(Bb)   IVm   bVIIx

(Bb)   I$^6_5$ VIx^{b9}

(Bb)   II   V

(Bb)   I   L.H.   L.H.

(B)   II   V

(B)   I   (A)   II   V^{b9}

(A)   I   (G)   II   V

21

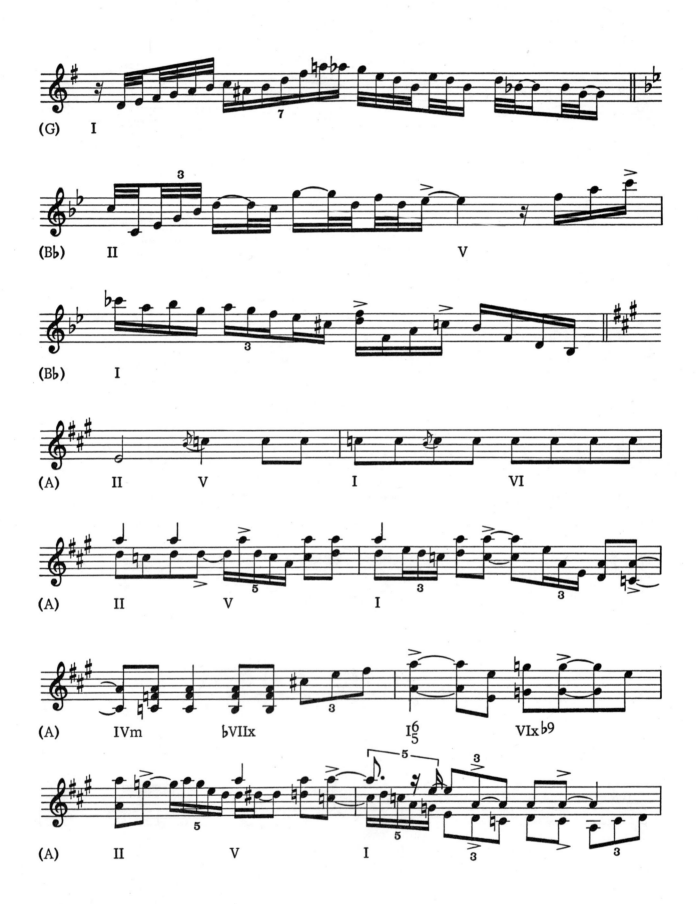

(G)   I

(B♭)   II   V

(B♭)   I

(A)   II   V   I   VI

(A)   II   V   I

(A)   IVm   ♭VIIx   I⁶₅   VIx♭9

(A)   II   V   I

(A)   I   I   VI

(A)   II   V   I

(A)   IVm   ♭VIIx

(A)   III   VIx

(A)   II   ♭13
                  V ♭9

(A)   I

(B♭)   II   V

23

(B♭)   I   VI

(B♭)   IIø   ♭13 / V ♭9

(B♭)   I

(B♭)   IVm   ♭VIIx

(B♭)   III   VIx

(B♭)   II   V

(B♭)   I   (B)   II   V

25

(A)   IVm   bVIIx   III   VIx

(A)   II   V   I

(A)   I   I   VI

(A)   II   V   I

(A)   IVm   bVIIx

(A)   III   VIx   II   b13
                                                                           V b9

(A)   I

(Bb)   II   V

(Bb)   I   VI

(Bb)   IIø   ♭13   3
                  V ♭9   I

(Bb)   IVm   ♭VIIx   III   VIx

(Bb)   II   V

(Bb)   I

(B)   II   V   I

Bill Evans'

PERI'S SCOPE

PERI'S SCOPE

Bill Evans

II   V   III   VI   II   V

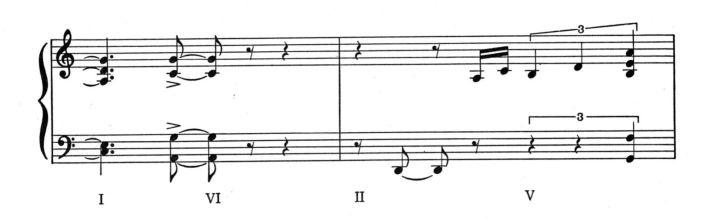

I   VI   II   V

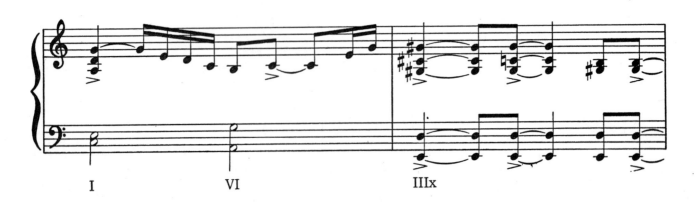

I   VI   IIIx

Used by Permission.

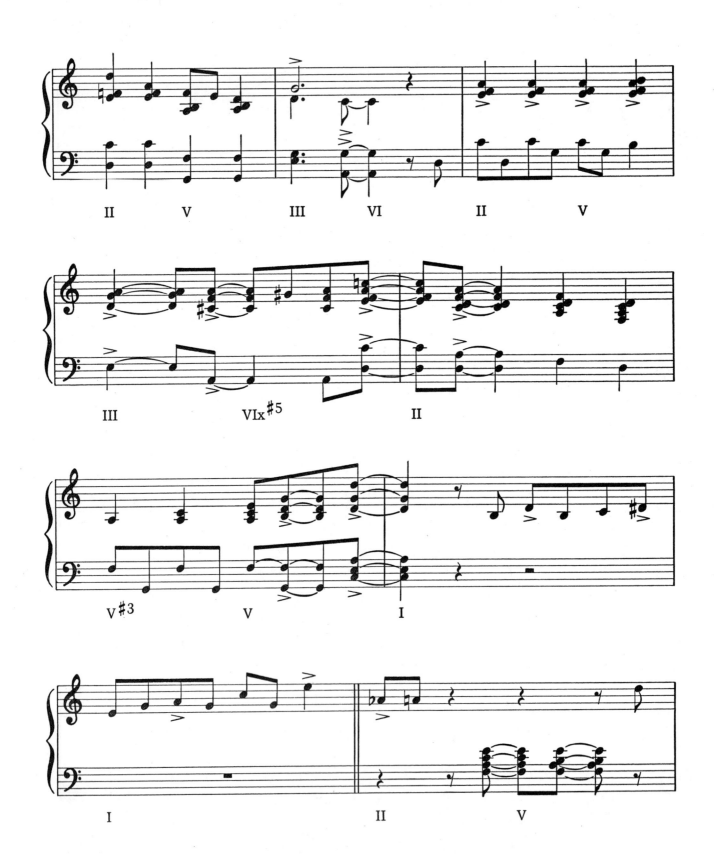

II   V   III   VI   II   V

III   VIx#5   II

V#3   V   I

I   II   V

32

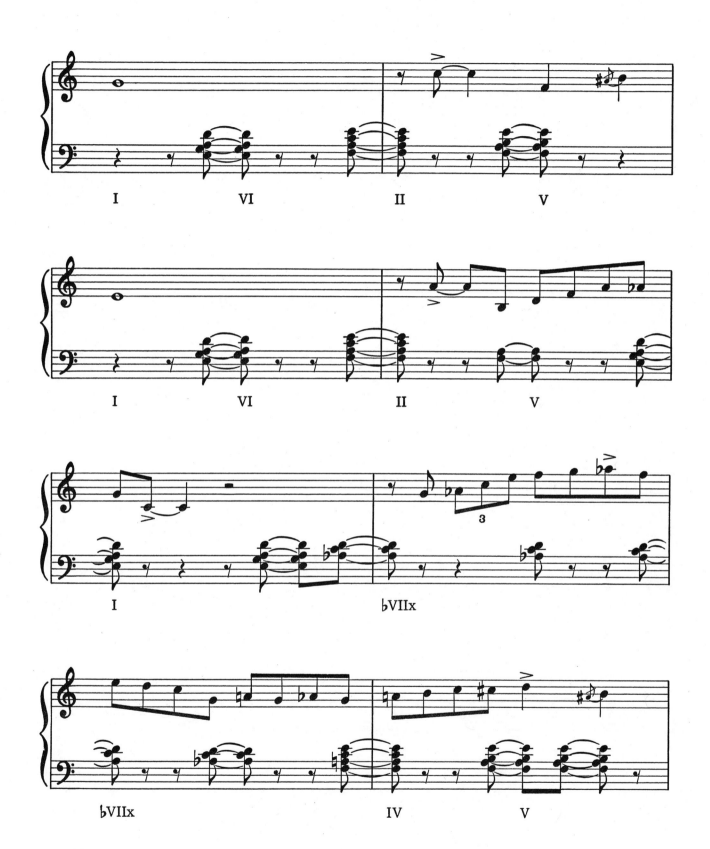

34

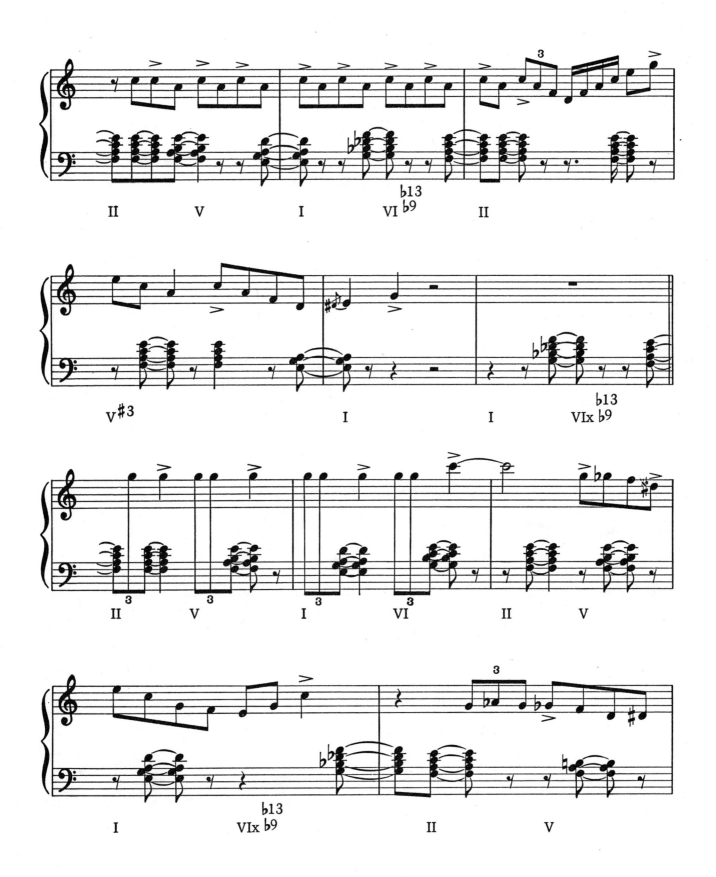

35

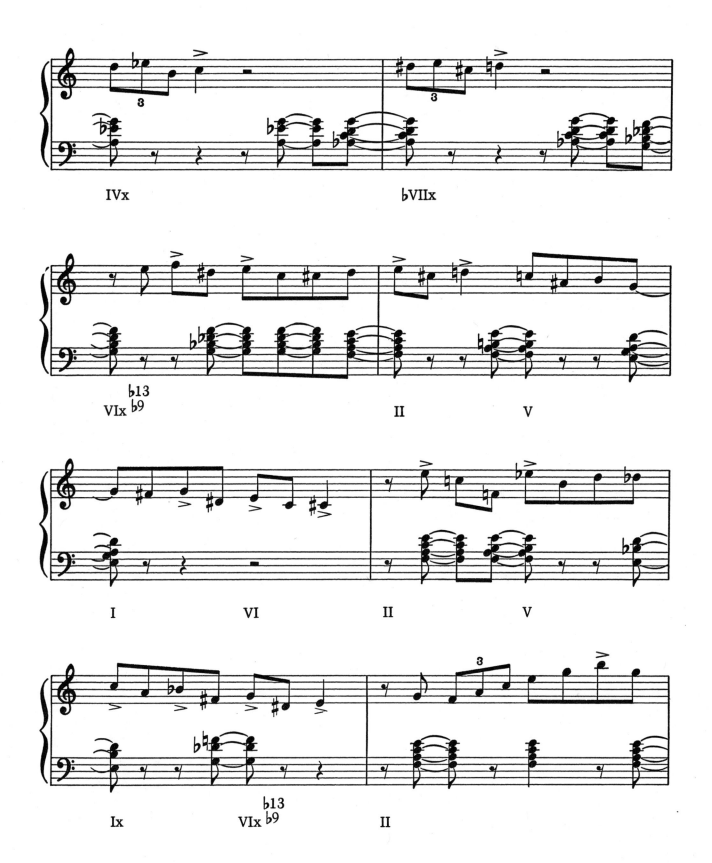

IVx   ♭VIIx

VIx ♭13 ♭9   II   V

I   VI   II   V

Ix   VIx ♭13 ♭9   II

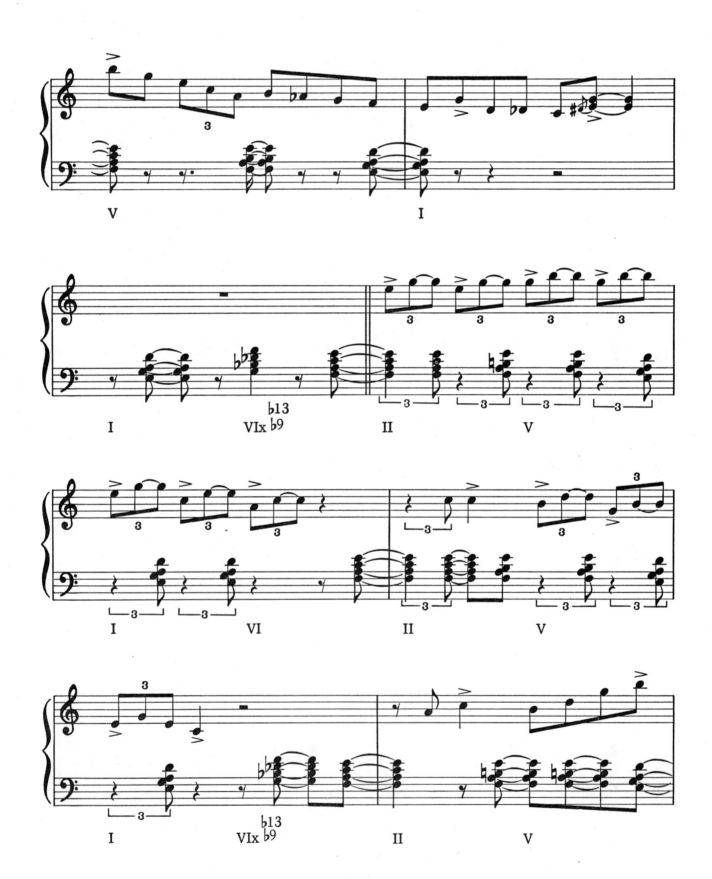

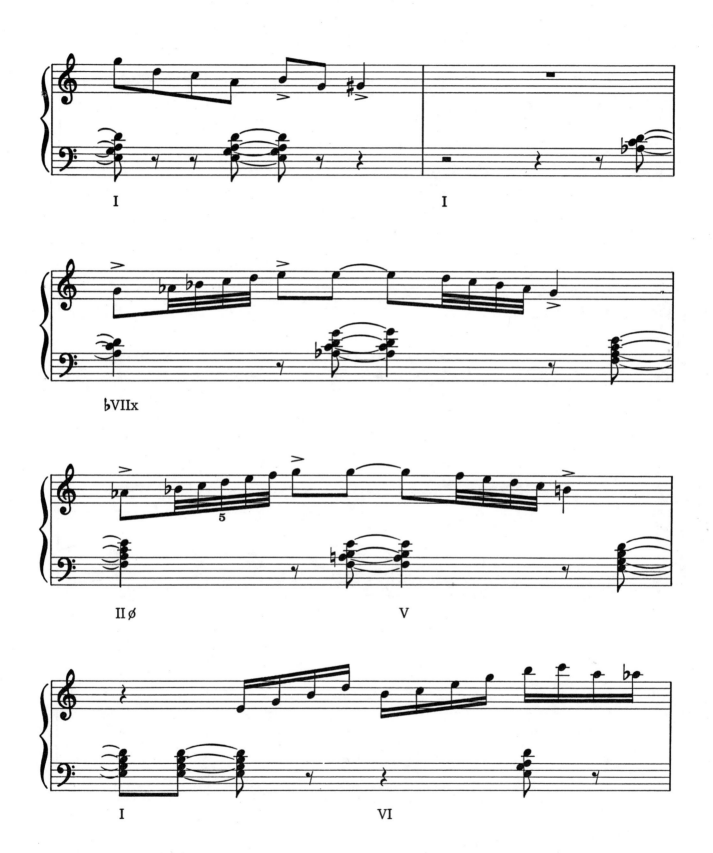

II   V♭9

I   V♯3

IVx

♭VIIx

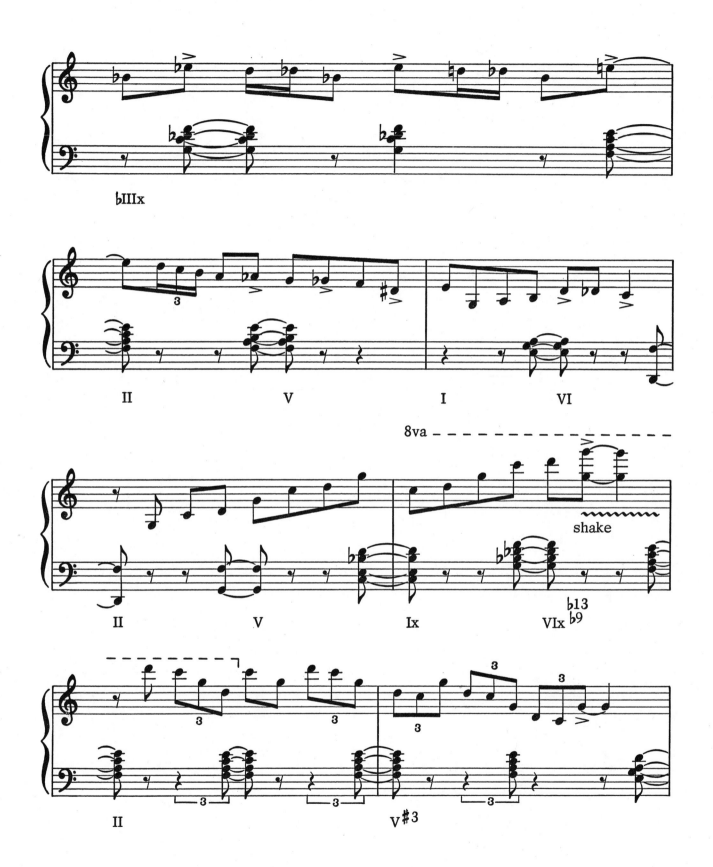

bVIIx   II   V

I   VI   II   V

IIIx#5   IV

IVx   bVIIx

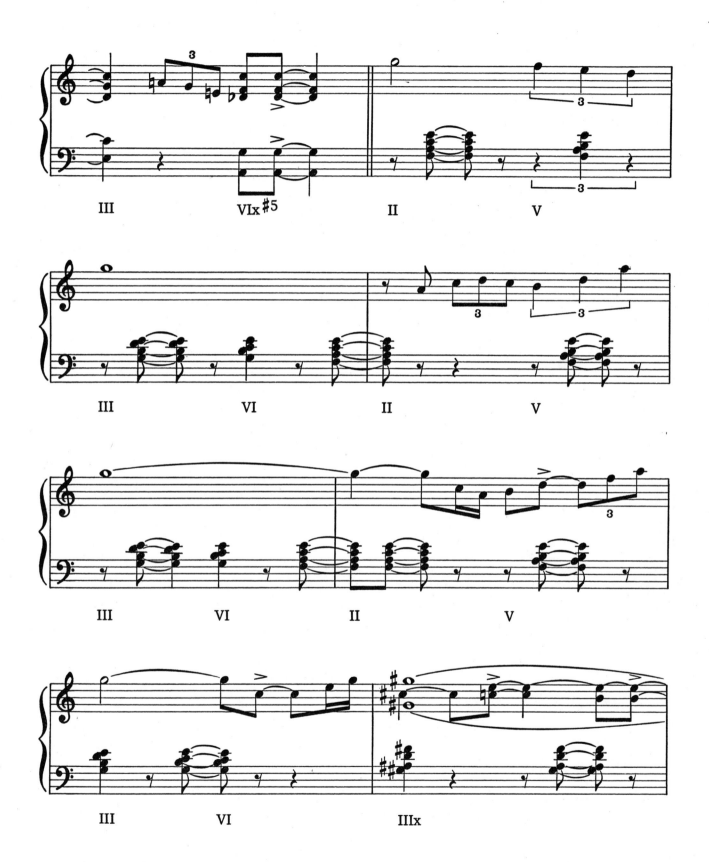

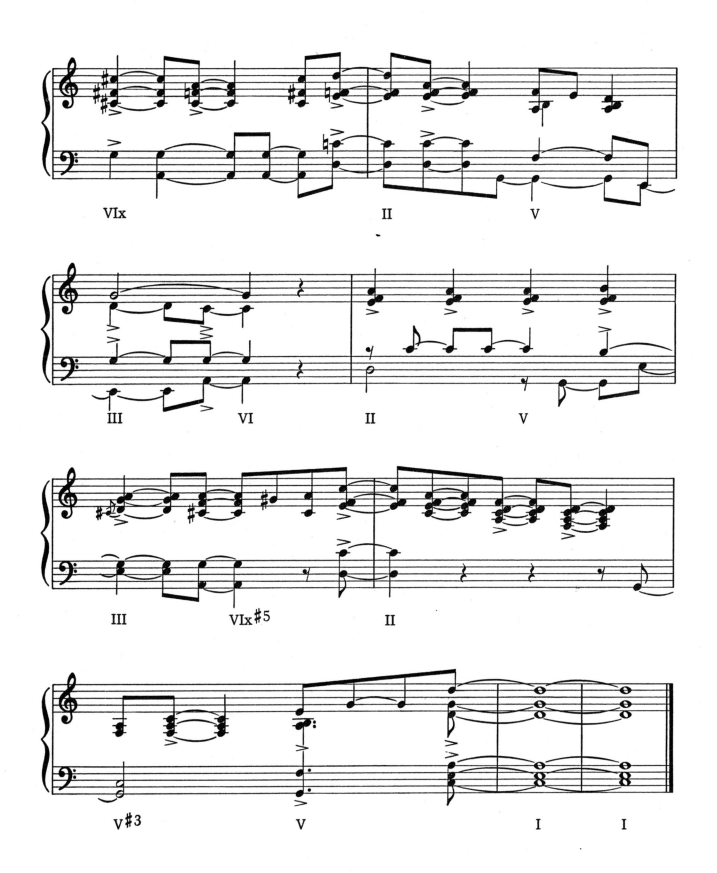

VIx   II   V

III   VI   II   V

III   VIx#5   II

V#3   V   I   I

General

The voicings to be considered in this section will be referred to as the (A) Form and the (B) Form simply to distinguish one from the other. These two *forms* constitute the basic textural sound of contemporary jazz piano. It is important to remind the student that these structures are not chords, since the roots, do not appear, and they are therefore incomplete structures. The voicings will be presented first, followed by a section dealing with solo piano in which the various devices of integrating roots and voicings will be described. Following this, sections on fragmentation, " 'comping" and the improvised line will complete the material on the (A) and (B) Forms.

The history of the (A) Form begins in the classical piano literature of the Nineteenth Century. This form first appeared in the piano works of Frederick Chopin and became one of the vernacular sounds of the Nineteenth-Century piano concerto. In this form, the *third* appears in the bass of the minor voicing, the *seventh* appears in the bass of the dominant voicing, and the *third* again appears in the bass of the major voicing. This is the older of the two forms and is usually more familiar to the average pianist for that reason.

The (B) Form appeared about one hundred years later in the piano compositions of Maurice Ravel. This form clearly reveals the poignant textures characteristic of the impressionistic music of the Twentieth century and represents the sound of "modernity" in contemporary orchestration. In this form the *seventh* appears in the bass of the minor voicing, the *third* appears in the bass of the dominant voicing, and the *seventh* or *added sixth* appears in the bass of the major voicing. As the student will learn, one form is an "inversion" of the other, although the term "inversion" is not proper because the root is absent, thus making the structure incomplete; the more appropriate term is "permutation."

The history of these forms in the popular music of America dates from the Mid-Thirties in the scores of Fletcher Henderson and Duke Ellington. Here the voicings appeared in the part-writing of the saxophone sections, and became the accepted sound for sax-section backgrounds for vocals and horn solos. In the beginning the (B) Form was seldom used, but by the Mid-Forties, this form had been permanently integrated with the (A) Form. Also during this period, guitarists explored these voicings, although the appearance of Charlie Christian completely changed the emphasis of the guitar from the vertical concept of Lang and Van Eps to the modern horizontal style.

Pianists began isolating these voicings in the Mid-Forties, first the (A) Form and later the (B) Form. These voicings are employed by modern pianists for many purposes. They are used in the left hand to support a melody, an improvised line, or with modified Shearing blocks in the right hand to form the two-handed "concerto" sound of the modern period. These same voicings are employed in the right hand, coupled with roots in the left as a major "'comping" device. Strangely enough, the indisputable master of this 'comping idiom is Horace Silver, who made a major transition in his style from the shell style of the previous decade. The student is strongly advised to listen to the more recent recordings of Silver in order to become acquainted with this aspect of the (A) and (B) Forms.

LESSON 2.

The (A) Form

(See the Introduction and Lesson 1 for a general description of the (A) and (B) Forms).

The general keyboard register of the (A) and (B) Forms appears in Fig. 1.

Fig. 1. 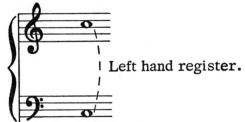 Left hand register.

These voicings will be initially studied on the basis of the II-V-I pattern in twelve keys — the basic cadence pattern of all jazz harmony. For the moment, we will consider these voicings in the right hand while playing the roots in the left hand. This device will enable the student to hear the entire structure before placing these voicings in the left hand without the roots.

Since the entire five-quality system may be easily derived from the II - V - I pattern, the following modal table will be employed:

CHORD QUALITY	MODE
Major	Ionian
Dominant	Mixolydian
Minor	Dorian
Half-Diminished	Dorian (modified)
Diminished	Dorian (modified)

50

If the student is not familiar with this material, it is suggested that a thorough study be made of Vol. I, Section VI.

The Ⓐ Form voicings are as follows:

II (Dorian) 3 5 7 2
V (Mixolydian) 7 2 3 6
I (Ionian) 3 5 6 2 (See Fig. 2.)

Fig. 2.

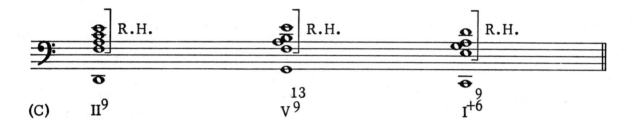

In Fig. 2 the formations are as follows:

II

D—root
F—minor third
A—perfect fifth   Chord — D minor ninth
C—minor seventh
E—ninth

V

G—root
F—minor seventh
A—ninth   Chord — G dominant nine thirteenth
B—major third
E—thirteenth

I

C—root
E—major third
G—perfect fifth   Chord — C major ninth added sixth
A—added sixth
D—ninth

(all intervals based on the *prevailing mode* of the chord)

51

In the tone row, 2 becomes 9, 6 becomes plus 6 in M and m, 6 becomes 13 in x (Fig. 3).

Fig. 3.

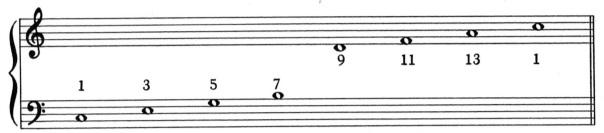

The explanation of 6 becoming 13 in the dominant chord may be tested by the student. Play C E G A, C E♭ G A and C E A B♭ as broken arpeggios, striking the A in each chord with more intensity in order to hear the relationship of the tone to the chord. Upon striking C E A B♭, the student will detect a color value of A not present in the remaining two chords. This value is formed by the specific presence of the major third and minor seventh comprising the dominant chord: this unique value is referred to as "Thirteen."

Figure 4 illustrates the (A) Form voicings for the remaining 11 keys. Figure 5 illustrates the inner-voice movement of each interval in the transition from II to V to I.

Fig. 4.

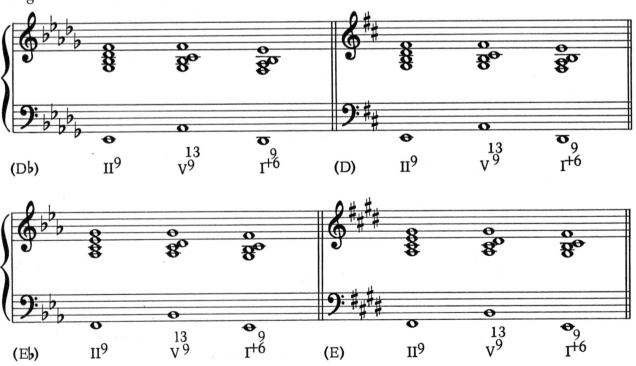

(F) II⁹ V⁹/13 I⁺⁶/9 (F♯) II⁹ V⁹/13 I⁺⁶/9

(G) II⁹ V⁹/13 I⁺⁶/9 (A♭) II⁹ V⁹/13 I⁺⁶/9

(A) II⁹ V⁹/13 I⁺⁶/9 (B♭) II⁹ V⁹/13 I⁺⁶/9

(B) II⁹ V⁹/13 I⁺⁶/9

Fig. 5.

(C)   3rd   7th   3rd   5th   9th   5th

(C)   7th   3rd   6th   9th   13th   9th

DRILL: Study and memorize the voicings in Figs. 2 and 4 for automatic facility.

Figure 6 is a bass line for "Stella by Starlight." This tune was treated in an inversion study in Vol. I, Lesson 24. The present bass line represents a conventional chord chart.

NOTE: The student is advised not to employ various trick devices of dealing with these voicings: i.e., II in Ⓐ Form involves a II root with a IV scale-tone chord. Such devices can only result in a permanently distorted visual and auditory conception of these important voicings.

Fig. 6.

pick-up
VI₂ // ♭Vm / VIIx / II / V / Vm / ♭V / IV / ♭VIIx / I VI /

♭V∅ VIIx / III / VI∅ ⁴₃ / III₂ / Io / VII / IIIx / VIx ♯⁵ / ♭IIIx / II ♯⁷ /

II III / IV ♭³ / ♭VIIx / III / VI VI₂ / ♭V∅ / VIIx / III∅ / VIx /

II∅ / ♭IIx / I / I //

STELLA BY STARLIGHT — By Ned Washington and Victor Young — Copyright © 1946 by Famous Music Corporation.

The Ⓑ Form

We will now consider the Ⓑ Form voicing. For reasons of texture, register and voice leading, it would be impossible to build an adequate harmonic system through the use of only one form.

The Ⓑ Form voicings are as follows:

II (Dorian) 7 2 3 5
V (Mixolydian) 3 6 7 2
I (Ionian) 6 2 3 5

The voicings are based upon the prevailing mode of the chord. In Fig. 1 the formations are as follows:

II

    D—root
    C—minor seventh
    E—ninth   Chord — D minor ninth
    F—minor third
    A—perfect fifth

V

    G—root
    B—major third
    E—thirteenth   Chord — G dominant nine thirteenth
    F—minor seventh
    A—ninth

I

    C—root
    A—major sixth
    D—ninth   Chord — C major ninth added sixth
    E—major third
    G—perfect fifth

Fig. 1. Key of C — Ⓑ Form

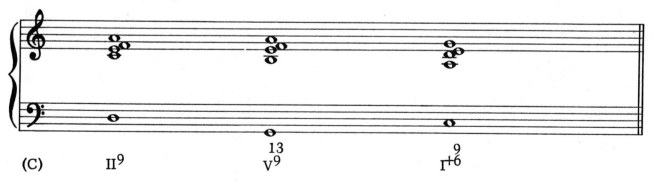

(C)   II^9 V$^{13}_9$ I$^{+6}_9$

Figure 2 illustrates the Ⓑ Form voicings for the remaining 11 keys. As with the Ⓐ Form, the Ⓑ Form voicings are illustrated in all keys. It is important for the student to become automatically familiar with both voicings in all keys for future extended studies.

Fig. 2.

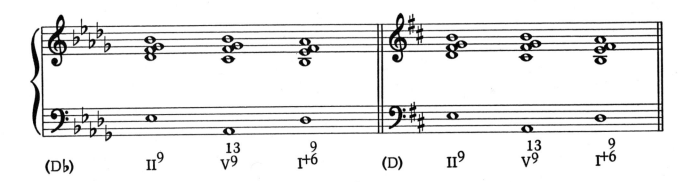

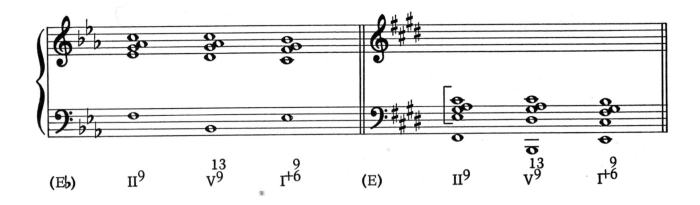

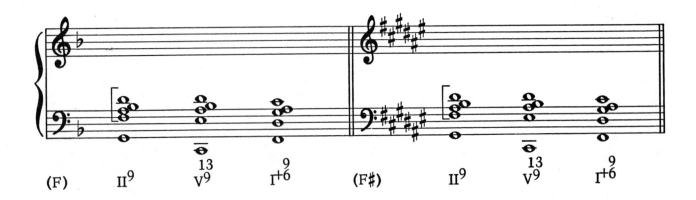

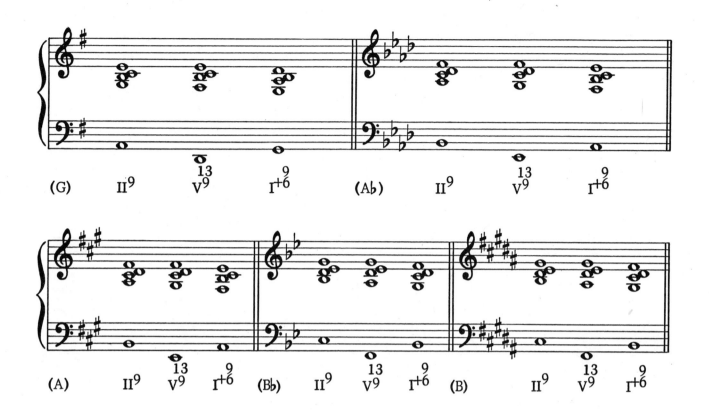

Fig. 3.

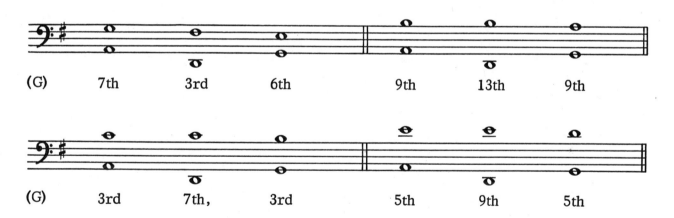

Fig. 3 illustrates the horizontal movement of the voices:

7th	becomes	3rd	becomes	6th
9th	becomes	13th	becomes	9th
3rd	becomes	7th	becomes	3rd
5th	becomes	9th	becomes	5th
II		V		I

Although they are not strictly speaking "inversions" (the root remains in the bass), Ⓑ Forms represent "permutations" of the Ⓐ Form (see Fig. 4).

Fig. 4.

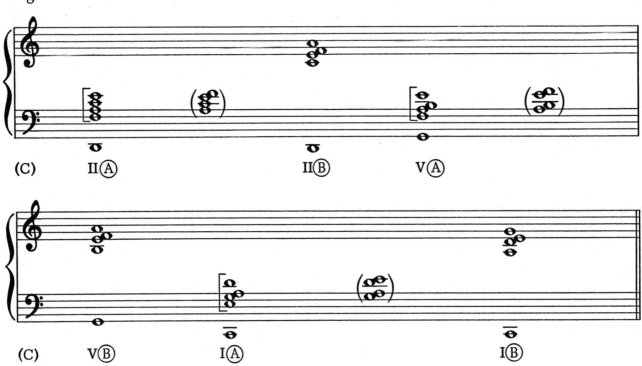

DRILL: Study and memorize the voicings in Figs. 1 and 2 for automatic facility.

Figure 5 is a bass line for "Ghost Of A Chance."

Fig. 5.

I / ♭IIx / IIIφ ♭IIIx / IIφ IVφ / III VI / II V / ♭VIIx VIx /

♭VIx V / I / ♭IIx / IIIφ ♭IIIx / IIφ IVφ / III VI / II ♭IIx /

I⁺⁶ ♯I / I⁺⁶ ♯Io / II♯♯⁷ II♯⁷ / II ♭IIx / I⁺⁶ II / III IV /

♭Vφ / VIIx / III ♭IIIo / II ♭IIx / I / ♭IIx / IIIφ ♭IIIx / IIφ IVφ /

III VI / II ♭IIx / I⁺⁶ / I⁺⁶ //

The Combined Ⓐ and Ⓑ Forms

The student will notice in playing the Ⓐ Form in Lesson 2 that as the II-V-I pattern ascends through the keys, the resonance of the voicings becomes thinner in the keys from F♯ to A♭; in A, B♭ and B the voicings are too low to convey an easily accessible sound.

Also in playing the Ⓑ Form in Lesson 3, the voicings from C to E♭ are again too thin to be effective; in the keys of E and F, voicings are placed too low.

To avoid these problems, the octave will be divided into two key areas:

Ⓐ Form II-V-I: keys C, D♭, D, E♭, E, F
Ⓑ Form II-V-I: keys F♯, G, A♭, A, B♭, B

This arrangement of the Ⓐ and Ⓑ Forms will be utilized in succeeding chapters.

DRILL: Repeat intensive study of II-V-I Ⓐ Form in keys C to F and II-V-I Ⓑ Form in keys F♯ to B (see Fig. 1).

Fig. 1.

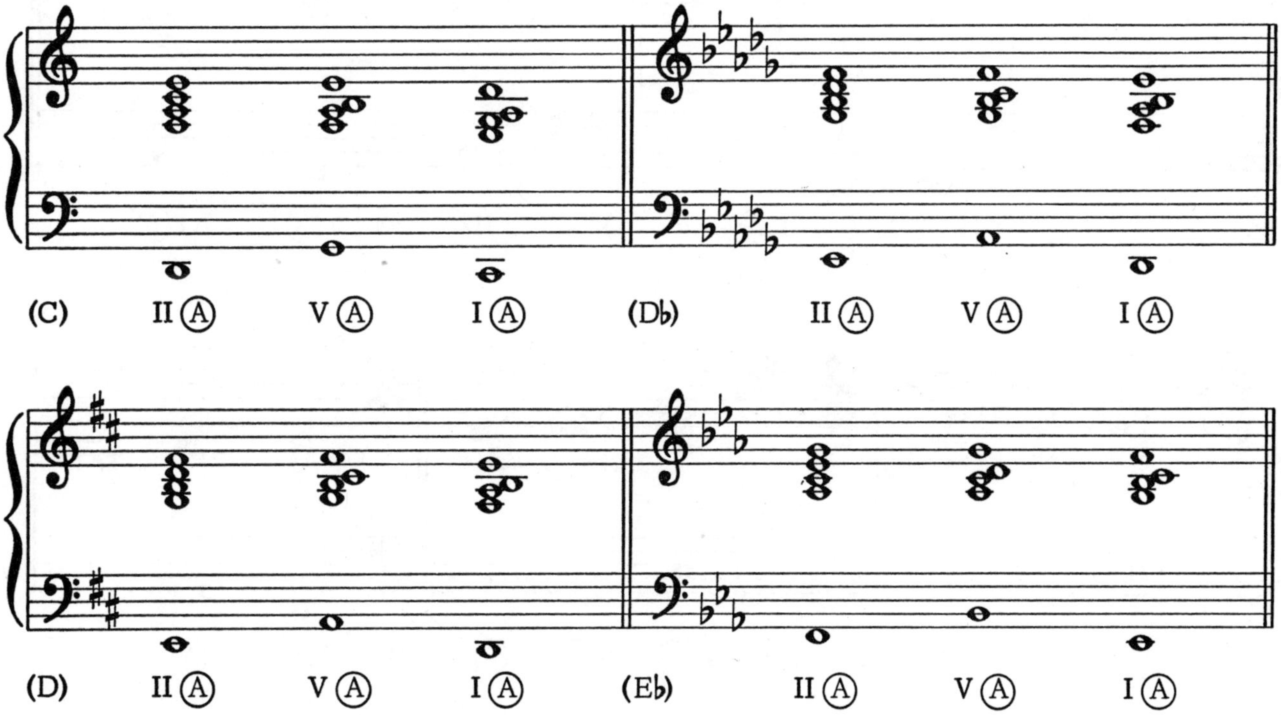

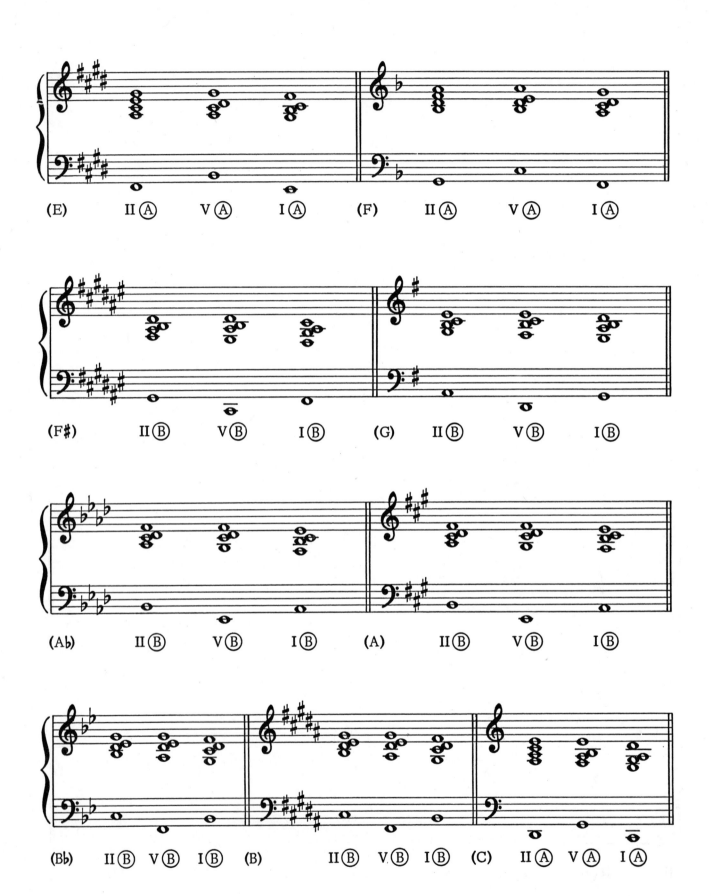

(E)   II Ⓐ   V Ⓐ   I Ⓐ   (F)   II Ⓐ   V Ⓐ   I Ⓐ

(F#)   II Ⓑ   V Ⓑ   I Ⓑ   (G)   II Ⓑ   V Ⓑ   I Ⓑ

(A♭)   II Ⓑ   V Ⓑ   I Ⓑ   (A)   II Ⓑ   V Ⓑ   I Ⓑ

(B♭)   II Ⓑ V Ⓑ I Ⓑ   (B)   II Ⓑ V Ⓑ I Ⓑ   (C)   II Ⓐ V Ⓐ I Ⓐ

60

Figure 2 is a bass line for "I Wish I Were In Love Again."

Fig. 2.

pick-up

♭IIx // I / IVx / I / IVx / I / IVx / III ♭IIIo / II ♭IIx / I /

IVx / I / IVx / I / IVx / III II / I̷x V̷m I̷x / ♭Vφ IVo / VI $^4_3$ ♭IIIo /

II ♭IIx / I $^{+6}$ IV / VII ♭VIIx / VI VIx $^{+5}$ / VI IIx / V ♭IIx / I /

IVx / I / IVx / I II / III VI / IIφ ♭IIx / I $^{+6}$ //

I WISH I WERE IN LOVE AGAIN (Lorenz Hart and Richard Rodgers) — Copyright
© 1937 by Chappell & Co., Inc. — Copyright Renewed. Used by Permission.

LESSON 5.

Left-Hand Major Voicing

Since the immediate purpose of the Ⓐ and Ⓑ voicings is to support
a right hand "trumpet" line, we will now consider these voicings in the
left hand.

In dealing with Ⓐ and Ⓑ voicings the same *temporary* or *parent-
key* principles employed in the improvising scales (Vol. I, Section VI)
will be used:

> Major: I or temporary I
> Dominant: V or temporary V
> Minor: II or temporary II

Half-diminished and diminished chords will be considered separately
in relation to a minor-dominant-major (II-V-I) framework.

Since the I chord will employ the voicing of the prevailing key:

I   Ⓐ   Form: keys C to F
I   Ⓑ   Form: keys F♯ to B

the only problem is that of IV, which will be treated as a temporary I. Thus in the key of C:

I   Ⓐ   Form
IV   Ⓐ   Form (temporary I of F)

However, in the key of E♭:

I   Ⓐ   Form
IV   Ⓑ   Form (temporary I of A♭)

RULE: The major chord is a I or a *temporary* I of a *parent key* and takes the voicing of that key:

Ⓐ Form: keys C to F
interval combination 3 5 6 2 (based on the Ionian mode of the chord)

Ⓑ Form: keys F♯ to B
interval combination 6 2 3 5 (based on the Ionian mode of the chord)

Figure 1 illustrates the 12 major chords in their appropriate voicing to be played in the left hand.

Fig. 1.

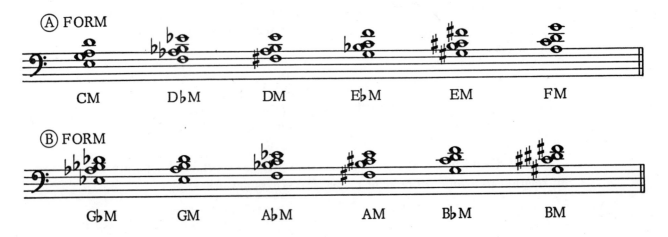

DRILL: Study Fig. 1 for automatic left-hand facility with the 12 major voicings. Figure 2 is a bass line for "I'll Take Romance" in F. Here the conversion from 3/4 to 4/4 is effected by removing one beat from each bar. Note the key changes.

Fig. 2.

(F) I + ⁶ VI / II IVo / III (D♭) V // I (F) IIϕ // VI ₂ ♯Io / II ♭IIx /

(F) I + ⁶ VI / II ♭IIx / I + ⁶ VI / II IVo / III (D♭) V // I (F) IIϕ //

(F) VI ₂ ♯Io / II ♭IIx / I + ⁶ ♯I / I + ⁶ VI // (D♭) II IVo / III ♭IIIo /

(D♭) II ♭IIM / Io I + ⁶ // (B) II V / I ♭Vϕ // (F) VI ₂ ♯Io / II ♭IIx /

(F) I + ⁶ VI / II IVo / III (D♭) V // I (F) IIϕ // VI ₂ ♯Io / II ♭IIx /

I + ⁶ / I + ⁶ //

"I'LL TAKE ROMANCE" By: Oscar Hammerstein II and Ben Oakland — © Copyright 1937 by Bourne, Inc., New York, N. Y. — Used by Permission.

LESSON 6.

Left-Hand Dominant Voicing

The dominant voicing is a V or a temporary V. If either a V or a temporary V belongs to keys C to F, use the Ⓐ Form; if it belongs to keys F♯ to B, use the Ⓑ Form.

Thus, in the key of C:

Ix	= temporary V of F:	Ⓐ Form
IIx	= temporary V of G:	Ⓑ Form
IIIx	= temporary V of A:	Ⓑ Form
IVx	= temporary V of B♭:	Ⓑ Form
V	= natural V of C:	Ⓐ Form
VIx	= temporary V of D:	Ⓐ Form
VIIx	= temporary V of E:	Ⓐ Form
♭IIx	= temporary V of G♭:	Ⓑ Form

RULE: The dominant chord is a V or a *temporary* V of a *parent key* and takes the voicing of that key:

Ⓐ Form: keys C to F
interval combination 7 2 3 6 (based on the Mixolydian mode of the chord).

Ⓑ Form: keys F♯ to B
interval combinations 3 6 7 2 (based on the Mixolydian mode of the chord).

63

Figure 1 illustrates the 12 dominant chords in their appropriate voicings to be played in the left hand.

Fig. 1.

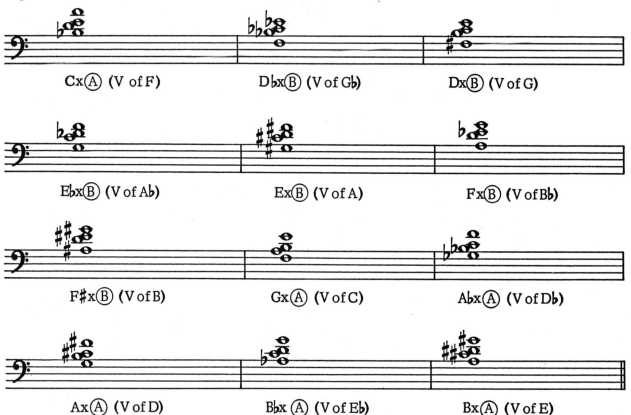

DRILL: Study Fig. 1 for automatic left hand facility with the 12 dominant voicings.

Figure 2 is a bass line for "I'm In The Mood For Love" in D♭.

Fig. 2.

I VI / II V / II ♭IIx ♭⁵ / I II / III ♭IIIo / II ♯♯⁷ II ♯⁷ / II IVo /

III ♭IIIx II ♭IIx / I VI / II V / II ♭IIx ♭⁵ / I II / III ♭IIIo /

II ♯♯⁷ II ♯⁷ / II ♭IIx ♭⁵ / I ⁺⁶ VI / II IVo / III ♭IIIx / II ♭IIx /

I VI / ♭Vφ IVx / III ♯⁷ III / VIφ IIx / II ♭IIx / I VI / II V /

II ♭IIx ♭⁵ / I II / III ♭IIIo / II ♯♯⁷ II ♯⁷ / II ♭IIx ♭⁵ / I ⁺⁶ //

LESSON **7.**

Left-Hand Minor Voicings

In Vol. I, Lesson 44, the problem of the minor chord was explored. In dealing with modes, any minor chord may imply II, III or VI of some key:

$$Cm = \text{II of B}\flat$$
$$= \text{III of A}\flat$$
$$= \text{VI of E}\flat$$

However, in building the minor voicing, *all minors become II or temporary II* of some *parent key*. Thus in the key of C:

Im	= temporary II of B♭:	Ⓑ	Form
II	= natural II of C:	Ⓐ	Form
III	= temporary II of D:	Ⓐ	Form
IVm	= temporary II of E♭:	Ⓐ	Form
Vm	= temporary II of F:	Ⓐ	Form
VI	= temporary II of G:	Ⓑ	Form
VIIm	= temporary II of A:	Ⓑ	Form
♭Vm	= temporary II of E:	Ⓐ	Form

All III and VI chords are treated as *temporary* II chords. See Vol. I, Lesson 44 for rule concerning the use of modes in the right hand.

RULE: The minor chord is a II or a temporary II of a *parent key* and takes the voicing of that key:

Ⓐ Form: keys C to F

interval combination 3 5 7 2 (based on the Dorian mode of the chord).

Ⓑ Form: keys F♯ to B

interval combination 7 2 3 5 (based on the Dorian mode of the chord).

Fig. 1 illustrates the 12 minor chords in their appropriate voicings to be played in the left hand.

Fig. 1.

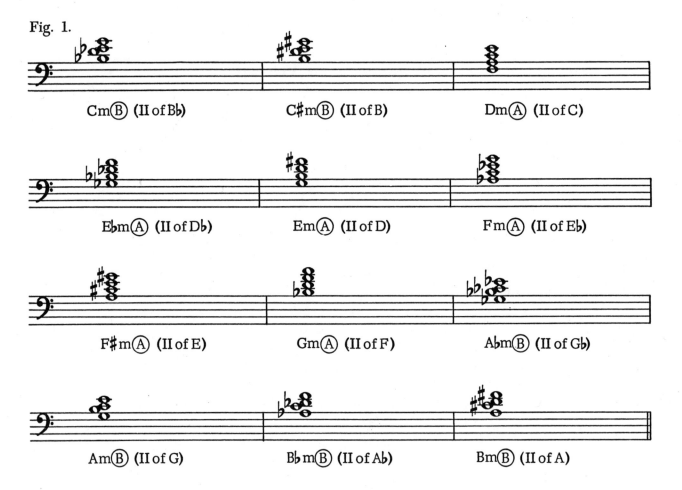

DRILL: Study Fig. 1 for automatic left-hand facility with the 12 minor voicings.

Figure 2 is a bass line for "I Get A Kick Out Of You" in Eb.

Fig. 2.

II / IVo / III / bIIIx / II / bIIx / I / VI / II / IVo / III / bIIIx /
II / bIIx / I^{+6} / VI / II / IVo / III / bIIIx / II / bIIx / I /
VI / II / IVo / III / bIIIx / II / bIIx / I^{+6} / #IVo / Vm / Ix$^{#3}$ /
Vm$_2$ / IV / IIIϕ / VIx / IIIϕ / bIIIx / II^{+6} / VII / IIIϕ bIIIx /
II$^{#7}$ II / VI / IIx / II / V / II / IVo / III / bIIIx / II / bIIx /
I / VI / II / V / IIIϕ / VIx / II / bIIx / I^{+6} / I^{+6} //

Left-Hand Half-Diminished Voicings

In Vol. I, Lesson 45, the half-diminished chord was treated as a VII or temporary VII, since that represents its position in any key. However, here we are dealing with a fundamental II-V-I (minor-dominant-major) pattern that does not account for the half-diminished and diminished qualities. In seeking a half-diminished voicing within a major-dominant-minor pattern, it seems reasonable to turn to the *minor voicing*, since it is nearest in structure to the half-diminished:

minor voicing   = m3, P5, m7, 9th = II or temporary II
half-diminished voicing = m3, o5, m7, 9th = II^{b5} or temporary II^{b5}

If we apply this interval principle to the Ⓐ and Ⓑ minor voicings, we derive the following combinations:

ϕ Ⓐ Form: 3 ♭5 7 2   ϕ Ⓑ Form: 7 2 3 ♭5
(based on the Dorian mode of the root)

Figure 1 illustrates the half-diminished Ⓐ Form on D. Figure 2 illustrates the half-diminished Ⓑ Form on A.

Fig. 1.   Fig. 2.

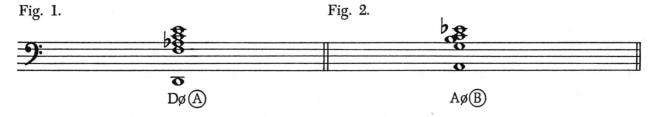

Dø Ⓐ   Aø Ⓑ

In playing Fig. 2, the student will notice the "harsh" sound of the Ⓑ Form; however, it is important that the student be aware that both the half-diminished and the diminished voicings represent contemporary mannerisms found in nearly all present-day keyboard and orchestral music. In other words, the student should not indulge a conservative attitude in these matters.

Actually, "hearing," as opposed to "listening," involves two levels of reaction:

1. Externalized listening dealing with emotion reactions to recordings, sound tracks, etc.
2. Internalized hearing dealing with those reactions to the resources employed by the student in his personal performance.

It is apparent that the externalized experience is broader, more indulgent and less arbitrary. The internalized tends to assume the active levels of experience felt by the student, which may be quite circumscribed.

Figure 3 illustrates the six half-diminished Ⓐ Form voicings derived by lowering the 5th of the minor Ⓐ Form (II ♭5 Ⓐ). The interval combination in each case is 3 ♭5 7 2, based on the Dorian mode of the root.

Fig. 3.

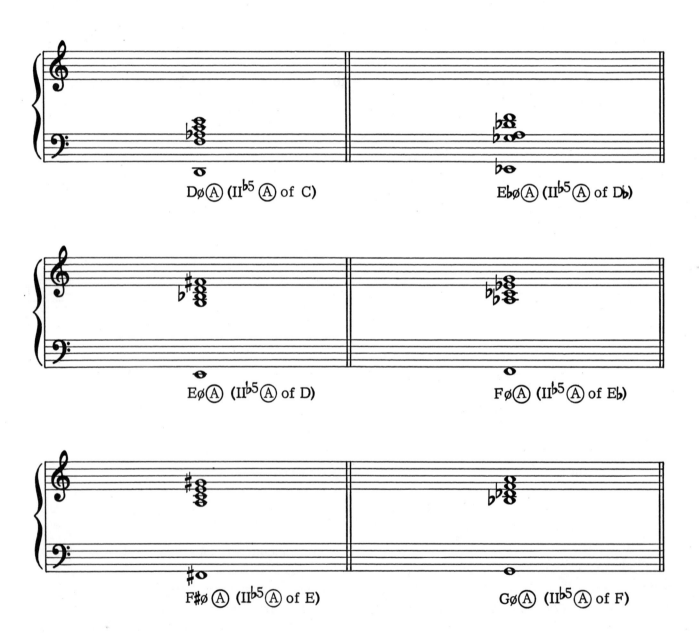

Dø Ⓐ (II♭5 Ⓐ of C)   Ebø Ⓐ (II♭5 Ⓐ of Db)

Eø Ⓐ (II♭5 Ⓐ of D)   Fø Ⓐ (II♭5 Ⓐ of Eb)

F#ø Ⓐ (II♭5 Ⓐ of E)   Gø Ⓐ (II♭5 Ⓐ of F)

Fig. 4.

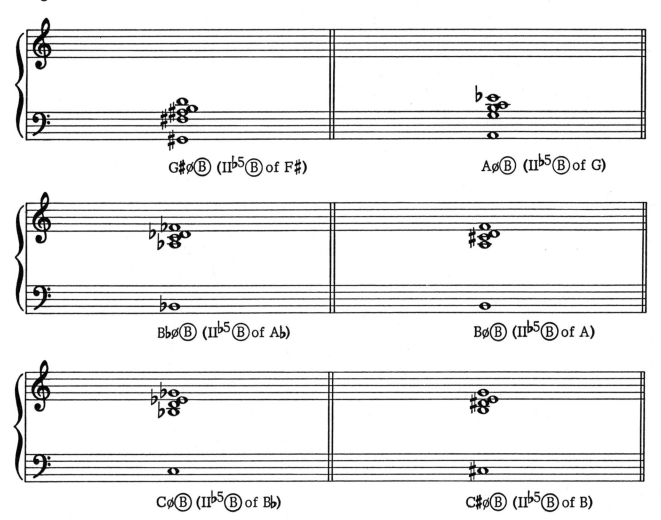

G#ø(B) (II♭5(B) of F#) Aø(B) (II♭5(B) of G)

Bbø(B) (II♭5(B) of Ab) Bø(B) (II♭5(B) of A)

Cø(B) (II♭5(B) of Bb) C#ø(B) (II♭5(B) of B)

Figure 4 illustrates the six half-diminished (B) Form voicings derived by lowering the 5th of the minor (B) Form (II♭5 (B)). The interval combination in each case is 7 2 3 ♭5, based on the Dorian mode of the root.

Thus in the key of C:

Iφ	= temporary IIᵇ⁵	of Bb:	(B) Form
IIφ	= temporary IIᵇ⁵	of C:	(A) Form
IIIφ	= temporary IIᵇ⁵	of D:	(A) Form
IVφ	= temporary IIᵇ⁵	of Eb:	(A) Form
Vφ	= temporary IIᵇ⁵	of F:	(A) Form
VIφ	= temporary IIᵇ⁵	of G:	(B) Form
VII	= temporary IIᵇ⁵	of A:	(B) Form
♭Vφ	= temporary IIᵇ⁵	of E:	(A) Form

RULE: The half-diminished chord is a II^{b5} or a temporary II^{b5} of a parent key and is treated as follows: In keys C to F: minor Ⓐ Form flat 5; interval combination: 3 ♭5 7 2 (based on the Dorian mode of the root). In keys F♯ to B: minor Ⓑ Form flat 5; interval combination: 7 2 3 ♭5 (based on the Dorian mode of the root).

DRILL: Study Figs. 3 and 4, playing the voicings in the right hand with the root in the left; also, play the voicings in the left hand.

Figure 5 is a bass line for "You'd Be So Nice To Come Home To" in C. Note key changes including the A minor sections.

Fig. 5.

pick-up
(a) V$^{♯3}$ // I^{+6} VI / II V / I^{+6} / VII // (F) II / ♭IIx / I I$_2$ /

(F) VI VI$_2$ // (a) II / V / VII / Im Im$_2$ / VI / IIx / II /

(a) V / I^{+6} VI / II V / I^{+6} / VII // (C) Vm / ♭V / IV^{+6} IV$_2$ /

(C) II / ♯IIo / III / IV^{+6} / IV ♯IVo / VI$_2$ ♭VIx / V$^{♯5}$ V /

(C) I^{+6} / I^{+6} //

YOU'D BE SO NICE TO COME HOME TO (Cole Porter) — Copyright © 1942 by Chappell & Co., Inc. — Used by Permission.

LESSON 9.

Left-Hand Diminished Voicings — Inversions

The diminished voicing has no "status" in the major scale-tone system. However, the *minor voicing* can easily be altered to diminished by *lowering the fifth and the seventh* (Symbol: II$^{b5}_{b7}$):

m3, p5, m7, 9th ⎫
      to   ⎬ or ⎧ minor voicing II or temporary II
m3, o5, o7, 9th ⎭   ⎨ diminished voicing II$^{b5}_{b7}$ or temporary II$^{b5}_{b7}$

If we apply this interval principal to the Ⓐ and Ⓑ minor voicings we derive the following combinations:

o Ⓐ Form = 3 ♭5 ♭7 2
o Ⓑ Form = ♭7 2 3 ♭5 (based on the Dorian mode of the root)

Figure 1 illustrates the diminished Ⓐ Form on D. Figure 2 illustrates the diminished Ⓑ Form on A♭. In both combinations forming the diminished voicing it is understood that the position of 6 in the Dorian mode actually functions as the 7th of the chord.

Fig. 1.   Fig. 2.

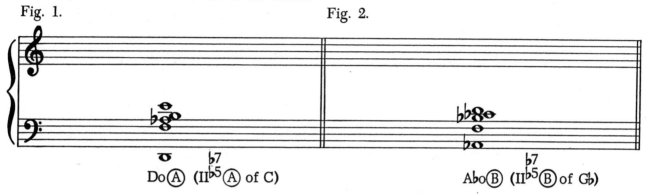

Do Ⓐ (II♭5 Ⓐ of C)   A♭o Ⓑ (II♭5 Ⓑ of G♭)

Again in playing Fig. 2, the student will notice a similar "harshness" noted in the half-diminished Ⓑ Form. In a later chapter modified versions of the half-diminished and diminished voicings will be discussed.

Fig. 3.   Fig. 4.

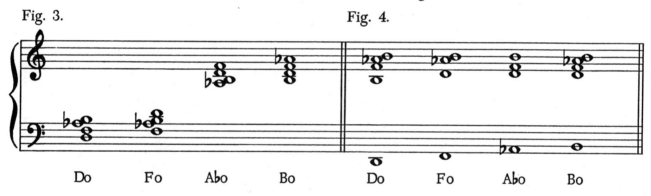

Do   Fo   A♭o   Bo   Do   Fo   A♭o   Bo

In Vol. I, page 46, we learned that the diminished chord always appears in root position (Fig. 3). However, each diminished chord also offers three permutations or voicings which may be used interchangeably, provided the root is respected. These permutations may appear in the root (Fig. 4) or in the chord (Fig. 5). (See note.)

Fig. 5.   Fig. 6.
                                               opposite form

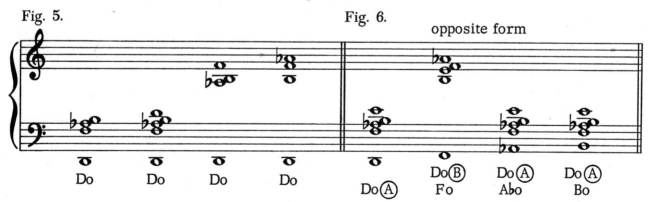

Do   Do   Do   Do   Do Ⓐ   Do Ⓑ   Do Ⓐ   Do Ⓐ
                                                        Fo   A♭o   Bo

These series also function with the Ⓐ and Ⓑ Form voicings, again in the root (Figs. 6 and 8) or the voicings (Figs. 7 and 9).

Fig. 7.

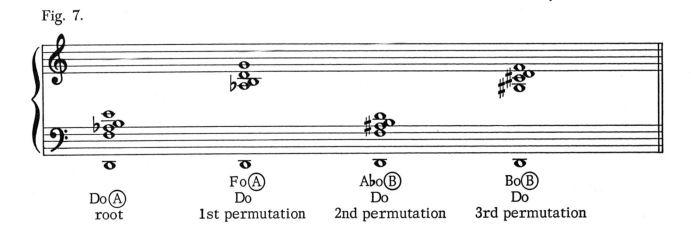

Do Ⓐ
root

Fo Ⓐ
Do
1st permutation

Abo Ⓑ
Do
2nd permutation

Bo Ⓑ
Do
3rd permutation

Fig. 8.

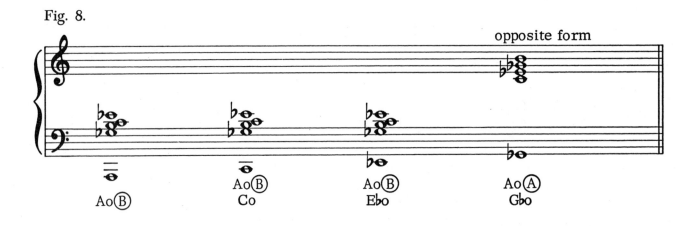

Ao Ⓑ

Ao Ⓑ
Co

Ao Ⓑ
Ebo

Ao Ⓐ
Gbo

Fig. 9.

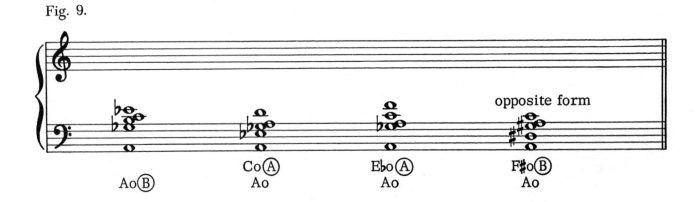

Ao Ⓑ

Co Ⓐ
Ao

Ebo Ⓐ
Ao

F#o Ⓑ
Ao

We shall return to the series in Figs. 6, 7, 8 and 9 later. For now, we shall illustrate the six Ⓐ and six Ⓑ Forms derived from the modified minor voicings (II^{b5}_{b7} or temporary II^{b5}_{b7}). See Figs. 12 and 13.

NOTE ON INVERSIONS: In Figs. 4 and 5, the basic rule prevailing in classical harmony of avoiding the doubling of the root, except when it appears in the soprano (top voice), has been respected.

The rules regarding doubling in Ⓐ and Ⓑ Forms vary somewhat, as illustrated in Fig. 6.

RULE: When dealing with inversions in Ⓐ and Ⓑ Forms, doubling of the root is permitted except when the root appears in the bass of the voicing; in this case, the *opposite form* should be employed.

See Figs. 10 and 11. In Fig. 10, I^6_5 Ⓐ forms an impermissible octave. In Fig. II, Ix_2 Ⓐ also forms an impermissible octave.

Fig. 10.

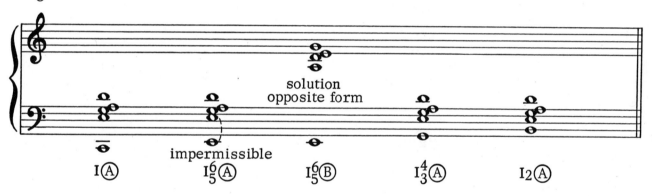

Fig. 11.

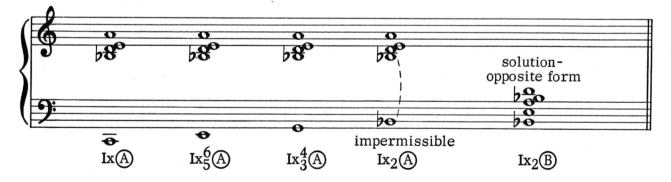

Figure 12 illustrates the six diminished Ⓐ Form voicings derived by lowering the fifth and the seventh of the minor Ⓐ Form voicing.

Fig. 12.

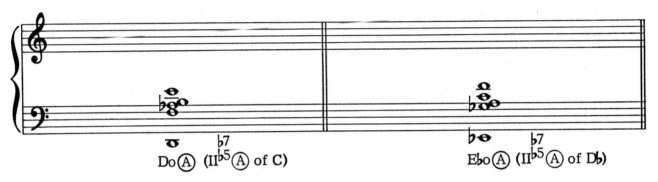

Do Ⓐ (II♭5 Ⓐ of C)   E♭o Ⓐ (II♭5 Ⓐ of D♭)

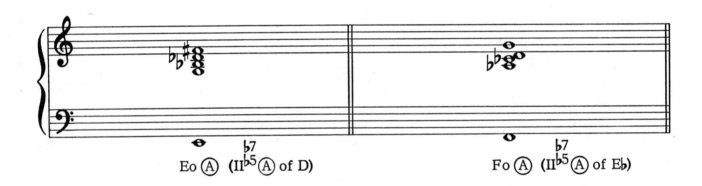

Eo Ⓐ (II♭5 Ⓐ of D)   Fo Ⓐ (II♭5 Ⓐ of E♭)

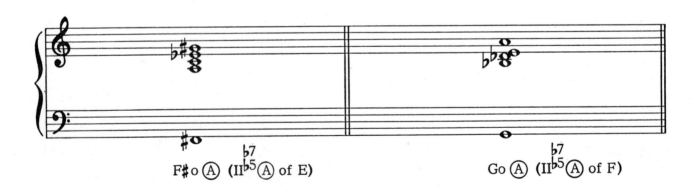

F♯o Ⓐ (II♭5 Ⓐ of E)   Go Ⓐ (II♭5 Ⓐ of F)

Figure 13 illustrates the six diminished Ⓑ Form voicings derived by lowering the fifth and the seventh of the minor Ⓑ Form voicing.

Fig. 13.

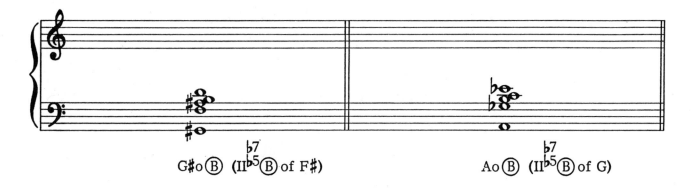

G#oⒷ (II♭5Ⓑ of F#)   AoⒷ (II♭5Ⓑ of G)

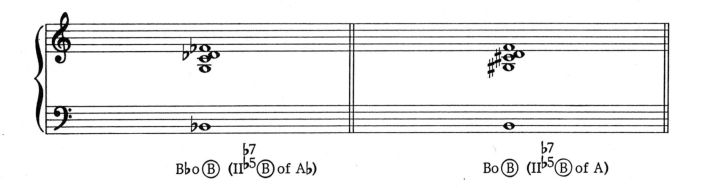

B♭oⒷ (II♭5Ⓑ of A♭)   BoⒷ (II♭5Ⓑ of A)

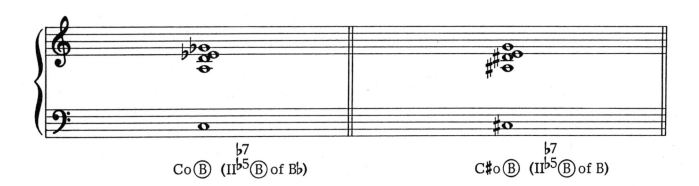

CoⒷ (II♭5Ⓑ of B♭)   C#oⒷ (II♭5Ⓑ of B)

NOTE: The diminished voicing of the Ⓐ Form is constructed by lowering the *inside* voices of the minor voicing; the diminished voicing of the Ⓑ Form is constructed by lowering the *outside* voices of the minor voicing.

In the key of C:

Io	= temporary $\text{II}^{\flat5}_{\flat7}$	of B♭:	Ⓑ	Form
IIo	= temporary $\text{II}^{\flat5}_{\flat7}$	of C:	Ⓐ	Form
IIIo	= temporary $\text{II}^{\flat5}_{\flat7}$	of D:	Ⓐ	Form
IVo	= temporary $\text{II}^{\flat5}_{\flat7}$	of E♭:	Ⓐ	Form
Vo	= temporary $\text{II}^{\flat5}_{\flat7}$	of F:	Ⓐ	Form
VIo	= temporary $\text{II}^{\flat5}_{\flat7}$	of G:	Ⓑ	Form
VIIo	= temporary $\text{II}^{\flat5}_{\flat7}$	of A:	Ⓑ	Form
♭Vo	= temporary $\text{II}^{\flat5}_{\flat7}$	of E:	Ⓐ	Form

RULE: The diminished chord is a $\text{II}^{\flat5}_{\flat7}$ or a temporary $\text{II}^{\flat5}_{\flat7}$ of a parent key and is treated as follows: In keys C to F: minor Ⓐ Form flat 5 flat 7; interval combination: 3 ♭5 ♭7 2 (based on the Dorian mode of the root). In keys F♯ to B: minor Ⓑ Form flat 5 flat seven; interval combination: ♭7 2 3 ♭5 (based on the Dorian mode of the root).

DRILL: Study Figs. 12 and 13 playing the voicings in the right hand with the root in the left; also play the voicings in the left hand.

Figure 14 is a bass line for "From This Moment On" in A♭. Note the transitions from f minor to the relative A♭ major.

Fig. 14.

(f) I $^{+6}$ / VI / II / V / I // (A♭) VI / Vm / ♭V / IV / IV $^{+6}$ / IV $^{♭3}$ /

(A♭) ♭VIIx / I / IV / (f) II / ♭IIx / I $^{+6}$ / VI / II / V / I // (A♭) VI /

(A♭) Vm / ♭V / IV / IV $^{+6}$ / IV $^{♭3}$ / ♭VIIx / I / VI / Vm / ♭V /

(A♭) IV / IV $^{+6}$ / IVm / ♭VIIx / I $^{+6}$ / VIIx / IIIφ $^{4}_{3}$ / VIx / VIIm /

(A♭) III / VI / IIx / V / ♭V / IVx // (f) V / I $^{+6}$ / VI / II / V / I //

(A♭) VI / Vm / ♭V / IV / IV $^{+6}$ / IVm / ♭VIIx / I / VIIx / IIIφ $^{4}_{3}$ /

(A♭) VIx / IIx / II ♭IIx / I $^{+6}$ / I $^{+6}$ //

LESSON 10.

Modulation Ⓐ and Ⓑ Forms

Now that we have completed the Ⓐ and Ⓑ Form voicings for the sixty chords, we can proceed to apply these voicings to a specific tune.

"Cherokee" in B♭ has been chosen as an interesting study in key modulation in a II-V-I pattern.

Figure 1 illustrates an Ⓐ - Ⓑ Form bass line for "Cherokee" in B♭. Note the key changes.

In normal group playing the roots would be played by the bassist. For now we will employ the simple device of playing the chord on the first beat of each bar and the root on the third beat. For a full sound the student is advised to pedal through each bar, thus connecting the chord with its root.

DRILL: Build a right hand improvisation on Fig. 1.

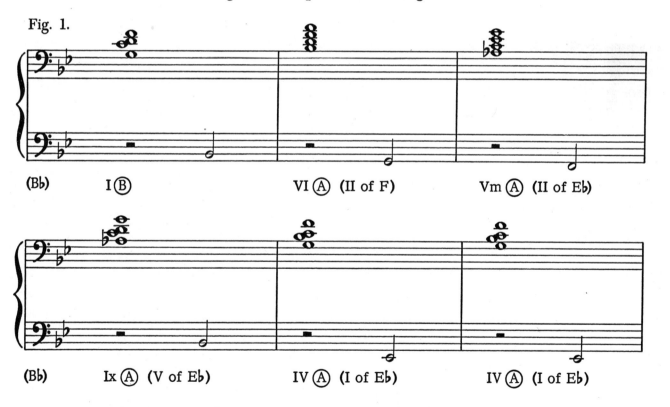

Fig. 1.

(B♭)   I Ⓑ   VI Ⓐ (II of F)   Vm Ⓐ (II of E♭)

(B♭)   Ix Ⓐ (V of E♭)   IV Ⓐ (I of E♭)   IV Ⓐ (I of E♭)

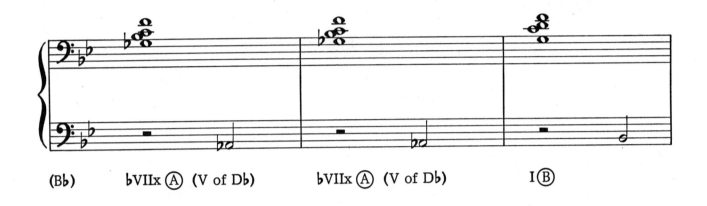

(B♭)   ♭VIIx Ⓐ (V of D♭)   ♭VIIx Ⓐ (V of D♭)   I Ⓑ

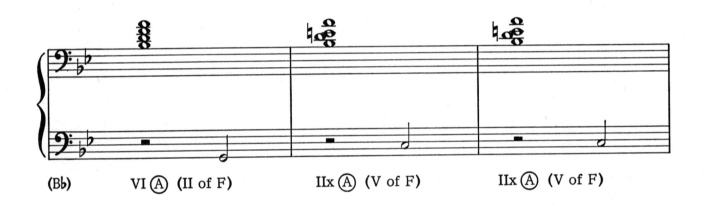

(B♭)   VI Ⓐ (II of F)   IIx Ⓐ (V of F)   IIx Ⓐ (V of F)

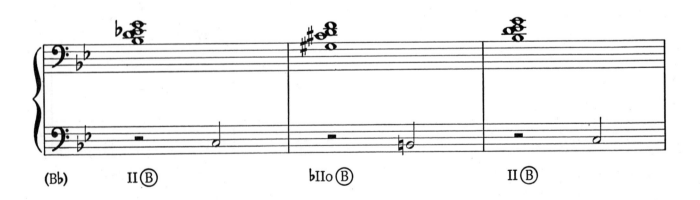

(B♭)   II Ⓑ   ♭IIo Ⓑ   II Ⓑ

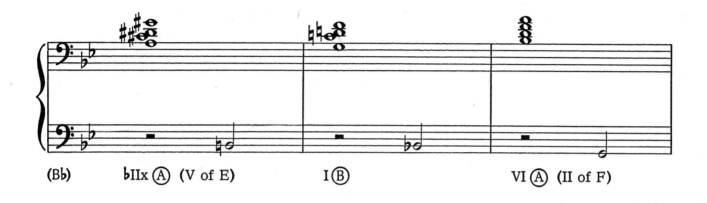

(B♭)   ♭IIx Ⓐ (V of E)   I Ⓑ   VI Ⓐ (II of F)

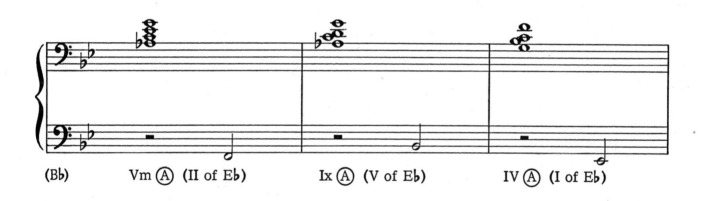

(B♭)   Vm Ⓐ (II of E♭)   Ix Ⓐ (V of E♭)   IV Ⓐ (I of E♭)

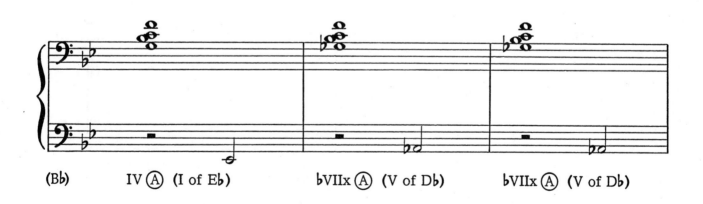

(B♭)   IV Ⓐ (I of E♭)   ♭VIIx Ⓐ (V of D♭)   ♭VIIx Ⓐ (V of D♭)

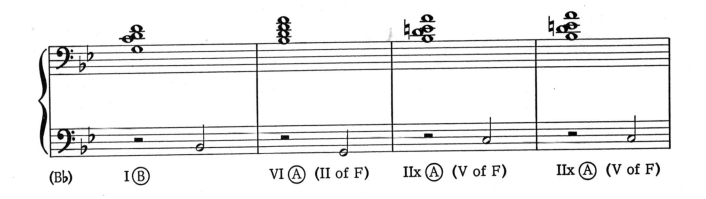

(Bb)   I Ⓑ   VI Ⓐ (II of F)   IIx Ⓐ (V of F)   IIx Ⓐ (V of F)

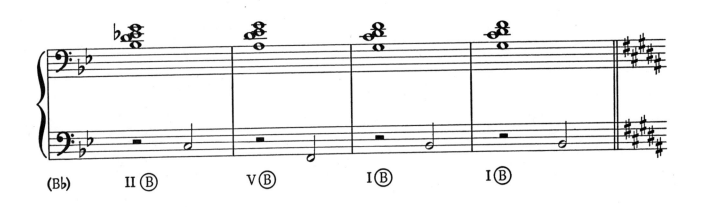

(Bb)   II Ⓑ   V Ⓑ   I Ⓑ   I Ⓑ

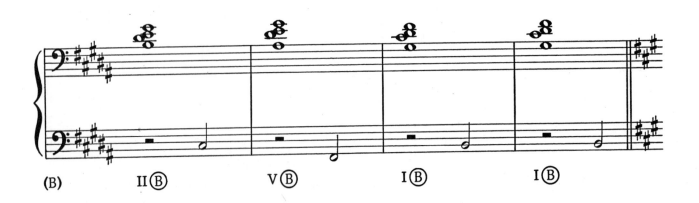

(B)   II Ⓑ   V Ⓑ   I Ⓑ   I Ⓑ

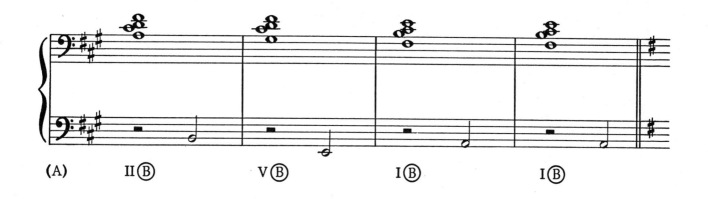

(A)   II Ⓑ   V Ⓑ   I Ⓑ   I Ⓑ

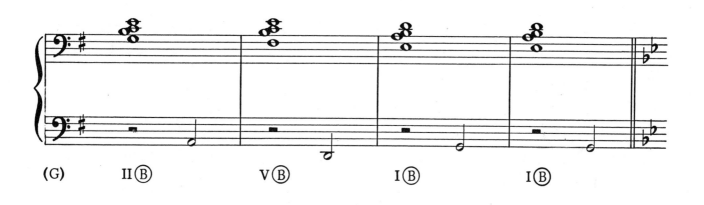

(G)   II Ⓑ   V Ⓑ   I Ⓑ   I Ⓑ

(B♭)   VI Ⓐ (II of F)   IIx Ⓐ (V of F)   II Ⓑ

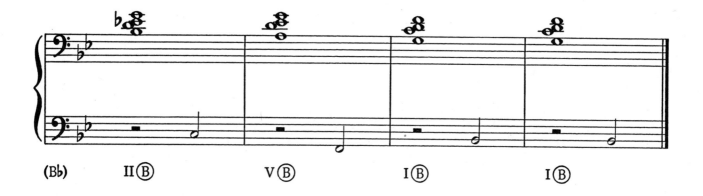

(B♭)   II Ⓑ   V Ⓑ   I Ⓑ   I Ⓑ

LESSON 11.

Alternate Ⓐ and Ⓑ Forms

In Vol I, Section IX the various patterns common to all jazz were considered. The importance of these patterns cannot be overestimated in dealing with any facet of jazz piano. This is particularly true of the Ⓐ and Ⓑ Form patterns, since they are constantly employed as "temporary" factors in shifting tonalities.

The following pattern drill is strongly recommended to insure the automatic facility necessary for employing these voicings. The student will note that the Ⓐ and Ⓑ Forms *alternate* in the chromatic patterns. The overlapping of the Forms in some patterns is to preserve smooth voice-leading; the C — F, F♯ — B key segments are for general voicing and may be occasionally suspended in the borderline keys (F, F♯, B and C). These patterns are to be played with the root in the left hand and the chord in the right. When the student has become familiar with the sonority of these voicings, the chords (omitting the roots) should also be played again in the left hand for an automatic facility.

Keys C to F

V Ⓐ — I Ⓐ (Note)
II Ⓐ — V Ⓐ — I Ⓐ
II Ⓐ — ♭IIx Ⓑ — I Ⓐ (Fig. 1)
I Ⓐ — VI Ⓑ — II Ⓐ — V Ⓐ — I Ⓐ (Fig. 2)
III Ⓐ — ♭IIIx Ⓑ — II Ⓐ — ♭IIx Ⓑ — I Ⓐ (Fig. 3)
VIIm Ⓑ — IIIx Ⓑ — VI Ⓑ — IIx Ⓑ — V Ⓐ — 1 Ⓐ (Fig. 4)

NOTE: The ability to proceed directly to V or temporary V without first passing through the related II is of the utmost importance.

V Ⓑ – I Ⓑ
II Ⓑ – V Ⓑ – I Ⓑ
II Ⓑ – ♭IIx Ⓐ – I Ⓑ (Fig. 5)
I Ⓑ – VI Ⓐ – II Ⓑ – V Ⓑ – I Ⓑ (Fig. 6)
III Ⓑ – ♭IIIx Ⓐ – II Ⓑ – ♭IIx Ⓐ – I Ⓑ (Fig. 7)
VIIm Ⓐ – IIIx Ⓐ – VI Ⓐ – IIx Ⓐ – V Ⓑ – I Ⓑ (Fig. 8)

Fig. 1.

(C)   II Ⓐ   ♭IIx Ⓑ   I Ⓐ   (D♭)   II Ⓐ   ♭IIx Ⓑ   I Ⓐ

(D)   II Ⓐ   ♭IIx Ⓑ   I Ⓐ   (E♭)   II Ⓐ   ♭IIx Ⓑ   I Ⓐ

(E)   II Ⓐ   ♭IIx Ⓑ   I Ⓐ   (F)   II Ⓐ   ♭IIx Ⓑ   I Ⓐ

Fig. 2.

(C)   I Ⓐ   VI Ⓑ   II Ⓐ   V Ⓐ   I Ⓐ   (Db)   I Ⓐ   VI Ⓑ   II Ⓐ   V Ⓐ   I Ⓐ

(D)   I Ⓐ   VI Ⓑ   II Ⓐ   V Ⓐ   I Ⓐ   (Eb)   I Ⓐ   VI Ⓑ   II Ⓐ   V Ⓐ   I Ⓐ

(E)   I Ⓐ   VI Ⓑ   II Ⓐ   V Ⓐ   I Ⓐ   (F)   I Ⓐ   VI Ⓑ   II Ⓐ   V Ⓐ   I Ⓐ

Fig. 3.

(C)   III Ⓐ   bIIIx Ⓑ   II Ⓐ   bIIx Ⓑ   I Ⓐ

85

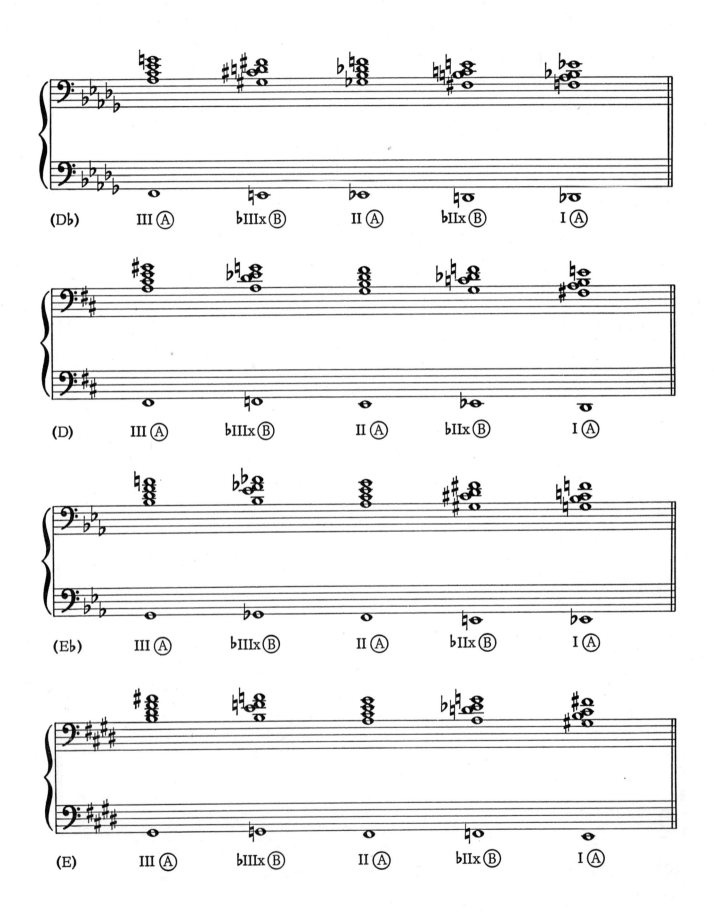

(F)   III Ⓐ   bIIIx Ⓑ   II Ⓐ   bIIx Ⓑ   I Ⓐ

Fig. 4.

(C)   VIIm Ⓑ   IIIx Ⓑ   VI Ⓑ   IIx Ⓑ   V Ⓐ   I Ⓐ

(Db)   VIIm Ⓑ   IIIx Ⓑ   VI Ⓑ   IIx Ⓑ   V Ⓐ   I Ⓐ

(D)   VIIm Ⓑ   IIIx Ⓑ   VI Ⓑ   IIx Ⓑ   V Ⓐ   I Ⓐ

Fig. 5.

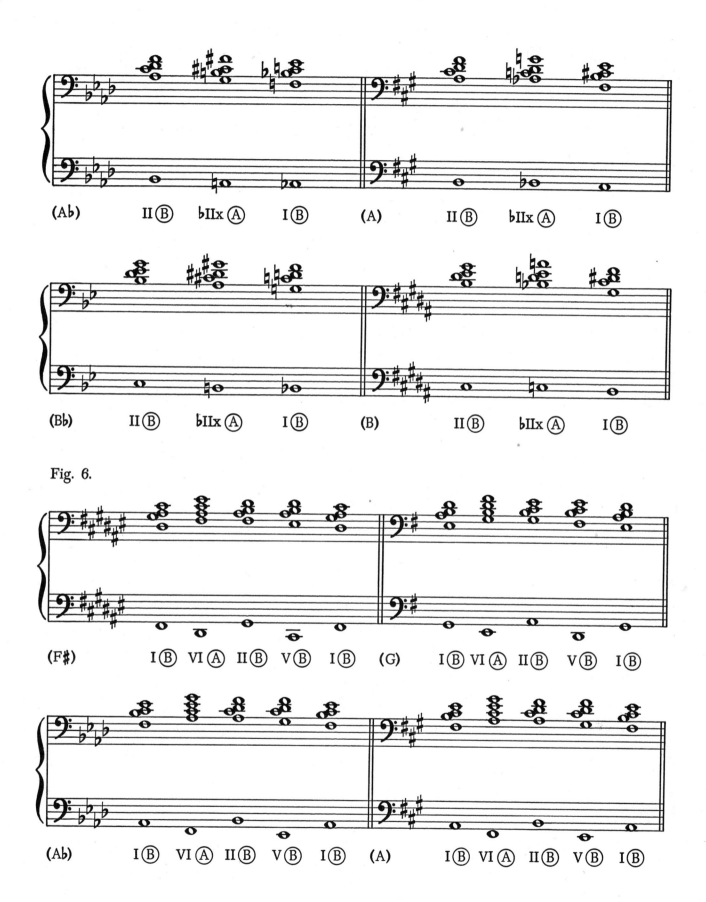

Fig. 6.

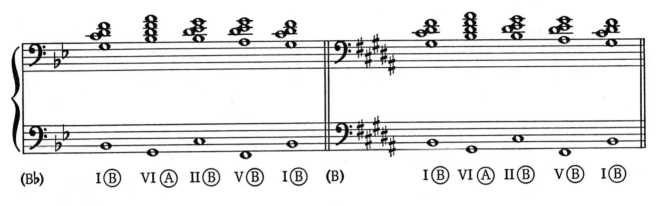

(Bb)   I Ⓑ   VI Ⓐ   II Ⓑ   V Ⓑ   I Ⓑ   (B)   I Ⓑ   VI Ⓐ   II Ⓑ   V Ⓑ   I Ⓑ

Fig. 7

(F♯)   III Ⓑ   ♭IIIx Ⓐ   II Ⓑ   ♭IIx Ⓐ   I Ⓑ

(G)   III Ⓑ   ♭IIIx Ⓐ   II Ⓑ   ♭IIx Ⓐ   I Ⓑ

(Ab)   III Ⓑ   ♭IIIx Ⓐ   II Ⓑ   ♭IIx Ⓐ   I Ⓑ

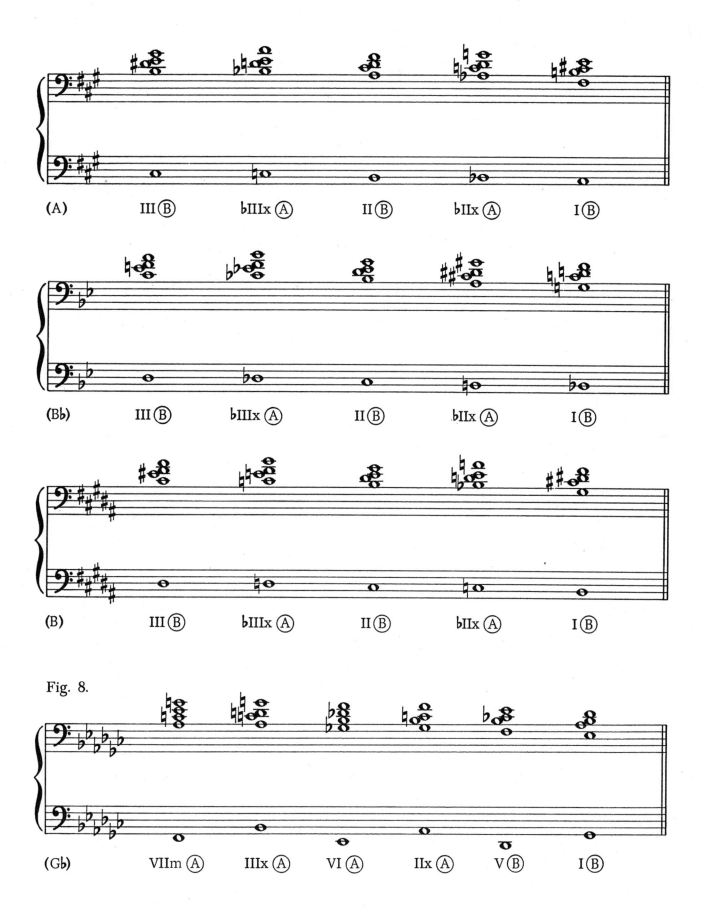

Fig. 8.

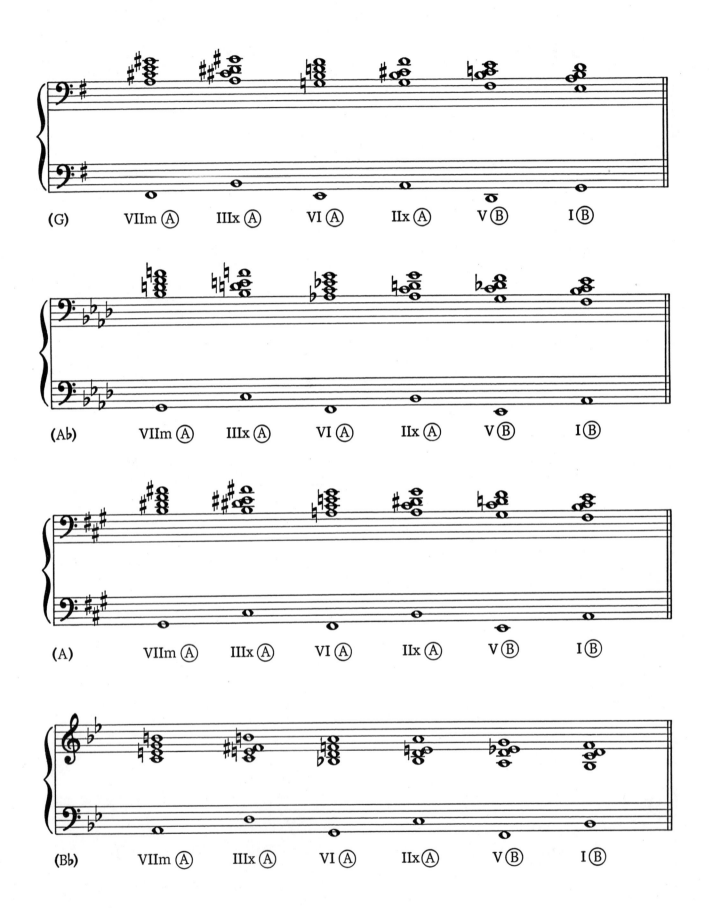

(G)   VIIm Ⓐ   IIIx Ⓐ   VI Ⓐ   IIx Ⓐ   V Ⓑ   I Ⓑ

(A♭)   VIIm Ⓐ   IIIx Ⓐ   VI Ⓐ   IIx Ⓐ   V Ⓑ   I Ⓑ

(A)   VIIm Ⓐ   IIIx Ⓐ   VI Ⓐ   IIx Ⓐ   V Ⓑ   I Ⓑ

(B♭)   VIIm Ⓐ   IIIx Ⓐ   VI Ⓐ   IIx Ⓐ   V Ⓑ   I Ⓑ

92

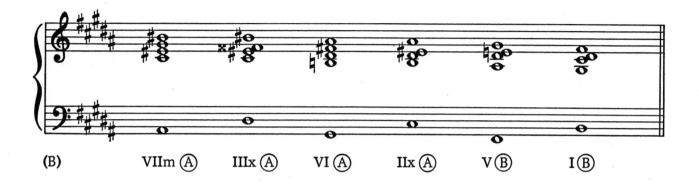

(B)   VIIm Ⓐ   IIIx Ⓐ   VI Ⓐ   IIx Ⓐ   V Ⓑ   I Ⓑ

Figure 9 is a bass line for "Embraceable You" in G that employs Ⓐ and Ⓑ Forms. Improvise on Fig. 9. Figure 9 employs a *chord-root* design in the left hand to add motion to the study. In general, a *chord-root* motion prevails in most modern playing in order to avoid the outmoded swing-bass sound of the traditional *root-chord*.

Fig. 9.

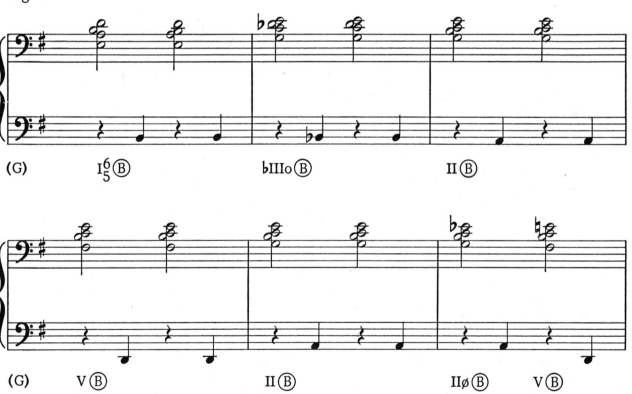

(G)   I$^6_5$ Ⓑ   ♭IIIo Ⓑ   II Ⓑ

(G)   V Ⓑ   II Ⓑ   IIø Ⓑ   V Ⓑ

94

95

The Altered Dominant Ⓐ and Ⓑ Forms — The Dominant Ⓒ Form

We learned in Vol. I, Lesson 56, that the dominant chord, in particular, lends itself to alteration. These alterations are easily assessible in the Ⓐ and Ⓑ Forms; the Ⓒ Form is a modified Ⓑ Form.

The basic alterations of the dominant chord are as follows:

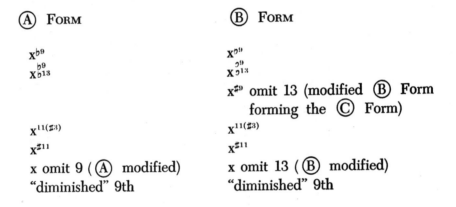

Ⓐ Form

x^{b9}
x^{b9}_{b13}

$x^{11(\sharp3)}$

$x^{\sharp11}$

x omit 9 (Ⓐ modified)
"diminished" 9th

Ⓑ Form

x^{b9}
x^{b9}_{b13}

$x^{\sharp9}$ omit 13 (modified Ⓑ Form forming the Ⓒ Form)

$x^{11(\sharp3)}$

$x^{\sharp11}$

x omit 13 (Ⓑ modified)
"diminished" 9th

(a) The dominant flat nine Ⓐ and Ⓑ Forms are illustrated in Fig. 1. Flat nine involves lowering the second of the voicing one half-step.

Fig. 1.

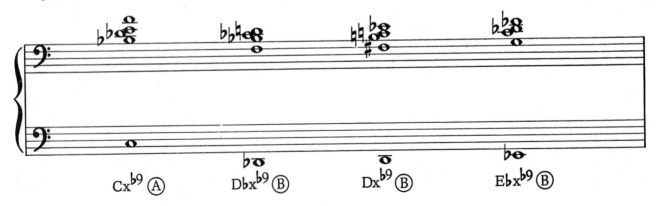

Cx^{b9} Ⓐ Dbx^{b9} Ⓑ Dx^{b9} Ⓑ Ebx^{b9} Ⓑ

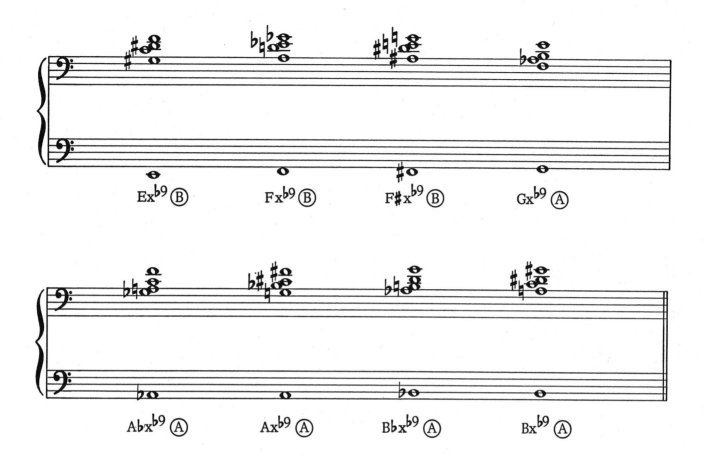

Ex^{b9} Ⓑ Fx^{b9} Ⓑ $F\#x^{b9}$ Ⓑ Gx^{b9} Ⓐ

Abx^{b9} Ⓐ Ax^{b9} Ⓐ Bbx^{b9} Ⓐ Bx^{b9} Ⓐ

(b) The dominant flat nine flat thirteen Ⓐ and Ⓑ Forms are illustrated in Fig. 2. Flat nine involves a lowered second; flat thirteen involves a lowered sixth.

Fig. 2.

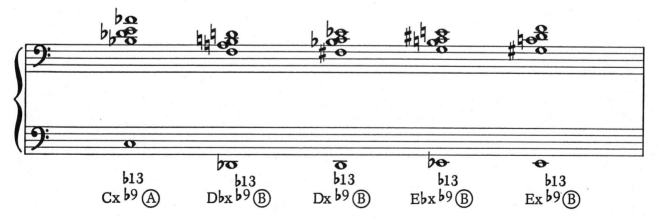

Cx^{b9}_{b13} Ⓐ Dbx^{b9}_{b13} Ⓑ Dx^{b9}_{b13} Ⓑ Ebx^{b9}_{b13} Ⓑ Ex^{b9}_{b13} Ⓑ

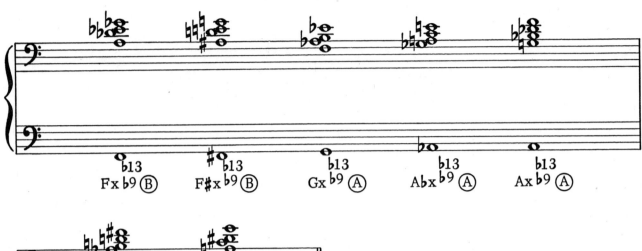

(c) The x$^{\sharp 9}$ omit 13 (augmented dominant ninth) occurs only in Ⓑ Form and is employed on all 12 dominants, including the Ⓐ Form area. Because of the frequent occurrence of this chord and the awkward symbol necessary to identify it, the letter Ⓒ will be used in future studies when referring to any x$^{\sharp 9}$ omit 13 (e.g. E x Ⓒ).

The principle of the dominant Ⓒ Form involves raising the ninth one half step and omitting the 13 of any of the 12 dominant Ⓑ Forms (see Fig. 3). The 13th must be omitted in order to achieve the characteristic "open" sound of the dominant augmented ninth.

Fig. 3.

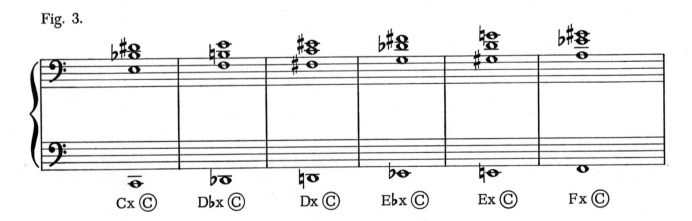

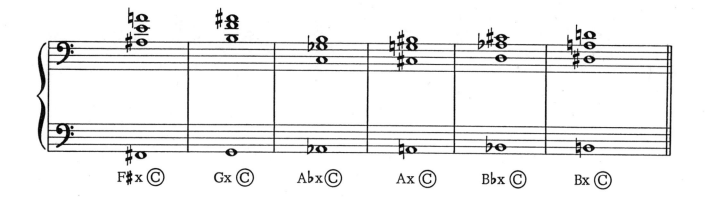

F#x©   Gx©   Abx©   Ax©   Bbx©   Bx©

This voicing, involving the illusion of a chord simultaneously containing a major and minor "third" (a harmonic cross-relation), is a familiar device and will be recognized as a common harmonic mannerism in the jazz-influenced compositions of George Gershwin.

(d) The x^{11} or "suspend 4," as it often appears in sheet music, represents the suspended dominant chord studied in Vol. I in the primitive form of $x^{\sharp 3}$. Figure 4 illustrates the x^{11}, Ⓐ and Ⓑ Forms, for the 12 dominant chords. In each case the normal resolution accompanies each x^{11} chord. The student should note that the x^{11} chord is actually a II voicing with a V root.

Fig. 4.

Cx^{11}Ⓐ   Cx Ⓐ   Dbx^{11}Ⓑ   Dbx Ⓑ   Dx^{11}Ⓑ   Dx Ⓑ   Ebx^{11}Ⓑ   Ebx Ⓑ

Ex^{11}Ⓑ   Ex Ⓑ   Fx^{11}Ⓑ   Fx Ⓑ   F#x^{11}Ⓑ   F#x Ⓑ   Gx^{11}Ⓐ   Gx Ⓐ

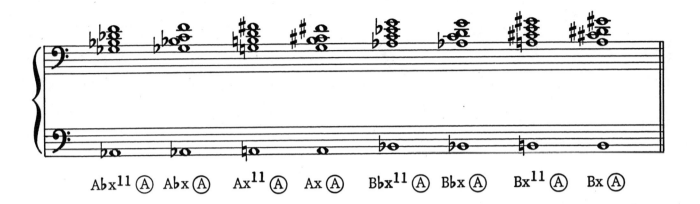

$Ab x^{11}$ Ⓐ $\quad$ $Ab x$ Ⓐ $\quad$ $A x^{11}$ Ⓐ $\quad$ $A x$ Ⓐ $\quad$ $Bb x^{11}$ Ⓐ $\quad$ $Bb x$ Ⓐ $\quad$ $B x^{11}$ Ⓐ $\quad$ $B x$ Ⓐ

(e) The $x^{\sharp 11}$ (augmented 11th) is a common ornamental dominant, often referred to as the "flatted fifth." Figure 5 illustrates the 12 dominant augmented 11th chords in Ⓐ and Ⓑ Forms. Although the $x^{\sharp 11}$ may be used as an isolated chord, it often appears as a segment of a familiar inner-voice movement on the dominant chord. Figure 5 illustrates this movement from 5 to $\flat 5$ ($\sharp 11$) to 4 ($\sharp 3$) and finally to a position of "rest" on 3.

Fig. 5.

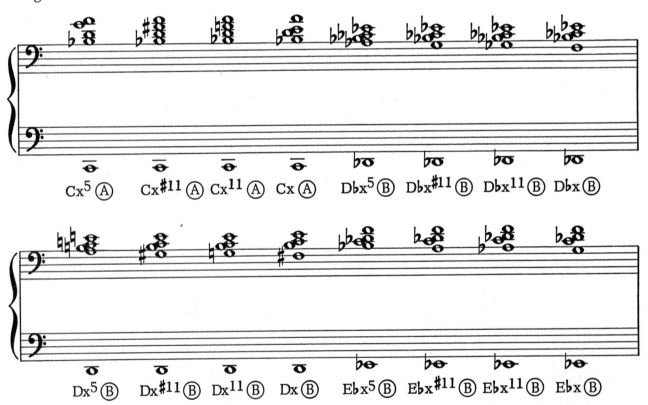

$C x^5$ Ⓐ $\quad$ $C x^{\sharp 11}$ Ⓐ $\quad$ $C x^{11}$ Ⓐ $\quad$ $C x$ Ⓐ $\quad$ $Db x^5$ Ⓑ $\quad$ $Db x^{\sharp 11}$ Ⓑ $\quad$ $Db x^{11}$ Ⓑ $\quad$ $Db x$ Ⓑ

$D x^5$ Ⓑ $\quad$ $D x^{\sharp 11}$ Ⓑ $\quad$ $D x^{11}$ Ⓑ $\quad$ $D x$ Ⓑ $\quad$ $Eb x^5$ Ⓑ $\quad$ $Eb x^{\sharp 11}$ Ⓑ $\quad$ $Eb x^{11}$ Ⓑ $\quad$ $Eb x$ Ⓑ

Ex^5Ⓑ $Ex^{\sharp 11}$Ⓑ Ex^{11}Ⓑ ExⒷ Fx^5Ⓑ $Fx^{\sharp 11}$Ⓑ Fx^{11}Ⓑ FxⒷ

$F\sharp x^5$Ⓑ $F\sharp x^{\sharp 11}$Ⓑ $F\sharp x^{11}$Ⓑ $F\sharp x$Ⓑ Gx^5Ⓐ $Gx^{\sharp 11}$Ⓐ Gx^{11}Ⓐ GxⒶ

Abx^5Ⓐ $Abx^{\sharp 11}$Ⓐ Abx^{11}Ⓐ AbxⒶ Ax^5Ⓐ $Ax^{\sharp 11}$Ⓐ Ax^{11}Ⓐ AxⒶ

Bbx^5Ⓐ $Bbx^{\sharp 11}$Ⓐ Bbx^{11}Ⓐ BbxⒶ Bx^5Ⓐ $Bx^{\sharp 11}$Ⓐ Bx^{11}Ⓐ BxⒶ

(f) The ninth is sometimes omitted from the dominant Ⓐ Form in order to gain clarity.

Fig. 6   Ⓐ modified

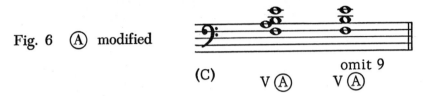

(C)   V Ⓐ   omit 9
                          V Ⓐ

(g) The 13th is sometimes omitted in the dominant Ⓑ Form, also in order to gain clarity.

Fig. 7   Ⓑ modified

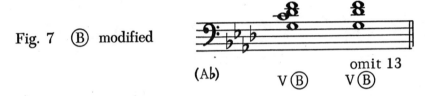

(A♭)   V Ⓑ   omit 13
                           V Ⓑ

(h) A unique relationship exists between any dominant chord and the diminished chord one-half step above. In Fig. 8 the superimposed D♭o chord over the C root forms the following intervals:

C - D♭:   flatted 9th
C - E: major 3rd
C - G: perfect 5th
C - B♭:   minor 7th

Formation — Cx^{b9}: This relationship also functions in any chord of the series (Fig. 9).

Fig. 8.

Cx^{b9}

Fig. 9.

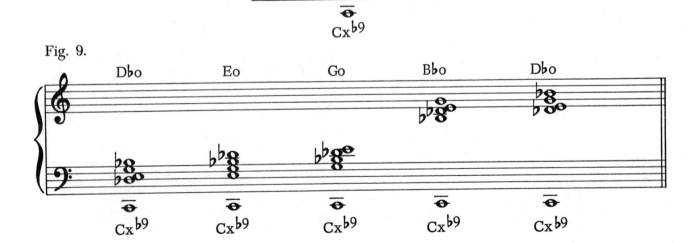

Dbo   Eo   Go   Bbo   Dbo

Cx^{b9} Cx^{b9} Cx^{b9} Cx^{b9} Cx^{b9}

102

Figure 9: This chord is often erroneously referred to as a "diminished" ninth. Referring to Fig. 10, if the dominant Ⓐ Form voicings of the D♭, E, G and B♭ diminished chords are superimposed over the C root, a dominant series is created which may be employed as an extension series on any dominant chord — see Lesson 29, Fig. 1, bars 18, 20. (This device was first illustrated in Lesson 9, Fig. 7 in the original diminished formation.)

Fig. 10.

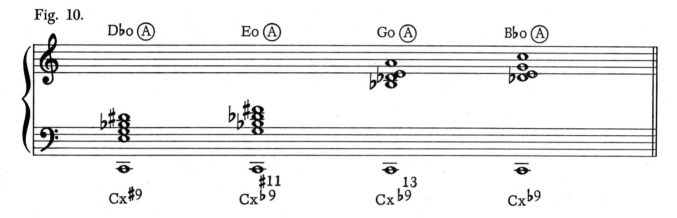

This minor third series may also be played in root position (see Fig. 11).

Fig. 11.

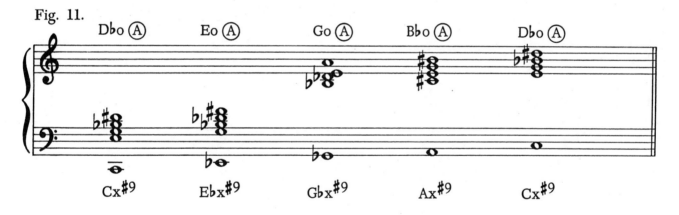

Figures 12 and 13 illustrate the identical formations for the Ⓑ Form.

Fig. 12.

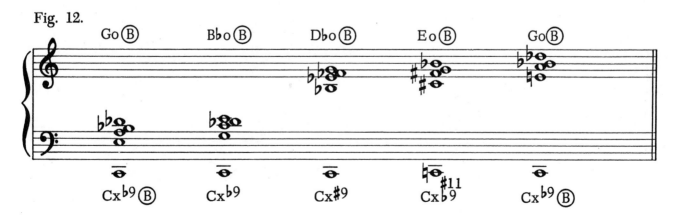

Fig. 13.

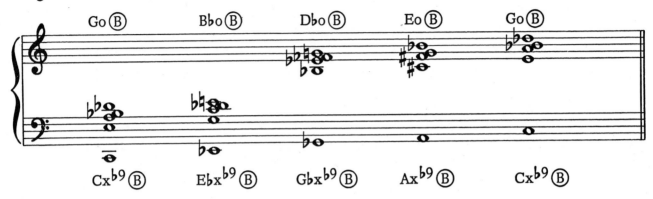

Figures 14 and 15 illustrates the identical formations for the dominant Ⓒ Form.

Fig. 14.

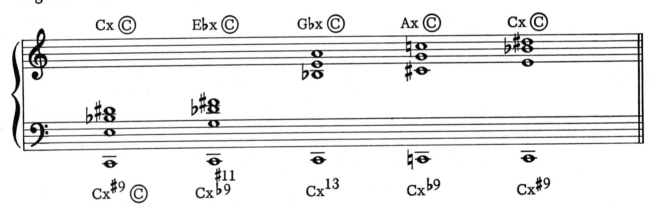

Fig. 15.

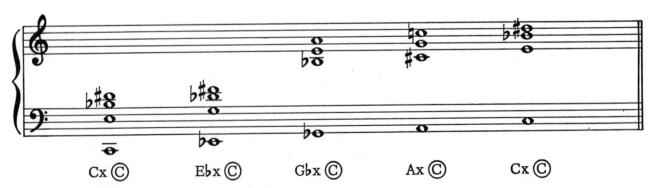

RULE: Any dominant chord may be extended by superimposing the diminished Ⓐ or diminished Ⓑ Form series one half step above the root (Figs. 10 and 12). A similar series may be built on the root employing the dominant Ⓒ Form (Fig. 14).

A further interesting relationship of this dominant-diminished superimposition is illustrated in Figs. 16 and 17.

Figs. 16.

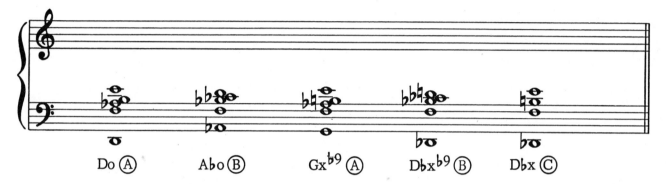

Fig. 17.

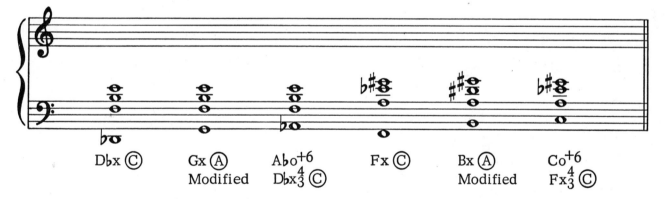

NOTE: Referring to Fig. 17, the diminished added sixth structure represents a root, seventh, third and the added sixth of the diminished scale of the root (021212121). There is a further implication of an dominant four-three structure in this voicing (A♭o⁺⁶ or D♭ x Ⓒ⁴₃; Co⁺⁶ or F x Ⓒ⁴₃); however, the o⁺⁶ feeling appears stronger and is more practical within the scope of normal jazz mechanics.

DRILL: Study Figs. 1 through 5 for automatic facility. Explore Figs. 6 through 17 on the 12 dominant positions.

Figure 18 is a bass line for "By Myself" in F, illustrating the use of the altered dominant chords.

Fig. 18.

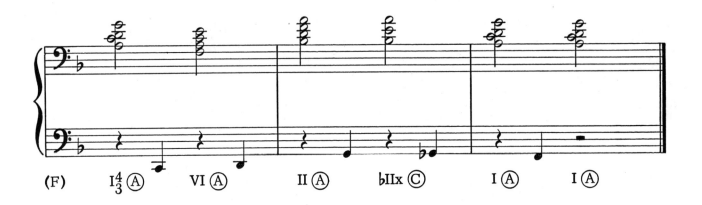

(F) $I\frac{4}{3}$ Ⓐ VI Ⓐ II Ⓐ ♭IIx Ⓒ I Ⓐ I Ⓐ

The Suspended Minor, Half-diminished and Diminished Ⓐ and Ⓑ Forms

The following table describes the alteration technique of the minor, half-diminished and diminished chords:

minor chord	♯♯7, ♯7	Fig. 1
half-diminished chord	♯7	Fig. 2
diminished chord	♯♯7	Fig. 3

Fig. 1. Fig. 2. Fig. 3.

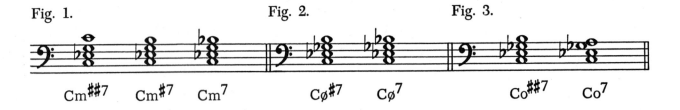

Cm♯♯7 Cm♯7 Cm7 Cø♯7 Cø7 Co♯♯7 Co7

The student will note that the suspended half-diminished and diminished chords are identical, although their resolutions are, of course, different.

Unlike the suspended dominant chord (V¹¹), which often passes to the succeeding chord while still suspended (V¹¹ - I), the three chords under consideration here usually resolve as in Figs. 1, 2 and 3 before proceeding to a new chord.

In the Ⓐ and Ⓑ Forms, the identical alterations appear. Figure 4 illustrates the Ⓐ Form in keys C to F and the Ⓑ Form in keys F♯ to B, employing the following patterns:

C to F: II²⁷ Ⓐ   II Ⓐ   ♭IIx Ⓑ   I Ⓐ
F♯ to B: II²⁷ Ⓑ   II Ⓑ   ♭IIx Ⓐ   I Ⓑ

Note that in moving from II to I through ♭IIx, the opposite form appears in the dominant.

Fig. 4.

(C)   II#7 Ⓐ II Ⓐ ♭IIx Ⓑ I Ⓐ   (D♭)   II#7 Ⓐ II Ⓐ ♭IIx Ⓑ   I Ⓐ

(D)   II#7 Ⓐ II Ⓐ ♭IIx Ⓑ   I Ⓐ   (E♭)   II#7 Ⓐ II Ⓐ   ♭IIx Ⓑ   I Ⓐ

(E)   II#7 Ⓐ II Ⓐ ♭IIx Ⓑ I Ⓐ   (F)   II#7 Ⓐ II Ⓐ   ♭IIx Ⓑ   I Ⓐ

109

(F#)   II#7 Ⓑ   II Ⓑ   ♭IIx Ⓐ   I Ⓑ   (G)   II#7 Ⓑ   II Ⓑ   ♭IIx Ⓐ   I Ⓑ

(A♭)   II#7 Ⓑ   II Ⓑ   ♭IIx Ⓐ   I Ⓑ   (A)   II#7 Ⓑ   II Ⓑ   ♭IIx Ⓐ   I Ⓑ

(B♭)   II#7 Ⓑ   II Ⓑ   ♭IIx Ⓐ   I Ⓑ   (B)   II#7 Ⓑ   II Ⓑ   ♭IIx Ⓐ   I Ⓑ

Figure 5 illustrates the suspended half-diminished chord in the following patterns:

C to F: $II\phi^{\#7}$ Ⓐ $II\phi$ Ⓐ   ♭IIx Ⓒ   I Ⓐ
F♯ to B: $II\phi^{\#7}$ Ⓑ $II\phi$ Ⓑ   V Ⓒ   I Ⓑ

The student will note that the ninth (2) of the suspended half-diminished (Fig. 5) and the suspended diminished (Fig. 6) has been omitted. This is necessary in order to avoid the diffuse sound of the suspension.

Fig. 5.

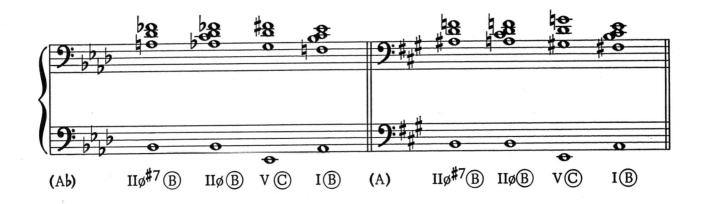

(Ab)   IIø#7 Ⓑ   IIø Ⓑ   V Ⓒ   I Ⓑ   (A)   IIø#7 Ⓑ   IIø Ⓑ   V Ⓒ   I Ⓑ

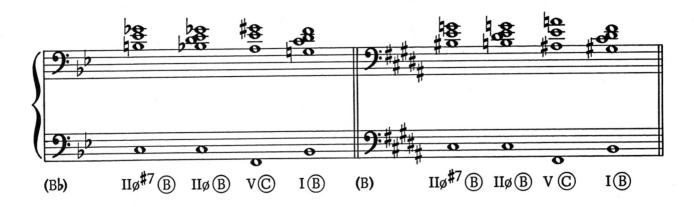

(Bb)   IIø#7 Ⓑ   IIø Ⓑ   V Ⓒ   I Ⓑ   (B)   IIø#7 Ⓑ   IIø Ⓑ   V Ⓒ   I Ⓑ

Figure 6 illustrates the suspended diminished chord in the following patterns:

C to F: bIIIo##7 Ⓐ   bIIIo Ⓐ   II Ⓐ   V♭13b9 Ⓐ   I Ⓐ
F♯ to B: bIIIo##7 Ⓑ   bIIIo Ⓑ   II Ⓑ   V Ⓒ   I Ⓑ

Fig. 6.

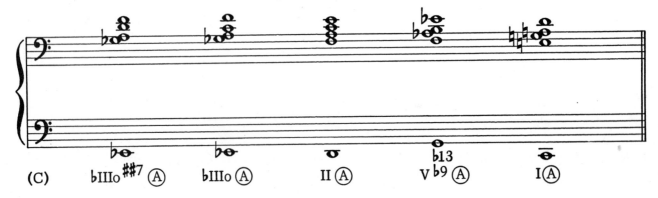

(C)   bIIIo##7 Ⓐ   bIIIo Ⓐ   II Ⓐ   V♭9b13 Ⓐ   I Ⓐ

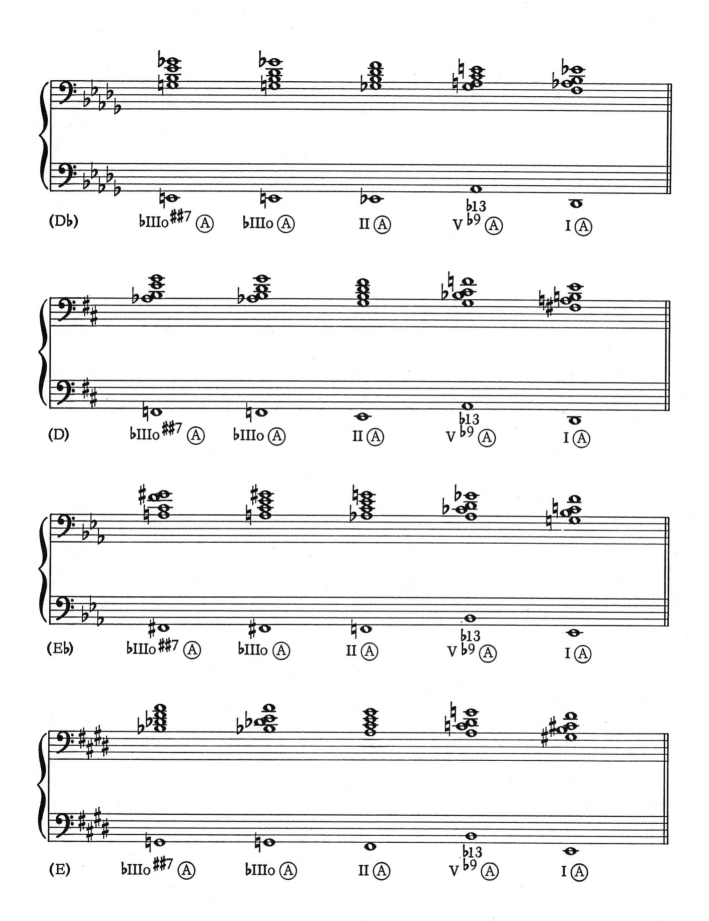

(Db)   bIIIo##7 Ⓐ   bIIIo Ⓐ   II Ⓐ   V b13 b9 Ⓐ   I Ⓐ

(D)   bIIIo##7 Ⓐ   bIIIo Ⓐ   II Ⓐ   V b13 b9 Ⓐ   I Ⓐ

(Eb)   bIIIo##7 Ⓐ   bIIIo Ⓐ   II Ⓐ   V b13 b9 Ⓐ   I Ⓐ

(E)   bIIIo##7 Ⓐ   bIIIo Ⓐ   II Ⓐ   V b13 b9 Ⓐ   I Ⓐ

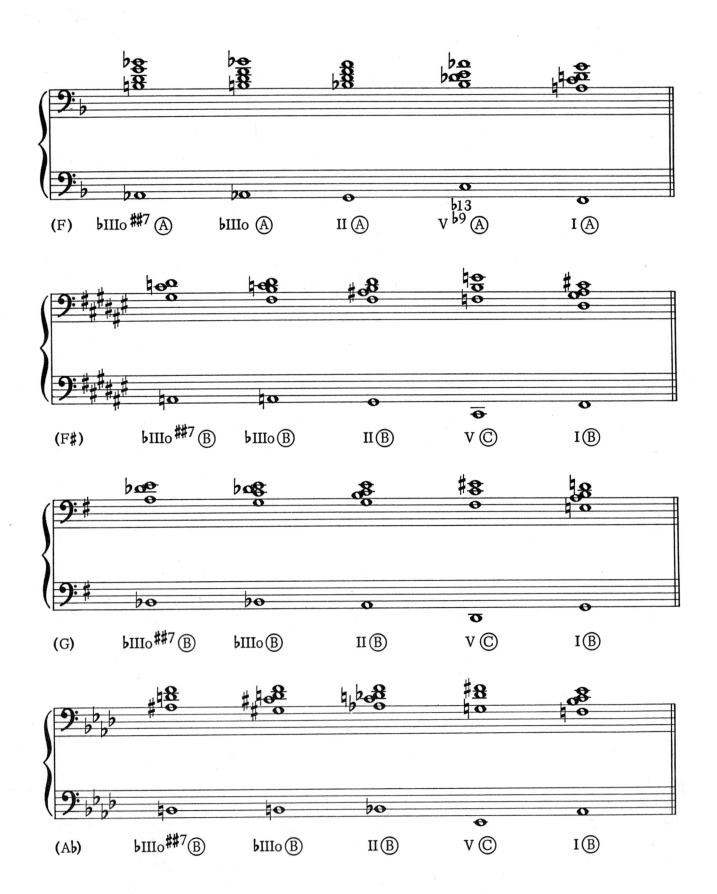

(F)   bIIIo ##7 Ⓐ   bIIIo Ⓐ   II Ⓐ   V b13 b9 Ⓐ   I Ⓐ

(F#)   bIIIo ##7 Ⓑ   bIIIo Ⓑ   II Ⓑ   V Ⓒ   I Ⓑ

(G)   bIIIo ##7 Ⓑ   bIIIo Ⓑ   II Ⓑ   V Ⓒ   I Ⓑ

(Ab)   bIIIo ##7 Ⓑ   bIIIo Ⓑ   II Ⓑ   V Ⓒ   I Ⓑ

114

Figure 7 is a bass line for "Better Luck Next Time" in F, illustrating the use of these various suspensions. In bar 29 the use of the m##7 chord is illustrated.

Fig. 7.

117

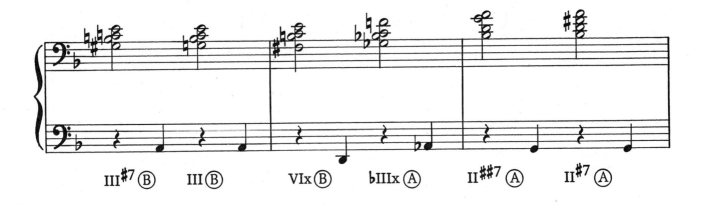

III#7 Ⓑ   III Ⓑ   VIx Ⓑ   bIIIx Ⓐ   II##7 Ⓐ   II#7 Ⓐ

II Ⓐ   bIIx Ⓒ   I Ⓐ   #I Ⓐ   I Ⓐ

Figure 8 illustrates the minor added sixth chord. In all cases of the added sixth ($^+$6) chord, the seventh is omitted and the *sixth tone of the prevailing mode* is added.

Fig. 8.

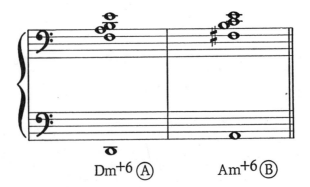

Dm$^+$6 Ⓐ   Am$^+$6 Ⓑ

LESSON 14.

Melodic Adjustment — Ⓐ and Ⓑ Forms

Although in jazz terms the principle of the Ⓐ and Ⓑ Forms is to establish an interesting harmonic underpinning for an improvised line, these forms are often employed to support a straight melody. As a result an occasional conflict will arise between a melodic tone and the voicing.

Major Chord: Conflict seldom arises with the major chord since most melodic tones fall in the appropriate *Ionian* mode.

Dominant Chord: Adjustments on the dominant chord are quite simply made since this chord allows for so many alterations. Fig. 1 illustrates the usual conflicts and their adjustments. In the seventh example of Fig. 1 the C♯ does not represent a conflict as much as it does a tension, which is permissible.

Fig. 1.

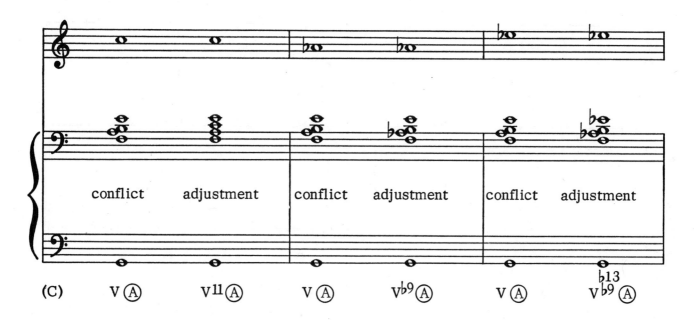

119

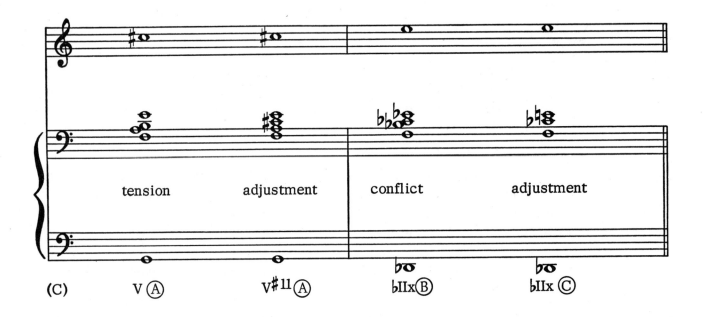

Minor Chord: The minor chords present the majority of conflicts in playing straight melody. The normal solution is to lower the ninth a major second to the eighth or octave of the root (Fig. 2). The symbol 8 over the Roman numeral indicates this adjustment.

Fig. 2.

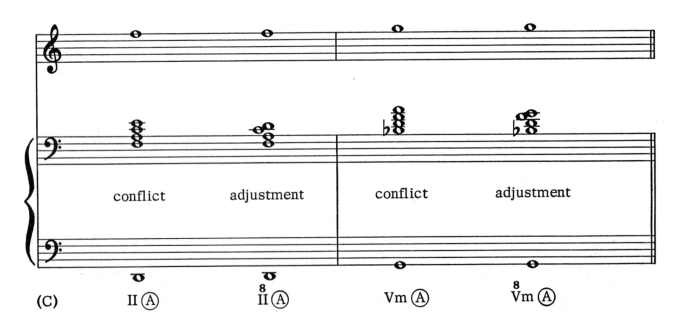

In dealing with minor and half-diminished chords, a special problem arises in all keys with the III Ⓐ and Ⓑ Form and VII Ⓐ and Ⓑ Form voicings, since the ninth of each voicing does not appear in the prevailing key (Fig. 3). This is due to the half steps in the major scale: 3-4 and 7-8. Here again, the ninth must be lowered to the octave in order to make an adjustment (Fig. 4). All other minor and half-diminished chords in melodic conflict follow these rules.

Fig. 3.

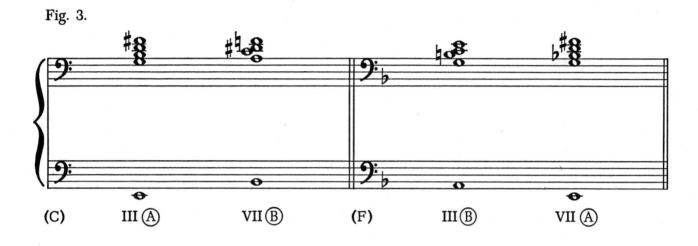

Fig. 4.

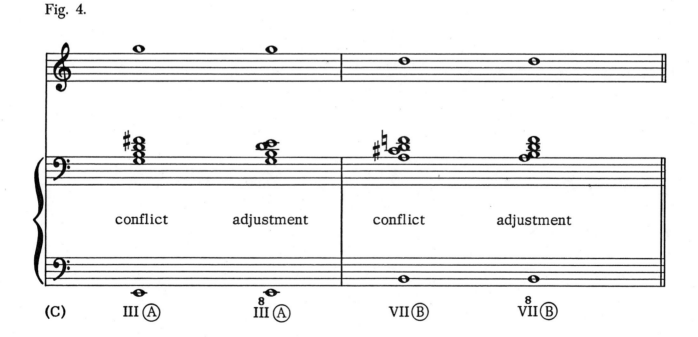

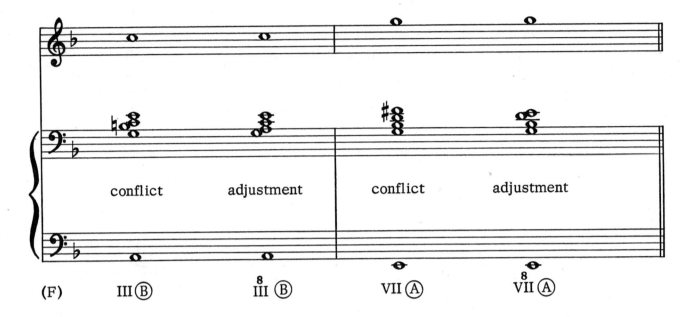

Diminished Chord: **Conflict seldom arises in the diminished voicings; in any case, the ninth in either Ⓐ or Ⓑ Forms may be lowered a whole step for consonance.**

Figure 5 illustrates the various adjustment problems in "Poor Butterfly" in D♭.

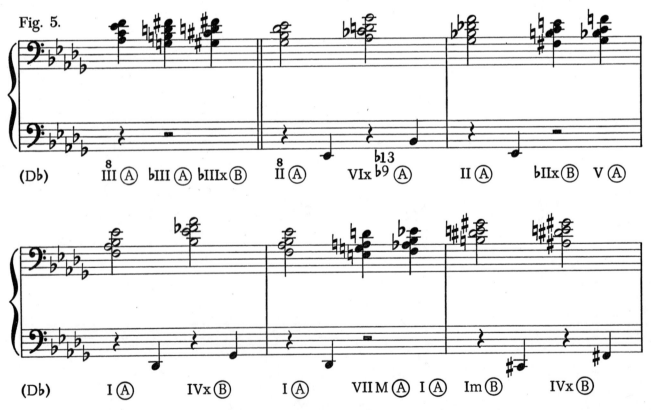

POOR BUTTERFLY — Copyright 1916 by Harms, Inc. — Used by Permission.

123

124

Right-Hand Modes with Ⓐ and Ⓑ Forms

In Vol. I, Section VI a thorough study of applying modes or *displaced scales* to jazz improvisation was made. In this study the following principles were established:

CHORD QUALITY	IMPROVISING FRAME
Major	Ionian Mode (1-1)
Dominant	Mixolydian Mode (5-5)
Minor II	Dorian Mode (2-2)
Minor III	Phrygian Mode (3-3) or temporary Dorian
Minor VI	Aeolian Mode (6-6) or temporary Dorian
Half-diminished	Locrian Mode (7-7)
Diminished	Semitone combination: 0 2 1 2 1 2 1 2 1

The general application of these modes to the Ⓐ and Ⓑ Forms is identical to that assigned the basic scale-tone chords in Vol. I.

Figure 1 illustrates the major Ⓐ and Ⓑ Forms with the appropriate modes.

RULE: The major Ⓐ and Ⓑ Forms employ the Ionian mode.

Fig. 1.

Ionian of C

Ionian of G

CMⒶ

GMⒷ

Figure 2 illustrates the dominant Ⓐ and Ⓑ Forms with the appropriate modes.

RULE: The dominant Ⓐ and Ⓑ Forms employ the Mixolydian mode. Altered dominants studied in Lesson 12 require similar adjustments in the appropriate modes.

Fig. 2.

Mixolydian of C

Mixolydian of G

Gx Ⓐ

Dx Ⓑ

In Vol. I, Lesson 44 the special problems of the minor chord were considered. These special problems rest with the fact that the minor chord appears in three positions of the diatonic scale — II, III and VI. We learned in Vol. I that:

> II is always II
> III may be III
> III may be temporary II
> VI may be VI
> VI may be temporary II

All other minors are considered as temporary II.

Figure 3 illustrates the minor Ⓐ and Ⓑ Forms with the appropriate modes for the function of II.

RULE: In all II chords or temporary II chords the minor Ⓐ and Ⓑ Forms employ the Dorian mode. Exceptions involving III (Phrygian) and VI (Aeolian) may still remain, although the Form itself is constructed as a temporary II.

Fig. 3.

Dorian of C

Dm Ⓐ (II of C)

Dorian of G

Am Ⓑ (II of G)

Figure 4 illustrates the minor Ⓐ and Ⓑ Forms with the appropriate modes for the function of III as a temporary II.

RULE: In functions in which III appears as a temporary II, the minor Ⓐ and Ⓑ Forms employ the Dorian mode of the temporary key.

Fig. 4.

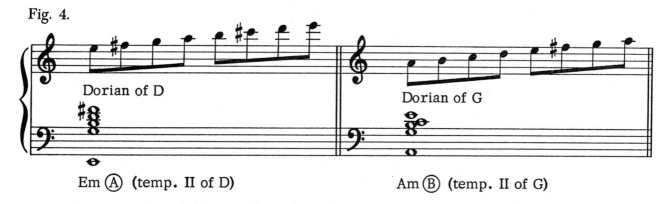

Dorian of D

Em Ⓐ (temp. II of D)

Dorian of G

Am Ⓑ (temp. II of G)

Figure 5 illustrates the minor Ⓐ and Ⓑ Forms with the appropriate modes for the function of III as III.

RULE: In functions in which III appears as III, the minor Ⓐ and Ⓑ Forms employ the Phrygian mode of the prevailing key. In this case the ninth *must* be lowered to eight (octave of the root).

Fig. 5.

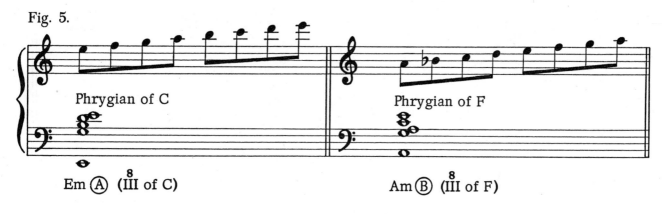

Phrygian of C

Em Ⓐ ($\overset{8}{\text{III}}$ of C)

Phrygian of F

Am Ⓑ ($\overset{8}{\text{III}}$ of F)

127

Figure 6 illustrates the minor Ⓐ and Ⓑ Forms with the appropriate modes for the function of VI as a temporary II.

RULE: In functions in which VI appears as a temporary II, the minor Ⓐ and Ⓑ Forms employ the Dorian mode.

Fig. 6.

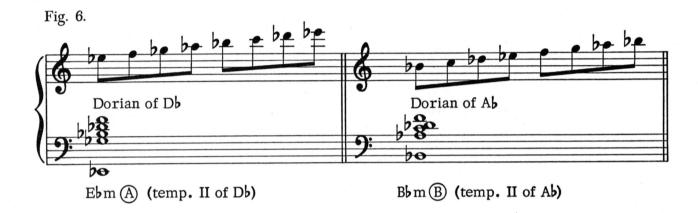

Dorian of D♭

E♭m Ⓐ (temp. II of D♭)

Dorian of A♭

B♭m Ⓑ (temp. II of A♭)

Figure 7 illustrates the minor Ⓐ and Ⓑ Forms with the appropriate modes for the function of VI as VI.

RULE: In functions in which VI appears as VI, the minor Ⓐ and Ⓑ Forms employ the Aeolian mode of the prevailing key. No adjustment of the ninth is necessary.

Fig. 7.

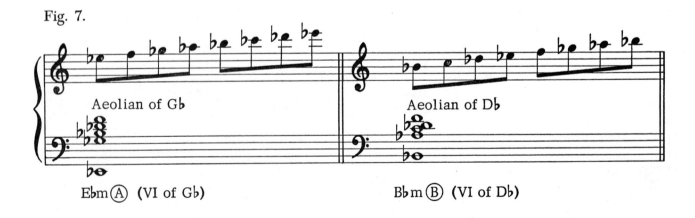

Aeolian of G♭

E♭m Ⓐ (VI of G♭)

Aeolian of D♭

B♭m Ⓑ (VI of D♭)

The half-diminished Ⓐ and Ⓑ Forms present a special problem, since the ninth employed in these voicings does not fall in the appropriate mode (Locrian 7-7) (see Fig. 8).

Fig. 8.

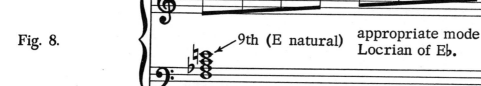

9th (E natural)   appropriate mode
                   Locrian of E♭.

Dø Ⓐ (temp. II♭5 of C)

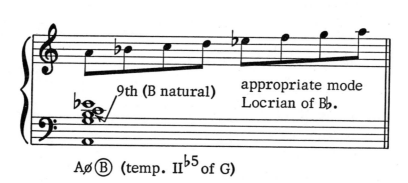

9th (B natural)   appropriate mode
                   Locrian of B♭.

Aø Ⓑ (temp. II♭5 of G)

The half-diminished chord, which is the weakest in terms of key inference of the four natural qualities (M, x, m, ø), is further weakened by the introduction of the ninth, since this tone destroys the tonic of the implied key. As a result, the half-diminished ninth Ⓐ and Ⓑ Form voicings assume the non-key reference found in the diminished chord. The most practical solution here is to build a tone-row similar in structure to that employed by the diminished chord. The tone-row is as follows:

0 2 1 2 1 2 2 1 1   (See Fig. 9)

RULE: The half-diminished Ⓐ and Ⓑ Forms employ the tone-row
0 2 1 2 1 2 2 1 1. The adjusted half-diminished (ø̆) takes the same tone row.

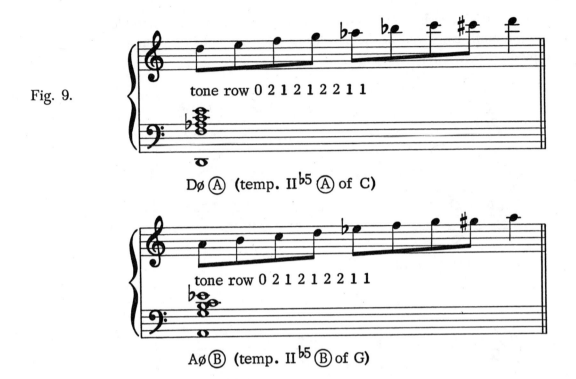

Fig. 9.

tone row 0 2 1 2 1 2 2 1 1

Dø Ⓐ (temp. II♭5 Ⓐ of C)

tone row 0 2 1 2 1 2 2 1 1

Aø Ⓑ (temp. II♭5 Ⓑ of G)

Figure 10 illustrates the diminished Ⓐ and Ⓑ Forms with the appropriate tone-row: 0 2 1 2 1 2 1 2 1.

RULE: The diminished Ⓐ and Ⓑ Forms employ the tone-row 0 2 1 2 1 2 1 2 1. The adjusted diminished (o) takes the same tone row.

Fig. 10.

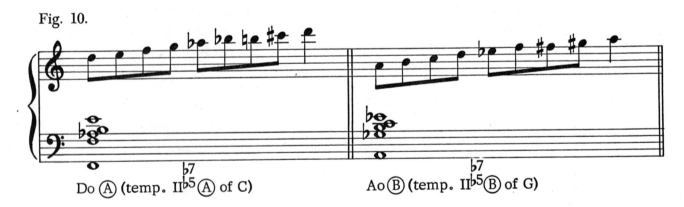

Do Ⓐ (temp. II♭5 Ⓐ of C)   Ao Ⓑ (temp. II♭5 Ⓑ of G)

DRILL: Explore the Ⓐ and Ⓑ Form voicings for the sixty chords with the appropriate modes or tone-rows. Figure 11 is a bass line for "Ten Cents a Dance" in E♭.

130

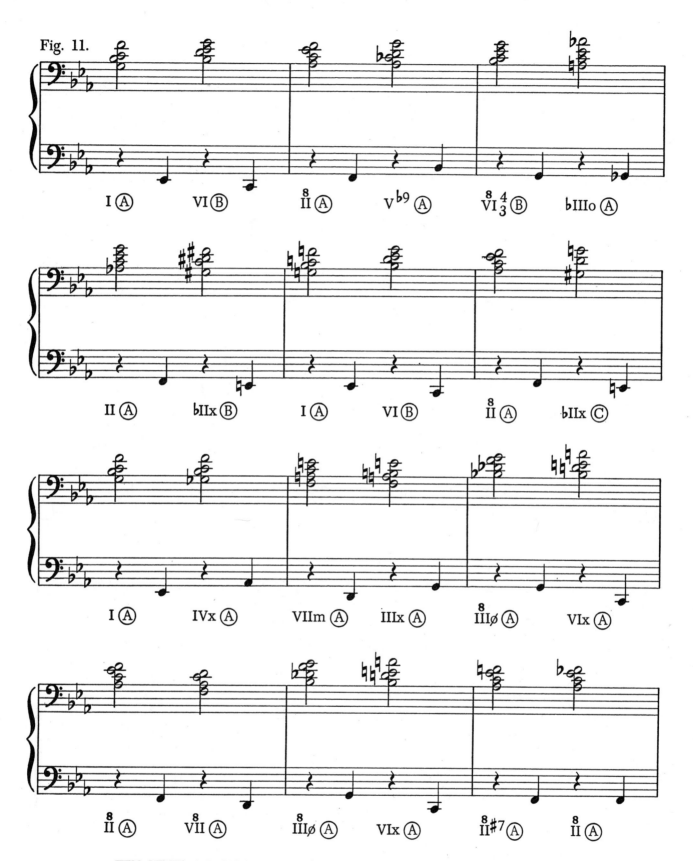

Fig. 11.

TEN CENTS A DANCE — Copyright 1930 by Harms, Inc. — Used by Permission.

131

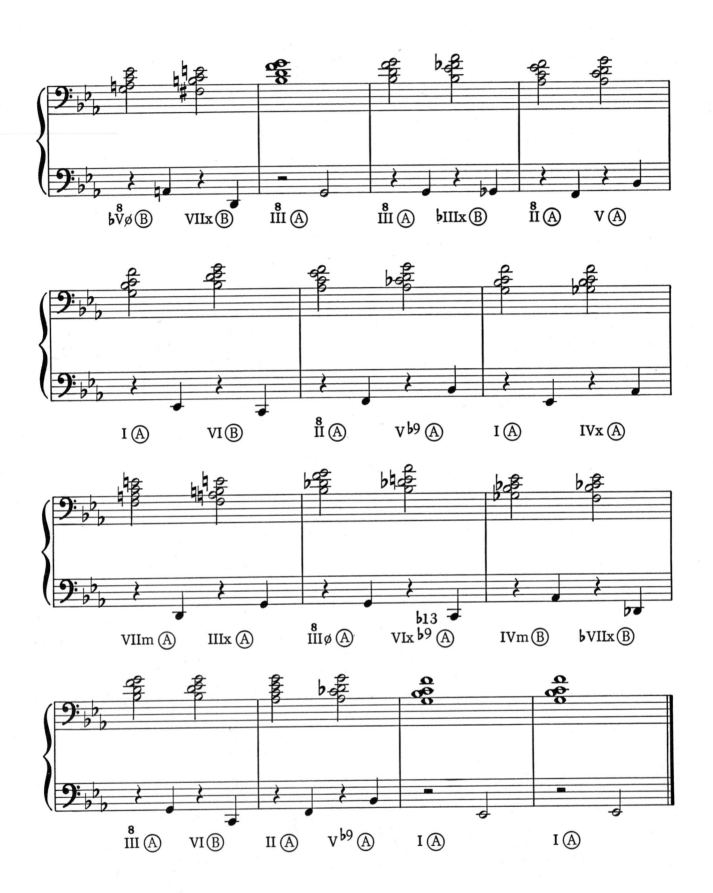

(A) and (B) Form Summation

In view of the complexity of the (A) and (B) Form system, this chapter will summarize the important facts considered in the previous fifteen lessons. This summation will bring not only a distillation of the material studied, but will also offer the student an easily accessible outline for convenient visual reference. In the following outline all interval combinations are based on the *prevailing mode of the chord.*

The Major Chord:

> I or temporary I of a parent key
> Keys C to F: (A) Form; 3 5 6 2 (Ionian Mode)
> Keys F♯ to B: (B) Form; 6 2 3 5 (Ionian Mode)

The Dominant Chord:

> V or temporary V of a parent key
> Keys C to F: (A) Form; 7 2 3 6 (Mixolydian Mode)
> Keys F♯ to B: (B) Form; 3 6 7 2 (Mixolydian Mode)

The Minor Chord:

> II or temporary II of a parent key
> Keys C to F: (A) Form; 3 5 7 2 (Dorian Mode)
> Keys F♯ to B: (B) Form; 7 2 3 5 (Dorian Mode)

The Half-Diminished Chord:

> II$^{\flat 5}$ or temporary II$^{\flat 5}$ of a parent key
> Keys C to F: (A) Form; 3 ♭5 7 2 (Dorian Mode)
> Keys F♯ to B: (B) Form; 7 2 3 ♭5 (Dorian Mode)

The Diminished Chord:

> II$^{\flat 5}_{\flat 7}$ or temporary II$^{\flat 5}_{\flat 7}$ of a parent key
> Keys C to F: (A) Form; 3 ♭5 ♭7 2 (Dorian Mode)
> Keys F♯ to B: (B) Form; ♭7 2 3 ♭5 (Dorian Mode)

Figure 1 illustrates the sixty jazz chords in their appropriate (A) and (B) Forms. The modified half-diminished and diminished (B) Forms are also included.

Fig. 1.

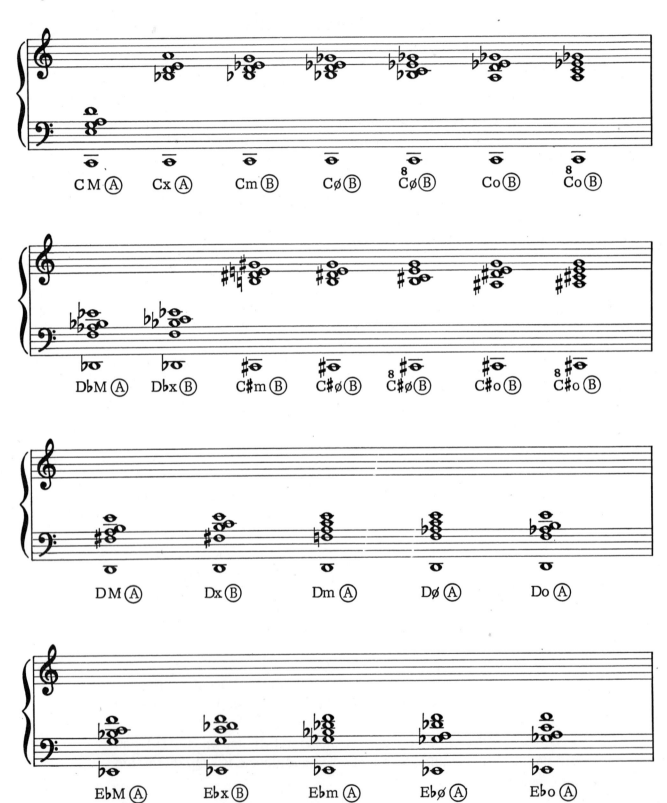

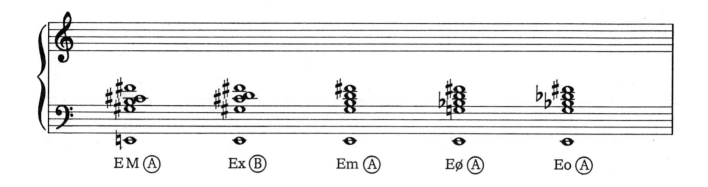

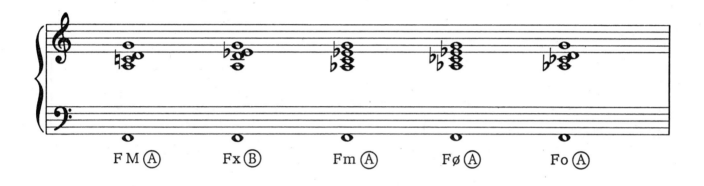

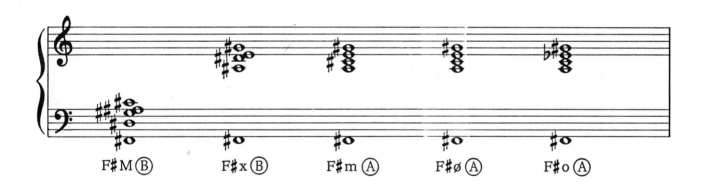

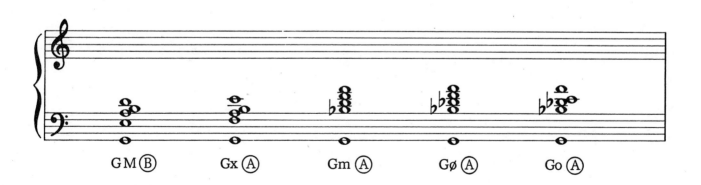

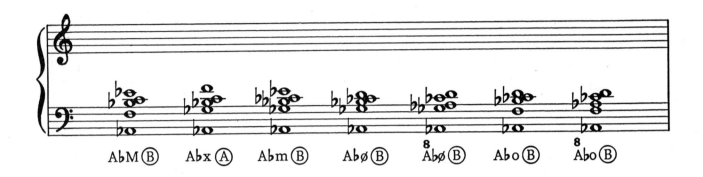

AbM Ⓑ   Abx Ⓐ   Abm Ⓑ   Abø Ⓑ   Abø Ⓑ   Abo Ⓑ   Abo Ⓑ

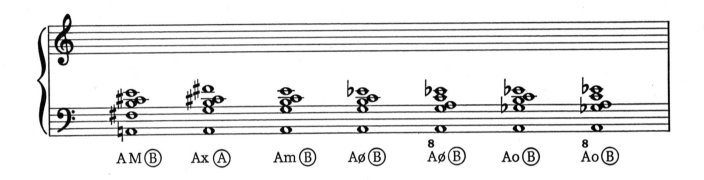

AM Ⓑ   Ax Ⓐ   Am Ⓑ   Aø Ⓑ   Aø Ⓑ   Ao Ⓑ   Ao Ⓑ

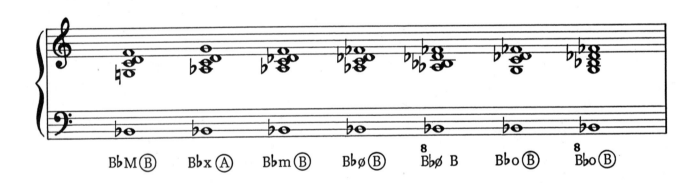

BbM Ⓑ   Bbx Ⓐ   Bbm Ⓑ   Bbø Ⓑ   Bbø B   Bbo Ⓑ   Bbo Ⓑ

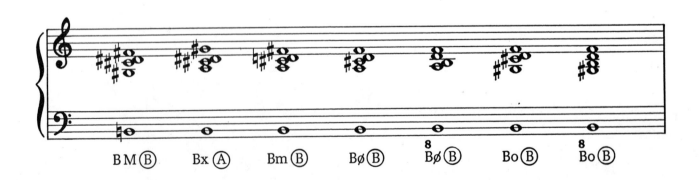

BM Ⓑ   Bx Ⓐ   Bm Ⓑ   Bø Ⓑ   Bø Ⓑ   Bo Ⓑ   Bo Ⓑ

Automatic, memorized facility with Fig. 1 is imperative in employing these forms of the sixty chords.

INVERSIONS: When an octave is formed between the bass note of the voicing and the root, use the opposite form.

Figure 2 illustrates a bass line for "Right As The Rain" in Ⓐ and Ⓑ Forms.

Fig. 2.

RIGHT AS THE RAIN (E. Y. Harburg and Harold Arlen) — Copyright © 1944 by The Players Music Corporation — Used by Permission.

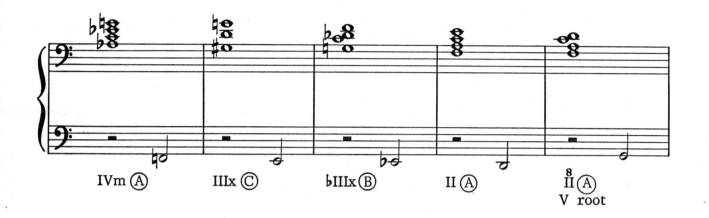

IVm Ⓐ   IIIx Ⓒ   bIIIx Ⓑ   II Ⓐ $\overset{8}{II}$ Ⓐ
V root

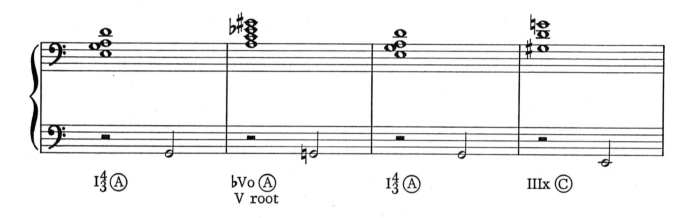

$I\tfrac{4}{3}$ Ⓐ   bVo Ⓐ $I\tfrac{4}{3}$ Ⓐ   IIIx Ⓒ
V root

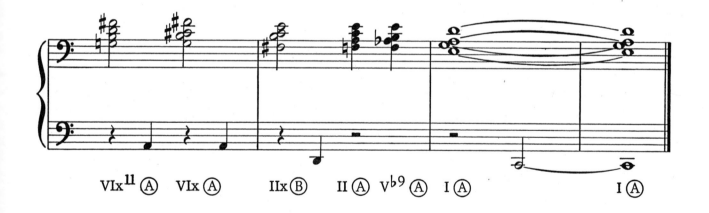

VIx^{11} Ⓐ   VIx Ⓐ   IIx Ⓑ   II Ⓐ V^{b9} Ⓐ   I Ⓐ   I Ⓐ

SECTION II

Solo Piano

LESSON 17.

Solo Piano (General)

The first systematic application of Ⓐ and Ⓑ Form idioms to modern popular piano was made by Cy Walter. Walter drew upon the various harmonic resources of Chopin, Scriabin, Albeniz, Debussy and Rachmaninoff to forge these elements into a handsome frame for a popular tune.

This stream of improvisation stems from the bravura pianists of the Nineteenth Century (Liszt, Busoni) and appears in an American line of descent from Leopold Godowsky through Herman Wasserman and George Gershwin to Walter.

The Ⓐ and Ⓑ Form voicings represent a practical distillation of harmonic devices found in Nineteenth- and early Twentieth-Century piano. Perhaps the most familiar employment of these idioms is in the classical piano concerto of the period. In general, the Ⓐ Form can be traced back to Chopin, the more modern Ⓑ Form derives from Ravel.

Cy Walter is an important figure is the development of modern vernacular piano and is undoubtedly the master figure of a school of pianism variously known as "society" or "cocktail" piano.

In the Forties the reaction within strict jazz ranks against the romantic individualism of the Thirties resulted in the re-assignment of the piano to the minor role of an accompanying unit in a rhythm section that occasionally played "horn-like" lines in the right hand, supported by 7-3 shells in the left (Bud Powell).

Post-Tatum piano is a non-solo, group piano style invariably supported by bass and drums. Isolated forays of solo explorations by Dave Brubeck, Dave McKenna, Lou Levy and others have been inconclusive, precisely because of the flagging nature of these explorations. As a result, general mainstream solo piano remains in a crippled state. Oscar Peterson and Bill Evans are the two figures in the contemporary scene capable of dealing with the problems of solo piano, but, up to this point, neither Peterson nor Evans has elicited any sustained interest in this medium. (See note.)

Walter is not a jazz pianist, yet his architectural approach to contemporary improvisation remains the finest expression of this ultimate challenge to all pianists — the keyboard as an unsupported "orchestra."

The name of Ellis Larkins should also be mentioned here, although this pianist has remained within the circumscribed limits of the accompanist's art.

NOTE: The original compositions of Powell ("Un Poco Loco," "Glass Enclosure," "Parisienne Thoroughfare," "Dusk in Sandi") are fantastic, surreal explorations in the tonal and rhythmic elements of contemporary jazz. Many of these compositions were performed unaccompanied. It would seem that any future developments in solo jazz piano would emanate from the point achieved by Powell in the late Forties.

The primary devices of contemporary solo piano are as follows:

1. Improvised lines (Vol. I)
2. Mixed positions (Vol. III, Section II)
3. 7-3-7 design (Vol. III, Section III)
4. Block chords (Vol. III, Section IV)
5. Ⓐ and Ⓑ Forms (Vol. IV, Section I)
6. Swing bass (modified) (Vol. IV, Section II)
7. "Walking" bass lines (Vol. IV, Section II)
8. Left-hand arpeggiation (Vol. IV, Section II)

Succeeding chapters will deal with modified swing bass, "walking" bass lines and left-hand arpeggiation. In general, it is permissible to employ any device considered in this present volume, or in previous volumes, when dealing with solo piano — surely a "moment of truth" for any jazz pianist.

SWING BASS (MODIFIED)

This idiom involves the Ⓐ and Ⓑ Forms supplemented by swing bass designs between the voicings and their roots.

"WALKING" BASS LINES

These lines simulate those played by a bassist in a modern jazz group. Such contrapuntal lines move in symmetry with the foot beat.

LEFT-HAND ARPEGGIATION

This is an ad-lib concerto device to create a harp-like underpinning for an ad-lib melodic line.

Figure 1 is a bass line for "But Not For Me" in E♭ employing Ⓐ and Ⓑ Forms.

Fig. 1.

pick-up

V♯³ // I VI / II ♭IIx / I / VI / IIx / II ♭IIx / Ix VI / Vm Ix / IV /
Ⓐ   ⒶⒷ Ⓐ Ⓒ   Ⓐ   Ⓑ   Ⓑ   ⒶⒸ   ⒷⒷ   ⒷⒷ   Ⓑ

♭VIIx / III / VI / II♯⁷ / II / ♭VIx / V♯³ / I VI / II ♭IIx / I / VI /
Ⓑ   Ⓐ   Ⓑ   Ⓐ   Ⓐ   Ⓐ   Ⓐ   ⒶⒷ Ⓐ Ⓒ   Ⓐ   Ⓑ

IIx / II ♭IIx / Ix VI / Vm Ix / IV / ♭VIIx / III / ♭IIIx / II / ♭IIx /
Ⓑ   Ⓐ Ⓒ   ⒷⒷ   ⒷⒷ   Ⓑ   Ⓑ   Ⓐ   Ⓑ   Ⓐ   Ⓒ

I⁺⁶ / I⁺⁶ //
Ⓐ   Ⓐ

BUT NOT FOR ME — Copyright 1930 by New World Music Corporation —
Used by Permission.

LESSON 18.

Root-Chord Patterns — Ⓐ and Ⓑ Forms

The principle of modified swing bass to be considered here demands
the ability of the student to make quick weight displacements from any
root to any chord or from any chord to any root.

This technique can best be achieved by drill studies based upon
our original II-V-I pattern appearing in varying root-chord designs. In
the following designs "R" will indicate the root; "ch" will indicate the
voicing (chord).

Design 1: R - ch - R - ch - R - ch

Fig. 1. Key of C

(C)   II Ⓐ   V Ⓐ   I Ⓐ

Fig. 2. Key of G

(G)   II Ⓑ   V Ⓑ   I Ⓑ

In general, the register employed by the roots is the second octave below middle C (Fig. 3). Roots may be played below, but seldom above, this octave.

Fig. 3.

root register

The technical problem of these quick displacements can be aided by the following suggestions:

1. Free swinging arm moving from a combined shoulder-elbow-wrist hinge movement
2. Non-visual drill to encourage muscular-tactile automation (since the hand moves faster than the eye, it is important to free any normal movement from a visual "lag")
3. Suggested "stagger" practice of mastering II root to II chord; II chord to V root; V root to V chord, etc.

Design 2: ch - R - ch - R - ch - R

Fig. 4. Key of D♭

(D♭)   II Ⓐ   V Ⓐ   I Ⓐ

Fig. 5. Key of A♭

(A♭)   II Ⓑ   V Ⓑ   I Ⓑ

144

Design 3: R - ch - ch - R - R - ch

Fig. 6.   Key of E♭

(E♭)   II Ⓐ   V Ⓐ   I Ⓐ

Fig. 7.   Key of A♭

(A♭)   II Ⓑ   V Ⓑ   I Ⓑ

Design 4: ch - R - R - ch - ch - R

Fig. 8.   Key of F

(F)   II Ⓐ   V Ⓐ   I Ⓐ

Fig. 9.   Key of B♭

(B♭)   II Ⓑ   V Ⓑ   I Ⓑ

DRILL: Practice these four designs on II-V-I patterns as follows:

	II	V	I
Keys C to F:	Ⓐ	Ⓐ	Ⓐ
Keys F♯ to B:	II	V	I
	Ⓑ	Ⓑ	Ⓑ

145

Figure 10 is a bass line for "Be My Love" in the key of G. Improvise on Fig. 10. Voicings and roots may be pedaled so long as the right-hand improvisation is not smeared.

Fig. 10.

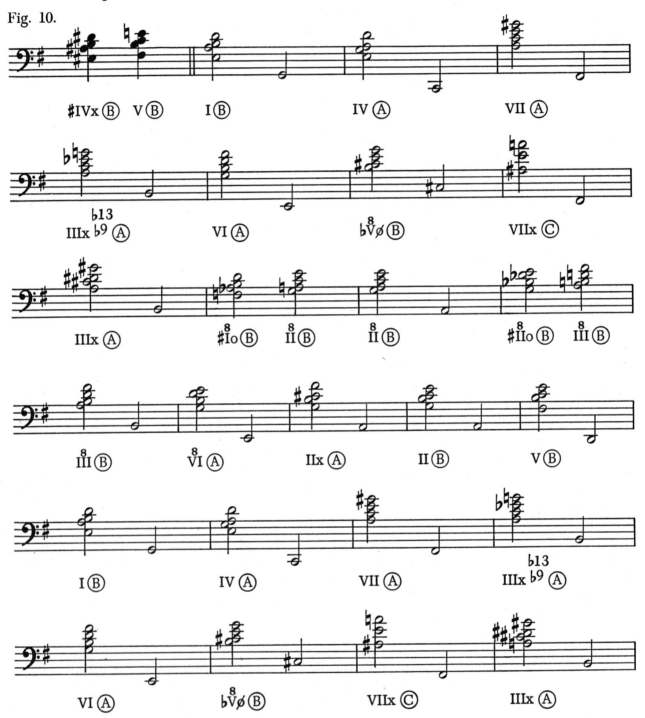

146

LESSON 19.

Root-Voicing, Voicing-Root Patterns,
Ⓐ and Ⓑ Forms — Ballad

Figure 1 illustrates a root-voicing, voicing-root treatment of a ballad. The principle here is one of constantly shifting patterns to sustain architectural interest. Each root-voicing or voicing-root unit may be pedaled, providing melodic or improvisational phrases are not smeared.

Figure 1 is a bass line for "My Ship" in the key of F.

NOTE: In bar 24 the use of the Ⓑ Form is to preserve the prevailing voice-leading.

147

Fig. 1.

148

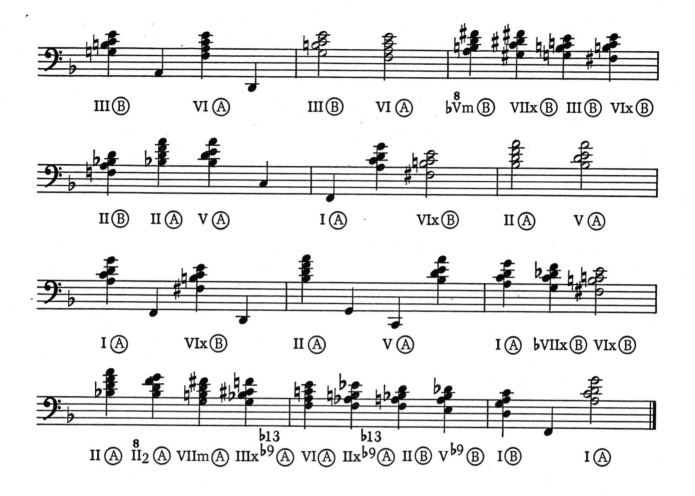

LESSON 20.

Root-Voicing, Voicing-Root Patterns,
Ⓐ and Ⓑ Forms — Bass Fifths

Figure 1 illustrates a root-voicing, voicing-root treatment of "Where Are You?" Here the fifth of each chord has been joined with the root in order to increase the resonance of the left-hand design. This device is most effective in slow, pedaled settings. It is only usable on qualities that employ perfect fifths (M, x, m); the diminished fifth sets up unsupportable overtones in the bass register. Inversions are also excluded.

Fig. 1.

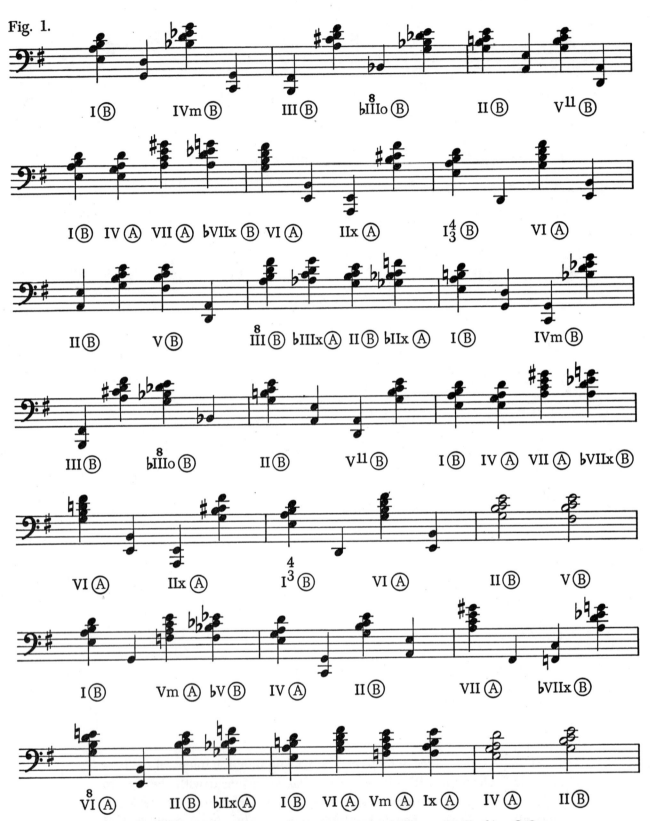

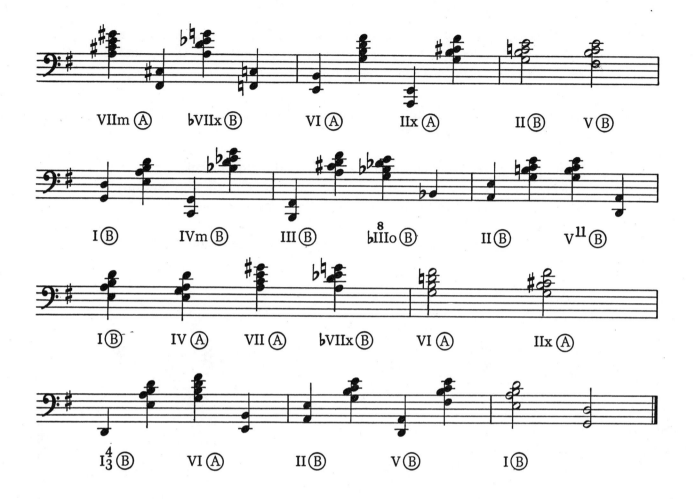

VIIm Ⓐ   ♭VIIx Ⓑ   VI Ⓐ   IIx Ⓐ   II Ⓑ   V Ⓑ

I Ⓑ   IVm Ⓑ   III Ⓑ   ♭IIIo Ⓑ   II Ⓑ   V^{11} Ⓑ

I Ⓑ   IV Ⓐ   VII Ⓐ   ♭VIIx Ⓑ   VI Ⓐ   IIx Ⓐ

I$^{4}_{3}$ Ⓑ   VI Ⓐ   II Ⓑ   V Ⓑ   I Ⓑ

LESSON 21.

Root-Voicing Patterns, Ⓐ and Ⓑ Forms — Minor Tonality

The minor scale-tone chords (Vol. I, Section 10) employ one quality (III—M$^+$) not found in the major scale system (Fig. 1).

Fig. 1.

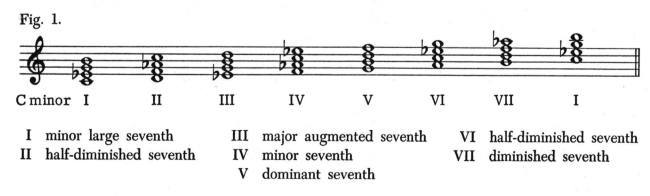

C minor   I   II   III   IV   V   VI   VII   I

I	minor large seventh	III	major augmented seventh	VI	half-diminished seventh
II	half-diminished seventh	IV	minor seventh	VII	diminished seventh
		V	dominant seventh		

The minor large seventh has been treated in Vol. IV, Lesson 13. The one unfamiliar chord is the major augmented seventh on III (symbol M⁺). The voicings for this chord are as follows:

        Ⓐ Form — 3 ♯5 7 2 (Ionian)
        Ⓑ Form — 7 2 3 ♯5 (Ionian)

These voicings are based on the Ionian mode of the root. In building these voicings, it is essential to insure the presence of the ♯5; this in turn requires the removal of the 6, since a half-tone clash occurs.

Figure 2 illustrates the six Ⓐ Form voicings for the major augmented chords.

Fig. 2.

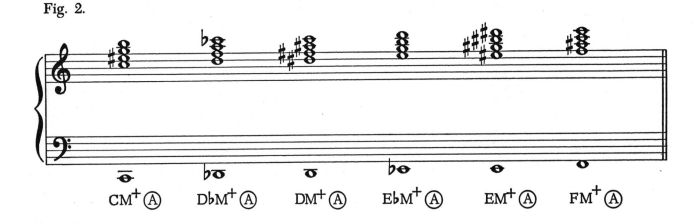

CM⁺Ⓐ   D♭M⁺Ⓐ   DM⁺Ⓐ   E♭M⁺Ⓐ   EM⁺Ⓐ   FM⁺Ⓐ

Figure 3 illustrates the six Ⓑ Form voicings for the major augmented chord.

Fig. 3.

G♭M⁺Ⓑ   GM⁺Ⓑ   A♭M⁺Ⓑ   AM⁺Ⓑ   B♭M⁺Ⓑ   BM⁺Ⓑ

152

NOTE: Fig. 4 illustrates a bass line for "You're My Thrill" in D minor. The figured bass is marked with reference to minor scale-tone chords in D minor (see Vol. I, page 163, Fig. 6). In bars 8 and 16, scale-tone chords have been used in place of the appropriate VI₂ⓑ and ♭VI₂Ⓐ, since both create impermissable octaves. The student is encouraged to work out similar solutions in addition to the general rule of employing the opposite form.

Fig. 4.

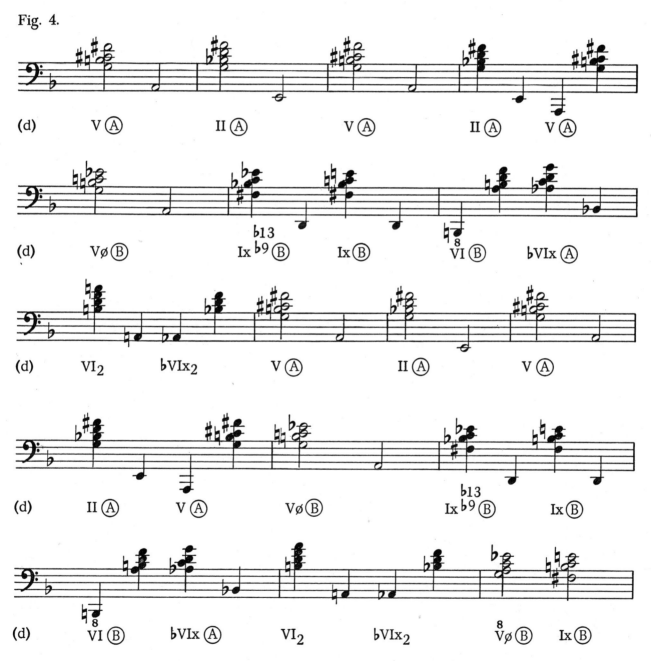

(d)   V∅ Ⓑ   ♭V Ⓐ   IV##7 Ⓐ   IV#7 Ⓐ   IV Ⓐ   IV₂ Ⓐ

(d)   VI Ⓑ   IIx Ⓑ   VI Ⓑ   IIx Ⓑ   V Ⓐ

(d)   IIIm Ⓐ   ♭VIx Ⓐ   V Ⓐ   II Ⓐ

(d)   V Ⓐ   II Ⓐ   V Ⓐ   V∅ Ⓑ

(d)   Ix♭9 Ⓑ   Ix Ⓑ   VI Ⓑ   ♭VIx Ⓐ

(d)   VI₂   IV Ⓐ   IIIx Ⓒ   IIx Ⓒ   ♭IIx Ⓒ   I+6 Ⓐ

154

LESSON 22.

Root-Voicing, Voicing-Root Patterns,
Ⓐ and Ⓑ Form — Superimposition

In tunes that employ the extended use of whole-note harmony (one chord to a bar), it is permissible and advisable to use both Ⓐ and Ⓑ Forms interchangeably in order to sustain interest. This means a free use of the Ⓐ Form in keys F♯ to B and of the Ⓑ Form in keys C to F.

This superimposition of the forms adds both rhythmic continuity and harmonic texture. The superimposed voicings should be pedaled to create a sonority in the left hand.

Figure 1 illustrates an application of this device to "This Is New" in the key of B♭.

Fig. 1.

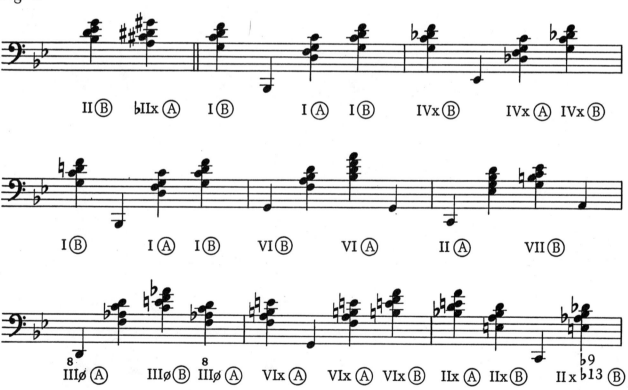

III Ⓐ   ³III Ⓑ   ³III Ⓐ   VI Ⓑ   VI Ⓐ   ⁸VI Ⓐ   ⁸IIø Ⓑ   ⁸IIø Ⓐ   IIø Ⓐ

♭13   ♭13

V♭⁹ Ⓐ   V♭⁹ Ⓑ   V Ⓑ   I Ⓑ   ♯I Ⓐ   ♯I Ⓑ   I Ⓑ   I Ⓐ

LESSON 23.

Root-Voicing Patterns, Ⓐ and Ⓑ Forms — 8/8 Time

The use of 8/8 time superimposed over a quarter-note foot beat is most familiar in the boogie-woogie idiom. In modern jazz this device has largely disappeared, although rhythm-and-blues groups still use it in a "shuffle" rhythm form.

However, used occasionally in slow ballads, this device can be effective in building a rhythmic and harmonic intensity not always present in tempi under ♩ = 80.

Figure 1 illustrates the use of 8/8 time in "I Fall In Love Too Easily" in the key of E♭.

In order not to break the continuity of the left-hand figure, it is suggested that the student cross his right hand over the left to strike the necessary roots. This cross-over technique must be integrated with the right-hand melodic phrase in the treble clef.

Figure 1 in this lesson and Fig. 1 in Lesson 24 are models. It is suggested that these devices be used sparingly to avoid monotony.

Fig. 1.

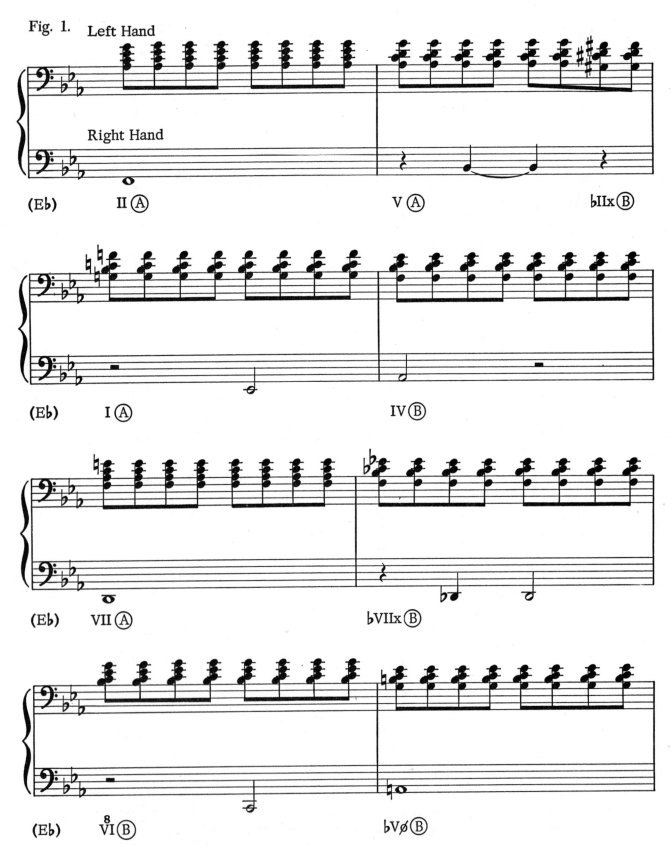

I FALL IN LOVE TOO EASILY (Lyric by Sammy Cahn, Music by Jule Styne) — ©
Copyright 1944 Leo Feist, Inc., New York, N. Y. — Used by Permission.

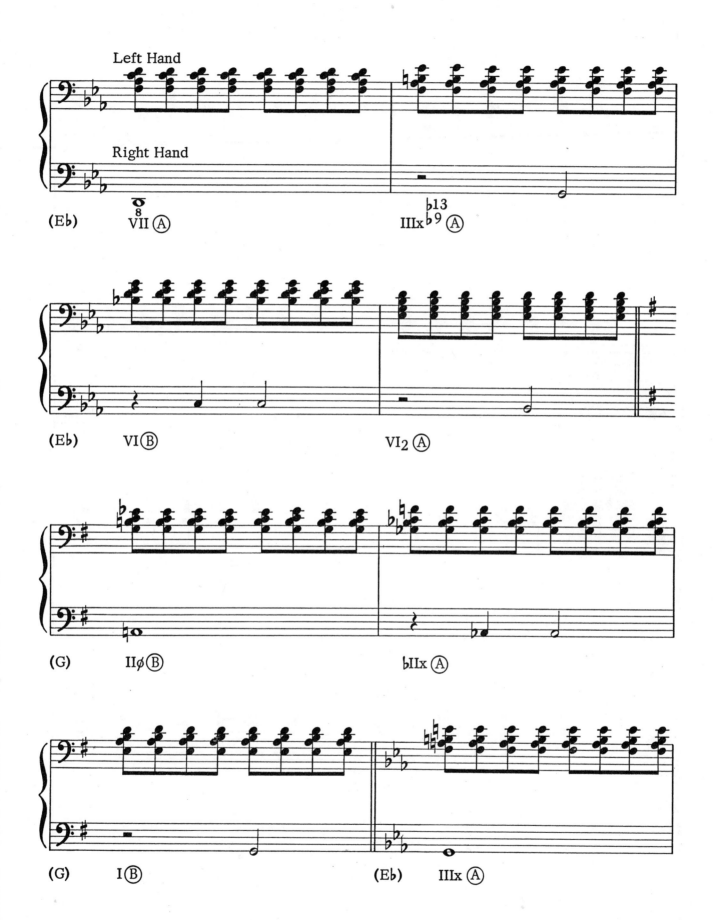

(Eb)   VII Ⓐ   IIIx ♭13♭9 Ⓐ

(Eb)   VI Ⓑ   VI₂ Ⓐ

(G)   IIø Ⓑ   ♭IIx Ⓐ

(G)   I Ⓑ   (Eb)   IIIx Ⓐ

159

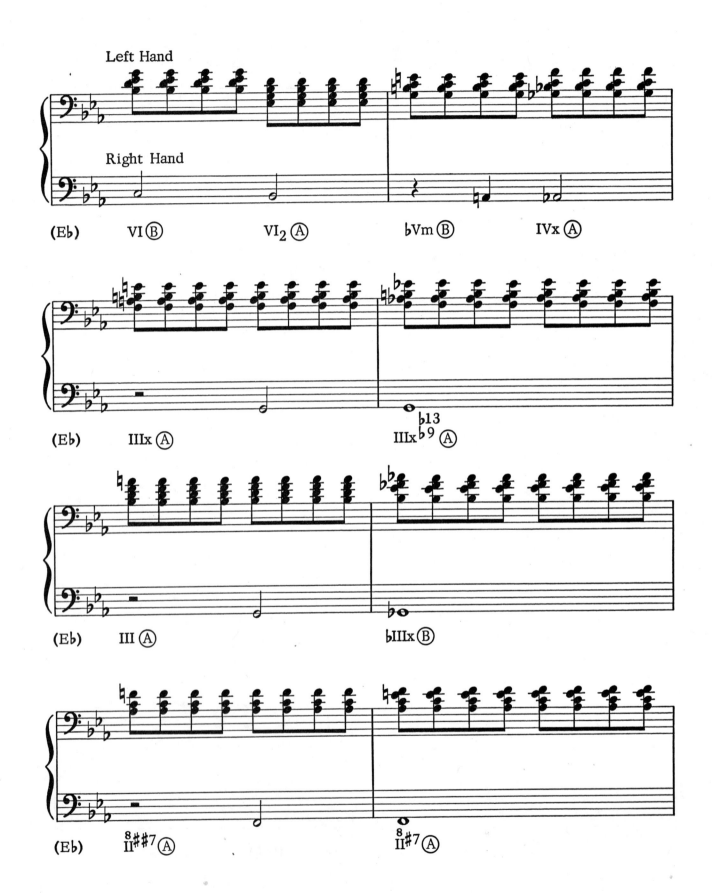

160

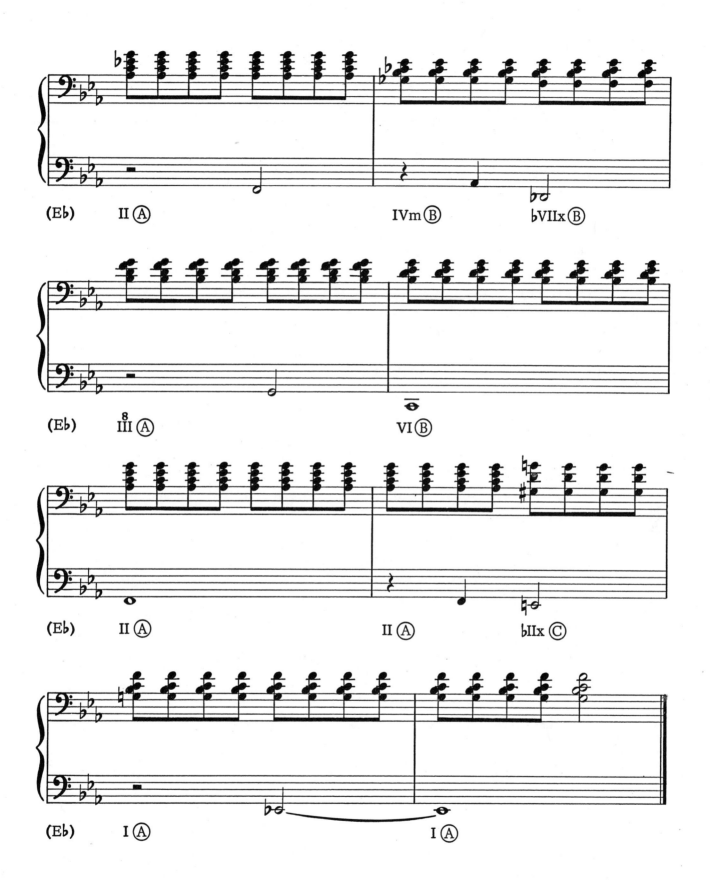

(E♭)   II Ⓐ   IVm Ⓑ   ♭VIIx Ⓑ

(E♭)   III Ⓐ   VI Ⓑ

(E♭)   II Ⓐ   II Ⓐ   ♭IIx Ⓒ

(E♭)   I Ⓐ   I Ⓐ

161

LESSON 24.

Root-Voicing Patterns, Ⓐ and Ⓑ Forms — 12/8 Time

A further development in this direction is the use of 12/8 time, the staple device of rock 'n' roll.

Actually 12/8 time has a very noble heritage, stemming from the folk elements of jazz pre-history. The juxtaposition of a 3/4 feeling over a 4/4 beat has always been an integral part of jazz rhythm, although the high classic stylists have usually employed this rhythmic element as one unit in an over-all composite of varying rhythms.

Figure 1 illustrates the application of 12/8 time on two simultaneous levels to the "Twelve-Bar Blues" in the key of B♭.

Harmonic 12/8 — left hand
Melodic 12/8 — right hand

A steady quarter-note foot beat (one to each triplet) should accompany this study.

The tension of this particular study is increased by the total absence of the natural tonic (major), which usually represents a function of resolution or "rest." This device is characteristic of the idiom. The student will also note that the entire study employs only the dominant chord, which further augments the tension. The "alliterative "effect created by the single melodic phrase played in varying "displacements" also tends to create a feeling of tension.

Roots have been added for right-hand cross-over.

Fig. 1.

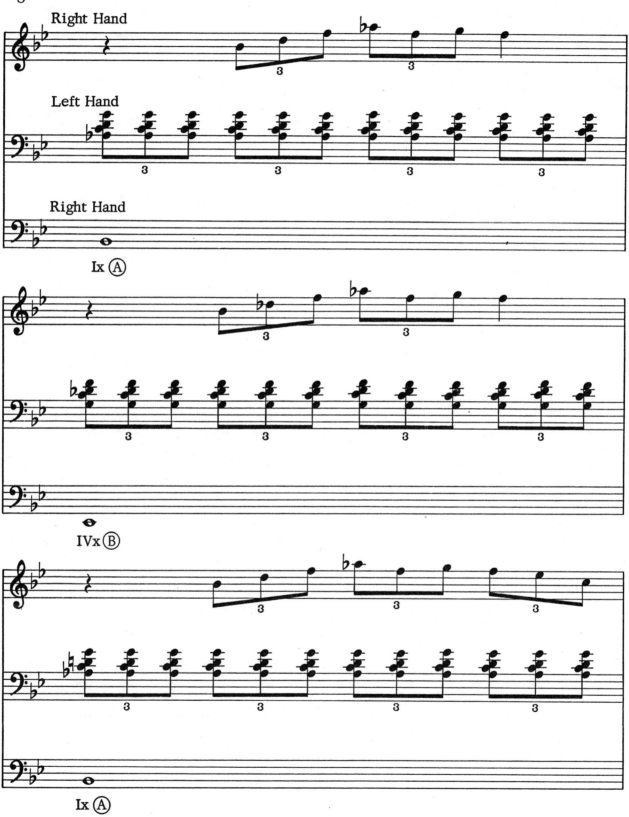

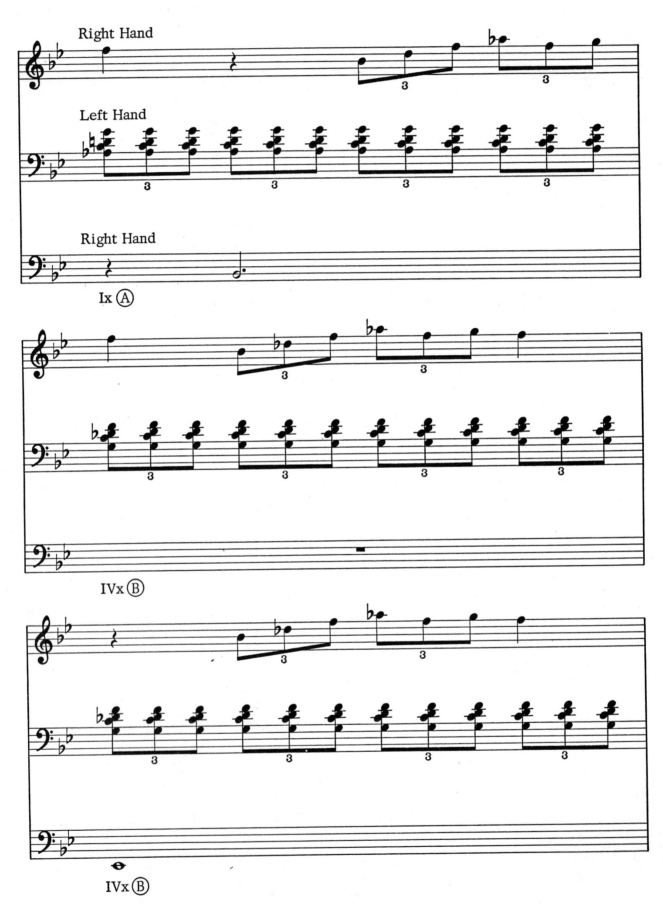

Right Hand

Left Hand

Right Hand

Ix Ⓐ

IVx Ⓑ

IVx Ⓑ

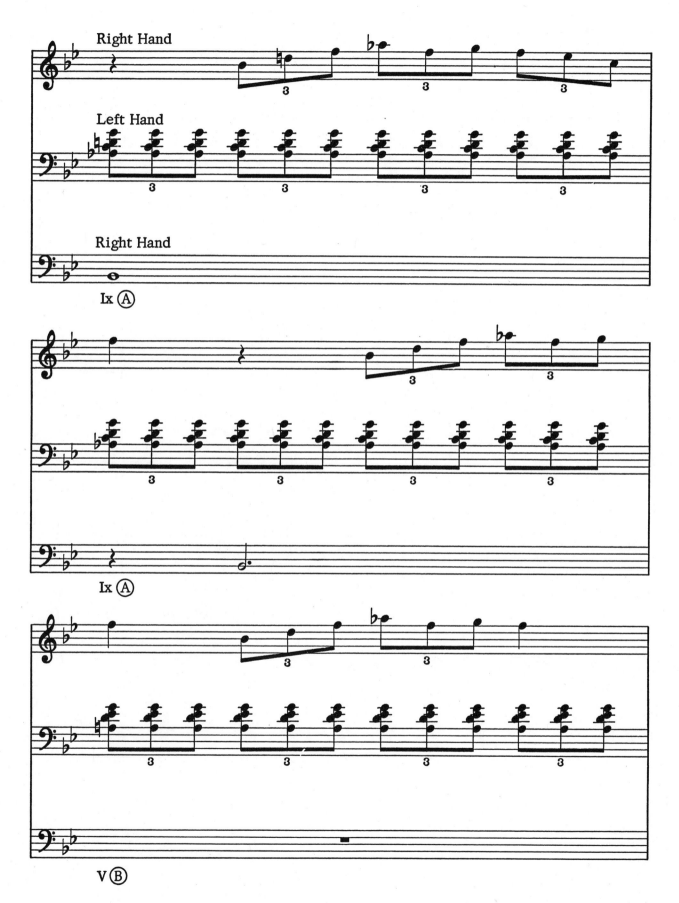

Ix Ⓐ

Ix Ⓐ

v Ⓑ

165

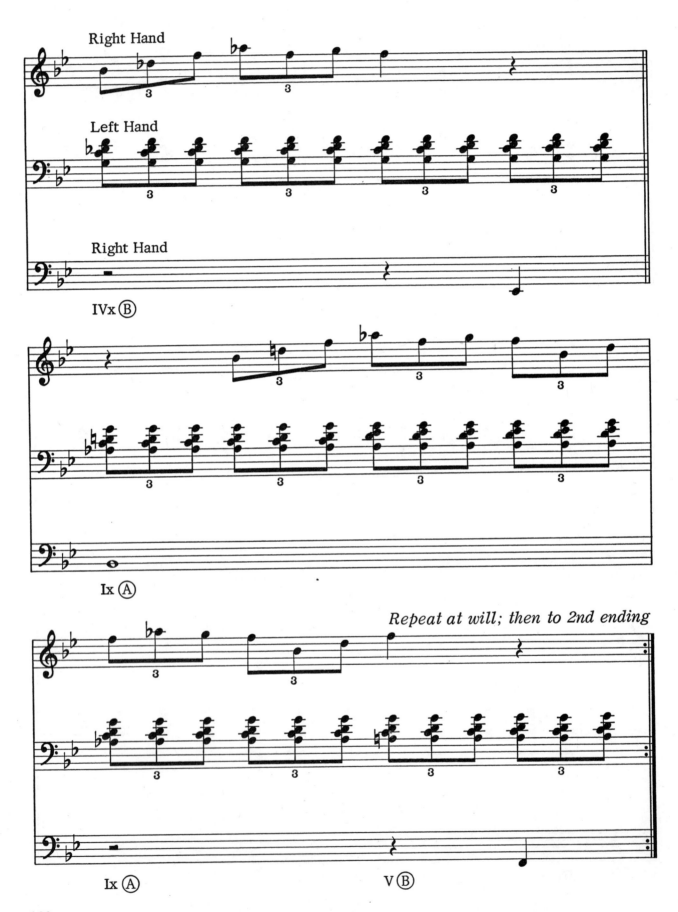

IVx Ⓑ

Ix Ⓐ

Repeat at will; then to 2nd ending

Ix Ⓐ   V Ⓑ

166

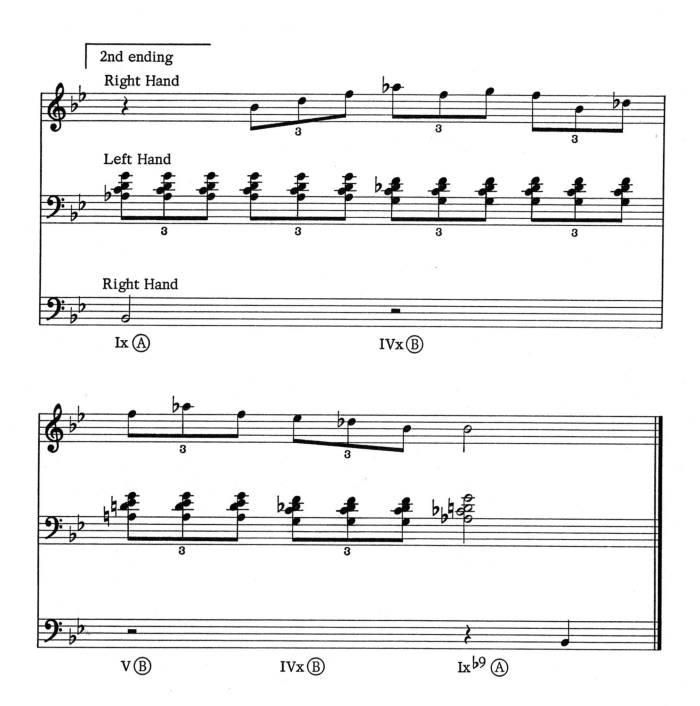

LESSON 25.

Root-Voicing Patterns, Ⓐ and Ⓑ Forms —
Bounce-Tempo Syncopated Swing Bass

In Vol. I, Lesson 34 the rhythmic essence of jazz was described as a composite of three simultaneous units of time:

melodic unit — eighth note (♪)

harmonic unit — half note (𝅗𝅥)

rhythmic unit — quarter note (♩)

We also learned in Volume I that the *variables* employed in the *melodic unit* or improvised line (in pianistic terms, the right hand) extend from eighth note to thirty-second note. See Volume II for a thorough analysis of the *harmonic* and *rhythmic variables* in jazz.

One of the basic devices of every jazz period has been the *superimposition* of the prevailing *unit* or the *variables* of one level *over* those of another level. For instance, in Volume III there is an analysis of swing bass — a *superimposition of the rhythmic unit* (quarter note) over the *harmonic unit* (half note). Also in Volume III, we saw a return to the original *harmonic unit* (half note) in the sections dealing with Bud Powell and Horace Silver.

In modern jazz piano the *melodic unit* (eighth note) and many of its *variables* (eighth note, thirty-second note) are often *imposed* over the *harmonic unit* (half note).

This superimposition of the rhythmic or the melodic unit and its variables may appear in the following forms:

1. Non-syncopation (Fig. 1)
2. Simple syncopation (Fig. 2)
3. Compound syncopation (Fig. 3)

168

Fig. 1.

Rhythmic
Superimposition

Harmonic Unit

Figured Bass

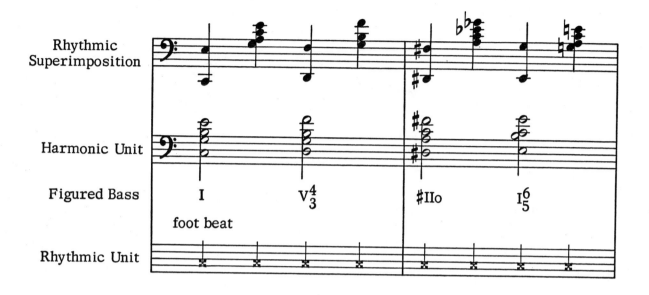

foot beat

Rhythmic Unit

Fig. 2

Melodic
Superimposition

Harmonic Unit

Figured Bass

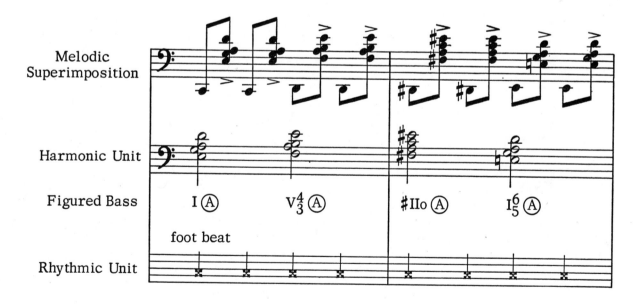

foot beat

Rhythmic Unit

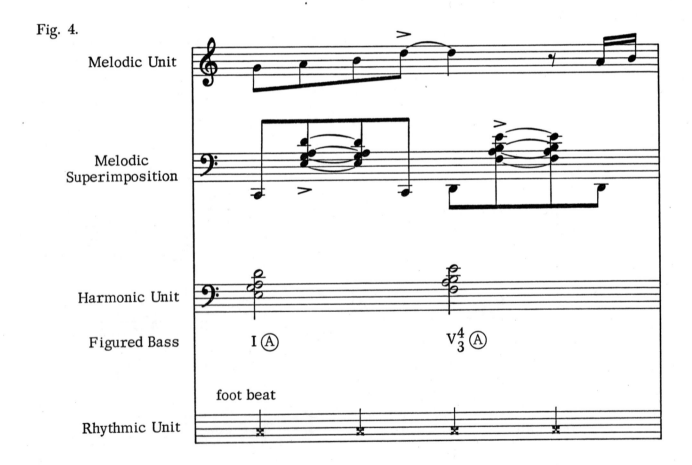

Fig. 3.

Fig. 4.

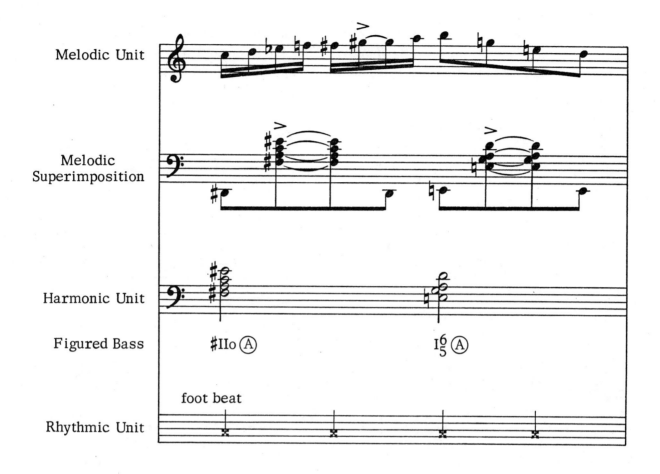

Simple syncopation employs only *accent*. Compound syncopation employs *notation* (tied and rest values) and *accent*.

In the preceding chapters we have explored non-syncopated rhythms; in this and in the following four lessons, simple and compound syncopation will be considered.

Figure 5 is a bass line for "Rose Room" in the key of A♭. The pedal may be used, provided the improvised line is not smeared; a steady quarter-note foot beat (left foot if pedaling with the right) should be present while playing Fig. 5.

ROSE ROOM (Words by Harry Williams, Music by Art Hickman) — © Copyright 1917, 1918, 1949 Miller Music Corporation, New York, N. Y. — Copyright Renewal 1945, 1946 Miller Music Corporation, New York, N. Y. — Used by Permission.

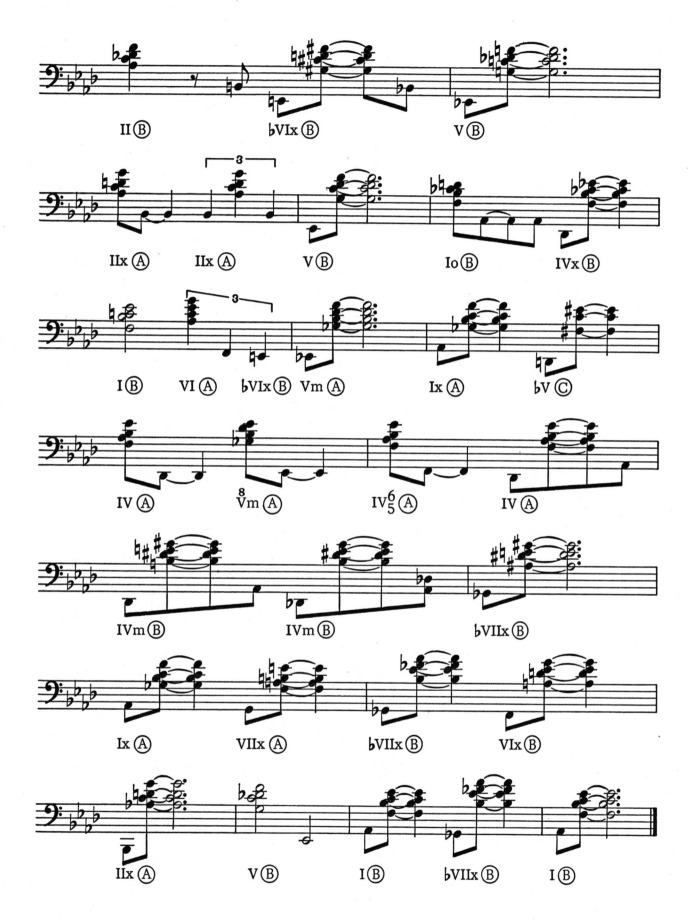

LESSON 26.

Root-Voicing Patterns, Ⓐ and Ⓑ Forms —
Bounce-Tempo Syncopated Swing Bass

Figure 1 is a bass line for "Ain't Misbehavin'" in the key of E♭, illustrating a syncopated bass. Improvise on this figure.

Fig. 1.

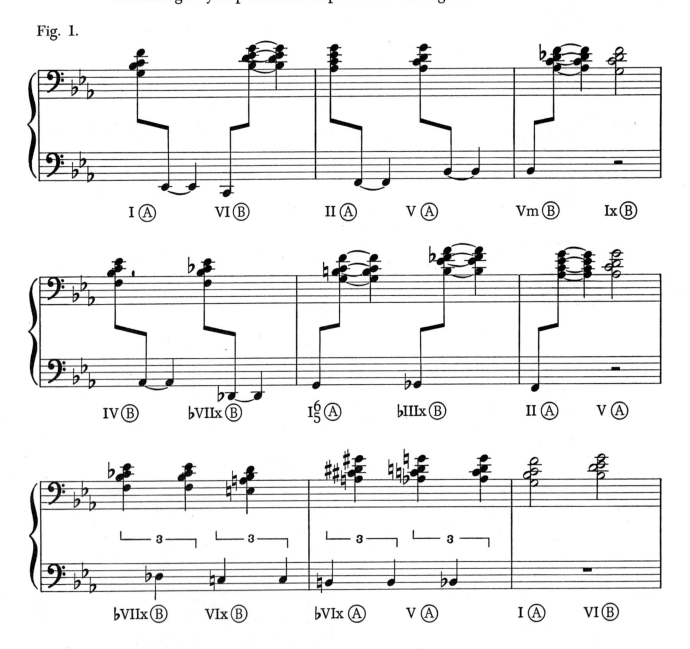

175

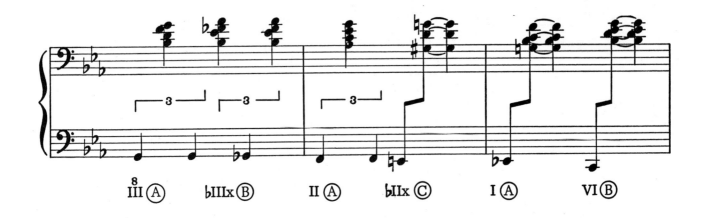

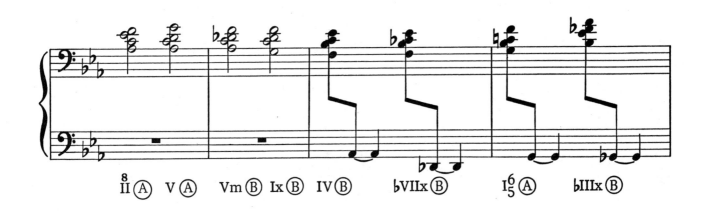

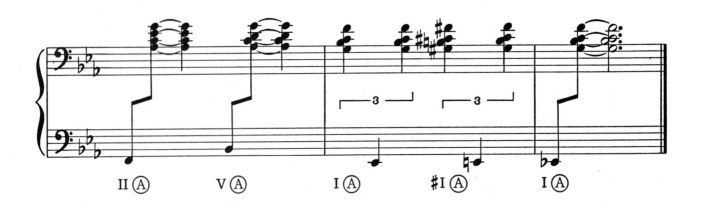

LESSON 27.

Root-Voicing Patterns, (A) and (B) Forms —
Up-tempo Syncopation

We have studied Left-hand syncopation employing tied values; now we will consider the use of the rest value in syncopation.

In Vol. I, Lesson 34 the various rest values employed in the improvised line (right hand) were illustrated. These rest values ranged from the whole rest (4 beats) to the sixteenth rest.

In general the rest values employed in the left hand are more restricted, since in some cases (whole rest, dotted half rest, half rest) the chord would completely disappear as a function in time.

The essential purpose of the rest value in the left hand is to "kick" the prevailing pulse by *anticipating* or *delaying* a chord.

Since the improvisor uses the symetrical pulsation of the chord chart as a point of departure into asymmetrical rhythmic and melodic areas, the disruption of harmonic time is usually slight and of short duration.

Figure 1 illustrates the normal eighth-note "kick" unit (tie) used to *anticipate* a chord.

Fig. 1.

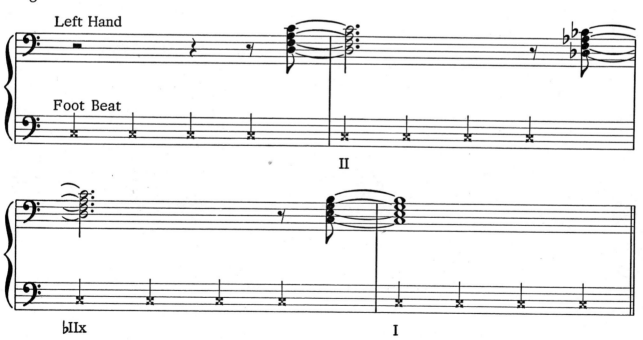

177

It is apparent in Fig. 1 that any further anticipation of each chord would seriously impair the improvised line which *must* proceed from an orderly chord chart (Fig. 2).

Fig. 2.

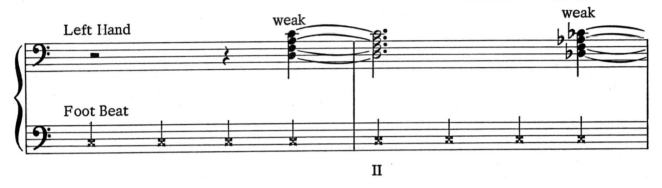

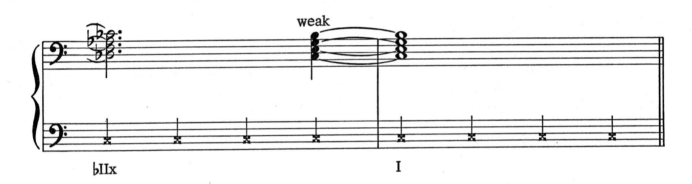

Figure 3 illustrates the normal eighth-note "kick" unit (rest) used to *delay* a chord.

Fig. 3.

In Fig. 3 the delaying unit may be increased (Fig. 4) but again, the improvised line that must proceed to the chord in its normal position will simply be left without support. Undoubtedly the most effective application of these anticiating and delaying elements is to limit them to the eighth-note unit (tie or rest) and to employ them interchangeably (Fig. 5).

Fig. 4.

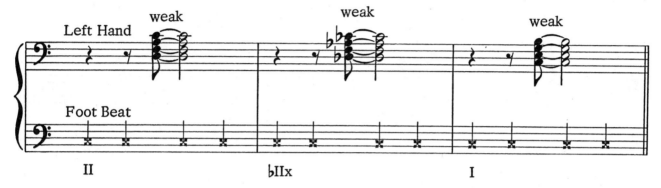

Overfrequent use of these devices can lead to a disturbance of the improvised line, which takes its essential *asymmetrical* character from its reference to a *symmetrical* underpinning.

Fig. 5.

Figure 6 illustrates a bass line for "The Lady Is A Tramp" in C. The anticipation and delaying of the chords is mixed with occasional non-syncopated elements. Constant syncopation can be as dull as no syncopation, since synocpation itself assumes non-syncopation. Bars 33 through 38 illustrate a "double-kick" of a single chord.

Roots have been omitted in the syncopated bars to permit the student to give the syncopation problem his undivided attention.

Fig. 6.

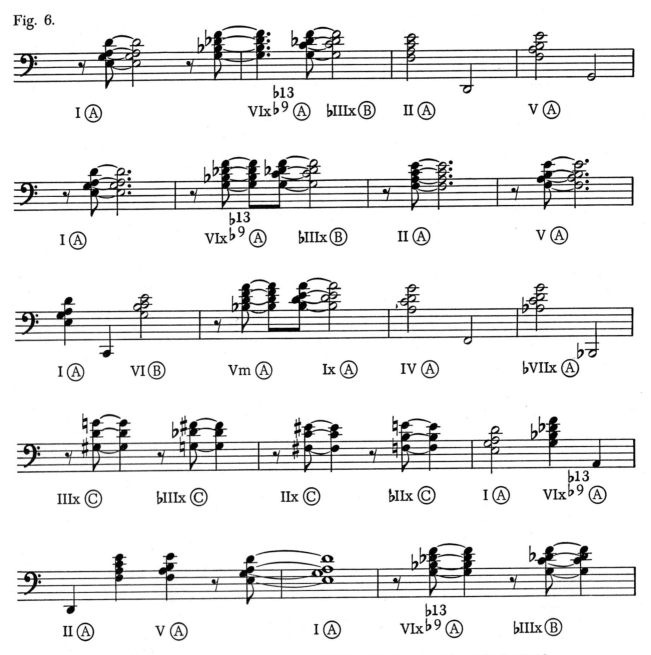

THE LADY IS A TRAMP (Lorenz Hart and Richard Rodgers) — Copyright © 1937 by Chappell & Co., Inc. — Copyright Renewed. — Used by Permission.

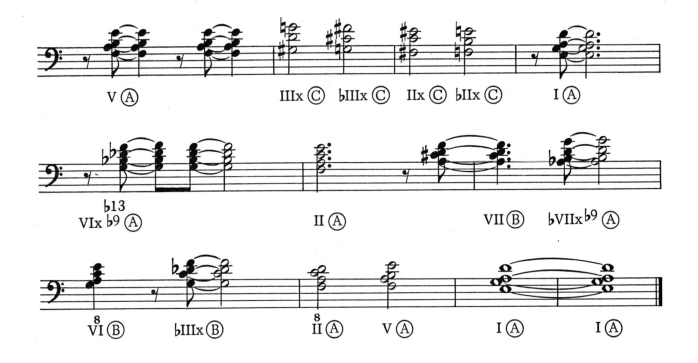

LESSON 28.

Root-Voicing Patterns, (A) and (B) Forms —
Up-Tempo Syncopation

Figure 1 illustrates an (A) and (B) setting for "Limehouse Blues" in A♭. All roots have been omitted here to avoid any cluttered sound in a traditionally "fast" tune. Improvise on Fig. 1.

Fig. 1.

LIMEHOUSE BLUES — Copyright 1922 by Ascherberg, Hopwood & Crew Ltd. — Used by Permission of Harms, Inc.

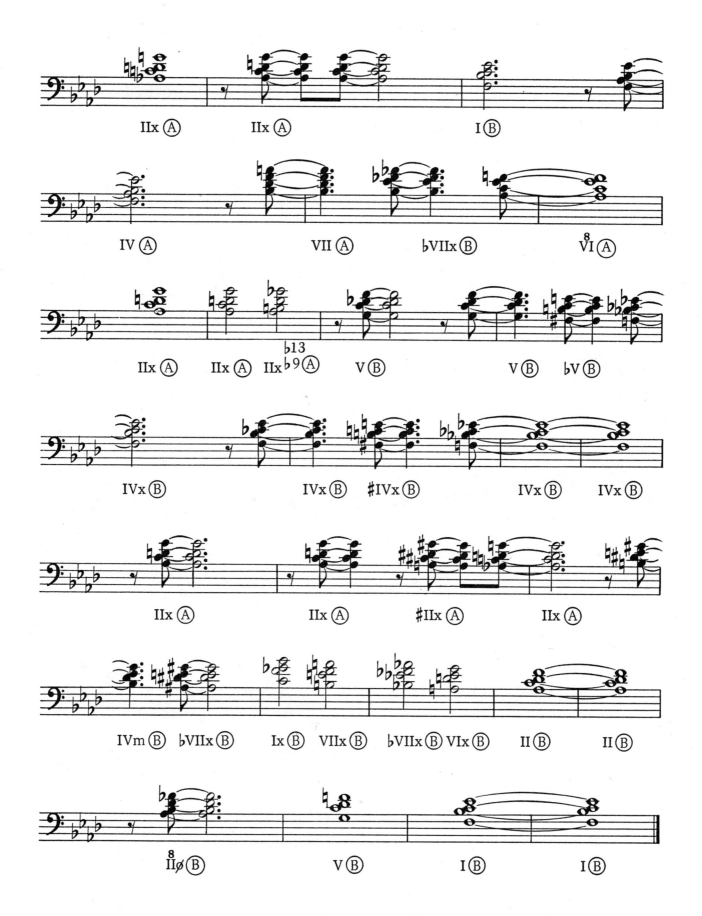

LESSON 29.

Root-Voicing Patterns, Ⓐ and Ⓑ Forms — Improvised

Since the purpose of the Ⓐ and Ⓑ Forms is to establish an interesting underpinning for an improvisation, we will here consider this final aspect of the solo style.

Figure 1 is an improvised line accompanied by an Ⓐ and Ⓑ Form bass line on "Peace" in B♭.

The student will note the integrated relationship between the hands in Fig. 1. In other words, a florid passage in the improvised line usually demands a quiet, unobtrusive accompaniment in the bass. On the other hand, a period of silence in the line should be "covered" by an interesting design in the left hand. This is no different from the principle of "alternating" interest found in any well-conceived classical composition for the keyboard.

Figure 1 should be pedaled cautiously.

Fig. 1.

PEACE — By Horace Silver, Ecaroh Music, Inc., 400 Central Park West, New York 25, New York — Used by Permission. — From the record BLP #4017 "Blowin The Blues Away" — (Horace Silver Quintet, Blue Note Records, Inc., New York).

185

(Db)   I Ⓐ

(Bb)   IIx Ⓑ   bIIx Ⓒ

(Bb)   I Ⓐ   VII Ⓑ   IIIx Ⓒ

(Bb)   VI Ⓑ   IIx Ⓑ

(B♭)   ♭II M Ⓐ   IIø Ⓑ   V♭9 Ⓑ

(B♭)   I Ⓐ   I Ⓐ

(A)   II Ⓑ   V♭9 Ⓑ   I Ⓑ   I₂ Ⓑ   VI Ⓑ VI₂ Ⓐ

(D♭)   IIø Ⓐ   V♭9 Ⓐ

(Db) I Ⓐ

(Bb) IIx Ⓑ   ♭IIx Ⓑ   I Ⓐ

LESSON 30.

Scale-Tone Chord Conversion to Ⓐ and Ⓑ Forms

Having mastered some familiarity with the Ⓐ and Ⓑ Forms, the student will naturally attempt the conversion of bass lines other than those appearing in the present volume to Ⓐ and Ⓑ Forms.

In converting bass lines appearing in Volumes I, II or III or simply in converting from sheet music, certain precautions must be exercised, although the principles of Ⓐ and Ⓑ application to any bass line are perfectly sound.

The following precautions, however, are well to keep in mind along with similar admonitions described in Vol. I, Lesson 76, as well as in Lessons 14 and 16 of the present volume.

THE MAJOR CHORD

The major chord is seldom a problem in either Ⓐ or Ⓑ Forms. The major *forms* also lend themselves easily to superimposition (Lesson 22).

THE DOMINANT CHORD

The dominant chord presents many problems but also offers many solutions (Lesson 12).

II-♭IIx-I was used extensively in Volume I as a substitute pattern for II-V-I. ♭IIx and V are interchangeable, of course, since both possess a compelling tendency to move to I; it is even permissible at times to superimpose one upon the other. Employing scale-tone chords, the following superimposition is derived.

Fig. 1. $\dfrac{\flat IIx}{V}$ — $V^{\flat 5}_{\flat 9}$

Fig. 2. $\dfrac{V}{\flat IIx}$ — $\flat IIx^{\flat 5}_{\flat 9}$

Fig. 1   Fig. 2

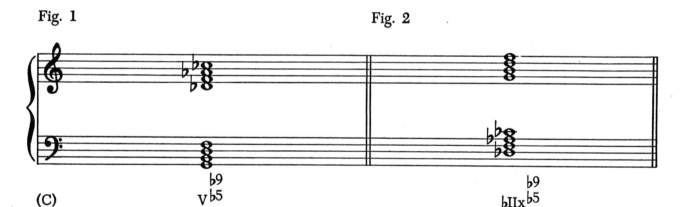

(C) $V^{\flat 5}_{\flat 9}$ $\flat IIx^{\flat 5}_{\flat 9}$

In general the Ⓐ and Ⓑ Forms employ V more often than ♭IIx. $x^{\flat 5}$ does not affect Ⓐ or Ⓑ Forms, since the fifth does not appear in the dominant voicing.

RULE: In conflicts involving ♭IIx, substitute V or ♭IIx Ⓒ. Any dominant of one *form* may be substituted by the dominant of the opposite *form*, an *augmented fourth* above or below.

189

Fig. 3.

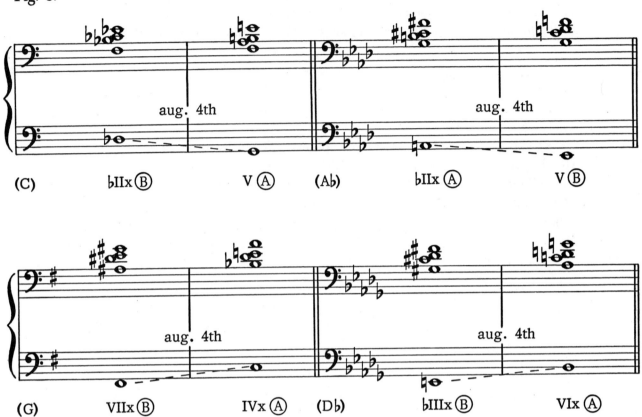

A further interesting aspect of this augmented fourth substitution is that of interchanging the roots and voicings of V and bIIx (Figs. 4 and 5).

Fig. 4.   Fig. 5.

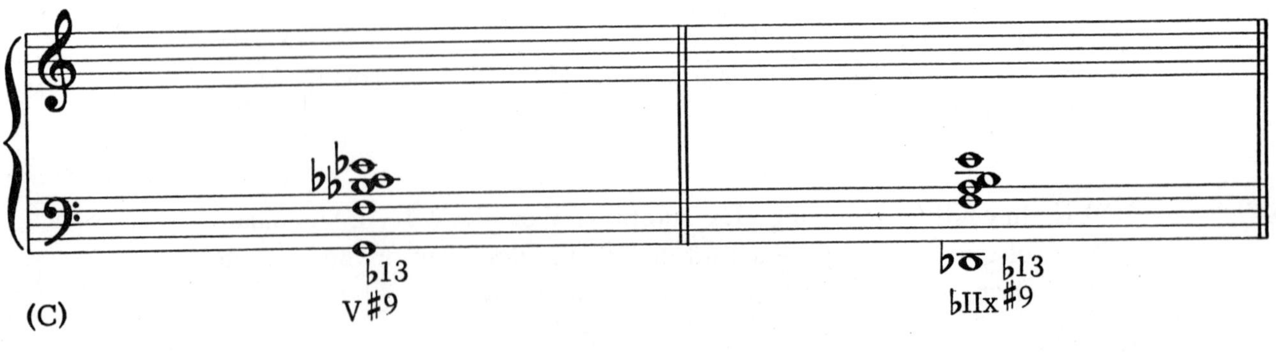

DOMINANT SUBSTITUTE TABLE

Cx	Ⓐ -	F♯x	Ⓑ -	Cx	Ⓒ
D♭x	Ⓑ -	Gx	Ⓐ -	D♭x	Ⓒ
Dx	Ⓑ -	A♭x	Ⓐ -	Dx	Ⓒ
E♭x	Ⓑ -	Ax	Ⓐ -	E♭x	Ⓒ
Ex	Ⓑ -	B♭x	Ⓐ -	Ex	Ⓒ
Fx	Ⓑ -	Bx	Ⓐ -	Fx	Ⓒ
F♯x	Ⓑ -	Cx	Ⓐ -	F♯x	Ⓒ
Gx	Ⓐ -	D♭x	Ⓑ -	Gx	Ⓒ
A♭x	Ⓐ -	Dx	Ⓑ -	A♭x	Ⓒ
Ax	Ⓐ -	E♭x	Ⓑ -	Ax	Ⓒ
B♭x	Ⓐ -	Ex	Ⓑ -	B♭x	Ⓒ
Bx	Ⓐ -	Fx	Ⓑ -	Bx	Ⓒ

THE MINOR CHORD

The problems of the minor chord have been fully treated in Lesson 14. Again, the student is warned of the tension of the III and VII, requiring in each case a lowering of the ninth a major second.

THE HALF-DIMINISHED CHORD

See Lesson 14.

THE DIMINISHED CHORD

See Lesson 14.

Figure 6 is a bass line for "I Concentrate On You" in the key of E♭. Convert Fig. 6 to Ⓐ and Ⓑ Forms and improvise. Note the modulation.

Fig. 6.

(E♭) I / I / I$^{\flat 3}$ / I$^{\flat 3}$ / Im / ♭IIIx / ♭III / ♭VIx / IIφ / ♭IIx /
Ⓐ   Ⓐ   Ⓐ   Ⓐ   Ⓐ   Ⓑ   Ⓐ   Ⓐ   Ⓐ   Ⓑ

(E♭) Im / Im$_2$ / ♭VIx / ♭IIx / I /♯I / I / I / I$^{\flat 3}$ / I$^{\flat 3}$ / Im / ♭IIIx /
Ⓐ Ⓐ   Ⓐ   Ⓑ Ⓐ Ⓐ Ⓐ Ⓐ   Ⓐ   Ⓐ   Ⓑ

(E♭) ♭III / ♭VIx // (G♭) II / ♭IIx / I / IV // (E♭) IIx $^{\flat 9}_{\flat 13}$ /
Ⓐ   Ⓐ   Ⓑ   Ⓐ   Ⓑ Ⓑ   Ⓑ

(E♭) ♭IIx / I / ♭V / IV / IVm / III^{8} / ♭IIIx / II^{8} / ♭IIx / I /
Ⓑ Ⓐ Ⓐ Ⓑ Ⓑ   Ⓐ   Ⓑ   Ⓐ   Ⓑ   Ⓐ

(E♭) ♭V / IV // (G♭) II ♭IIx / II$_2$ / I // (E♭) IIIφ^{8} VIx / IIx /
Ⓐ Ⓑ   Ⓑ   Ⓐ   Ⓐ   Ⓑ   Ⓐ   Ⓐ   Ⓑ

(E♭) V / V$^{\flat 9}_{\flat 13}$ / I$^4_3$ / I$^4_3$ / ♭Vφ / ♭Vφ / V$_2$ / I$^6_5$ / IIIx / III$^{\flat 9}_{\flat 13}$ /
Ⓐ Ⓐ   Ⓐ Ⓐ Ⓑ   Ⓑ   Ⓑ Ⓑ Ⓐ   Ⓐ

(E♭) IIIφ^{8} / VIx $^{\flat 9}_{\flat 13}$ / II $^{\sharp 7}$ / II / ♭VIx / ♭IIx / I / I //
Ⓐ   Ⓐ   Ⓑ   Ⓐ   Ⓐ   Ⓑ Ⓐ Ⓐ

NOTE: The opposite forms rule has been respected in bars 43, 53 and 54.

"Walking" Bass Line

In Vol III, Lesson 52 the problem of "walking" bass lines was introduced. In the same lesson the principle devices of "walking" lines were indicated as follows:

1. Arpeggios
2. Modes
3. Chromatic tones

In Vol. I, Lesson 55 the problem of non-modal or chromatic tones was raised. Of course, these non-modal tones could be considered "chromatic" tones, but a deeper principle seems involved here.

It is true, for instance, that in certain functions of a key the musical purposes of a bassist and a treble-clef oriented horn player (including pianists) seem to diverge, since the bassist strives to maintain the key center represented by the prevailing signature, while the horn player is usually intent upon fully exploring each new inflected key.

The following table indicates this horn-bass divergence in the various functions:

CHORD	HORN	BASS
Major I	Ionian	Ionian
Major IV	Ionian	Lydian
Dominant	Mixolydian	Mixolydian
Minor II	Dorian	Dorian
Minor III	{ Dorian / Phrygian	Phrygian
Minor VI	{ Dorian / Aeolian	Aeolian
Half-Diminished	Locrian	{ Tone Row 0 2 1 2 1 2 2 1 1 / Locrian
Diminished	Tone Row 0 2 1 2 1 2 1 2 1	Tone Row 0 2 1 2 1 2 1 2 1

A special problem for the bassist lies in the relative "weakness" of the half-diminished chord. Any half-diminished chord may infer the following:

1. VII of the prevailing major key
2. Temporary VII of a new major key
3. II of the prevailing minor key
4. VI of the prevailng minor key
5. Temporary II of a new minor key
6. Temporary VI of a new minor key

Numbers 1, 3, and 5 tend to take the Locrian mode.

Numbers 2, 4, and 6 tend to take the tone row 0 2 1 2 1 2 2 1 1.

A final consideration is that described in Lesson 15, in which the ninth of the half-diminished chord is a familiar consonance, the flatted ninth an impermissible extension (see Vol. I, Lesson 56).

Figure 1 illustrates a "walking" bass for "You Stepped Out Of A Dream" in C.

In building the melodic formations in the right hand, the following rules should be observed:

1. Each melodic tone should be accompanied by the 3rd and 7th of the prevailing chord (see Vol. 1, Leson 71).
2. The ornamental ninth should accompany each melodic tone, if possible.
3. On half-diminished and diminished chords, the diminished fifth should appear.

Fig. 1.

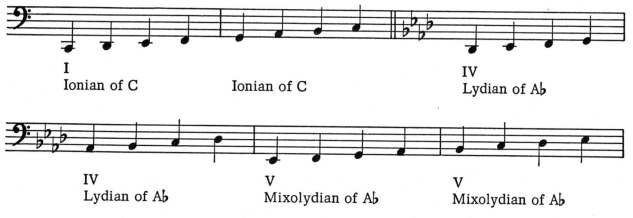

I
Ionian of C

Ionian of C

IV
Lydian of A♭

IV
Lydian of A♭

V
Mixolydian of A♭

V
Mixolydian of A♭

YOU STEPPED OUT OF A DREAM (Lyric by Gus Kahn, Music by Nacio Herb Brown) — © Copyright 1940 Leo Feist, Inc., New York, N. Y. — Used by Permission.

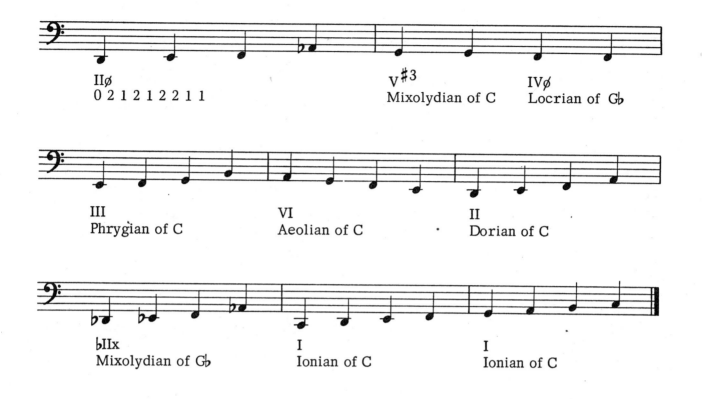

IIø
0 2 1 2 1 2 2 1 1

V$\sharp$3
Mixolydian of C

IVø
Locrian of G♭

III
Phrygian of C

VI
Aeolian of C

II
Dorian of C

♭IIx
Mixolydian of G♭

I
Ionian of C

I
Ionian of C

LESSON 32.

"Walking" Bass Line

Figure 1 is a "walking" bass line for "Blue Room."

In bars 9 and 10, the I-VI-II-V pattern is preserved, although the bass line avails itself of the "swing" of the long scale line.

In this and the following two studies, an added rhythmic factor is introduced that is used extensively by modern bass players. This is the ♪. ♪ "kick" employed to propel the pulse over a bar line. The sixteenth note in this case is often an appogiatura tone one half step above or below a "target" tone. This "target" tone is usually the prevailing root, although it may sometimes appear as the third, fifth or seventh of the chord.

A legato touch should prevail in these walking lines in order to avoid "air space" between tones.

Fig. 1.

(F)   II   V   IVm bVIIx III VIx   VI   IIx

(F)   II   V   I   #Io   II   #IIo

(F)   III   VI   II   V   I   VI Vm bV

(F)   IV   bVIIx   VI$\frac{4}{3}$ bIIIo II bIIx I^{+6}

LESSON 33.

"Walking" Bass Line

Figure 1 is a "walking" bass line for "The Way You Look Tonight" in the key of E♭.

Fig. 1.

(E♭)   I   VI   II

(E♭)   V   I   IIIø$\frac{4}{3}$ VIx

(E♭)   II##7   II#7   II   ♭VIo   Vm

(E♭)   Ix   IV^{+6} III ♭IIIx   II   ♭IIx

(E♭)   I^{+6} VI   II   VII$\frac{4}{3}$ III   VI

(E♭)   II   ♭IIx   I   VI   II

(E♭)   V   III   VIx   II

(E♭)   II$_2$ III$\frac{4}{3}$ II$\frac{4}{3}$ ♭VIo   Vm   ♭V

(E♭)   IV^{+6} III ♭IIIx II   ♭IIx   I^{+6} VI

198

(E♭)   II   IVo   III   VI   II   V   V₂

(G♭)   I   #Io   II

(G♭)   V   IVo   I$^6_5$ ♭IIIo

(G♭)   II   V   V₂   I$^6_5$

(G♭)   ♭IIIx   II   V   ♭IIx

(G♭)   I   IV   (E♭)   II

(E♭)   ♭IIx   I   VI

199

(E♭)   II   V   I   IIIø$^4_3$

(E♭)   VIx   II$^{\#\#7}$ II$^{\#7}$ II$_2$ V$^6_5$ II$^4_3$ ♭VIo

(E♭)   Vm   ♭V$^{♭5}$ IV   III ♭IIIx

(E♭)   II   ♭IIx   I^{+6} VI   II   V

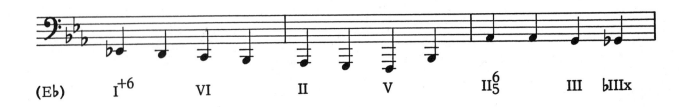

(E♭)   I^{+6} VI   II   V   II$^6_5$ III ♭IIIx

(E♭)   II   ♭IIx   I^{+6} #I$^{♭5}$ I^{+6}

LESSON 34.

"Walking" Bass Line

Figure 1 is a "walking" bass line for "Fine and Dandy" in the key of F.

Fig. 1.

(F)　　I_5^6　　　　♭IIIo　　　　II　　　　V　　IVo

(F)　　I_5^6　　　　♭IIIo　　　　II　　　　V

(B♭)　　II　　　　V　　　　I　　　　I^{+6}

(A♭)　　II　　　　V　　　　I　　IV

(F)　　II　　　V　IVo　I_5^6　　　　♭IIIo

FINE AND DANDY — Copyright 1930 by Harms, Inc. — Used by Permission.

(F)   II   V   IVo   I$\frac{6}{5}$

(F)   bIIIo   II   V   Vm

(F)   Ix   IV   IVm   bVIIx

(F)   III   VI   II   bIIx   I^{+6} I^{+6}

LESSON 35.

Left-Hand Arpeggiation —
The Scale-Tone Chords — Eighth Note

One of the important concerto devices indicated in Lesson 17 of this volume for supporting a right-hand melody or improvisation is the left-hand arpeggio moving in harp-like design in the bass register.

The major problem of building horizontal sonorities in the bass register is that of combining intervals that will form a clear, uncluttered frame for the right hand. This style must be pedaled.

Figure 1 illustrates the normal register for this arpeggiation.

202

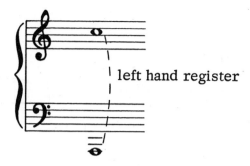

Fig. 1.   left hand register

Figure 2 illustrates a breakdown of Fig. 1 into two tonal areas:

 A-Section: A to C
 B-Section: C to C

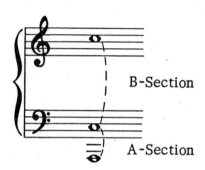

Fig. 2.   B-Section

                                          A-Section

(The student is not to confuse A- and B-Sections with Ⓐ and Ⓑ Forms; the terminology has been retained to aid the student's study of the various architectures.)

RULE: Generally in the A-Section, intervals of less than a *diminished fifth* should be avoided.

RULE: In the B-Section, all intervals are permissable.

Left-hand arpeggiation employs the identical structures utilized by the right hand in Vol. I:

1. Arpeggios
2. Modes

These structures may be used freely with the one interval restriction indicated for the A-Section. We will study two basic structures associated with this architecture:

1. Arpeggiated scale-tone tenth chords (Fig. 3)
2. Arpeggiated tone row: Root - 5-9-3-7 - reverse (Fig. 4)

Fig. 3.

Fig. 4.

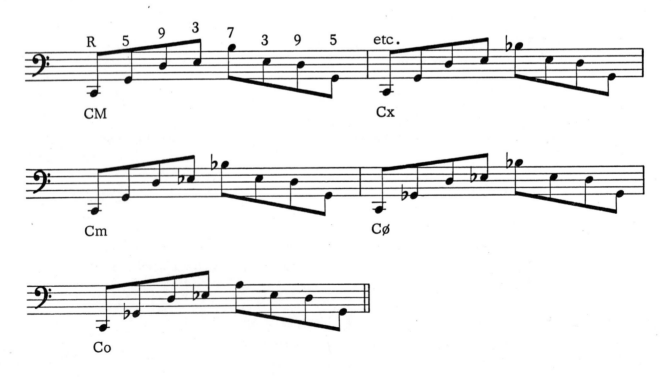

The scale-tone tenth chords may be arpeggiated in A- and B-Sections as follows:

A-Section: Root position (Vol. III, Lesson 18). R-5-3 (omit 7), Fig. 3.
A-Section: Inversions (Vol. III, Lesson 19) omit next to bottom note, Fig. 5.

(The 2 position in Fig. 5 is essentially in the B-Section, which allows normal arpeggiation.)

B-Section: Root position, Fig. 3; normal arpeggiation.
B-Section: Inversions, Fig. 5; normal arpeggiation.

These arpeggios may support a right-hand melodic line, either in single notes or in octaves with inner voices (See Vol. III, Lesson 51).

Fig. 5.

CM_5^6 CM_3^4 CM_2

DRILL: Using Lessons 18 and 19 as references, explore the various root-position and inversion arpeggios in the left hand.

Figure 6 illustrates an arpeggiated bass line for "We'll Be Together Again" in the key of C. This is essentially a non-jazz treatment, although the idiom is familiar to and is occasionally employed by all jazz pianists; it is to be played ad-lib (no quarter-note foot beat). Note the C-minor section in the bridge. This idiom must be pedaled in order to achieve a harp-like effect in the left hand.

Fig. 6.

(C)   bIIx   I^{+6} bVIx   II   V

(C)   VI   IIx^{b5}

"WE'LL BE TOGETHER AGAIN" — Copyright 1945 E.D.M. Music Publishers — Used by Permission.

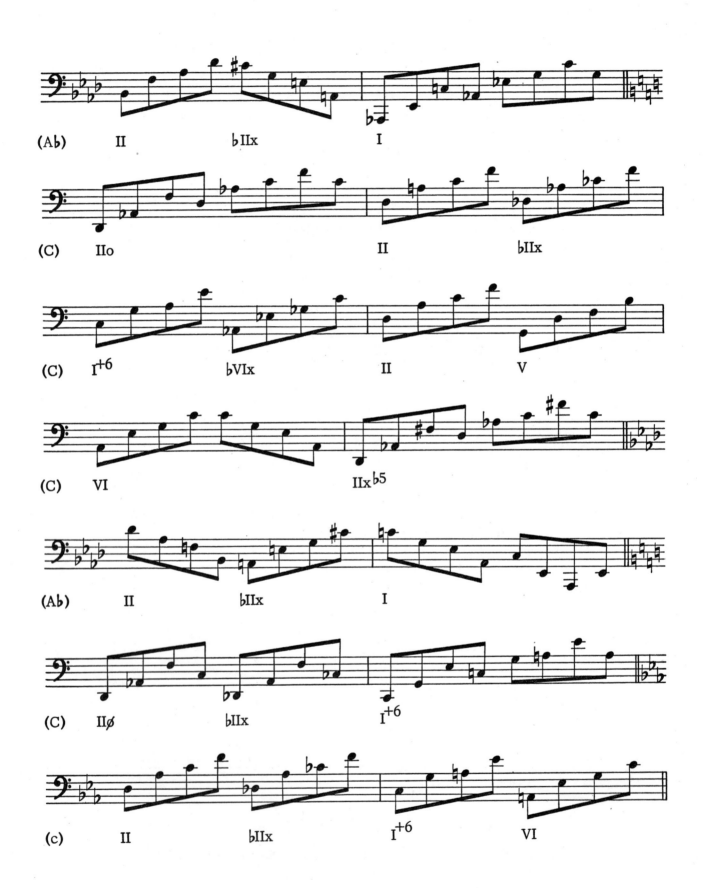

(A♭)   II   ♭IIx   I

(C)   IIo   II   ♭IIx

(C)   I⁺⁶   ♭VIx   II   V

(C)   VI   IIx♭5

(A♭)   II   ♭IIx   I

(C)   IIø   ♭IIx   I⁺⁶

(c)   II   ♭IIx   I⁺⁶   VI

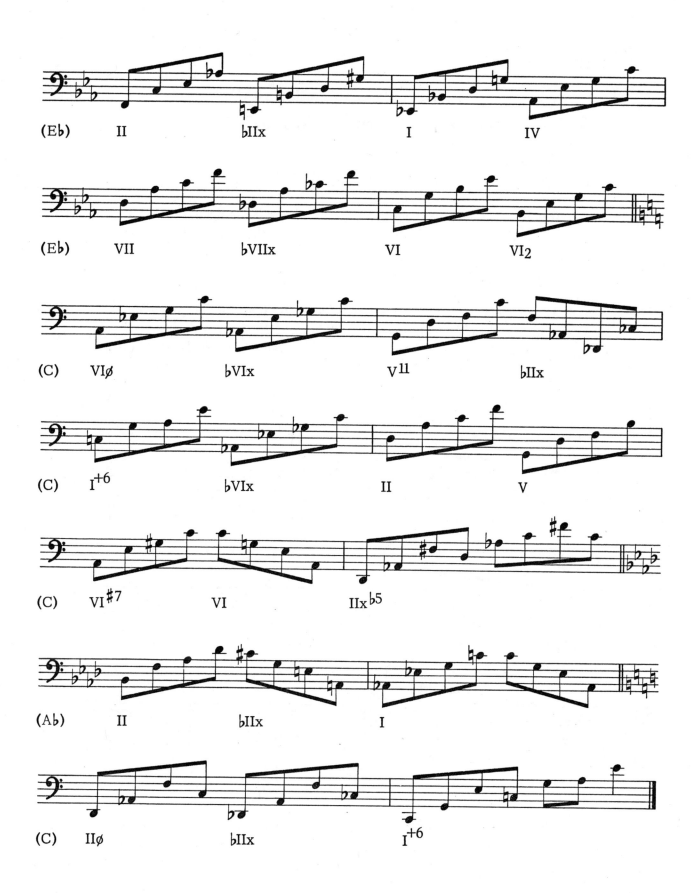

207

LESSON 36.

Left-Hand Arpeggiation —
Root-5-9-3-7-Reverse — Eighth Note

This design represents a practical reduction of idioms found in the piano compositions of Chopin, Liszt, Scriabin and Rachmaninoff.

It is easily applied to each of the five qualities. As indicated in Vol I, Lesson 56, the M, m, φ and o qualities take only the natural ninth; the dominant employs the flatted and augmented ninth in addition to the natural ninth — these extensions may also be used in this design (Fig. 1).

All references to root, 5, 3 and 7 refer to the tones of the *prevailing mode*. Nine is always a *major second* (whole step) from the root displaced up one octave. M, x and m ninths fall in the prevailing mode; the Locrian mode on half-diminished violates this principle, which necessitates the use of the major-second rule.

Fig. 1.

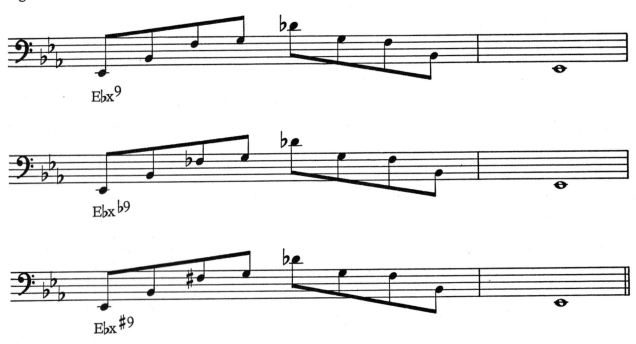

All R-5-9-3-7 designs employ the same fingering: 5-2-1-2-1 reverse. This fingering is maintained regardless of the relationship of black and white notes (Fig. 2).

208

Fig. 2.

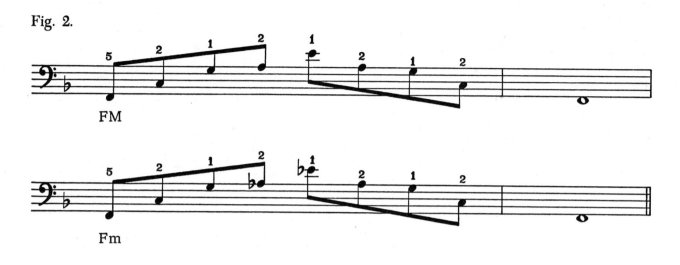

Figure 3 illustrates the R-5-9-3-7 design for the 60 chords.

Fig. 3.

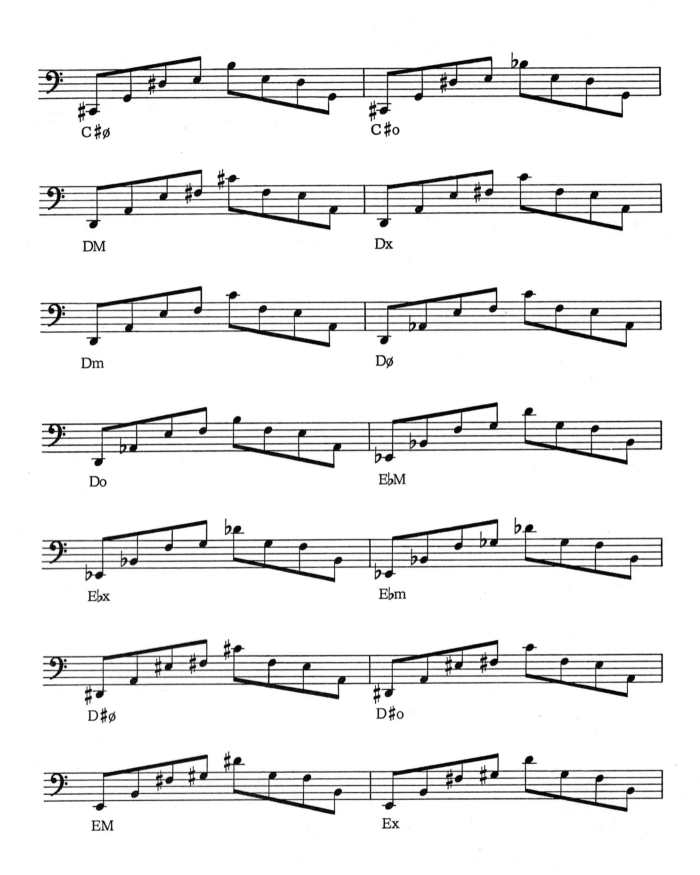

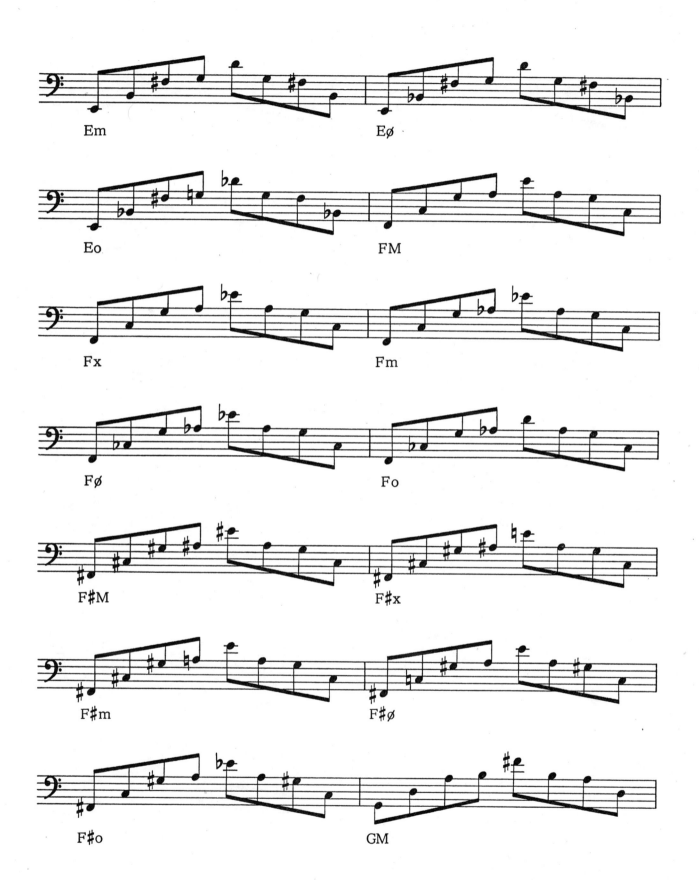

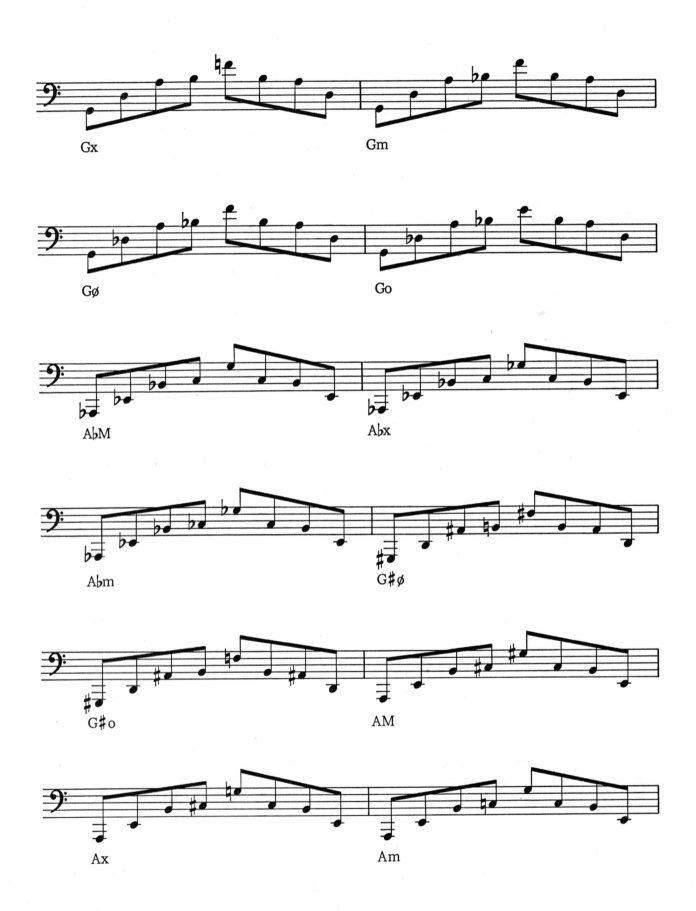

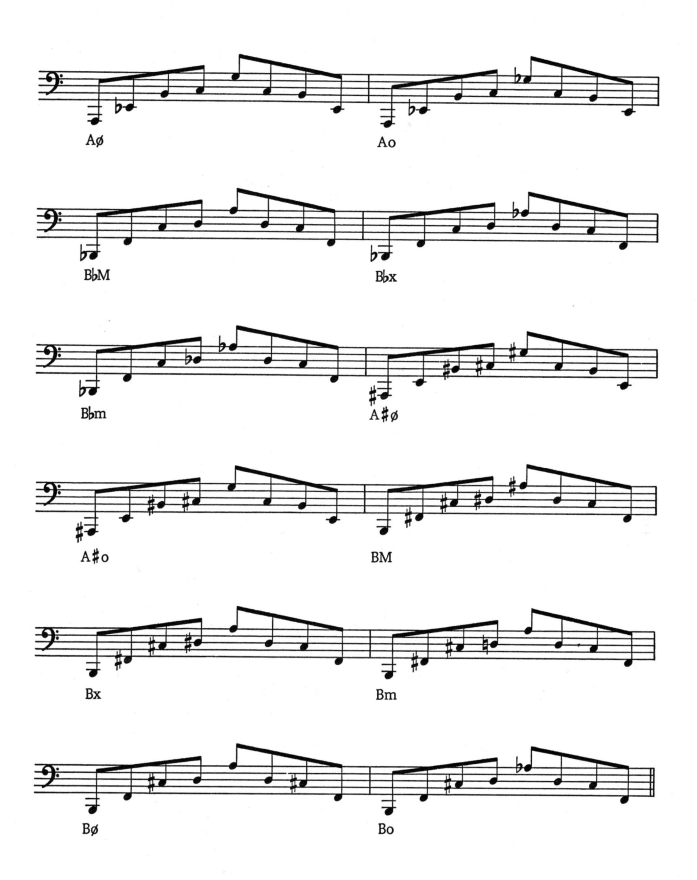

Figure 4 illustrates the 12 dominant ♭9 chords.

Fig. 4.

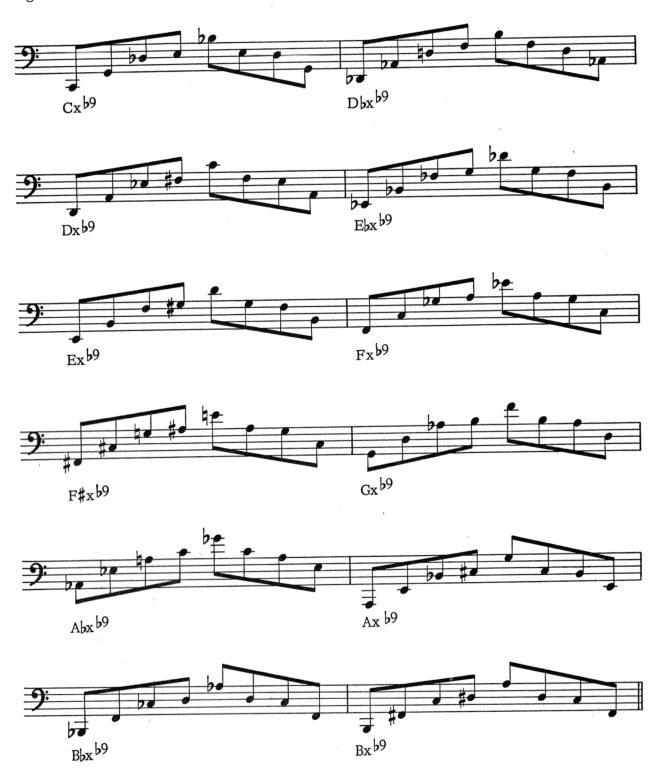

Figure 5 illustrates the 12 dominant ♯9 chords. Figures 4 and 5 appear only in root position and usually emanate in the A-section. This pattern, as well as those previously illustrated, must be pedaled in order to achieve the necessary sonority; speed is also an essential factor in attaining this sonority.

Fig. 5.

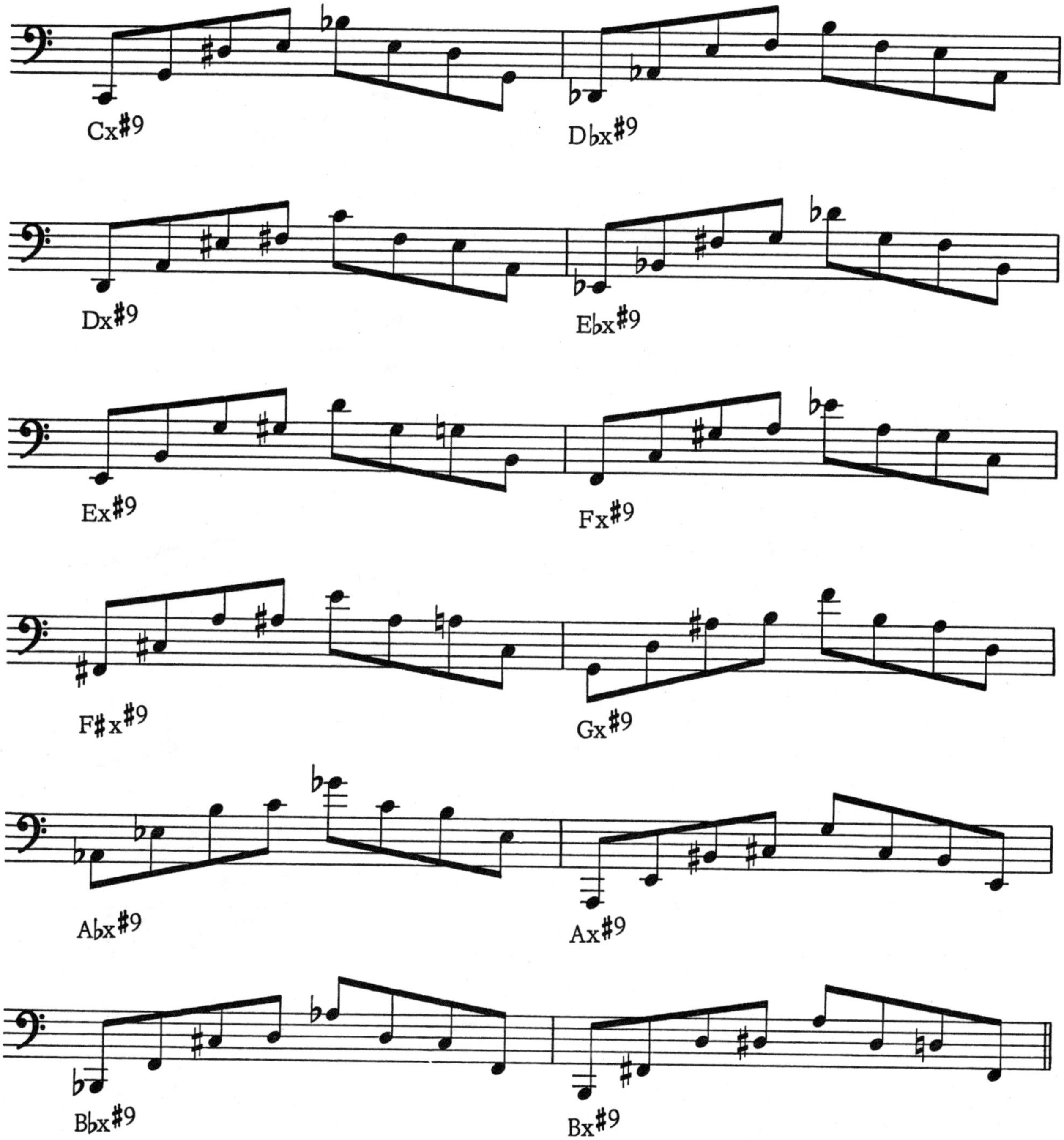

DRILL: Practice Figs. 3, 4 and 5 for automatic facility. Figure 6 is an arpeggiated bass line for "Jet" in the key of Eb.

Fig. 6.

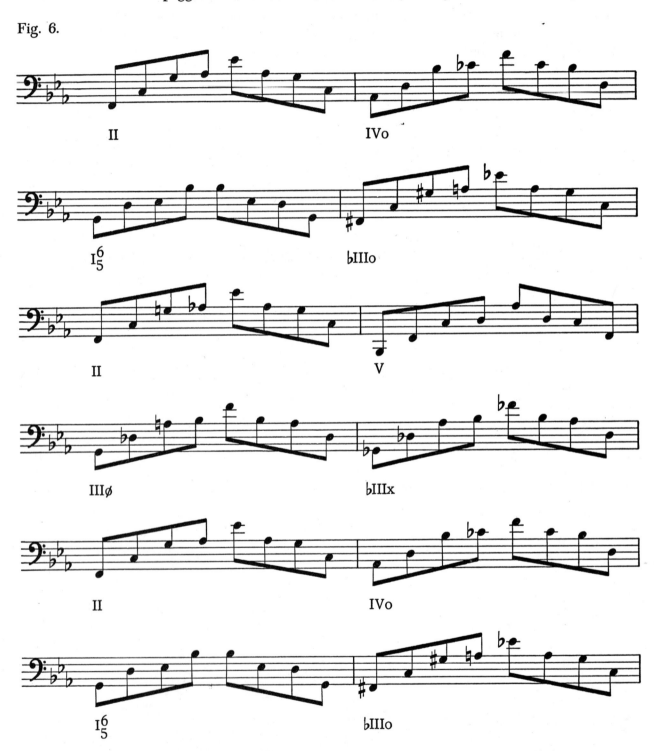

217

Left-Hand Arpeggiation, Mixed Elements —
Eighth-Note Triplet

Figure 1 illustrates a left-hand arpeggiation for "Sometimes I'm Happy" in the key of F.

Fig. 1.

I   ♯Io   II   IVo

III   ♭IIIx   II   ♭IIx

I   ♯Io   II   IVo

III   ♭IIIx   II   ♭IIx

SOMETIMES I'M HAPPY — Copyright 1927 by Harms, Inc. — Used by Permission.

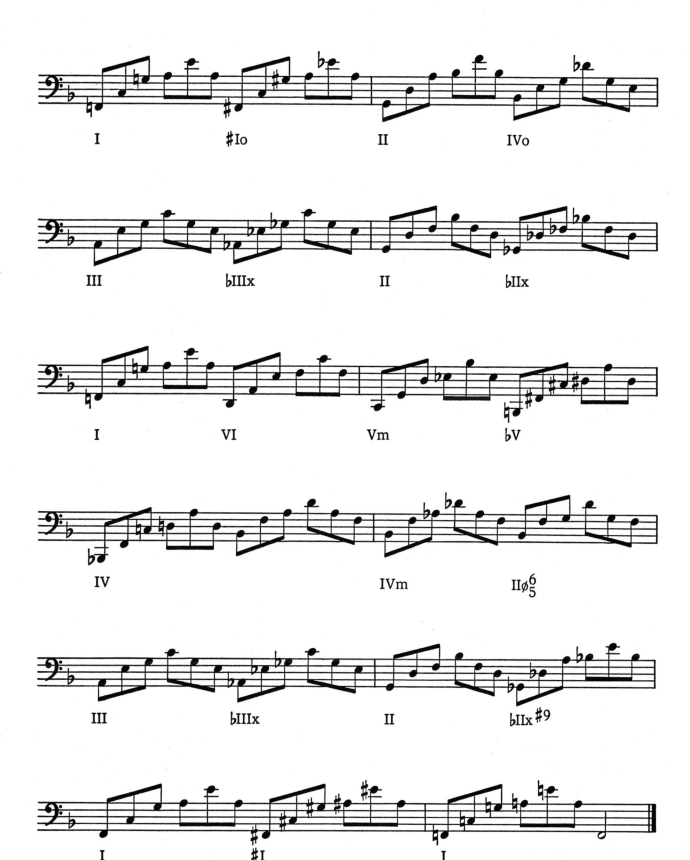

221

LESSON 38.

Left-Hand Arpeggiation, Mixed Elements — Sixteenth Note

Figure 1 illustrates an arpeggiated bass line for "It Never Entered My Mind" in the key of F.

Fig. 1.

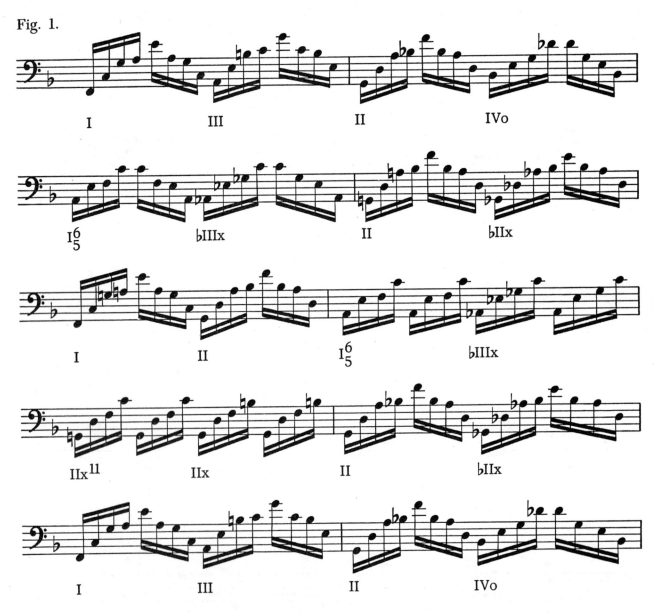

IT NEVER ENTERED MY MIND (Lorenz Hart and Richard Rodgers) — Copyright
© 1940 by Chappell & Co., Inc. — Used by Permission.

222

223

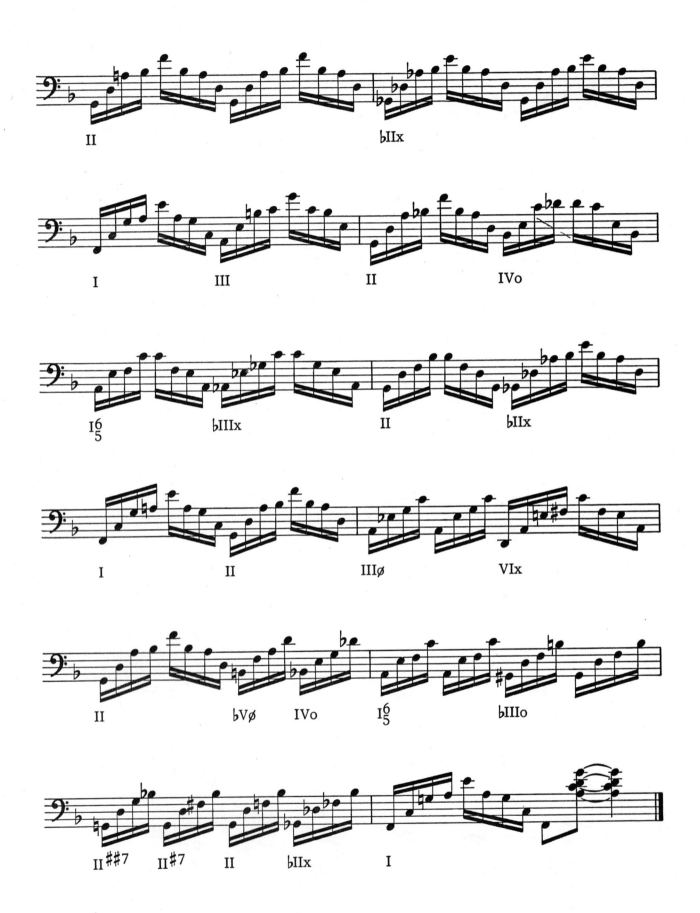

Left-Hand Arpeggiation, Ⓐ and Ⓑ Forms, and Modes

One of the natural devices for left-hand arpeggiation is the application of the Ⓐ and Ⓑ Forms. In joining the root and the voicing in a moving arpeggio, an effective underpinning is established for a melodic line.

Figure 1 illustrates an arpeggiated bass line for "Ruby" in C, employing Ⓐ and Ⓑ Forms in addition to modal fragments emanating from varying points based upon the mode of the prevailing chord. Elements studied in Lessons 35 and 36 appear also.

Fig. 1.

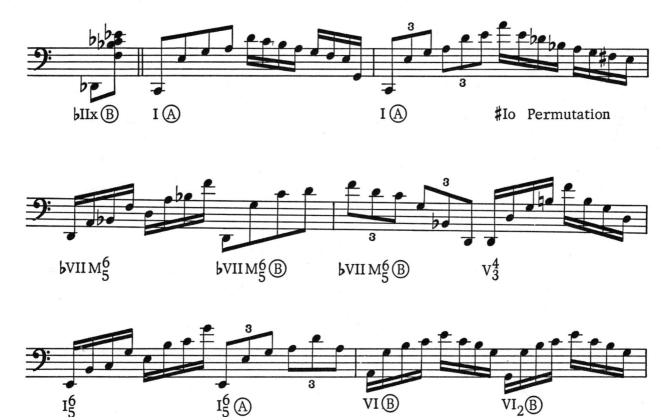

RUBY (Words by Mitchell Parish, Music by Heinz Roemheld) — © Copyright 1953
Miller Music Corporation, New York, N. Y. — Used by Permission.

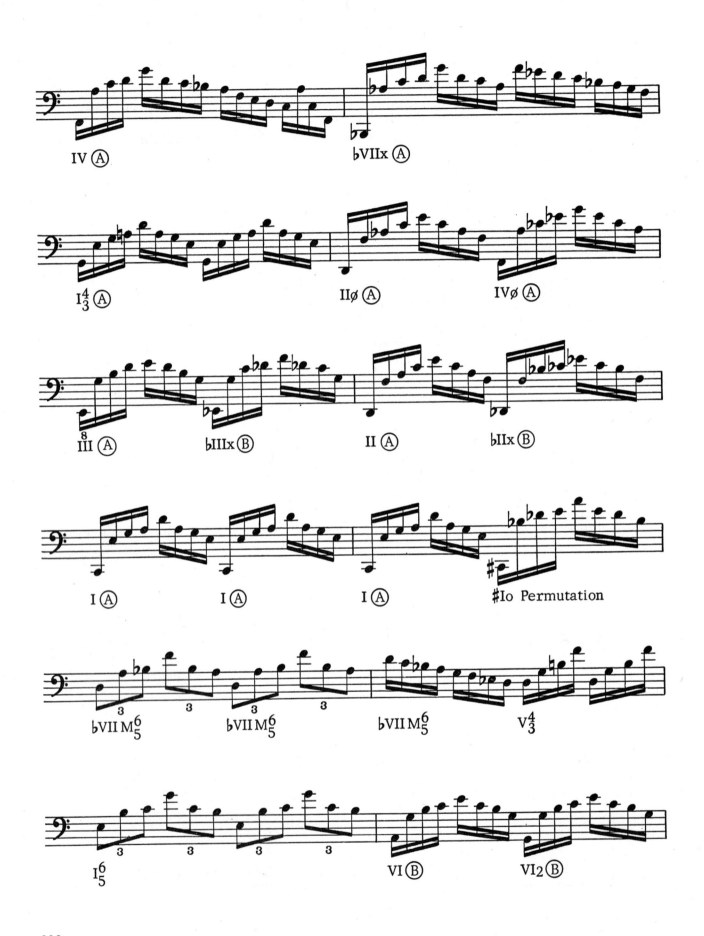

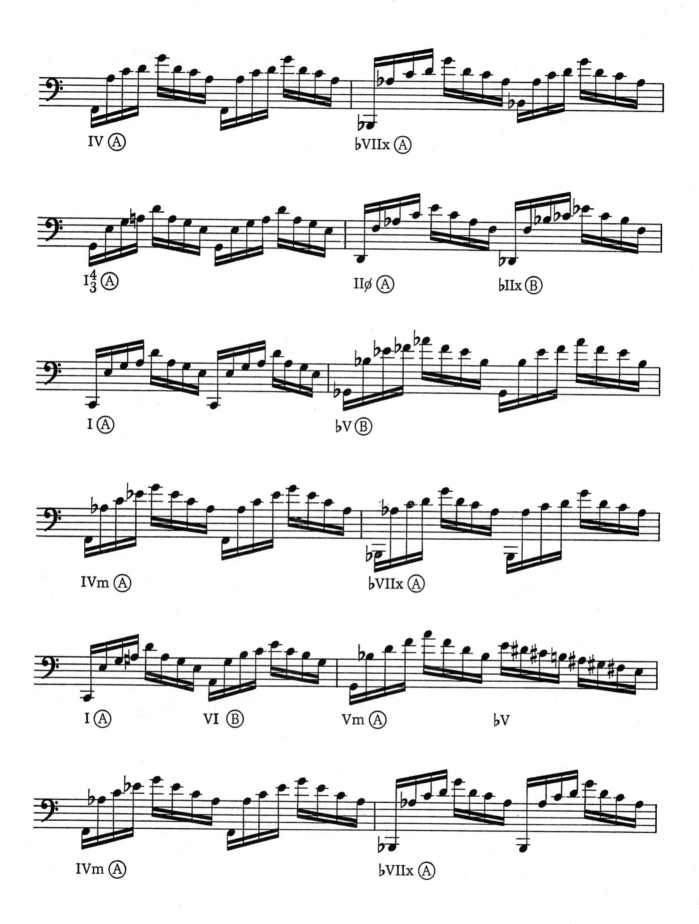

227

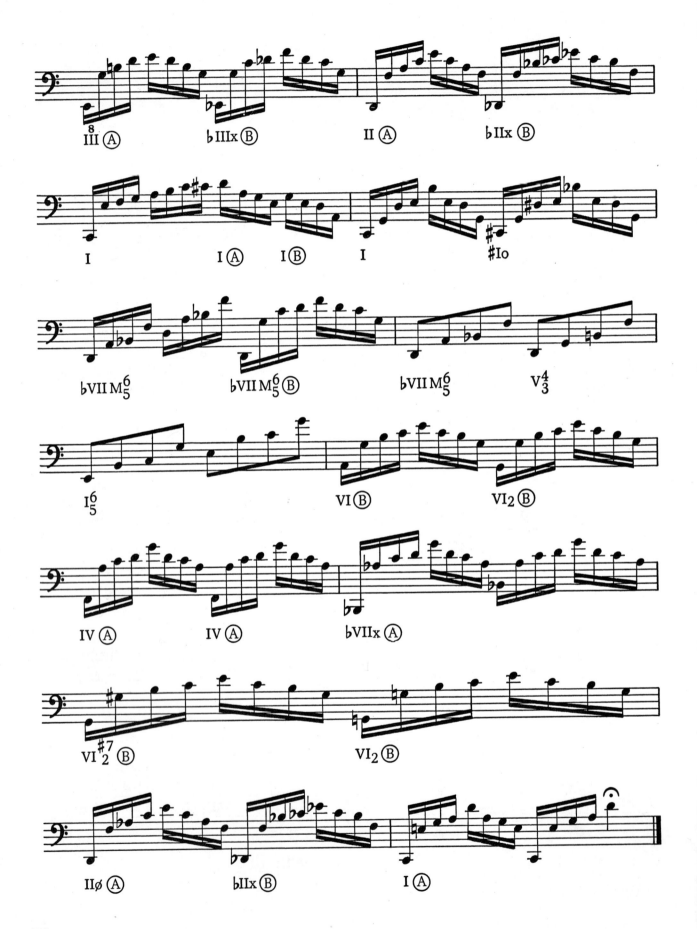

LESSON 40.

" 'Comping" (Accompanying)

A thorough analysis of the rhythmic elements of jazz appears in Vol. II. At this point we will consider the accompanying role of the piano in a rhythm section.

PRE-SWING BRAVURA PIANO

The pre-swing period (1920-1934), represented by Jelly Roll Morton, James P. Johnson, "Fats" Waller, Earle Hines and Willie "The Lion" Smith, was a wild careening joy ride of keyboard gymnastics, full of content, but with very little form. Since every pianist was a solo pianist (meaning he could play without accompaniment), it was sometimes no easy task to subdue him to the social tasks of playing with a rhythm section.

Both Hines and Morton made important contributions in this area (Waller generally remained unsubdued).

The following outline illustrates a typical rhythm section prior to 1930 with the rhythmic units for each componant:

Fig. 1. Pre-1930 Rhythm Section

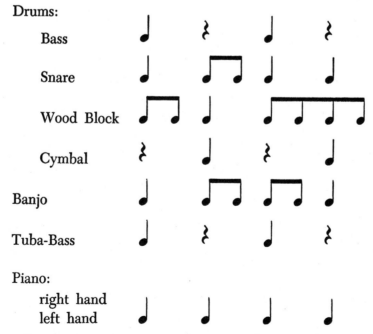

Here the pianist was committed to a rigid, unsyncopated 4/4 beat, often playing with both hands on each beat of the bar (Fig. 1).

Fig. 2 Swing (1932-1940) Rhythm Section

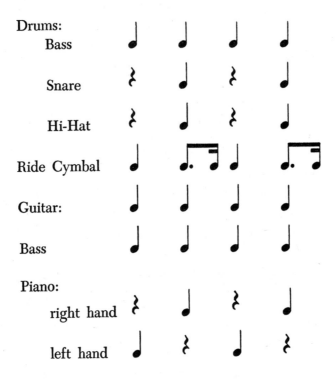

Here the pianist played an alternate left-hand root, right-hand-chord rhythmic pattern, still unsyncopated, but relieved by a more modern approach to both harmony and architecture (Fig. 2).

Fig. 3.   Modern (1940-Present)

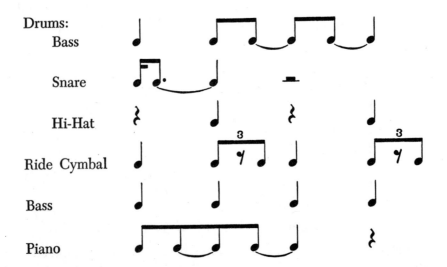

Here both piano and drums are relieved of the oppressive responsibility of maintaining a rigid 4/4 beat, which is now left to the bass. Chords are constantly "kicked" by the pianist, either through anticipation or by delaying (Fig. 3).

The principle devices of 'comping are open-position scale-tone chords — axis of 3rd and 7th (Vol. I, Lessons 68, 69, 70) and Ⓐ and Ⓑ Forms.

Figure 4 illustrates a 'comping line for "I Love You" in the key of F, employing both axis and Ⓐ and Ⓑ Forms (note the modulation). (Refer to recent Horace Silver recordings.)

Fig. 4.

(F)   ♯Io   IIø   ♭IIx

(F)   I   ♯Io   II

(F)   ♭IIx   I   #Io Ⓐ

(F)   IIø Ⓐ   ♭IIx Ⓑ

(F)   I   (A)   IIø

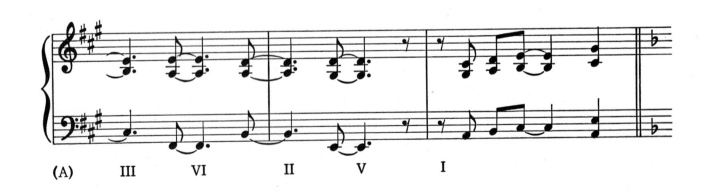

(A)   III   VI   II   V   I

(F)   ♭IIIo   II Ⓐ

(F)   ♭IIx Ⓑ   I Ⓐ   II Ⓐ   VIo Ⓐ   III Ⓑ

                                       2nd permutation

(F)   IIIø Ⓑ   ♭IIIx Ⓐ   II

(F)   V   IV   III   ♭IIIx   IIø Ⓐ   VIIo Ⓐ

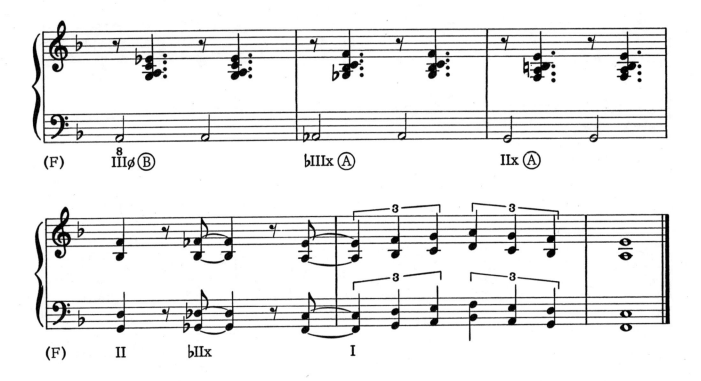

"Walking" open-position patterns moving internally against the prevailing chord are derived from the three traditional patterns studied in Vol. I, Lessons 62, 63, 64:

1. Circle of fifths
2. Diatonic
3. Chromatic

Diatonic and chromatic patterns rotating around the prevailing chord are the most commonly used (Fig. 5). Essential to this device is an automatic facility with the axis of the 3rd and 7th (see Vol. I, Section XI) in all scales and modal displacements. These walking lines are similar to those in Vol. III, Section 2, and Lessons 31 through 34 of Vol. IV.

Fig. 5.

LESSON 41.

Turnarounds

The problem of "Intros" was discussed in Vol. III, Lesson 28. In a normal jazz performance the following general format prevails:

Chorus 1. Statement of melody, harmonic chart, tempo, etc.
Chorus 2, etc. Unspecified number of improvised choruses.
Final Chorus. Restatement of melody, close.

Obviously, these repeated choruses must be joined by some smooth sequence of chords connecting the end of one chorus with the beginning of the next.

Most jazz tunes fall into the following structural categories:

1. 32-bar form, melody closing on bar 31 on M I chord.
2. 32-bar form, melody closing on bar 32 on M I chord.
3. 32-bar form, melody closing on bar 31 on m I chord.
4. 32-bar form, melody closing on bar 32 on m I chord.
5. 64-bar form, melody closing on bar 61 on M I chord.

This means that in forms 1 and 3 a two-bar (bars 31 and 32) turn-around is required.

In forms 2 and 4, a one-bar (32nd bar) turnaround is required.

In form 5, a four-bar (bars 61, 62, 63 and 64) turnaround is required.

RULE: The final melodic tone indicates the beginning of the turnaround.

The problem now remains to determine the chords to be employed. Since in any case the turnaround begins on either the M or m I chord, the question remains to find the most suitable chords to "connect" this I chord to the first chord of the tune (see Vol. III, Lesson 28).

The following categories include the principle initial chords (not including pick-up chords):

1. Tunes beginning on I chord
2. Tunes beginning on II chord
3. Tunes beginning on VI chord

In functions other than those considered, "cover" the turnaround by using a basic I-VI-II-V pattern; then proceed directly to the initial chord of the tune.

RULE: Turn-around patterns are determined harmonically by the initial chord and rhythmically by the closing bar of the melody.

A common turnaround device employed to sustain tension while passing from one chorus to the next is that of employing the fifth of the prevailing key (either major or minor) in the bass, while moving through a turnaround pattern in the right hand. This device is known as an *organ-point* or *pedal-point,* and may be joined with any basic pattern of the prevailing key (Fig. 1).

Fig. 1.

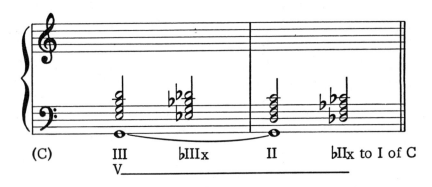

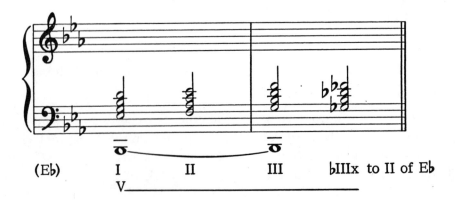

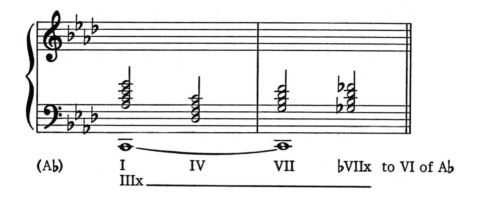

(A♭) I IV VII ♭VIIx to VI of A♭
IIIx

From the preceding the following solutions are suggested:

INITIAL CHORD	ENDING	TURN-AROUND
I	2 bars	I VI / II ♭IIx //
I	1 bar	I ♭IIx //
I	4 bars	I / ♭IIIx / IIx / ♭IIx //
Im	2 bars	I VIφ / IIφ ♭IIx //
Im	4 bars	I / VIφ / IIφ / ♭IIx //
II	2 bars	I II / III ♭IIIx //
II	1 bar	I ♯Io //
II	4 bars	I / ♭Vm VIIx / III / VIx //
VI	2 bars	I IV / VII IIIx //
VI	1 bar	I IIIx⁴₃ //
VI	4 bars	I / ♯Io / II II₂ / VII ♭VIIx //
all other	2 bars	I VI / II V //
all other	4 bars	I / VI / II / V //

Figure 2 illustrates a bass line for "Down By The River" in A♭.

Fig. 2.

I VI / IV IV₂ / II / V / I IV VII IIIx / VI IIx Vm Ix / IV III /

II V / I IV VII IIIx / VI VI₂ / IV VII / I͞I͞I V͞I ♯V͞Io / VII IIIx /

VI VI₂ ♭Vφ VIIx / III VIx / II V / I VI / IV IV₂ / II / V /

I IV VII IIIx / VI IIx Vm Ix / IV III / II V / I IV VII IIIx /

VI VI₂ / ♭Vm VIIx / III VIx / II III / IV V♯³ / I⁺⁶ / I⁺⁶ //

LESSON 42.

Building a Bass Line

In Vol. I, Lesson 76 the problem of converting sheet music to jazz was given some consideration.

The problems of conversion vary according to the individual composer; also, the time of the original copyright determines to some extent the accessibility of a logical chord chart. Again, some compositions that enjoy a permanent position in the popular literature originally appeared in musical comedies under specific dramatic conditions which may have imposed certain harmonic or rhythmic restrictions no longer applicable.

A case in point is "Small Hotel" from *On Your Toes* by Rodgers and Hart.

The bass line of the first eight bars that appeared in the original score is as follows:

I VI$_2^6$ / I VI$_2$ / I VI$_2$ / I VI$_2$ / II / II V / I VI$_2$ / I VI$_2$ //

This particular bass line was extremely effective for the dramatic situation prevailing in *On Your Toes* in 1936; however, for the present-day improvisor this harmonic setting seems inadequate for the "absolute" problem of improvisation compared with the "relative" problem of dramatic context.

The following solutions are offered to help establish a more effective underpinning for improvisation:

Solution 1

I / II / III / ♭IIIo / II / ♭IIx / I VI / II V //

Solution 2

I II / III IV / VI$_2$ IV / III ♭IIIo / II ♭IIo / II ♭IIx / I ♭IIIo / II ♭IIx //

Solution 3

I VI / II V$^{\sharp 3}$ / I II / III ♭IIIo / II III / IV IVø / III VI / II V //

238

Solution **4**

I I$_2$ / VI II$\phi{}^4_3$ / VI$_2$ IV / III $\flat$IIIo / II $\flat$IIo / II$_2$ VIIo / I$_2$ VI /
II$\phi{}^4_3$ V //

Solution **5**

I I$_2$ / VI VI$_2$ / $\flat$Vϕ IVx / III $\flat$IIIo / II V / Im IVx / III $\flat$IIIM /
II $\flat$IIx //

Solution **6**

I IVx / $\flat$VIIx $\flat$IIIx / $\flat$VIx $\flat$IIx$^{\sharp 5}$ / $\flat$V$^{\sharp 3}$ VIIx / III VIx / II V /
I $\flat$VIIx / $\flat$VIx V //

Solution **7**

$\flat$Vϕ IVm / III $\flat$IIIo / II^{+6} $\flat$IIo / II$_2$ / VII $\flat$VIIo / IV$^6_5$ $\flat$VIo /
VI$_2$ $\flat$V$^{\sharp 5}$ / IV III $\flat$III II //

Solution **8**

Vm $\flat$Vϕ / IV^{+6} IVm / III IV / $\sharp$IVo VI$_2$ / $\flat$V / IV IVo / III IV^{+6} /
$\sharp$IVx V //

Solution **9**

I$_2$ $\flat$V$\phi{}^6_5$ / II$\phi{}^4_3$ VI$_2$ / $\flat$Vm IVx / III $\sharp$IVo / V IV$^6_5$ / $\sharp$VIo VII /
I VI / $\flat$VIx V //

Solution **10**

III VI / II V$^{\sharp 3}$ / $\flat$Vm VIIx / IVϕ $\flat$VIIM / III VIx / II V / Im IVx /
$\flat$VIIx $\flat$IIIM //

There are other solutions, of course, but these represent the conventional patterns usually applied in such a situation. Sections of one solution may also be interchanged with those of another solution.

Figure 1 illustrates a bass line for "Small Hotel" in G Major. Note the modulation.

Fig. 1.

(G) I II / III IV / VI $_2$ IV / I $_5^6$ $\flat$IIIo / II $\flat$IIo / II $\flat$IIx / I VI /

(G) II $\flat$IIx / I II / III IV / VI $_2$ IV / I $_5^6$ $\flat$IIIo / II $\flat$IIo / II V //

(C) V IV / III II / I VI / II $\flat$IIx / I IV / VIIm IIIx / VI $\flat$Vϕ /

(C) VII IIIx // (G) II$^{\sharp 7}$ II / IIϕ $\flat$IIx / I II / III IV / VI $_2$ IV /

(G) I $_5^6$ $\flat$IIIo / II $\flat$IIo / II $\flat$IIx / I / I //

THERE'S A SMALL HOTEL (Lorenz Hart and Richard Rodgers) — Copyright © 1936 by Chappel & Co., Inc. — Copyright Renewed. — Used by Permission.

Convert Fig. 1 to the Ⓐ and Ⓑ Forms. Improvise on Fig. 1.

LESSON 43.

Modern "Funky" Piano — Modified Ⓐ and Ⓑ Forms

The appearance in the Fifties of a style of pianism rooted in the archaic blues indicated a partial return by jazzmen to the substrata elements of jazz that had existed at the turn of the century. These substrata elements include the following:

1. Eight-bar and twelve-bar archaic blues
2. Gospel music
3. 8/8 and 12/8 time signatures
4. Country, mountain and western idioms

Some of the leaders in this movement include: Ray Charles, John Williams, Horace Silver, Hampton Hawes, Mose Allison, Pete Jolly, Jimmy Guiffre and Les McCann.

Figure 3 illustrates an application of these various idioms to the 12-bar blues in the key of G.

The left hand employs the modified Ⓐ and Ⓑ Forms (Lesson 12). Modified Ⓐ and Ⓑ occur on the *dominant* chord only; modified Ⓐ omits the ninth, modified Ⓑ omits the thirteenth.

The use of the "off-beat" device in the left hand creates a tension of continually "kicking" each beat; this takes on the character of an inverted boogie-woogie (see Figs. 1 and 2).

Fig. 1.   Boogie-Woogie

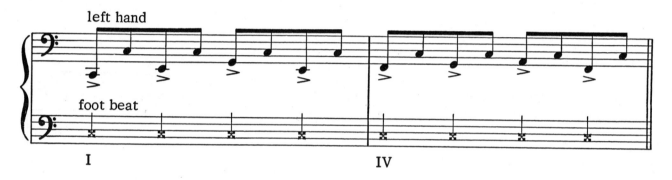

Fig. 2.   Inverted "funky" accent

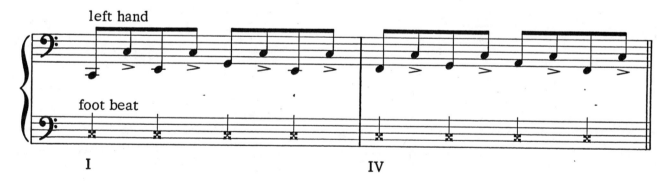

The unremitting use of this device can easily result in monotony unless it is joined with other rhythmic resources.

The use of only the dominant quality contributes to the general tension of the idiom. Bars 3 and 5 employ the upper chromatic dominants; bars 11 and 12 employ the same device extended to "cover" the necessary eight beats.

Fig. 3.

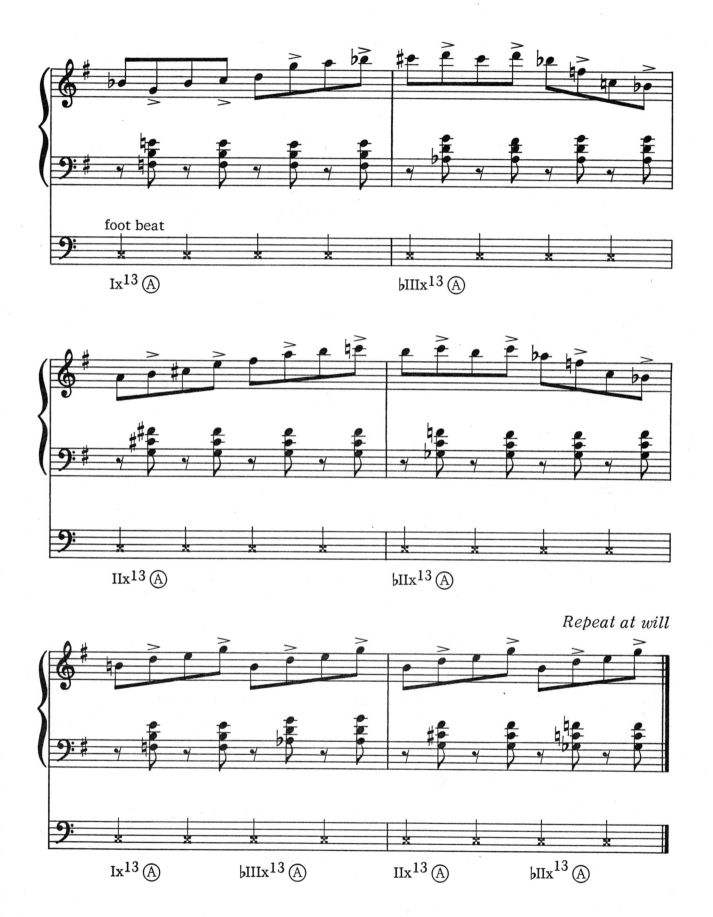

foot beat

Ix^{13} (A)   ♭IIIx^{13} (A)

IIx^{13} (A)   ♭IIx^{13} (A)

Repeat at will

Ix^{13} (A)   ♭IIIx^{13} (A)   IIx^{13} (A)   ♭IIx^{13} (A)

LESSON 44.

Harmonic Distortion

Occasionally the chord chart of a tune is distorted by substituting an *unrelated* but *familiar* pattern (organ point, circle of fifths) for the patterns dictated by the composition (Fig. 1).

Fig. 1.

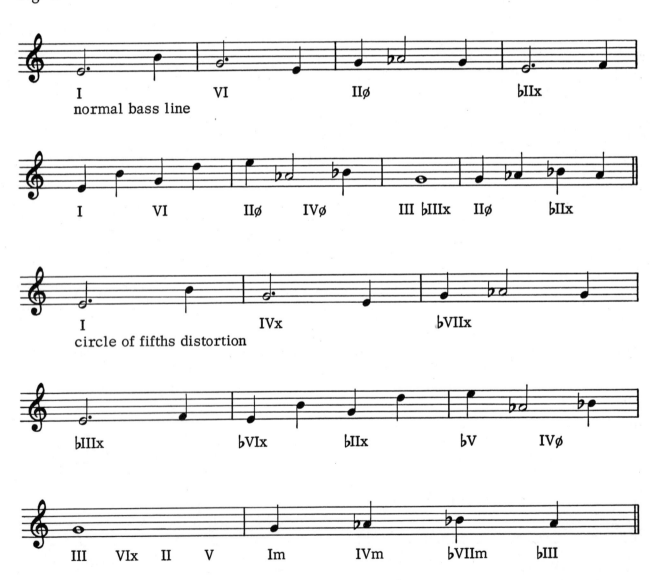

A further device involves the playing of the melody accompanied by a *parallel* harmonic structure. This is referred to as "parallel," since the identical intervals appear under each melodic "point." The prevailing chord chart is completely abandoned in this case and each formation is built *down* from each melodic tone. The descending tone-row is as follows:

> melody tone
> perfect fourth
> minor sixth
> major seventh
> ninth

(All intervals are figured from the melody down.) See Fig. 2.

Fig. 2.   Parallel distortion

Thus, in Fig. 2 we have:

MELODY	P4 BELOW	m 6 BELOW	M 7 BELOW	9 BELOW
E	B	G♯	F	D
B	F♯	D♯	C	A
G	D	B	A♭	F
A♭	E♭	C	A	G♭
F	C	A	G♭	E♭
D	A	F♯	E♭	C
E	B	A♭	F	D

Again, each formation is created by the melodic tone; the prevailing chord plays no part in the structure. Manually this structure functions identically with the block chords studied in Vol. III: four voices in the right hand; one in the left.

The student will recognize this formation as the Ⓐ Form of the diminished chord studied in Lesson 9. The use of this particular interval combination is arbitrary; of course; other combinations can be and are used. The effectiveness of this particular combination illustrated in Fig. 2 probably lies first in the resonance of the voicing itself, as well as in the peculiar relationship of the dominant and the diminished chords studied in Lesson 12.

The over-all effect of such a formation is one of extreme tension caused by both the parallelism itself and the strange "dominant-diminished" content of the voicings.

Copyright laws prevent the reproduction of a melody illustrating this medium. It is suggested that the student apply this idea to any melodic line, carefully following the indicated interval combination.

LESSON 45.

Building Chords in Fourths

In recent years there has appeared a trend in jazz pianism which, in terms of the rugged history of jazz piano, represents a rather startling, but musically effective joining of jazz and traditional "cocktail" idioms.

The left-hand structures are an extension of the modified Ⓐ and Ⓑ Forms in addition to the dominant Ⓒ Form (Lesson 12). The right hand employs a mixture of chords and running lines, heavily pedaled in order to achieve the deliberate vagueness and diffusion of tonal colors similar to the textures found in the Impressionism of the early Twentieth Century.

This extensive use of the *sostenuto pedal* as a basic device of this style has introduced a revolutionary conception of swing in which the time-honored, sharp, marcato touch has been replaced by a blurred, legato attack. The left-hand structures employ chords built in either perfect or augmented (tritone) fourths joined by various *root couplings;* the right-hand line generally avoids the traditional harmonic "hinges" (see Vol. I, pages 127-128) or chromatic appogiatura tones, raised to great eminence by alto saxophonist Charlie Parker (Fig. 1).

Fig. 1.

Instead, this new line concept employs the idea of superimposed thirds piled on top of each other in the manner of tenor saxophonist John Coltrane. In this conception the *horizontal* relationship of the chords is replaced by an intense *vertical* exploration of each individual harmonic function without the usual regard for the horizontal relation of any one vertical structure to the preceding or succeeding structure (Fig. 2).

Fig. 2.

The keyboard collation of these various factors is generally attributed to pianist Bill Evans; its intrinsic vitality will be best assessed by the passage of time.

The left-hand chords or voicings are derived from twenty-four basic structures — each of the twelve tones of the chromatic scale capable of supporting two formations. Various roots *(couplings)* may be joined to each of these twenty-four voicings. Fig. 3 illustrates the two voicings on G.

Fig. 3.

1.   2.

Voicing 1 consists of the following intervals:
    G to C — perfect fourth
    C to F — perfect fourth
Voicing 2 consists of the following intervals:
    C to C♯ — augmented fourth (tritone)
    C♯ to F♯ — perfect fourth

NOTE: Since the root is not present in either voicing 1 or 2, these voicings cannot be treated as a "chord" possessing an internal relationship of interval factors forming a "quality." In other words, the fact that voicing 1 contains a perfect fourth and a minor "seventh" has no meaning until a root is added to the voicing (see Fig. 4). Voicings 1 and 2 are simply artificial structures formed by piling various kinds of fourths on top of one another. Figure 4 illustrates the various *root couplings* of voicing 1.

Fig. 4.

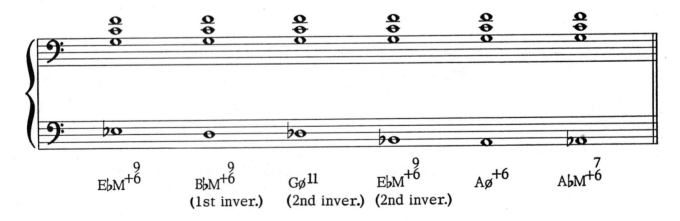

$E\flat M^{+6}_{\ 9}$ $B\flat M^{+6}_{\ 9}$ $G\emptyset^{11}$ $E\flat M^{+6}_{\ 9}$ $A\emptyset^{+6}$ $A\flat M^{+6}_{\ 7}$
          (1st inver.) (2nd inver.) (2nd inver.)

Figure 5 illustrates the various *root couplings* for voicing 2.

Fig. 5.

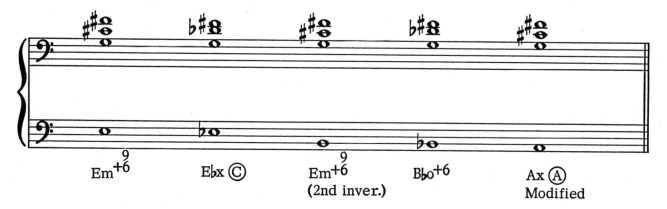

$Em^{+6}_{\,9}$ E♭x © $Em^{+6}_{\,9}$ B♭o^{+6} Ax Ⓐ
                         (2nd inver.)   Modified

The following tables represent an interval analysis of the *root couplings* illustrated in Fig. 4:

$E♭M^{9}_{+6}$ (E♭ major ninth chord with added sixth)
> E♭ — root
> G — third
> C — added sixth
> F — ninth

$B♭M^{9}_{+6}$ (B♭ major ninth chord wtih added sixth in *first* inversion)
> D — third
> G — added sixth
> C — ninth
> F — fifth

Gϕ¹¹ (G half-diminished eleventh chord in *second* inversion)
> D♭ — fifth
> G — root
> C — eleventh
> F — seventh

$E♭M^{9}_{+6}$ (E♭ major ninth chord with added sixth in *second* inversion)
> B♭ — fifth
> G — third
> C — added sixth
> F — ninth

Aϕ^{+6} (A half-diminished chord with added sixth; sixth tone of the Locrian mode of B$\flat$)

> A — root
> G — seventh
> C — third
> F — added sixth

A$\flat$M$^{7}_{+6}$ (A$\flat$ major seventh chord with added sixth)

> A$\flat$ — root
> G — seventh
> C — third
> F — added sixth

Here is an analysis of Fig. 5:

Em$^{9}_{+6}$ (E minor ninth chord with added sixth)

> E — root
> G — third
> C$\sharp$ — added sixth
> F$\sharp$ — ninth

E$\flat$x Ⓒ (E$\flat$ dominant augmented ninth chord)

> E$\flat$ — root
> G — third
> D$\flat$ — seventh
> F$\sharp$ — augmented ninth

Em$^{9}_{+6}$ (E minor ninth chord with added sixth in *second* inversion)

> B — fifth
> G — third
> C$\sharp$ — added sixth
> F$\sharp$ — ninth

B$\flat$o^{+6} (B$\flat$ diminished chord with added sixth; sixth tone of the B$\flat$ diminished scale)

> B$\flat$ — root
> G — seventh
> D$\flat$ — third
> F$\sharp$ — added sixth

Ax Ⓐ (A dominant thirteenth chord in Ⓐ Form modified)

      A — root
      G — seventh
      C♯ — third
      F♯ — thirteenth

Since the search for a chord or voicing usually begins at the root, the following table describes the *root-voicing couplings* of the *five qualities;* the interval distance in each case refers to the distance from the root *up* to the bass note of the voicing. In order to secure resonance, the root coupling is sometimes placed an octave below the original interval; this in no way affects the relationship of the particular root to the voicing.

QUALITY	VOICING	INTERVAL
M (root)	1	M3 up
M (root)	1	M7 up
M (1st inv.)	1	P4 up
M (2nd inv.)	1	M6 up
x (root)	2	M3 up
x (root)	2	m7 up
m (root)	2	m3 up
m (2nd inv.)	2	m6 up
φ (root)	1	m7 up
φ (2nd inv.)	1	+4 up
o (root)	2	M6 up

Voicings generally fall into the following register (Fig. 6).

Fig. 6.

Figure 7 illustrates the *root-voicing couplings* for the *five qualities* on each of the twelve tones. (See Vol. I, pages 25 and 26).

Fig. 7.

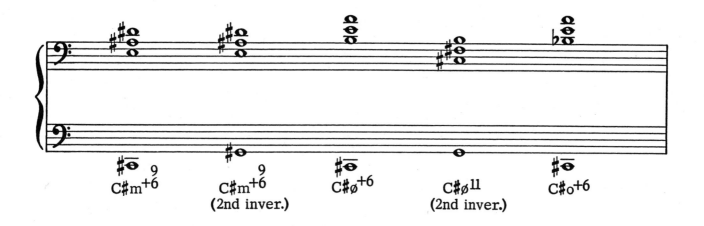

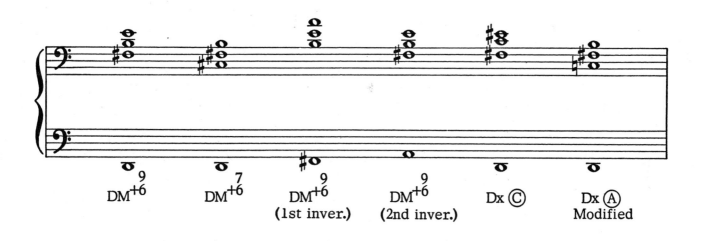

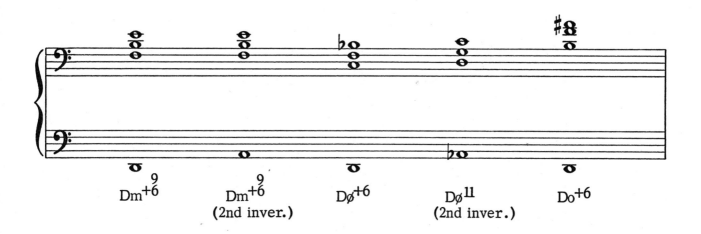

253

254

255

256

257

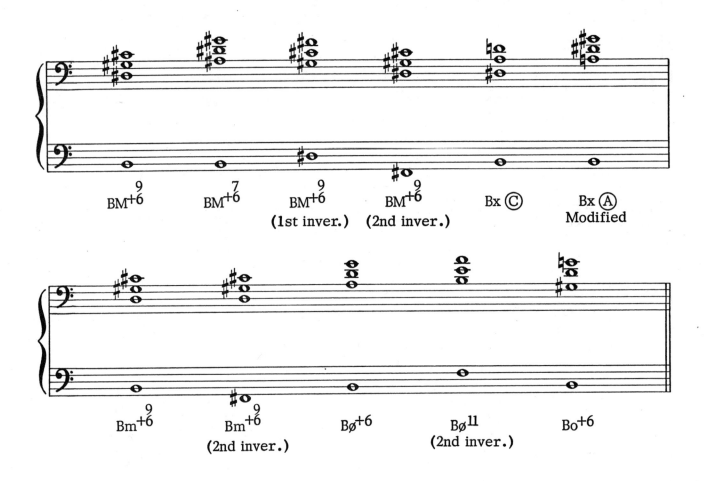

Figure 8 illustrates the various idioms employed in this style.

Fig. 8.

I (1) ♭V Ⓐ Modified

IVx Ⓐ Modified IIIM (1)

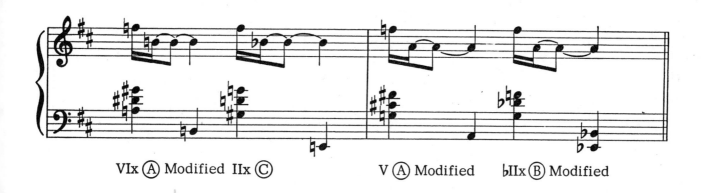

VIx Ⓐ Modified IIx Ⓒ V Ⓐ Modified ♭IIx Ⓑ Modified

I (1)

Im (2)

I (1)

♭V Ⓐ Modified

IVx Ⓐ Modified

260

IIIM (1)

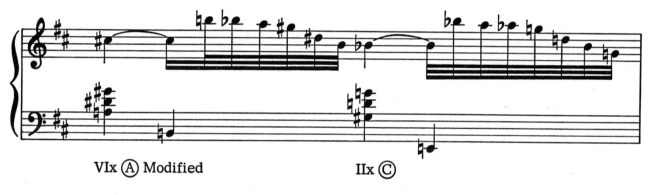

VIx (A) Modified   IIx (C)

V (A) Modified   bIIx (B) Modified

I (1)   Im (2)

I (1)   ♭V Ⓐ Modified

IVx Ⓐ Modified

IIIM (1)

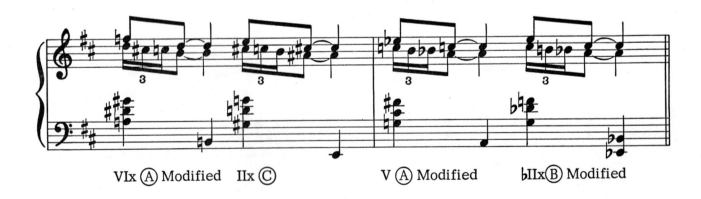

VIx Ⓐ Modified   IIx Ⓒ   V Ⓐ Modified   ♭IIx Ⓑ Modified

262

I (1)   Im (2)

I (1)   ♭V Ⓐ Modified

IVx Ⓐ Modified   III M (1)

VIx Ⓐ Modified   IIx Ⓒ

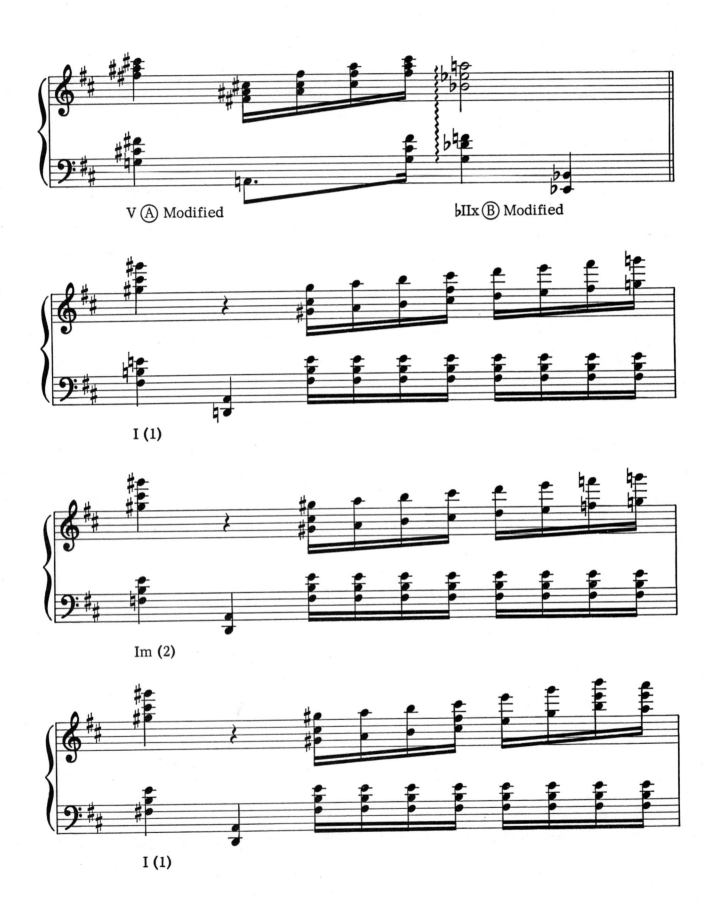

V Ⓐ Modified

♭IIx Ⓑ Modified

I (1)

Im (2)

I (1)

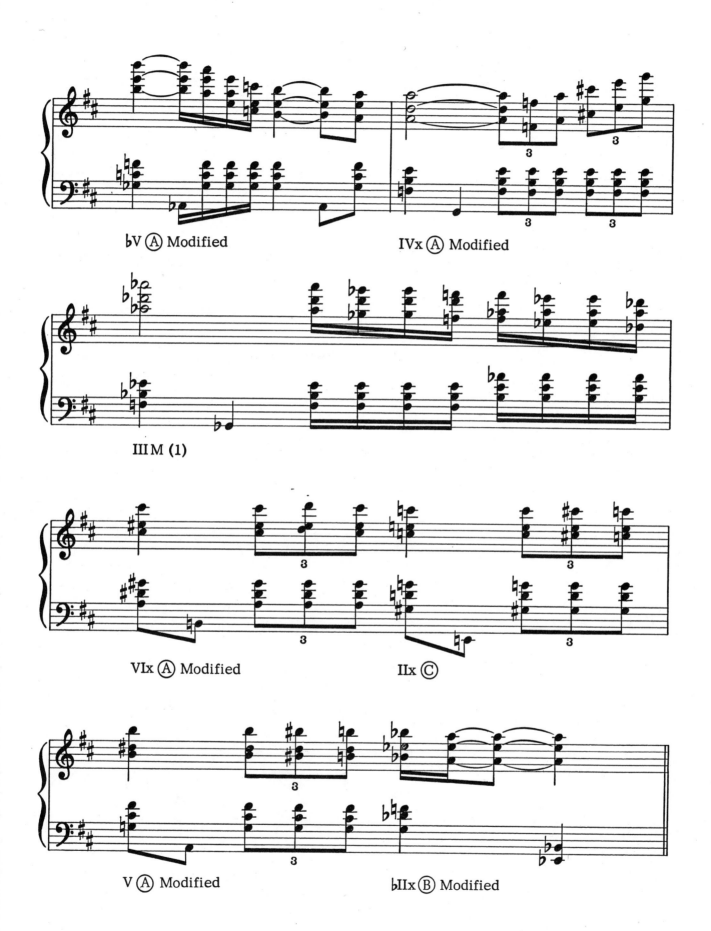

bV Ⓐ Modified

IVx Ⓐ Modified

IIIM (1)

VIx Ⓐ Modified

IIx Ⓒ

V Ⓐ Modified

bIIx Ⓑ Modified

265

I (1)   Im (2)

I (1)   ♭V Ⓐ Modified

IVx Ⓐ Modified   III M (1)

VIx Ⓐ Modified   IIx Ⓒ   V Ⓐ Modified   ♭IIx Ⓑ Modified

266

I (1)   Im (2)

I (1)   I (1)

LESSON 46.

Ⓐ and Ⓑ Forms with Shearing Block Chords

One of the most familiar pianistic sounds of the modern period has been the so-called "concerto sound" employing Ⓐ and Ⓑ Forms in the left hand and the Shearing block chords in the right. The sound derives its name from the similarity to the "*tutti*" sections of the Nineteenth- and Twentieth-Century piano concerto (i.e. Grieg, Tchaikovsky, Rachmaninoff).

The left-hand elements follow precisely the rules outlined in this volume; the right-hand chord blocks, however, will present problems to many pianists, since a normal hand span is incapable of re-creating the entire five-voice system in the right hand.

Figure 1 illustrates a chord block easily accessible in the conventional two-hand system described in Vol. III, but difficult or inaccessible for the average pianist in the right hand only.

Fig. 1.   

RULE: It is permissible to omit any or all of the inner voices of a block chord; but neither tone of the octave itself (the outside voices) can be omitted.

Thus, the following solutions would be permissible in modifying Fig. 1.

Fig. 2.

Solutions illustrated in Fig. 3 are impermissible.

Fig. 3.

These rules do not affect the use of single notes, thirds, fourths, fifths and sixths elsewhere described in this text. The seventh is usually avoided in the right hand, except in context with the Shearing block chords.

In selecting the inner voices to be retained in a modified chord block, the following suggestions should be kept in mind:

1. The third and seventh of a chord should be retained if possible.
2. The fifth may be omitted in M, x and m chords.
3. When the keyboard permits, two adjacent tones may be played by the thumb of the right hand (See Fig. 4).

Fig. 4.

4. The octave must remain intact.
5. In running passages, the open octave should be employed (see Vol. III, Lesson 53).

Figure 5 illustrates an Ⓐ and Ⓑ Form-block chord treatment of the melody illustrated in Vol. I, Lesson 7.

Fig. 5.

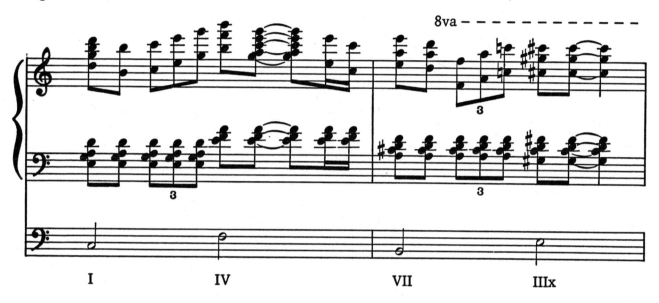

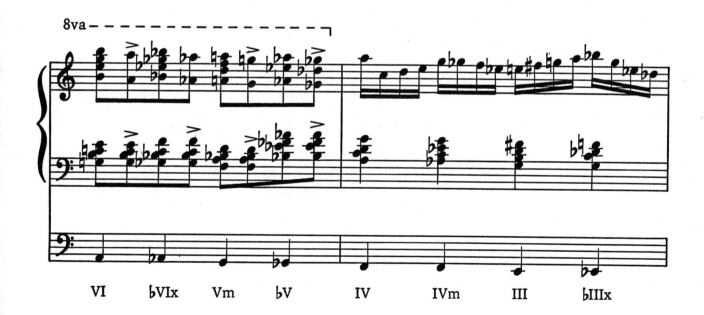

271

II   VII   III   VI

II   bIIx   I   VI

IVm   IVø

III   VI

bV∅   IVo

III   bIIIx   II   bIIx

In Fig. 5, the student will note that the basic device employed is that of rhythmic unison figures in the right and left hands. In this case, the rhythmic contour of each improvised phrase in the right hand is the determining factor; the left hand simply follows the right by repeating the prevailing voicing in rhythmic unison with the right-hand figure. This is basic; occasionally, this device may and should be abandoned in the interest of textural variety.

DRILL: Review Vol. III, Section IV.

Explore various melodies employing Ⓐ and Ⓑ Forms in the left hand, and melodic chord blocks in the right.

Employing similar mechanics, explore improvised lines on chord charts appearing in this and previous volumes.

LESSON 47.

The Modal Fourths

The history of jazz harmony has evolved three basic devices in building chord structures:

1. Alternate scale-tones or thirds (Tatum) — Fig. 1.
2. Consecutive scale-tones or seconds (Evans) — Fig. 2.
3. Double alternate scale-tones or fourths. (Avant-garde) — Fig. 3.

Fig. 1.

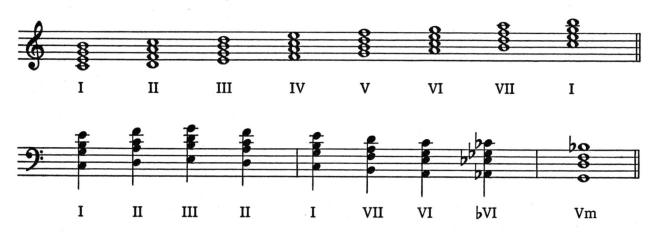

Fig. 2.

Ionian   Mixolydian   Dorian

Locrian   0 2 1 2 1 2 1 2 1

I   II   III   II   I   VII   VI   bVI   Vm

277

Fig. 3.

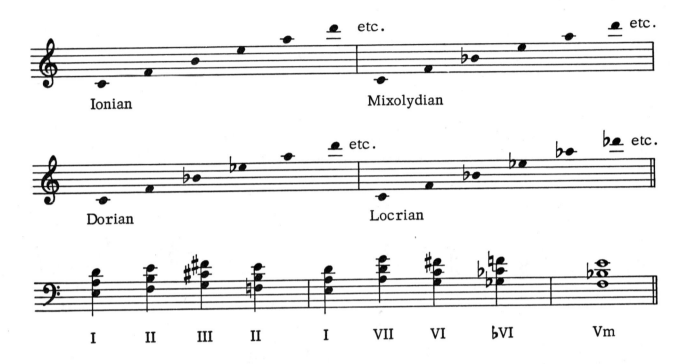

Ionian   Mixolydian

Dorian   Locrian

I   II   III   II   I   VII   VI   ♭VI   Vm

The basic structures of steps 1 and 2 have been fully explored in Vols. III and IV; the following figure illustrates the modal drill essential to the use of the contemporary fourth voicings on the M, x, m and φ qualities on C.

Fig. 4

Ionian of C   Mixolydian of F

Dorian of B♭   Locrian of D♭

This drill must be explored on the remaining eleven tones employing the M-x-m-φ modal system. The following table illustrates the tonal combinations for the seven positions of the Ionian, Mixolydian, Dorian and Locrian modes:

1-4-7
2-5-1
3-6-2
4-7-3
5-1-4
6-2-5
7-3-6

It is also possible to employ the positions of 1, 3, 5 and 7 in the diminished tone row:

1-5-8
3-7-2
5-1-4
7-3-6

Fig. 5.

0 2 1 2 1 2 1 2 1

Positions 2, 4, 6 and 8 are generally impractical. Figure 6 illustrates a minor blues chart (see Vol. I, Sec. X) that employs the fourth structures.

Fig. 6.

(d)　　　Im　　　　　　　　　Im　　　　　　　　Im

(d)   Im   IVm

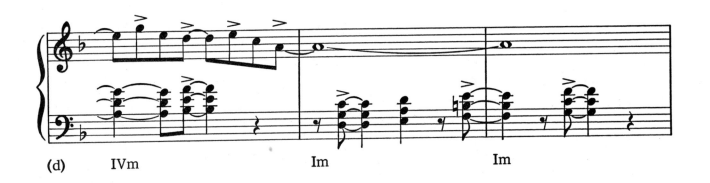

(d)   IVm   Im   Im

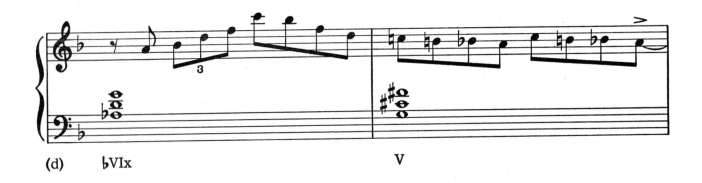

(d)   bVIx   V

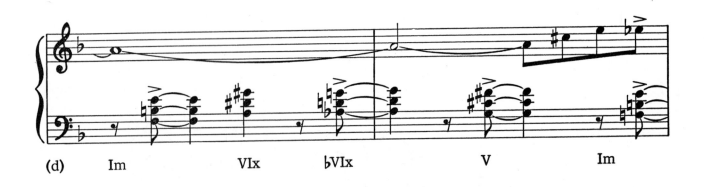

(d)   Im   VIx   bVIx   V   Im

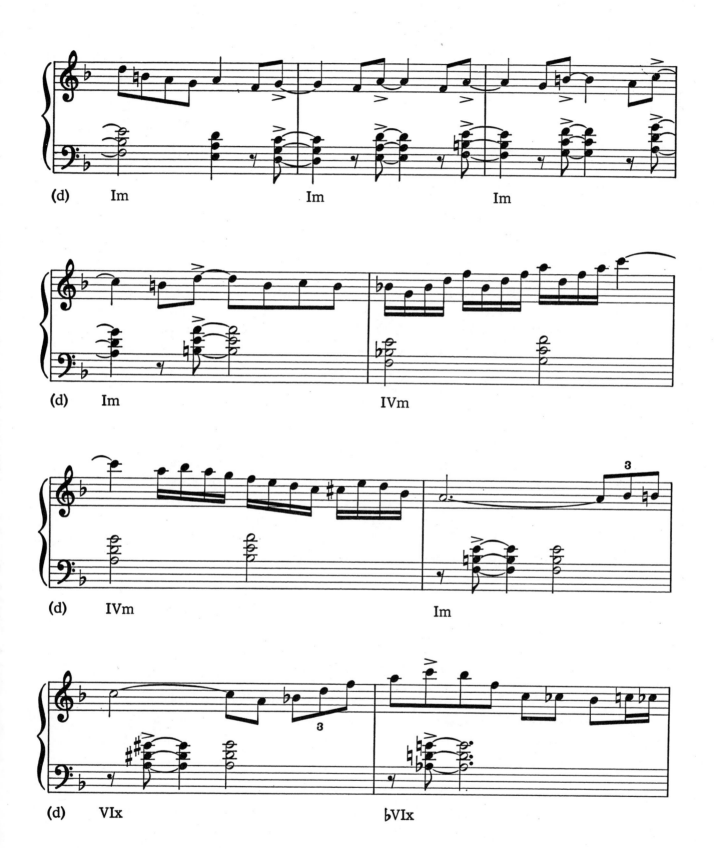

(d)   Im   Im   Im

(d)   Im   IVm

(d)   IVm   Im

(d)   VIx   ♭VIx

281

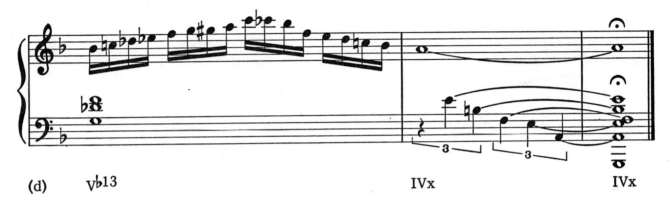

(d)   V♭13   IVx   IVx

DRILL: Practice Fig. 4 on the twelve tones of the chromatic scale. Apply the fourth structures to various bass lines.

NOTE: As illustrated in Fig. 6, the fourth structures are most effective when used in constantly shifting horizontal patterns. These patterns may appear in irregular fashion in any rhythmic pattern. This horizontal motion is essential, since any single structure can only weakly imply any particular chord value; appearing in "tandem," these structures are capable of infusing a chord chart with compelling tonal and rhythmic intensity. These structures also are essential in order to vary the textural sound of the Ⓐ and Ⓑ Forms; for effective application of this contemporary style, the fourth structures, as well as the modal fragments discussed in Lesson 48, *must* be integrated with the Ⓐ and Ⓑ Forms. The decision in these matters must rest with the individual student, of course, since they are based upon the particular factors appearing in the right hand at the moment of performance, as well as to the general, over-all emotional context prevailing at that time.

LESSON 48.

The Modal Fragments

The *modal fragments* represent clusters of model tones borrowed from the Spanish Impressionists. As the student will note, these fragments also represent segments of the Ⓑ Form voicings. The principle of extracting these fragments is as follows:

1. Determine the half-step positions in each mode.
2. Play both tones of the minor second, adding the *alternate note* of the mode above the top tone of the minor second. This structure usually appears in the left hand in the middle C area of the keyboard.

282

For instance, in Fig. 1, the half-steps appear on 3 and 7; the alternate tone in the mode above F is A, and the alternate step in the mode above C is E.

Thus, the fragments of the C major chord are:

E-F-A
B-C-E

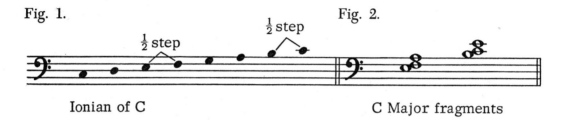

Fig. 1. Fig. 2.

Ionian of C C Major fragments

Figure 3 illustrates the modal fragments in G major.

Fig. 3.

G Major fragments

RULE: The major modal fragments employ the following combinations:

3-4-6
7-1-3

(based on the Ionian mode)

Figure 4 illustrates the half-step positions of the Mixolydian of F for the C dominant chord.

Figure 5 illustrates the modal fragments for the C dominant chord.

Fig. 4. Fig. 5.

Mixolydian of F C dominant fragments

RULE: The dominant modal fragments employ the following combinations:

3-4-6
6-7-2

(based on the Mixolydian mode)

Figure 6 illustrates the half-step positions of the Dorian of B♭ for the C minor chord.

Figure 7 illustrates the modal fragments for the C minor chord.

Dorian of B♭   C minor fragments

RULE: The minor modal fragments employ the following combinations:

2-3-5

6-7-2

(based on the Dorian mode)

Figure 8 illustrates the half-step positions of the Locrian of D♭ for the C half-diminished chord.

Figure 9 illustrates the modal fragments for the C half-diminished chord.

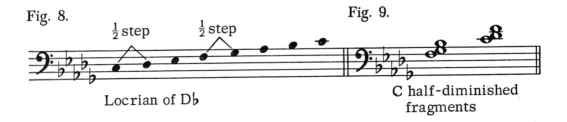

Locrian of D♭   C half-diminished fragments

RULE: The half-diminished modal fragments employ the following combinations:

1-2-4

4-5-7

(based on the Locrian mode)

Figure 10 illustrates the half-step positions of the C diminished tone row (0 2 1 2 1 2 1 2 1).

Fig. 10.

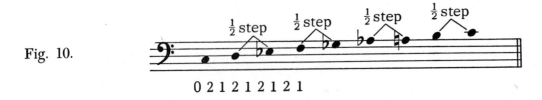

0 2 1 2 1 2 1 2 1

Figure 11 illustrates the tone-row fragments for the C diminished chord.

Fig. 11.

C diminished fragments

RULE: The diminished modal tone-row fragments employ the following combinations:

2-3-5
4-5-7
6-7-1
8-1-3

(based on the diminished tone row)

SUMMARY

Chord	Mode	Combination
Major	Ionian	3-4-6
		7-1-3
Dominant	Mixolydian	3-4-6
		6-7-2
Minor	Dorian	2-3-5
		6-7-2
Half-diminished	Locrian	1-2-4
		4-5-7
Diminished	0 2 1 2 1 2 1 2 1	2-3-5
		4-5-7
		6-7-1
		8-1-3

In choosing the most characteristic fragments from each mode, similar combinations, such as 3-4-6 of the Ionian and Mixolydian modes, are usually avoided. The following table illustrates the most common fragments of the five qualities:

major: 7-1-3
dominant: 6-7-2
minor: 2-3-5
half-diminished: 4-5-7
diminished: 4-5-7

Figure 12 illustrates the sixty fragment formations for the sixty chords.

Fig. 12.

DRILL: Practice Fig. 12 for automatic facility with the modal fragments.
Improvise on various charts integrating the modal fragments with
the (A) and (B) Forms and the fourth structures.

Figure 13 illustrates the use of the modal fragments in the contemporary style.

Fig. 13.

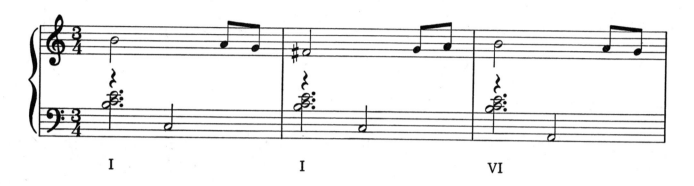

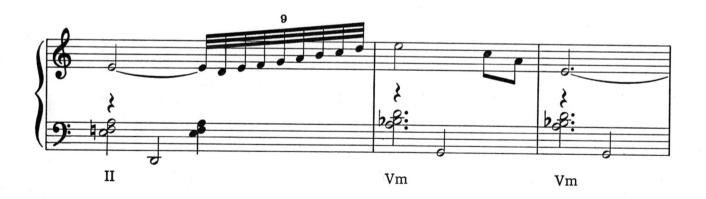